Christ Divided

Christ Divided

Antiblackness as Corporate Vice

KATIE WALKER GRIMES

FORTRESS PRESS
MINNEAPOLIS

CHRIST DIVIDED
Antiblackness as Corporate Vice

Cover design: Rob Dewey

Print ISBN: 978-1-5064-2799-7
eBook ISBN: 978-1-5064-3853-5

The paper used in this publication meets the minimum requirements of American National Standard for Information Sciences — Permanence of Paper for Printed Library Materials, ANSI Z329.48-1984.

Manufactured in the U.S.A.

Contents

Acknowledgments

I could not have written this book without the support of the following people: Professor Max Johnson, who first inspired me to start thinking about the relation between the sacraments and ethics; my Boston College cohortmates, Joshua Snyder, Michael Cagney, and Nichole Flores; my housemate, Michael Jaycox, who allowed me to try many of the ideas contained in this book out on him during impromptu conversations in our kitchen; the entire theology department at Boston College, especially James F. Keenan and M. Shawn Copeland, who did so much to help me make the transition from student to scholar; my patient and generous editor, Michael Gibson; my colleague Gerald Beyer, who never let me get too discouraged; my dear Sammy, who has inspired me more than he could ever understand; and perhaps most importantly, my Erin, who has been there for me through everything.

Preface

RESURRECTION PRACTICE

Resurrection may have changed Jesus's body, but it did not take his wounds away. Jesus greeted Mary Magdalene with hands that presumably still had jagged holes in them, and He visited the other apostles while sporting a deep gash in his side. But Jesus did not try to hide these wounds. To the contrary, he asked Thomas to place his finger inside of one of them. Imagine having a sword thrust deep into your side. Could you conceive of allowing, let alone inviting, anyone to stick her finger inside of it? But this is exactly what Jesus did. Due to the resurrection, a site of pain and vulnerability had been transformed into a pathway for self-communication and edifying intimacy; a cause of death had been turned into proof of life.

More than simply according other people the opportunity to cross over the borders of Jesus' own body, these resurrected wounds seem somehow connected to Jesus' newfound capacity to cross spatial borders. Just as Jesus's resurrected body could be safely entered, so it could enter spaces that otherwise would have been closed. As a result, the behavior of the resurrected Christ contrasts almost comically with that of his male apostles. They lock the doors, whereas Jesus's wounded body can pass through them. They hide themselves away; Jesus finds them anyway. They huddle fearfully together; Jesus is not afraid. Why? He has already been crucified. His body already has the holes that any crucifier would drive into it.

Only Doubting Thomas appreciates the meaning of the wounds on Jesus's resurrected body. Christians typically imagine Thomas as the model of how not to believe in Christ. We call him "doubting" as a slur. But Thomas was right to doubt Jesus's existence until he saw his wounds: Jesus could not have been his resurrected self unless he had retained the wounds he accrued on the cross. Thomas lacks faith not in Christ, but his friends' perceptions; he denies only that Jesus could be whoever we say he is. Thomas doubts in order to believe that Jesus Is Who He Is and that God can bring even the crucified back to life.[1]

Christ's encounter with Thomas dramatizes the future of all human life. If Jesus was "the first fruits of those who have died," as Christians hope he is, then would not our resurrected bodies also bear touchable evidence of the wounds that we accrued during our lifetimes?[2] And would we not also be eternally in the presence of the wounds that we helped to inflict upon others? Given that some Christian thinkers have argued that God would raise all of the dead to embodied life—not just those bound for heaven—before casting final judgment on them, it is possible that not even the damned can escape the wounds of history. If this speculation proves accurate, then hell would also be full of the wounded bodies of the resurrected.[3]

Reflecting upon this unsettling possibility enables us to zero in on what would comprise the most striking difference between heaven and hell. In heaven, wounds, such as those on Jesus's radically open body, would enable connection; in hell, they would isolate and traumatize. The wounded character of Jesus's resurrected body also helps to shed light on the nature of life this side of death. Perhaps life in this world—the one that still awaits the fullness of redemption—differs from hell primarily because, although our wounds still hurt and kill us, we alone can hope for the arrival of a world in which wounds bring people together rather than tear them apart. If hell has any occupants, they will have lost even that.

This thought experiment does not simply appease our curiosity about the life that will arrive at the end of history; it provides a framework with which to assess how we ought to live in history. History, even its more gruesome episodes, happens, and it can never be undone. Or, perhaps the wounded character of Jesus's resurrected body suggests that God does not wish to undo it. We acquire our identities in history and over the course of our sin-scarred lifetimes. Like Jesus, we bring our wounds with us into the afterlife. And like

1. John 20:19–31.
2. 1 Corinthians 15:20 New Revised Standard Version.
3. See, for example, Thomas Aquinas, *Summa Theologiae*, Supplementum Q.75.2.

Thomas, we can know the resurrected Lord only if we are willing to touch and look upon his wounds. We can inhabit the reign of God only if we are willing to know others and be known by them in this way as well.

Jesus's resurrected life therefore teaches us the following about racism: we cannot escape our racial history, not even by dying. Why? We do not overcome history by leaving it behind. God does not want us to forget. God will not let us forget. In heaven, there will still be wounds, both the ones we have suffered and the ones we have inflicted. When we confront the wounds of our racial history, we practice for the Resurrection and testify to our hope in it. We express our desire for its arrival. We enact our trust that the truth lies where the Resurrected Christ told us it did: in the wounds of the crucified. We lean upon our faith in a God who can bring even the most gruesomely brutalized bodies back to life, thereby turning old wounds into signs of new life.

Introduction

I grew up in a town in which it was impossible to forget that race and place mattered. Depending on whom you asked, Marion, Ohio was either a really small town or a bonafide city. Its 30,000 residents were arranged into a nearly perfect display of spatialized socioeconomic status: in general, the wealthiest neighborhoods existed on the city's east side and grew progressively less so as one traveled west; a similar pattern held with respect to race: while only a few black people resided on the city's south side, the north side contained neighborhoods equally divided between white and black.[1]

Our twelve public elementary schools funneled into three middle schools, each of which was marked by and took pride in an identity inflected by socioeconomic antagonisms. Intercity athletic competitions turned into showdowns between the north-side school that was full of so-called "hoods" and the south-side school that was home to the so-called "preps." These games between the disproportionately black Wildcats and the disproportionately white and upper-middle-class Bulldogs were always the most emotionally intense; the school on the west side, which was working class and in the middle in terms of racial mixture, just did not elicit the same type of hate from its counterparts. Still, everyone knew her place.

When we all entered the town's lone public high school as freshmen, the ire directed toward us by those who lived outside of our city made the old animosities seem small in comparison. The students who attended the overwhelmingly white schools out in the country

1. Matthew Bloch, Amanda Cox, and Tom Giratikanon, "Mapping Segregation: New government rules will require all cities and towns receiving federal housing funds to assess patterns of segregation," *The New York Times*, July 8, 2015. Accessed June 8, 2017, https://www.nytimes.com/interactive/2015/07/08/us/census-race-map.html?mcubz=2&_r=0.

falsely imagined our schooldays as interrupted by gang fights and our hallways pockmarked by gunshots. An adult spectator at an athletic event once called us "city trash." We played basketball games every season at a rural high school in a neighboring county where even adults sometimes shouted racial slurs from the stands. During a football game against a longtime rival, one of their fans threw a glass bottle at our lone black cheerleader and broke her nose. When we dared to enter the sprawling and shiny gyms that belonged to the suburban Columbus schools, we elicited a particular type of condescension: to them, we were not just too black, but white trash as well. When we would play against a predominately black school from the so-called "inner city" that only truly big cities could have, we felt our comparative whiteness reflected back at us. We were whoever our opponents were not. It was us against everybody, and we liked it that way.

My hometown affiliations notwithstanding, I am still white and upper middle class. I admittedly write this book against the grain of my own racially habituated being. Discussions about racial evil can make me feel defensive not just because of what they reveal about me, but perhaps even more so for what they suggest about my ancestors. I love my parents and grandparents, and, even though I did not know any of them, I feel a sort of love for my earlier ancestors as well. I want to be able to defend them against all charges of participation in racial evil, whether interpersonal or structural. I want to establish them as the exception to the rule of whiteness. Perhaps more than anything, I want to protect the stories I like to tell about them. I suspect I am not the only white person who feels this way.

I cling to these stories because I want to inherit only the good things my ancestors were. I want to be the descendant of striking Irish coalminers and the great-granddaughter of a city councilman and a postman respectively.[2] I want to count myself as the successor of the man who emigrated from Ireland and earned his citizenship fighting for the Union Army and of the Irish American women who stretched one man's wages into food for an entire extended family during the Great Depression. I want to be the granddaughter of the woman who worked as a nurse and held us all together with her love, and the man who found himself on an aircraft carrier in the North

2. David M. Emmons, *The Butte Irish: Class and Ethnicity in an American Mining Town, 1875–1925* (Chicago: University of Illinois Press, 1990), 52–54; Mark Bulik, *The Sons of Molly Maguire: The Irish Roots of America's First Labor War* (New York: Fordham University Press, 2015).

Atlantic surrounded by hostile Germans and still survived. I love to tell those stories.

But I hate that these are not the only stories I have to tell. I hate that the house my father grew up in and which I visited as a child was built as a part of the New Jersey Levittown, a postwar housing development infamous for its exclusion of black homeowners.[3] I regret that the university my grandpa loved so fiercely was all white when he went there.[4] I wince when I remember that a German immigrant ancestor received a parcel of Ohio farmland in exchange for fighting with General Winfield Scott in Mexico City.[5] I feel uneasy that my great-grandparents were young adults when the entire black population of our shared hometown hurriedly boarded the first train out of the county in order to escape an impending mass lynching.[6] I do not know what they thought about this event. It would break my heart if they felt anything but disgust, outrage, or sadness.

Most of all, I hate how I cannot keep the good stories entirely separate from the bad. Would my great-grandfather have found that job as a mailman—the one that enabled him not just to withstand the Great Depression, but also to save up enough money to send my grandmother to college at the end of it—had the postal service not systematically rejected black applicants?[7] The benefits of whiteness extended even to my ancestors who were otherwise oppressed. Consider my Irish forebears who lost their land and language to British conquest and then survived both the Great Hunger and the anthracite mineshafts of eastern Pennsylvania. As perceived through the lens of

3. Tom Hester, "Willingboro: A Half-Century of Suburbia," NJ.com, accessed July 25, 2016, http://www.nj.com/news/index.ssf/2008/10/willingboro_a_half_a_century_o.html; James Wolfinger, *Philadelphia Divided: Race and Politics in the City of Brotherly Love* (Chapel Hill: University of North Carolina Press, 2011).

4. Margaret Fosmoe, "1947 Saw First Black Notre Dame Grads," *South Bend Tribune*, February 26, 2009, http://articles.southbendtribune.com/2009-02-26/news/26729743_1_black-men-black-student-rotc.

5. "A War of Violence and Violations: The Consequences of Conquest: A Conversation with Antonia I. Castañeda," PBS, http://www.pbs.org/kera/usmexicanwar/aftermath/violence.html. Accessed July 25, 2016; "Jacob Schoenlaub," *The History of Marion County, Ohio: Containing a History of the County, Its Townships, Towns, Churches, Schools, Etc.; General and Local Statistics; Military Record; Portraits of Early Settlers and Prominent Men; History of the Northwest Territory; History of Ohio* (Marion, OH: Leggett, Conaway, 1883), 626.

6. "Quiet Night Follows Trouble of Monday: More Than 200 Negroes Leave the City," *The Marion Daily Star*, February 3, 1919; Associated Press, "Negroes Leaving Marion," *The Alliance Review and Leader* (Alliance, Ohio), February 4, 1919.

7. Philip F. Rubio, *There's Always Work at the Post Office: African American Postal Workers and the Fight for Jobs, Justice, and Equality* (Chapel Hill: University of North Carolina Press, 2010), 57–59.

anti-imperialism or economic injustice, they perhaps appear as heroic underdogs. But they too found relative prosperity by accessing a profession that excluded blacks.[8] I do not mind acknowledging that my ancestors were white. I hate admitting that it mattered so much. Regardless of how I feel about it, I have inherited this entire history. I cannot escape this past by pretending it does not exist. I am more than just the stories I like to tell.

The same could be said for the Catholic Church. Like religious people in general, we Catholics defend the honor of our church as instinctively as we would our family members. Accusations of racial evil are particularly upsetting. We white Catholics want our church to be the church of labor priests, scrappy immigrants, and former cultural outsiders who made this country their own. These are the stories white Catholics prefer to tell. But black Catholics know that these are not the only stories. They also recall, for example, segregated parishes and communion lines, exclusion from parochial schools and fraternal organizations, and white Catholic mobs that assembled to protect the racial purity of the neighborhoods they claimed as their own.[9]

Indeed, black Catholics have been articulating the theological implications of the church's persistent white supremacy for centuries.[10] They have been resisting white supremacy for just as long.[11] As a white person, there is nothing that I could say about the church's twisted relationship to white supremacy that black Catholics have not already said, thought, or suffered.[12] More than just unoriginal, this

8. Ronald L. Lewis, *Black Coal Miners in America: Race, Class, and Community Conflict, 1780–1980* (Lexington: University Press of Kentucky, 1987), x.

9. LaReine-Marie Mosely and Albert J. Raboteau, *Uncommon Faithfulness: The Black Catholic Experience*, ed. M. Shawn Copeland (Maryknoll, NY: Orbis, 2009); Cyprian Davis, *The History of Black Catholics in the United States* (New York: Crossroad, 1995); Diana L. Hayes and Cyprian Davis, eds., *Taking Down Our Harps: Black Catholics in the United States* (Maryknoll, NY: Orbis, 1998).

10. For a history of the primarily Protestant abolitionist theology of the Black Social Gospel that emerged at the end of the nineteenth century, see Gary Dorrien, *The New Abolition: W.E.B. Dubois and the Black Social Gospel* (New Haven: Yale University Press, 2015).

11. For more on this history, see Jamie Therese Phelps, *Black and Catholic: The Challenge and Gift of Black Folk: Contributions of African American Experience and Thought to Catholic Theology* (Milwaukee: Marquette University Press, 1997); Lincoln Rice, *Healing the Racial Divide: A Catholic Racial Justice Framework Inspired by Dr. Arthur Falls* (Eugene, OR: Wipf & Stock, 2014); Cyprian Davis, *Stamped with the Image of God: African Americans as God's Image in Black*, ed. Jamie T. Phelps (Maryknoll, NY: Orbis, 2004); Davis, *The History of Black Catholics in the United States*; Mosely and Raboteau, *Uncommon Faithfulness*; Hayes and Davis, *Taking Down Our Harps*.

12. Katie Geneva Cannon, *Katie's Canon: Womanism and the Soul of the Black Community* (New York: Continuum, 1995).

book comes far too late—I write nearly five hundred years after the arrival of the first African slave to the Catholic Americas, and non-black Catholic theology has yet to recognize chattel slavery's fundamental theological significance. As a result, there is nothing a white Catholic theologian needs to do except to listen to these black voices and reconsider everything, especially Catholic theology, in light of what she has allowed herself to hear. How can we Catholics fully love a church we do not truly know?

LISTENING IN ORDER TO LOVE

In 1932, lay black Catholic activist Dr. Arthur Falls described Catholic racism as not an assortment of isolated events but "an organized act of intolerance" such "that the very structure of the Catholic Church made . . . discrimination an almost built-in part of this structure." For this reason he contended that the church comprised not the Mystical Body of Christ, but "the Mythical Body of Christ."[13] On April 18, 1968, the fifty-eight members of the Black Catholic Clergy Caucus echoed Falls, proclaiming "the Catholic Church in the United States . . . primarily a white racist institution [that] has addressed itself primarily to white society."[14] One year later, the National Black Sisters' Conference decried the way in which "our powerlessness [as black people] is reflected in every social institution of American society, including the Church."[15] Nearly sixty years have passed since these declarations. Yet today the U.S. Catholic Church, while less white, remains corporately antiblack.

But prevailing categories cause theologians both to misidentify the operation of what we commonly identify as "racism" and to overestimate the church's racial innocence. Bringing the wisdom of generations of black Catholics into conversation with contemporary scholarly accounts of racism both within the field of theology and without, this book diagnoses antiblackness supremacy as a corporate vice that inhabits the body of Christ. In order to do this, it proposes two discursive shifts within the field of Catholic theology: first, theologians ought to exchange what I call "the white privilege approach"

13. Rice, *Healing the Racial Divide*, 94.
14. Albert J. Raboteau, *A Fire in the Bones* (Boston: Beacon, 1996), 134.
15. "The Survival of Soul: National Black Sisters' Conference Position Paper, 1969," in *"Stamped with the Image of God": African Americans as God's Image in Black*, ed. Cyprian Davis and Jamie Phelps (Maryknoll, NY: Orbis, 2003), 115.

to racial inequality, which centers its descriptive and rhetorical attention on "the unearned advantage" that white people accrue simply by being white, for what I call "the white supremacy approach," which instead focuses on the power and dominance that white people amass and exercise; and second, they ought to acknowledge the existence of what I call "antiblackness supremacy" and recognize its uniquely foundational role in prevailing processes of racialization and racial hierarchy.[16]

In the Catholic academy, antiracist scholars attribute racial inequality not just to the biased beliefs of bigoted whites, but also to the presence of white privilege, which provides "whites" with advantages it denies to people of color.[17] Catholic theologians and bishops have adopted this "white privilege" approach to racial inequality, seeking to make white Catholics aware of and then responsible for dismantling this racial privilege.[18] But, in relying so heavily upon the language of "white privilege," antiracist scholars obscure more than they illuminate.[19]

Why? Although white privilege exists as a social reality, it does not suffice as a description of racial evil.[20] Despite the intentions of

16. Peggy McIntosh, "White Privilege: Unpacking the Invisible Knapsack" (pdf), Independent School (Winter 1990) vol. 49 issue 2.

17. Peggy McIntosh, "White Privilege and Male Privilege," *Privilege: A Reader* (2003): 147–60; P. McIntosh, "White Privilege: Unpacking the Invisible Knapsack," *Race, Class, and Gender in the United States: An Integrated Study* 4 (1988): 165–69; Paula S. Rothenberg, *White Privilege: Essential Readings on the Other Side of Racism*, 4th ed. (New York: Worth, 2011); Shannon Sullivan, *Revealing Whiteness: The Unconscious Habits of Racial Privilege* (Bloomington: Indiana University Press, 2006).

18. Laurie M. Cassidy and Alexander Mikulich, eds., *Interrupting White Privilege: Catholic Theologians Break the Silence* (Maryknoll, NY: Orbis, 2007); Maureen O'Connell, *Compassion: Loving Our Neighbor in an Age of Globalization* (Maryknoll, NY: Orbis, 2009).

19. Curiously, the so-called white privilege approach to racial equality predominates among white Catholic ethicists but less so among their Protestant counterparts. It is not clear to what extent this reflects the influence of denominational differences or whether it is mere coincidence. See, for example, Christopher Pramuk, *Hope Sings, So Beautiful: Graced Encounters Across the Color Line* (Collegeville, MN: Liturgical, 2013); O'Connell, *Compassion: Loving Our Neighbor in an Age of Globalization*. In her work, *That They May Be One: Catholic Social Teaching on Racism, Tribalism, and Xenophobia* (Maryknoll, NY: Orbis, 2008), Dawn Nothwehr tends to use the term "white supremacy" to describe historical forms of racial injustice and the term "white privilege" to capture its contemporary operation. Other scholars like Karen Teel use the terms "racism," "white privilege," and "white supremacy" relatively interchangeably; see *Racism and the Image of God* (New York: Palgrave Macmillan, 2010). Mary C. Doak similarly refers to nonwhite people's "lack of power and privilege" in "Cornel West's Challenge to the Catholic Evasion of Black Theology," *Theological Studies* 63, no. 1 (2002): 94. Interestingly, white Protestant theologians Jennifer Harvey and James Perkinson, who both favor the discourse of white supremacy, represent exceptions to this.

20. Here I agree with Roger Haight's argument that white privilege "is an objectively ambigu-

those who deploy it, the white privilege approach to racial inequality tends to devolve into an unproductive and obfuscating comparison of individuals. I call this the "What About Oprah? Defense." As I have argued before, this rhetorical strategy points to the economic prosperity, power, and acclaim enjoyed by prominent black individuals such as Oprah Winfrey, Barack Obama, or Michael Jordan as evidence that racial injustice no longer prevails.[21] In response, adherents of the "white privilege approach" attempt to avoid this individualistic understanding through extensive explanation. Despite the eloquence with which scholars remind their readers of the structural character of white privilege, this language of white privilege continues to be misunderstood. This reflects not so much the interpretive shortcomings of the reader as it does the imprecision of the term itself.[22]

Ultimately, the phrase "white privilege" does not name what it purports to define. In the introduction to the seminal *Interrupting White Privilege*, Laurie Cassidy and Alex Mikulich explain that "for the purposes of this volume, we invited the reader to consider racism as 'a system by which one race maintains supremacy over another race through a set of attitudes, behaviors, social structures, ideologies, and the requisition power needed to impose them.'"[23] In a similar way, Margaret Pfeil claims that "white privilege, in general terms, functions systemically, invisibly, and without name while at the same time conferring power."[24] Indeed, as these scholars seemingly recognize, more than just privileged whiteness exists as an identity of power. Why not name it as such?[25]

ous category and conceptually adds nothing to what is described and characterized as racism." Cassidy and Mikulich, eds., *Interrupting White Privilege*, 90.

21. For recent examples of the "What About Oprah?" Defense, see "No, Oprah, America Isn't Racist: Column," *USA TODAY*, accessed January 18, 2016, http://www.usatoday.com/story/opinion/2013/11/24/oprah-obama-racist-bbc-freedom-medal-column/3693405/; "Oprah, Obama, and the Racism Dodge," *National Review Online*, accessed January 18, 2016, http://www.nationalreview.com/article/364359/oprah-obama-and-racism-dodge-jonah-goldberg; Fox Nation, "O'Reilly Clashes with Harvard Professor over Oprah: She's 'Indicting' America as a Racist Nation," *FoxNation.com* (January 18, 2016), http://nation.foxnews.com/2013/11/19/oreilly-clashes-harvard-professor-over-oprah-shes-indicting-america-racist-nation; Daniel Schorr, "A New, 'Post-Racial' Political Era in America," NPR.org, accessed January 18, 2016, http://www.npr.org/templates/story/story.php?storyId=18489466.

22. This section also appears in Katie Walker Grimes, *Fugitive Saints: Catholicism and the Politics of Slavery* (Minneapolis: Fortress Press, 2017), xiii.

23. Cassidy and Mikulich, *Interrupting White Privilege*, 2.

24. Ibid., 128.

25. For a more in-depth critique of "the white privilege approach," see Katie Grimes, "Black Exceptionalism: Anti-blackness Supremacy in the Afterlife of Slavery," eds. Vincent W. Lloyd and Andrew Prevot, *Anti-Blackness and Christian Ethics* (Maryknoll, NY: Orbis, 2017).

The white privilege approach also errs by portraying antiblackness as just one form of oppression among many others rather than a unique principle of social organization. It provides no way to attend to differences among differences, nor does it allow us to recognize ranks within social hierarchies. For example, under the conceptual influence of the white privilege approach, even Cassidy and Mikulich, two of very few white Catholic theologians to place racism at the center of their scholarship, claim that "the matrix of domination contains few pure victims or oppressors."[26] Even if true, their maxim obfuscates: while no one qualifies as "pure victim," only black people suffer victimization by antiblackness supremacy just as only nonblack people advance by means of it. The discourse of privilege encourages this very obfuscation. If white people possess white privilege, then so must men of all races possess male privilege as must heterosexuals benefit from straight privilege. And indeed they do. But rather than enabling us to attend to the intersections of economic, sexual, and racial oppressions, this framing impedes the intersectional analysis pioneered by black feminist scholars like Kimberlé Crenshaw: only distinct entities can intersect.[27]

Even worse, the language of white privilege allows almost everyone to position herself as analogously, if not equally, oppressed as black people. In addition to misrepresenting social reality, this à la carte approach to oppression makes black demands for equality less coherent. Indeed, if the overwhelming majority of human beings possess privilege in varying amounts based upon their unique bundle of identities, we lose our bearings quite quickly. In this view, a wealthy, able-bodied, heterosexual, cisgender African American male qualifies as vastly more privileged and therefore oppressive than a middle-class, masculine of center, physically disabled white lesbian. Whiteness, like blackness, ultimately becomes an individual condition.

Again, this effect often occurs against the wishes of white antiracist theologians. For example, Pfeil attempts to distinguish racial injustice from other forms of injustice when she depicts "those oppressed by structures of white privilege" as "arguably the most oppressed both

26. Cassidy and Mikulich, *Interrupting White Privilege*, 3. See also Karen Teel, *Racism and the Image of God*.
27. Kimberlé Crenshaw, "Mapping the Margins: Intersectionality, Identity Politics, and Violence against Women of Color," *Stanford Law Review* 43, no. 6 (1991), 124.

within the U.S. Catholic Church and in U.S. society."[28] But the framework of white privilege that she employs provides no way to justify this preference. A critical reader surely wonders what makes *white* privilege more oppressive than other forms of privilege, especially when everyone possesses different amounts and bundles of privilege. Indeed, such individualizing reflects less a misunderstanding of the concept of privilege than it does a reasonable interpretation of it. Peggy McIntosh developed her theory of white privilege because she perceived sexism and racism as analogous conditions: if men have male privilege, then white people have white privilege.[29] But herein lies the problem: due to antiblackness supremacy's unique connection to the exceptional condition of slavery, racism, and other forms of social injustice, including sexism, are not interchangeable evils. Although they intersect, they do not unfold within the same plane.

This language of white privilege also overestimates the possibility and importance of white agency and self-reform. Portraying white privilege rather than white supremacy as the ultimate evil, ethicists typically focus on ways to conduce white people to make more racially just choices. But if supremacy ultimately animates the evil heart of whiteness, then white power and agency represent not the solution, but the problem. The phrase "white supremacy" compels theologians to care less about how to persuade whites to do the right thing and more on what they need to be made to do.[30] In contrast to theologian Christopher Pramuk, who exhorts academics to "ask how [antiracist discourse] will be communicated to ordinary white Christians in the pews," the white supremacy approach to racial inequality encourages the church to focus much more intently on empowering black people.[31] Naming the relation between race and power, the phrase "white supremacy" possesses both a rhetorical effectiveness and a descriptive accuracy that the term white privilege lacks.[32]

28. Ibid., 129. Maureen O'Connell also deploys the discourse of white privilege in her work *Compassion.*

29. Peggy McIntosh, "White Privilege: Unpacking the Invisible Knapsack." http://ted.coe.wayne.edu/ele3600/mcintosh.html.

30. Despite her embrace of the term "white supremacy," I contend that Jennifer Harvey also places too much confidence in white agency. It is not enough to describe racial evil as white supremacy, we must also recognize its corporate operation. *Whiteness and Morality: Pursuing Racial Justice Through Reparations and Sovereignty* (New York: Springer, 2007), 41–42.

31. Pramuk, *Hope Sings, So Beautiful*, 5.

32. White Protestant ethicist Jennifer Harvey also tends to prefer the discourse of white supremacy to that of white privilege. See, for example, *Whiteness and Morality*.

The white privilege approach also prevents theologians from repairing ethical frameworks they rightly diagnose as broken.[33] For example, Cassidy, Mikulich, and Pfeil locate the inadequacy of "traditional Catholic moral categories of guilt and innocence" in their inability to explain how we can "be accountable to something we do not intend, or be complicit in something [in which] we do not consciously participate."[34] Highlighting the way in which "the language of cooperation with evil does not get at the radical nature of the moral conundrum of being white," these authors instead identify the moral problem at the heart of whiteness as one of "complicity in maintaining our white privilege even if we do not intend it."[35] In order to interrupt thought patterns that make "racism and white privilege [appear] to be abstract and separate from [white people like] me," they propose the concept of complicity for its capacity to obliterate the "assumption of distance that allows [white people like] me to [under]estimate how much I am actually participating in what is distinct from me."[36] But perhaps white people struggle to envision their "entanglement with oppression" in part because the discourse of privilege portrays whiteness as not what white people do, but something white people carry around with them.[37] Indeed, McIntosh famously figures white privilege as a knapsack, that is, an accessory whites carry around outside of their bodies.

Ultimately, what I term "the complicity approach to white racial evil" does not in fact prevent "racism and white privilege [from] continuing to be abstract and separate from me" as Cassidy and Mikulich argue. When they define "complicity" as "the ways that whites benefit from, consciously and unconsciously participate in, and contribute to the policies, institutions, and social structures that create, sustain, and perpetuate hyper-incarceration" and other components of white supremacy, they still situate racial evil as an entity existing outside of the white subject.[38] Rather than successfully explaining how "white superiority and racial oppression goes to the soul of white identity," they figure white supremacy more like a shady friend from high

33. An earlier version of part of the argument made in this chapter appears in Grimes, "Black Exceptionalism."

34. Alex Mikulich et al., *The Scandal of White Complicity in US Hyper-Incarceration: A Nonviolent Spirituality of White Resistance* (New York: Palgrave Macmillan, 2013), 8.

35. Ibid., 9.

36. Ibid., 8.

37. Ibid., 9.

38. Ibid., 33.

school who comes around every now and then and lures you into committing various acts of mischief, or like a slightly unsavory businesswoman with whom you occasionally collaborate and from whose questionable ethics you frequently reap profits.[39] In truth, whites do not simply collaborate with and benefit from racial evil; it lives within them, and they enact it directly with their bodies and not just through their interactions with structures. Cassidy, Mikulich, and Pfeil surely recognize this, but the moral framework they provide does not.[40] They are right about the destination, but wrong about how to get there.

Cassidy, Mikulich, and Pfeil favor the concept of "complicity" for a second reason: they believe it allows them to explain how white people can "be accountable to something we do not intend, or be complicit in something [in which] we do not consciously participate." But in so doing, they let white people off far too easily.[41] Locating intentionality primarily or even entirely in what the mind consciously acknowledges, these scholars underestimate intention's embodied, unconscious, and non-mental operation. In truth, white people *do* intend the white supremacist vices we embody, regardless of whether we do so consciously.

Third, the concept of complicity sometimes slips into incoherence. On the one hand, Cassidy and Mikulich describe racial injustice as an evil that white people do not intend, but, on the other hand, they accuse whites of participating in, maintaining, and otherwise supporting life-denying structures of sin. But how can an unintentional action of any sort qualify as an instance of maintenance or participation? For example, if a young child possessed a fascination for the can of wax sitting in her mother's garage and loved the sensation of smearing the wax in circles all over her mother's freshly painted car, we would not credit this child with "maintaining" the car. No, we would simply wipe our brow and breathe a sigh of relief that this child's curiosity made for an easy cleanup. Neither would we charge a person who was walking along a crowded sidewalk and unknowingly shielded a fleeing shoplifter from the sight of pursuing shopkeepers with "participating" in theft.

The lights of white agency have been dimmed: if white people did not intentionally create racism, how can we be sure they can inten-

39. Ibid.
40. Ibid., 9.
41. Mikulich et al., *The Scandal of White Complicity*, 8.

tionally dismantle it? Even worse, in describing racism as an often-unintended outcome of vaguely described actions, scholars portray it as an accidental catastrophe we have not bothered to clean up yet. This inevitably, even if implicitly, casts racially conscious whites more like Good Samaritan saviors than the unrepentant thieves that we are. Again, this critique does not claim that these leading ethicists actually believe this about whites; it argues only that they have not yet developed a moral framework that explains how individual whites can personally intend the white supremacist world they inhabit. So-called racism seems like something that happens but not so much like anything anyone actually does.

MOVING BEYOND EXISTING ETHICAL FRAMEWORKS

The discourse of white privilege should not bear all the blame. Just as ethicists underestimate the individual guilt of whites because we lean too heavily on the discourse of white privilege, we have leaned so heavily on the discourse of white privilege partially because we lack the means by which to judge white people guilty for a sin like white supremacy.[42] This book seeks to rectify this by introducing what I call a theory of corporate virtue and vice. While traditional virtue theory describes the relation between the habits and character of individuals, corporate virtue theory describes the relation between the habits and character of social bodies. Taking the next step along the long path that previous theological ethicists have been paving, this new account of moral habituation more convincingly reconciles the individual and social aspects of racial evil.

Despite both the late-twentieth-century turn to the body in theology and the rising popularity of Pierre Bourdieu's concept of habitus among scholars of social injustice, theological ethicists have yet to fully embrace the thoroughly embodied character of all moral processes.[43] Overlooking the way in which intention operates through the body, ethicists struggle to describe racial habituation as partially unconscious yet completely voluntary. Here one error spawns another. Lacking the means by which to describe the body's

42. For a summary of critiques of "assertions about the complicity of an entire group of people in violence," see Elisabeth T. Vasko, *Beyond Apathy: A Theology for Bystanders* (Minneapolis: Fortress Press, 2015), 16.

43. See, for example, Mikulich et al., *The Scandal of White Complicity*, 10, 76–81, 130, 161, 171, 177, 182.

role in habituation adequately, antiracist theologians are left with a nearly impossible task: they must attempt to convince all whites to shoulder the burden of repairing structures that white people cannot remember breaking in the first place. The concept of complicity in structural or social sin seemingly provides a way out of this bind: the notion of structural sin says something about all white people without saying anything definite about any white person in particular; the notion of complicity then attempts to place the individual white person at the scene of the crime, that is, in a morally significant relation to these racialized structures. But the expansive adaptability of "the complicity approach" provides no way to make the mundane sins of white supremacy visible. We know what is happening, but we do not know who is doing it.

This theory of corporate virtue and vice makes these sins much more visible.[44] Prioritizing the body both descriptively and rhetorically, it qualifies as corporate in two senses of the term. First, it envisages human beings as more than just individuals with a social disposition who are shaped by the social structures they help to build. It understands that, in a real sense, human beings also are the corporate bodies they comprise. In response, a corporate theory of virtue sharpens our perception of the guilt of white individuals while also providing the means to transcend the conceptual limits of individualized moral accounting. Put another way, this theory more convincingly convicts whites as individuals precisely by displacing the individual as the sole, basic unit of ethical measurement.[45]

Second, in addition to conceiving of the human person as part of a racial whole that exceeds the sum of its parts, this theory of corporate virtue illuminates the role the body plays in habituation. More than simply offering a more adequate explanation for how individual whites become socially constructed by white supremacy, this turn to the body intensifies the individual white person's moral responsibil-

44. In positing the existence of corporate racial virtue that all people, even non-Christians, are capable of acquiring, I do affirm the existence of what Aquinas would term "pagan virtues." But in describing corporate virtue as available to nonbelievers, I do not deny the role that God's grace plays in moral transformation. Like Jennifer Herdt, I "underscore the graced character of *all* virtue acquisition." God's grace does not extend to Christians only. Aquinas, ST I–II.65.2; II–II.23.7; II–II.136.3; see also Jennifer A. Herdt, "Redeeming the Acquired Virtues," *Journal of Religious Ethics* 41, no. 4 (2013): 730–31, 734.

45. My theory of corporate virtue and vice does not necessarily conflict with Vasko's bystander ethics. White people are bystanders to certain instances of racial violence and injustice, but they are not only bystanders. My claim is that white people have racial vices, not that they are committing racial sins every moment of their lives. (*Beyond Apathy*, 18.)

ity for the world around her and the world inside of her. Contrary to the claims of Cassidy, Mikulich, and Pfeil, whiteness is not a "conundrum." It only appears particularly vexing because we insist on asking it only as a question to which we already know the answer. Rather than an exception to the rules of ordinary moral problems, the phenomenon of racial evil exposes theological ethics' weak spots—as long as we name it correctly. In order to better describe the operation of racial evil, I propose the following two adjustments: first, we ought to supplement the interrelated concepts of complicity and structural sin with a theory of corporate virtue and vice, and second, we ought to favor the discourse of white supremacy to that of white privilege.[46]

But, despite its superiority to the term "white privilege," the descriptor white supremacy harbors dangers of its own, even when it is classified as a corporate vice. Just as the white privilege approach portrays, for example, black men and white women as somehow equally underprivileged, the phrase white supremacy falsely figures "people of color" as equally and "monolithically . . . victimized under white supremacy." This "people-of-color-blindness," Jared Sexton explains, "misunderstands the specificity of antiblackness" and misperceives both slavery and its afterlife "as a form of . . . racial oppression among others."[47] Sociologist George Yancey anticipates this insight when he argues that "a black/nonblack dichotomy" explains the operation of race better than the conventionally favored "white/nonwhite dichotomy."[48]

Thus, rather than focusing solely on the ways in which nonblack people of color experience disadvantage by not qualifying as "white," these scholars urge us to center our attention on the way in which whites and nonblack people of color accrue power and privilege by not qualifying as "black." Even if nonblack people of color do not occupy the ontological position of "master," they enjoy immunity from the ontological position of "slave."[49] Thus, in addition to preferring "white supremacy" to "white privilege," theologians ought to speak even more frequently of the condition I call "antiblackness supremacy." Just as white supremacy describes the fact that white people, both as groups and as individuals, possess more power

46. This section also appears in Grimes, "Black Exceptionalism."

47. Jared Sexton, "People-of-Color-Blindness: Notes on the Afterlife of Slavery," *Social Text* 28, no. 2 103 (June 20, 2010): 48.

48. George A. Yancey, *Who Is White?: Latinos, Asians, and the New Black/Nonblack Divide* (Boulder, CO: Lynne Rienner, 2003), 21.

49. Sexton, "People-of-Color-Blindness," 36.

than people of color, both as groups and as individuals, the phrase "antiblackness supremacy" identifies the fact that nonblack people, both as individuals and as groups, amass power due to this country's pervasive antiblackness. In this way, nonblack life comes at the expense of black life. Although the term "antiblackness supremacy" describes a different reality than does the phrase "white supremacy," it shares the latter's ethical clarity. It avoids individualizing; it places a rhetorical spotlight on the relation between racial evil and power; and it is compatible with a theory of corporate virtue. The term "antiblackness supremacy" in fact surpasses "white supremacy" in rhetorical precision because it specifies the racial system that emerged from and attempts to preserve the legacy of black slavery.

I call this form of supremacy "antiblackness" rather than "antiblack" in order to surpass the limits of individual thinking. While the word "antiblack" draws our attention primarily to black individuals and therefore encourages the type of comparative accounting that occurs when we attempt to calculate degrees of white privilege, the more expansive adjective "antiblackness" includes the black individual but also goes beyond her. The term "antiblackness" also better captures the way in which racialized power makes a performative argument about the body. In this way, nonblack people perceive "blackness" as a crime of which not all black people are equally guilty.[50] The word "antiblackness," though not a verb, indicates action unmistakably; the word is emphatically performative. Menacingly kinetic, it bears witness to the otherwise untold violence of our racial order with every breathed escape and every sharp hand sign.

Why not just advocate for the term "antiblackness"? Because slavery represents a relation that is sustained by and in turn provides a distinct form of power, the term "antiblackness supremacy" describes

50. Amaryah Armstrong, "Blackness and Value; Part 2: On Whiteness as Credit," *Women in Theology*, February 11, 2015, http://womenintheology.org/2015/02/11/blackness-and-value-part-2-on-whiteness-as-credit/; Amaryah Armstrong, "On the Theo-Political Vision of Macklemore; Or, Why Proximity & Intimacy ≠ Solidarity," *Women in Theology*, June 16, 2013, http://womenintheology.org/2013/06/16/on-the-theo-political-vision-of-macklemore-or-why-proximity-intimacy-≠-solidarity/; see also literature scholar Yago Colás's argument about the way in which, although professional basketball players Steph Curry and LeBron James are both black, James is perceived, even if implicitly, as embodying a certain style of blackness that Curry receives credit for rejecting. "A Desire Named Steph Curry | Between the Lines," accessed January 27, 2016, http://yagocolas.com/index.php/2015/06/16/a-desire-named-steph-curry/; Yago Colás further explores the performative dimensions of blackness in *Ball Don't Lie: Myth, Genealogy, and Invention in the Cultures of Basketball* (Philadelphia: Temple University Press, 2016).

the source and core character of racial injustice by naming it. In so doing, the term "antiblackness supremacy" maintains the link between the oppression of black people and enslavement in a way the appellation "antiblackness" cannot. In identifying antiblackness as supremacy, we better position ourselves to track the shifting operation of this power and push back against it.

These caveats notwithstanding, the phrase "antiblackness supremacy" undoubtedly sounds syntactically wooden. But, rather than being a weakness, such awkwardness represents a strength. Precisely because it does not roll easily off the tongue, "antiblackness supremacy" operates in interruptive fashion; it cannot be aesthetically assimilated. Unlike the phenomenon of antiblackness supremacy, whose routine pervasiveness, like camouflage, can make it appear not to exist at all, the phrase "antiblackness supremacy" cannot be rendered ordinary, mundane, or familiar.[51] It sticks out precisely because it does not fit within sentences the way that we expect it to.[52]

In introducing the concept of "antiblackness supremacy," this book unabashedly advocates a type of black exceptionalism that insists upon the uniqueness of antiblackness.[53] The historical specificity of antiblackness supremacy ought to change the way scholars speak about racial evil: in addition to situating their subjects in relation to white supremacy, theologians who reflect upon the experience of nonblack people of color must also account for these communities' empowering participation in the vice of antiblackness.[54] Rather than denying the difference between either white and nonwhite or mestizo and Asian American, for example, this move recognizes antiblackness as the animating center of all racial hierarchy. As such, the study of antiblackness supremacy provides a uniquely privileged epistemological vantage point from which to assess any facet of this country's racial landscape.[55]

By reserving the term "white supremacy" for only those conditions

51. Saidiya V. Hartman, *Scenes of Subjection: Terror, Slavery, and Self-Making in Nineteenth-Century America*, 1st ed. (New York: Oxford University Press, 1997), 3, 4.

52. This section also appears in Walker Grimes, *Fugitive Saints*, xiii.

53. An earlier version of this argument for black exceptionalism appears in Katie Grimes, "Black Exceptionalism."

54. Michelle A. Gonzalez, *Afro-Cuban Theology: Religion, Race, Culture, and Identity* (Gainesville: University Press of Florida, 2011), 9; Miguel De La Torre, "Masking Hispanic Racism: A Cuban Case Study," *Journal of Hispanic/Latino Theology* 6, no. 4 (1999): 57–73; Miguel A. De La Torre, "Beyond Machismo: A Cuban Case Study," *Annual of the Society of Christian Ethics* (1999): 213–33.

55. Sexton, "People-of-Color-Blindness," 48.

that empower whites over and against all peoples of color with relative, though not absolute, uniformity, we do not dim our outrage at white supremacy. Both white supremacy and antiblackness supremacy continue to operate as corporate vices in both the church and the world. Rather than supplying an excuse to ignore the reality of white supremacy, the concept "antiblackness supremacy" allows us to understand it better. Antiblackness supremacy exists as not a type of white supremacy, but its originating cause. Even more than white supremacy empowers and preserves the purity of whites, it feeds off the negation of blackness and black people.[56] For this reason, while antiblackness supremacy might survive the demolition of a specifically white supremacy, white supremacy undoubtedly would crumble without the antiblackness that upholds it. More than simply enabling antiblackness, scholars who ignore the supremacy it conveys ultimately empower whiteness, even as they try to dismantle or disarm it. For this reason, scholars ought to vigorously resist all calls to "move beyond the black-white binary."[57] As Sexton recognizes, this push serves less to de-center whiteness than to obscure blackness and to diffuse the demands of black power.[58]

ANTIBLACKNESS SUPREMACY AND THE "BROWNING" OF AMERICA

Especially in the field of Catholic theology, this black exceptionalism might not be popular. Many Catholic theologians and leaders anticipate the rapidly approaching future in which Latino/as will outnumber whites in both society and the church. Misperceiving unsullied whiteness as our nation's anchoring injustice, these Catholic theologians tend to portray this "browning of America" as the dawn of a new reality in which racial division gives way to the reconciling power of mestizaje.[59] Misidentifying a precious obsession with the

56. Natasha Howard, "Black in the Non-Black Imagination: How Anti-Black Ideology Shapes Non-Black Racial Discourse," PhD diss., University of New Mexico, 2011, 14. http://gradworks.umi.com/34/60/3460981.html. James Perkinson has also recognized this; see *White Theology: Outing Supremacy in Modernity* (New York: Palgrave Macmillan, 2004), 153, 172.

57. Jared Sexton, *Amalgamation Schemes: Antiblackness and the Critique of Multiracialism* (Minneapolis: University of Minnesota Press, 2008), 2, 6; Howard, "Black in the Non-Black Imagination," 60, 67.

58. Jared Sexton, "Proprieties of Coalition: Blacks, Asians, and the Politics of Policing," *Critical Sociology* 36, no. 1 (2010): 90.

59. Néstor Medina, *Mestizaje: Remapping Race, Culture, and Faith in Latina/o Catholicism* (Mary-

preservation of a white racial purity founded upon a type of "not even one-drop rule" as an integral and even foundational tenet of white supremacy, white Anglo scholars in particular misinterpret the racial significance of both rising rates of so-called interracial marriage and the entrance of large numbers of immigrants from Latin America and Asia into the United States.[60] But, as Néstor Medina highlights, ideologies of mestizaje can promote antiblackness even as they de-center whiteness.[61]

Why? Nonblack people of color along with immigrants of all races typically demonstrate their suitability for citizenship or ecclesial membership by asserting their difference from the native-born descendants of black slaves.[62] This benefit accrues even when antiblackness occurs unconsciously. Whiteness and humanness come into existence and maintain their coherence not *sui generis* but through contrasting negation with blackness. As Frantz Fanon recognizes, even when certain groups can never fit within the prevailing parameters of whiteness, they gain admission into the category of the human "simply . . . [by] not being a nigger."[63] We U.S.-Americans will not miscegenate or immigrate our way out of antiblackness supremacy.[64]

The antiblackness supremacy approach ultimately encourages theologians to acknowledge the uniqueness of both Africanized slavery and its ongoing afterlife. For this reason, theologians ought to resist the temptation to compare the nonblack Catholic experience to the black experience even implicitly. They ought to employ the phrase "people of color" only when describing a condition that truly encompasses all nonwhite peoples, and they should deploy the term "white supremacy" only when condemning structures that oppress all nonwhite peoples with relative uniformity. In classifying all nonwhite people as uniformly "of color," we amplify the ability of nonblack political projects to "allegorize themselves as revolts against slavery." Inattention to the specificity of antiblackness supremacy similarly enables the purportedly pan-racial, but often white-dominated,

knoll, NY: Orbis, 2009), 11, 14, 49–51; Arlene Dávila, *Latino Spin: Public Image and the Whitewashing of Race* (New York: New York University Press, 2008), 1.

60. Sexton, *Amalgamation Schemes*, 5.

61. Medina, *Mestizaje*, 48–50.

62. Howard, "Black in the Non-Black Imagination," 110, 112–13.

63. Frank B. Wilderson III, *Red, White & Black: Cinema and the Structure of US Antagonisms* (Durham, NC: Duke University Press, 2010), 37.

64. Yancey, *Who Is White?*, 3–4.

LGBT rights movement, which sometimes styles itself "the new civil rights movement."[65] Rather than an act of solidarity with black political movements, this type of unintended political blackface in fact undermines black power.[66] When the worker, nonwhite immigrant, or LGBT person advocates for social and civil equality, she often does so on the backs of blacks.[67]

Theologians also ought to interrogate the ways in which antiblackness supremacy makes the story of Asian American and Latino/a immigration similar to, but not identical with, that of the Europeans who came to this country during the last two centuries.[68] Simply by coming to the United States as immigrants rather than slaves, nonblack Latino/as and Asian Americans inherit structural antagonism to black descendants of slaves.[69] For example, although black Latino/as can be treated like native-born black people despite the ameliorating power of their immigrant status, they experience this condition not as Latino/as but as those who are visibly descended from this hemisphere's black slaves. Scholars should therefore resist the temptation to gather "black" and "Latino/a" into a single category of racial experience.[70] And, without denying the sociocultural validity of political salience of Latino/a identity, Catholic scholars in particular ought to follow the advice of Latino/a scholars such Medina and Jorge Aquino and much more rigorously attend to the way racial difference and hierarchy exists not around this category but within it.[71] By ignoring the whiteness, blackness, and antiblackness of Latino/a people, Catholic theologians obscure much more than they illuminate. For example, although black Latino/as can be treated like native-born blacks despite the ameliorating power of their immigrant

65. See, for example, the popular opinion site "The New Civil Rights Movement." http://www.thenewcivilrightsmovement.com/about_david.

66. Yancey, *Who Is White?,* 42.

67. Wilderson, *Red, White & Black*, 58.

68. Howard, "Black in the Non-Black Imagination," 74, 77, 112; Tamara K. Nopper, "Minority, Black and Non-Black People of Color: 'New' Color-Blind Racism and the US Small Business Administration's Approach to Minority Business Lending in the Post-Civil Rights Era," *Critical Sociology* 37, no. 5 (September 1, 2011): 652; Tamara K. Nopper, *Beyond the Bootstrap: How Korean Banks and U.S. Government Institutions Contribute to Korean Immigrant Entrepreneurship in the United States* (Ann Arbor, MI: ProQuest, 2008), 58.

69. Sexton, "People-of-Color-Blindness Notes on the Afterlife of Slavery," 40.

70. The racialization of *Latinidad* occurs in Protestant theology as well. For example, Harvey tends to refer to "Latino" and "black" as distinct, non-overlapping identities rather than distinct but often overlapping ones. Harvey, *Whiteness and Morality*, 20.

71. Jorge Aquino, *"Ni Blanquitos, ni Negritos": Race, Nation, and Identity in United States Latino/a Theology*, PhD diss., Graduate Theological Union, 2006, 5–6, 13.

status, they experience this condition not as Latino/as but as those who are visibly descended from this hemisphere's black slaves. Scholars of all types should thus resist the temptation to gather "black" and "Latino/a" together into a single category of racial experience.[72]

ANTIBLACKNESS AND ECONOMIC INJUSTICE: TWO DISTINCT FORMS OF EVIL

Rather than calling attention away from other forms of evil, the antiblackness supremacy approach enhances our ability to understand them precisely. This holds especially true with respect to the relation between race and class. Scholars and activists still struggle to understand how we can combat class oppression and so-called racism with equal vigor. Too often, opposition to one is perceived as, and in some cases functions as, a distraction from resisting the other partially because we have not yet devised a way of distinguishing one from the other. Rather than denying the interaction between economic injustice and racial evil of all kinds, the term "antiblackness supremacy" prevents us from collapsing the latter into the former.

Of course, we cannot detach the pursuit of black freedom from questions of economic justice entirely.[73] Antiblackness has always operated as a campaign of coordinated plunder. But current categories tempt us to envision antiblackness supremacy as just a racialized form of economic injustice.[74] Antiracist scholars and activists

72. Gonzalez, *Afro-Cuban Theology*, 6. In recent years, African American and Latino/a theologians have begun to engage in cross-cultural dialogue much more explicitly. See, for example, Anthony B. Pinn and Benjamin Valentin, eds., *The Ties That Bind: African American and American/Latino/a Theologies in Dialogue* (New York: Bloomsbury Academic, 2001).

73. The founders of the Black Lives Matter Movement—Alicia Garza, Patrisse Cullors, and Opal Tometi— argue for something similar with respect to other forms of differences and injustice; they encourage people to "lift up Black lives as an opportunity to connect struggles across race, class, gender, nationality, sexuality and disability." Black Lives Matter: HerStory, http://blacklivesmatter.com/herstory/. Accessed January 6, 2016.

74. For several recent examples of this tendency, see "Baltimore Riots Sparked Not by Race but by Class Tensions between Police, Poor—Washington Times," accessed January 27, 2016, http://www.washingtontimes.com/news/2015/apr/29/baltimore-riots-sparked-not-by-race-but-by-class-t/?page=all; Chris McGreal Ferguson and Missouri, "Blame Poverty, Not Race, Say Ferguson's White Minority," *The Guardian*, August 23, 2014, sec. US news, http://www.theguardian.com/world/2014/aug/23/ferguson-michael-brown-blame-poverty-not-race; Lydia DePillis, "Police Union: 'We Don't Believe It's an Issue of Race. We Believe It's an Issue of Poverty,'" *The Washington Post*, December 4, 2014, https://www.washingtonpost.com/news/storyline/wp/2014/12/04/police-union-on-brown-and-garner-we-dont-believe-its-an-issue-of-race-we-believe-its-an-issue-of-poverty/.

often struggle to explain how impoverished white people, for example, derive racialized power at the expense of affluent black people. Failing to distinguish antiblackness from economic oppression similarly prompts liberal policymakers to misidentify the pursuit of economic justice as the best way to combat racial inequality. But U.S. history provides us little reason to search for economic solutions to racial problems: after all, the most progressive legislative package in U.S. history, the New Deal, passed into law only because disproportionately black sharecroppers and domestic workers were barred from receiving from many of its most significant benefits.[75] Imprecise accounts of the relation between race and class also encourage leftists occasionally to succumb to the belief that racial inequality will disappear when capitalism does. But the antiblackness supremacy rooted in the European enslavement of Africans pre-existed capitalism; it first flourished in the late medieval monarchies of Spain and Portugal, which were neither capitalist nor neoliberal.[76] Ultimately, while capitalism and antiblackness supremacy certainly have been great allies, antiblackness supremacy could likely would outlast the demise of the economic system it helped to create.[77] Primarily economic solutions cannot solve primarily racial problems.

Because it traces antiblack racism back to slavery, the antiblackness supremacy approach provides scholars a steadier method of disentangling racial and economic injustice. Slavery comprises more than a condition of extremely uncompensated labor. For this reason, antiblackness supremacy represents more than just a particularly clever way of accumulating capital and controlling the working class: it instead preserves the pleasures and power of racialized slavery to all those it positions as nonblack, even those who are impoverished and otherwise marginalized.[78] The antiblackness supremacy approach also

75. Ira Katznelson, *When Affirmative Action Was White: An Untold History of Racial Inequality* (New York: W.W. Norton, 2005), xiv, 17, 22, 36–37, 42–44. For an example of how white socialists benefited at the expense of black people, see Dubois, *Darkwater*, 27, 66, 138. During this time, President Franklin Roosevelt also forced thousands of Japanese Americans into internment camps.

76. See Matthew Lange, James Mahoney, and Matthias vom Hau, "Colonialism and Development: A Comparative Analysis of Spanish and British Colonies," *American Journal of Sociology* 111, no. 5 (March 2006): 1416, 1421, 1422, 1436–37, and 1453.

77. Eric Eustace Williams, *Capitalism & Slavery* (Chapel Hill: University of North Carolina Press, 1944); Edward E. Baptist, *The Half Has Never Been Told: Slavery and the Making of American Capitalism* (New York: Basic Books, 2014).

78. Nor do I deny that socialist or other anticapitalist scholars can be simultaneously antiracist; I claim only that anticapitalist forms of labor organization do not necessarily overturn antiblackness supremacy.

clarifies the relation of race and class, positioning scholars to uncover the ways in which our economic order, no matter what shape it takes, seeks to suture blackness's association with slave status both materially and discursively.

The antiblackness supremacy approach amplifies our ability to identify which aspects of contemporary economic reality do in fact arise from the afterlife of slavery. Rather than simply analyzing how economic injustice intersects with antiblackness supremacy, this concept highlights the way in which the contemporary economic reality carries forward or attempts to "revivify . . . the [contested] association between blackness and slave status."[79] For example, while conventional analyses would tend to portray black people as more likely to experience poverty than their white counterparts, the antiblackness supremacy approach might instead distinguish black poverty for the way it imposes a unique stigma and inflicts unique dishonor on blackness and the people who are perceived as embodying it. It might also note how we imagine impoverished black people as uniquely dangerous: the exploited whites of Appalachia might be economically marginalized, but they are not corralled into ghettos and prisons. Black people then do not experience more of the same type of poverty that other groups experience; they alone experience antiblackness through impoverishment.

At the same time, the antiblackness supremacy approach lacks the rhetorical weaknesses of both the white privilege and white supremacy approaches: it better explains why wealth does not accord a black person immunity from antiblackness supremacy just as poverty does not deprive a white person of the power antiblackness supremacy provides.[80] For this reason, it more adeptly grasps the fact that the growth of the black middle class does not necessarily signal the demise or diminishment of slavery's afterlife: black people can experience varying levels of class exploitation yet still shoulder the weight of a common antiblackness supremacy. Under this framework, we can recognize that a black factory worker in postwar Detroit, for example, suffers under both antiblackness supremacy and class alienation whereas his white co-worker only endures the latter. Rather than obscuring the reality of class-based oppression, distin-

79. Walker Grimes, *Fugitive Saints*, xii.
80. Wilderson, *Red, White & Black*, 37.

guishing it from antiblackness supremacy makes the struggle against class exploitation both more coherent and more viable.[81]

Ultimately, more than simply considering racial injustice in light of Catholic theology, this book endeavors to reconsider Catholic theology in light of racial injustice. Catholic theologians too often assume that Catholic theology already possesses the tools both to fix the problem and to construct the new reality. When we white Catholic theologians bother to talk about racism, we typically attempt to make race fit within existing theological concepts and approaches. We have not even considered that the history and ongoing reality of white supremacy and antiblackness supremacy ought to change everything. In response, this book places the story of black slavery and its ongoing afterlife at the center of Christian life and theological reflection.

81. This applies to other forms of nonracial injustice as well. In this way, for example, the Black Lives Matter Movement, which was founded by three queer black women—Patrisse Cullors, Opal Tometi, and Alicia Garza—is simultaneously "queer affirming," "transgender affirming," and "unapologetically black." In fact, one could argue that the movement's unapologetically black character enhances its ability to be queer and transgender affirming. In contrast, those who attempt to affirm blackness and black people by being unapologetically queer would end up centering whiteness and white people. "Black Lives Matter: Founding Principles," http://blacklivesmatter.com/guiding-principles/. Accessed January 6, 2016.

PART I

Defining White Supremacy and Antiblackness Supremacy

Rather than being merely the fantasy of neo-Nazi and skinhead extremists, white supremacy operates as a governing principle.[82] Put simply, white people, as a group and as individuals, have more power than do peoples of color as groups and as individuals. Although white supremacist power has pressed down upon all the peoples of color who have inhabited lands colonized by Europeans and their American heirs, it has not done so uniformly: white supremacy exercises different forms and degrees of power over different racial groups. White supremacy has also adjusted the parameters of whiteness: not everyone who qualifies as white in one time and place will qualify as white in another. Adapting strategically, white supremacy does whatever it needs to do in order to survive.

This flexibility characterizes white supremacy even today. In this history, themes recur uncannily, at once familiar and brand new.

82. Zeus Leonardo, "The Souls of White Folk," *Race Ethnicity and Education* 5, no. 1 (2002): 33–34; Howard Winant, *The World Is a Ghetto: Race and Democracy Since World War II* (New York: Basic Books, 2002), 31.

Both shifting and solid, white supremacy exists more like a remix than a refrain. But even as white supremacy adjusts itself, its relation to antiblackness remains the same: it feeds off antiblackness even more than it requires the preservation of pure whiteness. For this reason, antiblackness and the supremacy it accords provide the best frame of reference by which to measure and assess white supremacy's strategically adaptive operation in history.

Before we can narrate the history of antiblackness supremacy, we must distinguish it from other forms of domination like patriarchy, classism, or racism against nonblack people. Unlike other asymmetrical power relations, antiblackness supremacy alone bears the imprint of black slavery. Unfortunately, however, contemporary Westerners typically misunderstand slavery. Contrary to prevailing notions, slavery is best understood as neither a condition of unpaid labor nor the experience of un-freedom that comes from being owned by another human being. While slaveownership can be driven by a thirst for endless profit, even in the Americas, women and men owned slaves for a range of noneconomic reasons. Nor does unencumbered independence supply slavery's antithesis: many people possess "claims, privileges, and powers in" other people. For example, the wife has property rights in her husband; the professional sports owner has the right to trade his star.[83] What, then, is slavery?

As Orlando Patterson clarifies, slavery represents "the permanent, violent domination of natally alienated and generally dishonored persons."[84] Let us describe these characteristics in greater detail. First, the phrase "violent domination" possesses a specific meaning. More than simply coercive as other asymmetrical power-relations are, slavery sustains itself through the deployment of direct violence. For example, although the capitalist certainly deploys power to coerce the proletariat into working for him, he does not drive the proletariat into his fields or sweatshops by beating or mutilating him as the slave master does.[85] And while other instances of racial evil undoubtedly sustain themselves through violence, both structural and interpersonal, the slave is kept in line through a unique form of violence.

Second, the slave's relative powerlessness stems from a unique source: "[I]t was always originated (or was conceived of as having

83. Orlando Patterson, *Slavery and Social Death: A Comparative Study*, 1st ed. (Cambridge, MA: Harvard University Press, 1985), 25, 27.
84. Ibid., 13.
85. Ibid., 4.

originated) as a substitute for death, usually violent death."[86] Purportedly deserving criminal death, the slave lives only through her master's power. The ideology of slavery figures the slave master as not a violent thief but a merciful pardoner; slavery casts even newborn slaves as criminal bodies. But his pardon proves truly conditional: the slave master grants this stay of execution only as long as the ransomed captive accepts her condition of powerlessness before him. This relation transforms the slave into the ultimate and infinitely fungible human surrogate. Living only at her master's mercy, the slave purportedly owes him everything and anything.[87] Slavery further differs from other forms of domination in a third way. It alone renders its victims natally alienated and socially dead. Unlike immigrants, women, the proletariat, or sexual minorities, slaves

> were not allowed freely to integrate the experience of their ancestors into their lives, to inform their understanding of social reality with the inherited meanings of their natural forebears, or to anchor the living present in any conscious community of memory.[88]

Indeed, while the immigrant or refugee may leave his mother and motherland, Hartman's work reminds us that the slave alone loses them.[89]

In the Americas, this natal alienation extended even to native-born slaves of African descent, as the relationships enslaved women and men forged with each other "were never recognized as legitimate or binding." Slave couples were frequently sold away from each other and slaves of both sexes often had to submit to sex with their master. Nor could enslaved parents keep their children's masters from selling them to another master in another part of the world.[90] Illustrating the mutually enriching relation between the slave's relative powerlessness and the slave's natal alienation, in 1930, a U.S. American ex-slave recalled an occasion in which his older sister

> was fooling with the clock and broke it, and my old master taken her and tied a rope around her neck—just enough to keep it from choking her—and tied her up in the backyard and whipped her I don't know

86. Ibid., 5.
87. Ibid., 4–5.
88. Ibid., 5.
89. Saidiya Hartman, *Lose Your Mother: A Journey Along the Atlantic Slave Route* (New York: Macmillan, 2008), 103.
90. Patterson, *Slavery and Social Death*, 6.

> how long. There stood mother, there stood father, and there stood all the children and none could come to her rescue.[91]

Just as parents could not protect their children, so enslaved children could not inherit from their parents. Denied a heritage, an enslaved person belonged only to her master: only the master or those empowered by him could exercise rights over the slave just as the slave had obligations only to her master.[92] Bearing the shame of a criminal and the ignominy of a bastard, slaves had no honor to protect. This expulsion from socially specific systems of honor and status further disempowered enslaved people. Unsurprisingly, then, slavery becomes its own justification: slaves are subjected to extraordinary levels of violence because they are uniquely dishonored; they are uniquely dishonored in turn because they are subjected to extraordinary levels of violence. The fact that they are beaten and killed with impunity proves that they deserve to be beaten and killed with impunity.

Natally alienated, violently disciplined, and uniquely dishonored, enslaved people are turned into 'the ultimate human tools.'[93] Because they are allowed to live through their master alone, they are expected to live for him alone, that is, they are reduced to an extension of his will.[94] Deprived of the protections that kinship and community ordinarily provide, they can be used for nearly any task. Their humanity in fact makes them infinitely fungible.[95] Unlike inanimate instruments or beasts of burden, for example, which can perform a limited number of very specific tasks, the slave's humanity enables her to do almost anything. This also helps to explain why overly economic analyses of slavery can be misleading: throughout history, slaves have been used as scribes, skilled artisans, wet nurses, musicians, sex objects, royal advisors, entertainers, soldiers, and manual laborers. Slaves ultimately provide their masters with not wealth, but a very specific form of power and honor: rather than perceiving wealth as the ultimate end of slavery, we ought to recognize wealth as merely one means to the end of masterly power and honor.

For these reasons, while other types of asymmetrical power relations, such as patriarchy, heterosexism, or economic exploitation,

91. Ibid., 8.
92. Ibid., 5.
93. Ibid., 302.
94. Ibid., 204.
95. Frank B. Wilderson III, *Red, White & Black: Cinema and the Structure of US Antagonisms* (Durham, NC: Duke University Press, 2010), 32.

may bear a partial resemblance to certain features of the master-slave relationship, the slave ultimately suffers a reality beyond analogy. For example, when an enslaved person performs the same type of labor as an exploited member of the proletariat, these figures do not experience slightly different versions of a common oppression as many scholars imply. The slave and the proletariat exist not as occasionally converging points on a continuum of misery, but on entirely different planes of domination. The slave who labors alongside a member of the proletariat does so as the victim of a double oppression: he is both enslaved and alienated from the product of his labor.

Patterson's schema further enables us to distinguish the evils of slavery from those of patriarchy: even the most violently dominated wife exercises rights and enjoys privileges that the most well-treated slaves lack. Plus, marriage accords unenslaved women honor they would otherwise lack. Enslaved women, on the other hand, remain dishonored and stigmatized even when allowed to contract marriages. Further distinguishing slavery from patriarchy, even unmarried, unenslaved women can call upon the protection of friends just as they can offer it. Largely for this reason, unenslaved women can defend the integrity of their bodies much more effectively than enslaved women, who are considered categorically rapeable.[96] Slavery's components work in mutually intensifying fashion: in contrast to enslaved women who are considered without honor, unmarried, unenslaved women have honor that could be defended. In this way, for example, so-called 'spinsters' may have lagged behind their married sisters in social status, but they still belonged to their families of origin. In this same way, even if sexist statutes prohibited them from inheriting their fathers' property, unenslaved girls and young women still counted as somebody's daughter.

The slave also differs from the colonized subject. Although slavery can help to construct colonial projects, it does not accompany coloniality necessarily. People can be violently colonized without being systematically enslaved just as they can be systematically enslaved without being violently colonized.[97] Africanized slavery diverges from coloniality not just conceptually, but genealogically: its origins lie in not a generalized colonial moment, but the specific power relation of slavery. And although these forces often have acted as

96. Jennifer A. Glancey, *Slavery in Early Christianity* (Minneapolis: Fortress Press, 2006), 12.

97. Santiago Slabodsky, *Decolonial Judaism: Triumphal Failures of Barbaric Thinking* (New York: Springer, 2014), 27, 29, 55.

great allies, they also can operate independently from each other. Decolonial projects, while worthwhile, will not necessarily dismantle antiblackness supremacy. The particular brand of slavery that has structured life in the West carries an addition characteristic: one could be reduced to slavery simply for having a body that came to be categorized as "black." Colonial relations too can be racialized, of course.[98] But colonization racializes the relation between civilized woman or man and barbarian while Africanized slavery racialized the relation between slave and master. Thus, black Americans ultimately endure the afterlife not of coloniality, but slavery.[99]

The uniquely embodied character of Africanized slavery explains why it continues to inhabit human bodies as the corporate vice of antiblackness supremacy. Racialization imbued Africanized slavery with a self-perpetuating momentum: it could live on even after it was abolished. This corporate vice of antiblackness supremacy instills in moral agents a drive to associate blackness with slave status; it both results from and helps to sustain a structural habitat that produces and enables this association; it provides nonblacks, and especially whites, dominating power as well as the masterly pleasure. This formulation encourages us to understand antiblackness supremacy as neither a scheme of impoverishing class differentiation nor a species of generalized racism, but a way of extending the approximated pleasures and power of black slave mastership to as many people as possible.[100] Importantly, the powers and pleasures of mastership extend far beyond the merely economic just as mastership itself extends even to those individuals who do not own slaves. Precisely because the master-slave relationship has been racialized, all white people, regardless of wealth, income, gender, sexual orientation, or colonial status, had access to these supra-economic powers and pleasures. For this same reason, all black people endured the disempowerment, degradation, and indignity of servility even if they never spent a single day as

98. Sub-Saharan Africans were racialized as slaves centuries before they were racialized as colonizable barbarians. As Slobodsky explains, "the modern narrative of barbaric Africa would not become hegemonic until the Enlightenment." *Decolonial Judaism*, 54.

99. In linking antiblackness to slavery in this way, my approach differs from, but does not necessarily conflict with, that offered by Cornel West. While West traces a genealogy of the "internal dynamics of the structure of modern discourse in the late seventeenth and eighteenth centuries in western Europe—or during the Enlightenment," my framework would begin at the symbolic start date of Africanized slavery: 1441, when Portugal first sent slave-kidnapping missions to the west coast of Africa. *Prophesy Deliverance! An Afro-American Revolutionary Christianity* (Philadelphia: Westminster, 1982), 47, 38.

100. Wilderson, *Red, White & Black*, 14.

a slave. Uniquely marked by the stigma of slavery, visibly African-descended inhabitants of the Americas occupy a unique position in a world still animated by the afterlife of slavery.

Of course, black women, children, and men always have struggled against these forces of natal alienation and social death.[101] The afterlife of slavery thus undoubtedly includes not just the vices of antiblackness supremacy, that is, the drive to associate blackness with slave status, but also the various forms of black resistance to this construction. The history of racialized power is not limited just to what white people did to black people, but includes what black people did for themselves. More than simply honoring the agency of black Americans, this recognition reminds us of how often white people have had to be coerced into accepting gains in racial justice. With few exceptions, slave masters ceased slaveholding only involuntarily. Unsurprisingly, then, abolition achieved the end of chattel slavery, but it did not neutralize white people's drive to link slavery with blackness. It deprived unrepentant advocates of antiblackness supremacy only of the most effective means by which to maintain the stigmatizing relation between blackness and slave status. After abolition, antiblackness supremacy would have to codify the sclerotic connection between blackness and slave status through other means. Still today, the afterlife of slavery remains a site of contestation and struggle.

But blackness entails more than the consequences of antiblackness; it represents the social life lived in and against forces of social death.[102] While processes of racialization produced mechanisms of domination, they also provided a space for resistance and self-creation. This vital self-creation leaves ample space for black individuality. Although antiblackness unfolds in relatively uniform fashion, the lives of actual black people do not.[103] This book focuses on antiblackness not to deny what Fred Moten terms "the terribly beautiful vitality" of blackness, but in order to upend the life-denying power of antiblackness.[104]

Given the parasitic character of slave mastership and its vicious afterlife—white life feeds off black life, strategically claiming it as

101. Patterson, *Slavery and Social Death*, 5.

102. Jared Sexton, "The Social Life of Social Death: On Afro-Pessimism and Black Optimism," *InTensions* 5 (2011): 15.

103. Here I attempt to respond to, without necessarily adopting, the critique Victor Anderson offers in *Beyond Ontological Blackness: An Essay on African American Religious and Cultural Criticism* (New York: Continuum, 1995).

104. Fred Moten, "The Case of Blackness," *Criticism* 50, no. 2 (2008): 188.

its own—white Catholic theologians need to begin to learn how to theorize about white supremacy without assuming that its end will somehow also be good news for white people.[105] Antiblackness supremacy similarly desires that black people live only if they submit to social death; it believes that black people live not by right, but only by white largesse and mercy. It perceives black agency and spatial freedom as dangerous, disobedient, and often violent. It treats black people as instruments that must remain in their place unless and until nonblack people decide to use them. Thus, more than simply learning to believe that black lives matter, white theologians may have to theorize about white supremacy as though only black (or at least nonwhite) lives matter. Of course white people are human beings endowed with equal dignity as children of God. But in our antiblack society, white claims to humanity often come at the expense of black life and freedom. For this reason, the church can stand against antiblackness supremacy only if it is willing to truly and decisively take a stand against those of us who perpetrate it. Indeed, if Christians truly desire that black people be liberated from antiblackness supremacy, they ought to remember both the God who delivered the Israelites from slavery by drowning the Egyptian army that pursued them and the Messiah who promised not just blessings to the poor but also woes to the rich.[106] Antiblackness has made whiteness and blackness antagonists; the church should not pretend it is otherwise.[107]

For this reason, the church ought to make a preferential option for black life and acquire a strategic detachment to white salvation and moral purity. Too often, white theological speech about racial injustice devolves into a misguided preoccupation with the moral lives of whites. In this way, for example, Pfeil argues that in addition to "serving the end of justice for all people of color harmed by white privilege," white acts of racial love "also represent the path of Christian salvation for white people."[108] White supremacy indeed ought to be damned to hell. But the church ought to pursue the eradication of antiblackness supremacy no matter its impact upon whites. In a similar way, the church should place black life above even the noblest ideological commitments. Rather than confining racial justice to the

105. Patterson, *Slavery and Social Death*, 336, 338.

106. In invoking Exodus in this way, I do not mean to use a "social justice" reading of this story to in any way deny or minimize the fact that this story also and perhaps even primarily tells of the Jewish people's status as God's chosen and uniquely beloved people.

107. Wilderson, *Red, White & Black*, 29.

108. Cassidy and Mikulich, *Interrupting White Privilege*, 129.

consequences of principled pacifism, for example, the church should place nonviolence in the service of black life and liberation.[109] While the former strategy supports black life and liberation to the extent that nonviolence allows, the latter adopts nonviolence to the extent that it serves black life and liberation.[110] We white people may hope that justice comes nonviolently, but we have no business telling black people how to get free.[111]

109. See, for example, the way in which Pfeil identifies pacifism as an unconditional norm and unbreakable rule, even for nonwhites. "A Spirituality of White Nonviolent Resistance to the Reality of Hyper-incarceration," in eds. Cassidy, Mikulich, and Pfeil, *The Scandal of White Complicity in US Hyper-Incarceration*, 147–58.

110. Here, I favor Perkinson's approach to Pfeil's. See, James W. Perkinson, *White Theology: Outing Supremacy in Modernity* (New York: Palgrave Macmillan, 2004), 220. For another critique of white theologians' affinity for nonviolence, see James Cone, *God of the Oppressed* (Maryknoll, NY: Orbis, 1997), 204.

111. For an example of how the history of black survival and resistance can challenge white insistence on unconditional pacifism, see Charles E. Cobb Jr., *This Nonviolent Stuff'll Get You Killed: How Guns Made the Civil Rights Movement Possible* (Philadelphia: Basic Books, 2014). Here, I offer not an apology for violence, but a plea that white people stop telling black people to be nonviolent.

1.

Antiblackness and World History

This book ultimately aims to analyze the ethical life of racism in the contemporary United States. But it cannot do this without considering the nearly global story of black slavery. Especially as Latin American immigrants and their descendants comprise a growing share of the population of the United States, geographically narrow accounts of antiblackness encourage us to misinterpret the racial significance of the country's changing demographic landscape.[1] Unlike other studies of racism both within the field of theology and without, this book re-narrates the racial history of the Americas as united by antiblackness supremacy. Admittedly, I am not a trained historian; I have not cleaned off the dusty covers of primary texts fashioned centuries ago. But more than simply repackaging historical arguments for a theological audience, this book innovatively reinterprets them according to a philosophical framework inspired by Saidiya Hartman, Jared Sexton, Fred Moten, and Frank Wilderson—a group of scholars sometimes referred to as "Afro-pessimists."[2] Adopting a hermeneutic of

1. Ruben Rosario Rodriguez's call to "move beyond the black white binary" as well as his argument for mestizaje as a type of solution to U.S.-style white supremacy epitomizes this misunderstanding. *Racism and God-talk: A Latino/a Perspective* (New York: New York University Press, 2011), 17–18, 25.

2. While these scholars do not necessarily all embrace this term, the designation "afro-pessimism" is often used to refer to their work due to the way they enlist Orlando Patterson's definition of slavery as social death to argue that black social life in the United States unfolds within what Hartman terms "the afterlife of slavery." Because they cogently differentiate antiblackness from other forms of domination, their work is both supported by and serves to clarify attempts to construct a historical account of the workings of race in the world.

mutual correction, I in turn have shaped my definition of antiblackness supremacy in light of the history I uncover here.

This history attempts to explain a curious commonality. Incredibly, despite sometimes-vast cultural, religious, and economic differences, every European country that colonized the Americas did so with the assistance of not just black slaves, but Africanized slavery. While indigenous slavery and European indentured servitude played a substantial role in the first decades of Iberian and English colonization of the Americas, these practices proved relatively fleeting.[3] Nor would any other European nation submit any non-African group of people to systematized slavery for any extended period of time.[4] Thus, even though indigenous people endured enslavement, slavery did not demarcate indigenous identity as it did blackness.[5]

In pursuit of the supremacy that only Africanized slavery could provide, the following European countries and their merchants engaged in and were empowered by the transatlantic trade in black slaves: Belgium, Denmark, England, France, Germany, the Netherlands, Norway, Portugal, Spain, and Sweden. Many of these countries also managed to establish American colonies stocked with black slaves: Denmark, England, France, the Netherlands, Norway, Portugal, Spain, and Sweden. Other entities—Courland, the Knights of Malta, and Scotland—attempted similar colonization projects, but had much less success. Those who could not seize control of the slave trade felt left behind. For example, as late as the turn of the twentieth century, Germans would bemoan their inability to master black flesh, either in the Americas or in Africa, as their European rivals had. Nor would any other European nation submit any non-African group of people to systematized slavery for any extended period of time.[6]

3. Alan Gallay, *Indian Slavery in Colonial America* (Lincoln: University of Nebraska Press, 2009), 11.

4. Even though indigenous people endured enslavement, slavery did not demarcate indigenous identity as it did blackness. For a more in-depth discussion of the differences between black and indigenous racialization with respect to genocide and slavery, see Wilderson, *Red, White & Black*, 10. A recently published book argues that indigenous slavery was in many ways "more insidious" than the enslavement in inflicted upon Africans. However, because Reséndez seems to classify all conditions of coerced labor as "slavery," he overestimates the similarity between the mechanisms of indigenous and black oppression. Andrés Reséndez, *The Other Slavery: The Uncovered Story of Indian Enslavement in America* (Boston: Houghton Mi in Harcourt, 2016), 4.

5. For a more in-depth discussion of the differences between black and indigenous racialization with respect to genocide and slavery, see Wilderson, *Red, White & Black*, 10.

6. David Olusoga and Casper W. Erichsen, *The Kaiser's Holocaust: Germany's Forgotten Genocide and the Colonial Roots of Nazism* (London: Faber & Faber, 2011), 27, 34, 41, 110.

Black slavery helped to structure the political, economic, cultural, and social life throughout the Americas. Black slaves toiled in the colonial precursors of every Central American nation; they cut sugarcane, mined for precious metals, and attended to the wishes of urban masters in the Andean colonies that would give rise to Ecuador, Peru, and Bolivia.[7] Black slaves helped give social life even to the overwhelmingly white South American nations of Argentina, Uruguay, and Paraguay.[8] In the United States and Brazil, the institution of slavery would outlast colonial independence. And even Canada practiced black slavery for the first three centuries of its history.[9] How did these people come to agree on black slavery when they disagreed about so much else?

IMPERIAL ORIGINS: BLACK SLAVERY IN EARLY MODERN EUROPE

Other scholars have argued that racism created race. The history of black slavery simply makes this insight more specific. Not racism in general, but antiblackness in particular first brought whiteness into existence. Ultimately, black slavery emerged before whiteness did. Indeed, the story of white supremacy begins not in 1492 on the island of Hispaniola but nearly fifty years earlier, in 1444, in Portugal.[10] In service of this country's imperial rivalry with the Muslim world, mariners dispatched by Prince Henrique sailed down the western coast of Africa, attacked a community along the Senegal River, kidnapped 234 of its residents, and returned to Portugal to sell these human captives as slaves.[11] Of course these people were not

7. Sherwin K. Bryant, *Rivers of Gold, Lives of Bondage: Governing through Slavery in Colonial Quito* (Chapel Hill: University of North Carolina Press, 2014); Frederick P. Bowser, *The African Slave in Colonial Peru, 1524-1650* (Stanford, CA: Stanford University Press, 1974).

8. Michael T. Luongo, "Argentina Rediscovers Its African Roots," *New York Times*, September 12, 2014, http://www.nytimes.com/2014/09/14/travel/argentina-rediscovers-its-african-roots.html; John M. Lipski, "Afro-Paraguayan Spanish: The Negation of Non-Existence," *Journal of Pan African Studies (Online)* 2, no. 7 (December 1, 2008): 2–37; Nathaniel C. Nash, "Montevideo Journal; Uruguay Is on Notice: Blacks Want Recognition," *New York Times*, May 7, 1993, http://www.nytimes.com/1993/05/07/world/montevideo-journal-uruguay-is-on-notice-blacks -want-recognition.html.

9. Afua Cooper, *The Hanging of Angélique: The Untold Story of Canadian Slavery and the Burning of Old Montreal* (Athens: University of Georgia Press, 2007), 7.

10. José F. Buscaglia-Salgado, *Undoing Empire: Race and Nation in the Mulatto Caribbean* (Minneapolis: University of Minnesota Press, 2003), 48, 79.

11. Cooper, *The Hanging of Angélique*, 27; Katie Geneva Cannon, "Christian Imperialism and

the first slaves brought to the Christian kingdoms of Iberia. Iberian Christians already had been enslaving foreign Muslims captured outside their borders as the purportedly well-deserved spoils of just war.[12] And, within their borders, these Christian sovereigns sought to establish religious supremacy by sentencing some of their Muslim vassals to a lifetime of slavery as punishment for certain crimes.[13] Fifteenth-century Christians also purchased non-Muslim Tartars, Circassians, Russians, Greek Orthodox Christians, and newly conquered Canary Islanders on the open market. They even owned a few black African slaves who had reached the peninsula by way of the Arab-controlled trans-Saharan slave trade.[14] In these ways, slavery helped Christian sovereigns jockey for geopolitical supremacy in the crowded and heavily contested Mediterranean and North African worlds.[15]

Portugal's midcentury plunder of coastal African communities accorded both Iberian kingdoms a dramatic advantage in this intraregional contest for religious supremacy.[16] In Africa, they found new supplies of gold, ending their reliance on the Muslim merchants who monopolized the existing trans-Saharan trade in gold. There they also found new sources of slaves, which they could exchange for even more gold acquired elsewhere along the West African coast.[17] Facilitating this trade, Portuguese mariners would establish a series of militarized trading forts, called factories, at Arguim, a coastal town in Mauritania, in 1448; in 1460 in Sierra Leone; and in 1470 on Ghana's Gold Coast they built the notorious slave fortress called Elmina.[18]

But this new profit source posed a problem. These valuable West African slaves did not meet existing Iberian criteria for enslavement: they were neither Muslim enemies of war nor were they purchased from foreign traders. Seeking to justify their plunder, Henrique's pirate crusaders originally classified the people they plucked from the

the Transatlantic Slave Trade," *Journal of Feminist Studies in Religion* 24, no. 1 (Spring 2008): 127.

12. Debra Blumenthal, *Enemies and Familiars: Slavery and Mastery in Fifteenth-Century Valencia* (Ithaca, NY: Cornell University Press, 2009), 22.

13. Ibid., 1.

14. Blumenthal, *Enemies and Familiars*, 1.

15. Scott L. Waugh and Peter Diehl, *Christendom and Its Discontents: Exclusion, Persecution, and Rebellion, 1000–1500* (New York: Cambridge University Press, 2002), 272.

16. Kenneth Wolf, "The 'Moors' of West Africa and the Beginnings of the Portuguese Slave Trade," *Pomona Faculty Publications and Research* (January 1, 1994): 451, 454.

17. Herbert S. Klein, *The Atlantic Slave Trade* (New York: Cambridge University Press, 1999), 10.

18. Blumenthal, *Enemies and Familiars*, 27–28.

coasts of West Africa as "moors." But as Gomes Eanes de Zurara, Henrique's royal biographer, noted, they categorized these captives as enslaveable enemies of the faith "without having any certain knowledge as to whether these men were moors or Gentiles, or as to what kind of life or manner of living they had." This politically convenient taxonomic ruse had one wrinkle. They classified these new captives as not simply "Moors," but "black Moors." This blackness, de Zurura reasoned, marked them as cursed descendants of Ham.[19] Although these new slaves were pagans, he concluded, their blackness allowed them to be enslaved as though they were defiant Muslims.[20]

What I call the incipient corporealization of slave status would only intensify as the size of the peninsula's black African slave population increased. Before the rise of black slavery, newly acquired slaves in cities like Valencia would be brought before a bailiff general so that he could verify the legitimacy of their captivity. Products of the same culturally diverse and deeply interconnected Mediterranean world, the majority of these slaves shared a common language, such as Arabic or Spanish, with the bailiff general. For this reason, they could "testify" to the legitimacy of their capture.

But the slaves transported from the western coast of Africa spoke neither Arabic nor Spanish. Their inability to "confess" their guilt as their Moorish counterparts could have proved to civil authorities that they had been unlawfully detained. It instead prompted the bailiff general to amend the criteria by which he ascertained "infidel" status: not the enslaved person's verbal testimony, but the perceived character of her body verified her enslaveability.[21] Consider one bailiff general's rationale for declaring 119 black Africans "*catius de bona Guerra*": "it is obvious and apparent by the appearance of them" that these captives were "infidels, from the lands and lineage of infidels." As infidels, he concluded, they qualified as "enemies of the holy Catholic faith and of the high lord King" and therefore deserved to be enslaved.[22] Anticipating a central aspect of both Africanized slavery and its ongoing afterlife, these black people were perceived as guilty

19. For more on the religious history of the Curse of Ham in the late medieval and early modern Mediterranean, see, David M. Goldenberg, *The Curse of Ham: Race and Slavery in Early Judaism, Christianity, and Islam* (Princeton, NJ: Princeton University Press, 2003).

20. Jonathan Schorsch, *Jews and Blacks in the Early Modern World* (New York: Cambridge University Press, 2004), 147.

21. Blumenthal, *Enemies and Familiars*, 42–43.

22. Ibid., 43–44.

criminals less for what they did than for what types of bodies they possessed.[23]

In transforming blackness into a title of enslavement in this way, these Iberians reversed the relation between slavery and geopolitical supremacy. Previously, Spanish Christians had enslaved certain people because they belonged to non-Catholic lands and clung to non-Christian status; their right to capture Muslims as slaves, for example, signaled Christian sovereignty over their lands. After 1444, they increasingly would begin to assess the sovereignty of certain lands by referencing the bodies of the people these lands produced. More than simply representing place, race would provide a means by which to make it.[24] In associating blackness with slave status, antiblackness supremacy would make what I call a performative argument about the body and the land that produced it. Iberian Christians convinced themselves that black people were inherently enslaveable by treating them as such. In time, it would become an argument that nearly every white person would come to accept as true.

More than simply emerging as a new marker of subjugation, blackness would fracture preexisting Spanish notions of Christian supremacy. For example, in the middle of the sixteenth century, the Spanish city of Seville contained a population 10 percent black and mulatto. Despite their status as among the only residents of Seville who lacked Muslim or Jewish ancestry without a shadow of a doubt, the city's black Christians were not honored as Christians of pure blood. When processing through town as members of the black confraternity Nuestra Senora de los Angeles, for example, they suffered insults and violent assault from the crowd of white Christians who gathered to mock them.[25] The rules of honor and civic belonging had changed. Blackness now mattered more than Christian status and heritage. Even public displays of Christian fidelity could not erase the newly embodied stigma of slavery: black Christians appeared as criminals in need of discipline and punishment.

This trade in black slaves also would change Portugal forever. A little over a century after Prince Henrique's 1444 mission to the western shores of Africa, nearly 33,000 black slaves had been shipped to

23. For more on the role that anti-Islamic ideologies played in the emergence of antiblackness supremacy, see Katie Walker Grimes, "'Birtherism' and Anti-Blackness: The Anti-Islamic Ante-Life of Africanized Slavery," *Political Theology*, forthcoming.

24. Willie James Jennings, *The Christian Imagination: Theology and the Origins of Race* (New Haven: Yale University Press, 2011).

25. Buscaglia-Salgado, *Undoing Empire*, 81–83.

Portugal. They eventually comprised one-tenth of the population of Lisbon, while the Portuguese city of Evora contained more black residents than white.[26] Until slavery's abolition in the 1750s, Portuguese masters treated the black captives held on their soil like true slaves: they sold family members away from each other, subjected their black property to rape and other forms of sexual abuse, enlisted enslaved women as breeders, and typically sold the surviving babies on the domestic slave market. Anticipating a pattern that would shape the Americas, even though Portuguese masters attempted to consign their black slaves to a state of social death, these black women and men contributed mightily to the country's social and cultural life. Afro-Portuguese slaves and freed people would leave a lasting imprint on the country's cultural, economic, and social life.[27] Most notably, in the nineteenth century, black slaves from Portuguese-held Brazil would contribute to the creation of what the Portuguese people still claim as their national music, *fado*.[28]

Portuguese-controlled trade in black slaves would enrich not just the Iberian Peninsula, but also nearly the entirety of Europe. In so doing, it would help knit Europe together—already in the late fifteenth century, white supremacy, like white solidarity, came by means of antiblackness and the masterly power it accorded. Especially after the king of Spain granted the Portuguese the exclusive royal rights to ship black slaves to his colonies in the Americas in 1518, the slave trade surpassed the gold trade in importance and profitability. But Portugal could not metabolize all the wealth this trade generated. Other Europeans picked up the slack. In addition to financing Portugal's overseas voyages, businessmen from Italy, Germany, Holland, England, France, Scandinavia, and Flanders purchased the peninsula's imported goods, including black slaves, and sold them throughout Europe.[29] In many places, such as Holland and England, black slaves would serve as an important marker of wealth and social status.[30]

Like the Spanish, the Portuguese did not simply hold black slaves; they also forged a stigmatizing link between slave status and even un-enslaved blackness. Reflecting the emerging racialization of the

26. Cooper, *The Hanging of Angélique*, 33.
27. A. Saunders, *A Social History of Black Slaves and Freedmen in Portugal, 1441-1555* (New York: Cambridge University Press, 1982), 1.
28. Kimberley DaCosta Holton, "Fado Historiograhy: Old Myths and New Frontiers," *Portuguese Cultural Studies* 1 (2014): 9–13.
29. Cooper, *The Hanging of Angélique*, 31.
30. Bryant, *Rivers of Gold, Lives of Bondage*, 16, 18.

relation between master and slave, Portuguese King Manuel's early sixteenth-century slave code grouped free black people into the same legal category with enslaved ones and subjected them to the same set of discriminatory restrictions and punishments. This code also drew a sharp line between white and black: white violators typically received fines while black rule-breakers were subjected to whippings. Because even free black people were treated like slaves, the Portuguese also began to perceive themselves as not just Catholic or Lusitanian, but white.[31] Why did Iberians seize upon race so easily? Perhaps blackness emerged as a new title of enslavement in part because it provided Christian Iberia a better method of marking and constructing the difference on which their dominance depended. While Iberian Christians expressed increasing anxiety about the indiscernibility of the Jewish or Muslim body, the black body provided incontrovertible visual evidence of slave status.[32]

Black slavery also empowered other persecuted people. Locked in a state of oscillating conflict with Catholic Iberians, Muslim and Jewish Europeans nonetheless possessed a significant investment in the whiteness antiblackness supremacy upheld, even if they were partially excluded from it.[33] Although Portuguese Muslims and Jews could not achieve full equality with Christians, they could at least be masters of black slaves.[34] After their expulsion from first Spain and then Portugal, Jewish refugees to the Netherlands supplied a large portion of slaves to Brazil and Dutch-held colonies, such as Surinam and Curaçao, during the late seventeenth century.[35] Between 1630 and 1760, these businessmen would transport nearly all of 85,000 of Curaçao's kidnapped black slaves. Another mistreated religious minority used Africanized slavery to their advantage: after they were expelled from France, the Protestant Huguenots financed a major share of their former homeland's seventeenth-century transatlantic trade in black flesh.[36]

31. Blumenthal, *Enemies and Familiars*, 42. For an in-depth study of Jewish participation in black slavery as it pertains to contemporary black-Jewish relations, see Jonathan Schorsch, *Jews and Blacks in the Early Modern World* (Cambridge: Cambridge University Press, 2004).
32. D. Nirenberg, "Enmity and Assimilation: Jews, Christians, and Converts in Medieval Spain," *Common Knowledge* 9, no. 1 (January 1, 2003): 138–46.
33. Cooper, *The Hanging of Angélique*, 56.
34. Ibid., 36.
35. Ibid., 57; Schorsch, *Jews and Blacks in the Early Modern World*, 62. The history of Jewish participation in the transatlantic slave trade has sometimes been used to justify antisemitism. I strongly denounce this as both illogical and unjust.
36. Cooper, *The Hanging of Angélique*, 62–63.

The black slave trade also helped to rewrite the rules of European international conflict and competition. Between the sixteenth and nineteenth centuries, European nations tussled both for imperial position in the Americas and slave-trading advantage on the West African coast. Although European powers also colonized and exploited vast swaths of the Asian continent, they inflicted prolonged and institutionalized slavery only on the African-descended. After both the abolition of black slavery in the Americas and their revolutionary expulsion from all corners of the Western Hemisphere, European powers used their commitment to suppressing African slavery as a pretext to bring nearly the entire African continent under their direct colonial control.[37] In the late nineteenth century, Germany pressed Africans into slavery not to sell them on international markets, but to build up their new colonies in East and Southwest Africa.[38] The Africanization of slavery positioned all black Africans, even those who were not enslaved, "as slaves in relation to the rest of the world."[39] As its near complete absence from the contemporary mapping project Google Street View symbolizes, sub-Saharan Africa continues to occupy a space of nonexistence and "darkness" in the international imagination.[40]

THE ESTABLISHMENT OF ANTIBLACKNESS SUPREMACY IN THE IBERIAN AMERICAS

By the time Christopher Columbus reached the shores of the island he would name "Hispaniola," Europeans had been buying and selling black Africans in significant numbers for more than fifty years. As a result, "indigenous Americans were incorporated into a world already formed through antiblackness."[41] Thus, even from the very begin-

37. Gwendolyn Midlo Hall, *Slavery and African Ethnicities in the Americas: Restoring the Links* (Chapel Hill: University of North Carolina Press, 2009), xiv.

38. Olusoga and Erichsen, *The Kaiser's Holocaust*, 68, 159, 167, 220.

39. Frank B. Wilderson III, *Red, White & Black: Cinema and the Structure of US Antagonisms* (Durham, NC: Duke University Press, 2010), 95; J.-A. Mbembé, *On the Postcolony* (Berkeley: University of California Press, 2001), 13–14.

40. "Coverage of Google Street View," *Wikipedia, the Free Encyclopedia*, July 15, 2015, https://en.wikipedia.org/w/index.php?title=Coverage_of_Google_Street_View&oldid=671512363.

41. Tryon Woods, "The Fact of Antiblackness: Decolonization in Chiapas and the Niger River Delta," *Human Architecture: Journal of the Sociology of Self-Knowledge* 5, no. 3 (June 21, 2007): 324.

ning, the indigenous inhabitants of Spanish and Portuguese America would occupy a distinct racial position in the emerging imperial hierarchy. The *encomienda*, uniquely imposed upon indigenous people, and slavery, uniquely imposed on black people, provided two distinct ways of extending Spanish royal sovereignty over the Americas.[42] Rather than ranking oppressions, I merely distinguish them: black and indigenous people were racialized differently.

The *encomienda* and its replacement, the *mita* system, differed from slavery in several ways. First, Spanish law required indigenous communities to provide their *encomenderos* with a fixed amount of labor or goods. In eighteenth-century Paraguay, for example, *encomenderos* extracted sixty days of labor per year from able-bodied indigenous men aged eighteen to forty-nine.[43] The black slave, on the other hand, was used however his master saw fit. Nor did the law limit how his master could use him.[44] Second, indigenous people could not be sold away from family or community.[45] They stayed with and in turn were confined to a given piece of land: when an *encomendero* died, his title did not transfer to his heirs or next of kin; it reverted to the Crown. A black slave, on the other hand, remained attached to an individual person, her master.[46] She could be bought, sold, or bequeathed to anyone. Third, for this reason, while indigenous peoples certainly experienced social and cultural disruption, only the black slave suffered social death and natal alienation. Fourth, the black slave "faced types of physical violence that it was not possible to impose on wage laborers, including indigenous people, as masters literally drove their slaves to work harder and faster with the whip."[47]

42. Bryant, *Rivers of Gold, Lives of Bondage*, 25. A recently published book argues not just that we have underestimated the scope of indigenous slavery, but that it was in many ways "more insidious" than the enslavement inflicted upon Africans. Andrés Reséndez, *The Other Slavery: The Uncovered Story of Indian Enslavement in America* (Boston: Houghton Mifflin Harcourt, 2016), 4. However, because Reséndez seems to classify all conditions of coerced labor as "slavery," he overestimates the similarity between the mechanisms of indigenous and black oppression.

43. James Schofield Saeger, "Survival and Abolition: The Eighteenth Century Paraguayan Encomienda," *The Americas* 38, no. 1 (July 1, 1981): 61.

44. Saidiya V. Hartman and Frank B. Wilderson III, "The Position of the Unthought," *Qui Parle* 13, no. 2 (April 1, 2003): 188.

45. Timothy J. Yeager, "Encomienda or Slavery? The Spanish Crown's Choice of Labor Organization in Sixteenth-Century Spanish America," *Journal of Economic History* 55, no. 4 (December 1, 1995): 843.

46. Saeger, "Survival and Abolition," 62.

47. Frank T. Proctor, *Damned Notions of Liberty: Slavery, Culture, and Power in Colonial Mexico, 1640–1769* (Albuquerque: University of New Mexico Press, 2010), 30.

Fifth, slavery in any time or place reduces its victims to infinitely fungible, usable bodies; they could be used for any purpose. The corporealization of slavery only intensified the association that conceived of the slave as a body.[48] As historian Sherwin Bryant details, because they "were branded, watched, whipped, castrated, and otherwise made to announce their presence in the form of a belled iron collar, slaves embodied 'exemplary, because exceptional, punishment'" in a way the subjugated Indian did not.[49] The spectacle of the enslaved black body announced white power simply by existing.[50]

In identifying *encomienda* and black slavery as two distinct modes of racial governance, I contest what I term the "labor thesis" of early American racialization typically proffered by scholars of this period. According to this thesis, Iberian imperialists turned to African slavery in order "to meet growing labor needs" after Spanish disease, warfare, and domination devastated the indigenous population.[51] In addition to neglecting the differences between slavery and the *encomienda*, the labor thesis leaves several questions unanswered. First, if Spanish colonists turned to African slavery only as a replacement for the depleted pool of Indian labor, why did they import African slaves into regions where the indigenous population remained relatively robust, such as Quito?[52] Second, if these Iberian colonists imported African slaves in order to keep the indigenous population from dying off, why did they use slaves for other, relatively nonlethal purposes, such as wet-nursing?[53] Third, even if the Spanish initially had begun to acquire larger numbers of African slaves solely in order to replace indigenous people in the mines and plantations, why did they then spend so much time and energy seeking to keep black and indigenous people apart? Why would they care what color their laborers were?

The labor thesis errs most by failing to explain why Spanish colonists believed subjugated indigenous people, but not Africans and their descendants, a population worthy of protection against

48. Jennifer A. Glancy, *Slavery in Early Christianity* (Minneapolis: Fortress Press, 2006), 3, 7.

49. Bryant, *Rivers of Gold, Lives of Bondage*, 20.

50. Ibid., 20, 26, 46, 81.

51. See for example Proctor, *Damned Notions of Liberty*, 15; Junius P. Rodriguez, *Slavery in the United States: A Social, Political, and Historical Encyclopedia* Vol. One, (Santa Barbara, CA: ABC-CLIO), 80-81; Theodore W. Allen, *The Invention of the White Race: The Origins of Oppression in Anglo-America* (London: Verso, 1997), 7-8.

52. Bryant, *Rivers of Gold, Lives of Bondage*, 1–2, 5–6.

53. Proctor, *Damned Notions of Liberty*, 32.

enslavement.[54] Contrary to the oversimplified conclusions arising from the labor thesis, the Spanish Crown did not abolish Indian slavery simply so that a depleted labor pool could replenish itself. Indeed, even after the size of the indigenous population surged and then stabilized in the eighteenth century, the Crown did not seek to reduce this revitalized demographic to slavery. This reticence proves especially significant given that slavery surpassed the *mita* in profitability. The Spanish Crown instead protected its conscripted Indian vassals from slavery because "improving its miserable Indios were requirements of colonial sovereignty and legitimacy."[55]

For this reason, while Spanish colonists, theologians, and royal officials debated the status of the Indian and fought over their treatment, they did not deem black slavery a moral question worthy of discussion. More than simply failing to liberate the black slave, Spanish colonial society did not even consider her. Associated with enslavement, black people occupied what Saidiya Hartman terms "the position of the unthought."[56] In the nearly four centuries of Spanish colonial American slaveholding, only two Spaniards ever expressed written opposition to this vicious practice.[57] No Bartolomé de las Casas fought for the sake of America's black slaves.[58] The Spanish Court hosted no great debate about their humanity—their slave status proved settled and commonsensical.[59]

Further undermining the labor thesis, Iberian colonists considered indigenous people different from African slaves from the moment they arrived in the Americas—long before the irruption of a labor shortage. In this way, for example, the first Spaniards who stepped foot on the island they would name "Hispaniola" generally "treated the Taínos as legally free subjects." Sharing this perception, Queen Isabella allowed for the enslavement only of those Indians—the purportedly cannibalistic Caribs and other groups who prosecuted unjust wars—who violated natural law. In fact, as historian David Abulafia

54. Aníbal Quijano, "Coloniality of Power and Eurocentrism in Latin America," *International Sociology* 15, no. 2 (June 1, 2000): 217.

55. Bryant, *Rivers of Gold, Lives of Bondage*, 2.

56. Hartman and Wilderson, "The Position of the Unthought," 185.

57. David Brion Davis, *The Problem of Slavery in Western Culture* (New York, Oxford University Press, 1966), 190.

58. Woods, "The Fact of Antiblackness," 324–25.

59. For an overview of Las Casas' famous debate against Juan Ginés de Sepúlveda, see ed. Francis Patrick Sullivan, SJ, *Indian Freedom: The Cause of Bartolomé de las Casas (1484-1566) A Reader* (Kansas City, MO: Sheed & Ward, 1995), 289-90.

reports, she "was furious when she was sent shiploads of Taino slaves."[60] The Queen felt no such outrage at the indiscriminate enslavement of black Africans, however. In the same year she condemned Indian slavery, she "imposed a head tax of 2 ducats on any black slave arriving in the Indies." Five years later in 1517, she ordered the shipment of 4,000 captive Africans to the Americas as one of her first acts of governance there.[61] Rather than a response to fluctuating and unforeseen American economic circumstances, Queen Isabella helped to establish her sovereignty over the Indies by differentiating African from Indian on the basis of their enslaveability.

The labor thesis fails to comprehend the significance of this fact because it mistakenly begins the story of white supremacy with Columbus's 1492 voyage. But as previously demonstrated, the story does not begin there. Only by placing Iberian beliefs about and treatment of black and indigenous people in their pre-Columbian context can we fully make sense of them. When Spanish and Portuguese colonists intensified the transatlantic trade in black slaves, they drew upon the notions of order and dominance that had begun to emerge on the Iberian Peninsula in response to the events of 1444. In the century or so before Columbus crossed the Atlantic, Iberian Christians increasingly believed that territory should not just be governed by a Christian sovereign, but also inhabited solely by Christian subjects. Due to their obstinate rejection of Christian sovereignty, Muslims, whether foreign or domestic, qualified as uniquely enslaveable and unfit to exercise sovereignty. But as demonstrated by their 1340s encounter with the "cave-dwelling" inhabitants of the Canary Islands, they related to uncontacted pagans somewhat differently.[62] While Muslims had chosen both to reject Christianity and to refuse the sovereignty of its monarchs, these people were simply ignorant of both and therefore devoid of culpability for their condition. For this reason, pagans ordinarily deserved slavery only if they resisted their proper place in the Iberian imperial realm or violated natural law.[63]

The Spanish brought these religiously inflected ideologies of imperial space with them when they stumbled upon the Americas, classifying the Taínos as a new type of Canary Islander and sometimes

60. David Abulafia, "Stripped Assets: The Opening of the Atlantic and the Discovery of Mankind," *History Today* 58, no. 5 (May 1, 2008): 41.

61. Bryant, *Rivers of Gold, Lives of Bondage*, 16.

62. Abulafia, "Stripped Assets," 39.

63. Ibid., 41.

calling the West Indies the "New Canaries."[64] Although he was disappointed that these people were not Christians, Columbus was relieved to report that they were not Muslims or Jews.[65] For these reasons, when the Spanish Crown claimed the Taínos as its vassals, it incorporated them into the Spanish kingdom as not slaves, but "docile" and "gentle" subjects in need of protection from their purportedly cannibalistic Carib persecutors.[66] Due to their pagan status, they were subordinate but free.

But if the racialization of indigenous peoples initially followed the preexisting patterns of religious domination that governed Iberian interaction with Muslims and Canary Islanders, what I call the intensifying Africanization of slavery continued to defy them. The Spanish did not attempt to distinguish Africans by custom or moral character as they had the Taínos and Caribs; nor did they sort sub-Saharan Africans by religious affiliation as they had everyone else. While some enslaved Africans surely professed devotion to Islam, some would have qualified as so-called pagans, and others were baptized Kongolese Christians who had been living under the authority of a Christian sovereign since 1490.[67]

But they did not treat pagan Africans as potentially redeemable innocents in need of protection. According to Iberian lore, indigenous people, childlike and uncorrupted, had humbly accepted the Spanish offer of Christian conversion, while Africans, descended from Ham, initially rejected it and would have to be converted against their wills.[68] For this reason, Spanish missionaries especially feared that the imported African "would hamper the Christianization of the Indian" through either his associations with Islam or his savage paganism.[69] Expressing this ideology, the sixteenth-century Spanish monarch Felipe II accused the African of transmitting to the Indian "faults which can corrupt and pervert the benefice that we,

64. Ibid., 39.
65. Ibid., 40.
66. David Abulafia, *The Discovery of Mankind: Atlantic Encounters in the Age of Columbus* (New Haven: Yale University Press, 2008), 110, 127.
67. Saunders, *A Social History of Black Slaves and Freedmen in Portugal, 1441–1555*, 7; Linda M. Heywood and John K. Thornton, *Central Africans, Atlantic Creoles, and the Foundation of the Americas, 1585–1660* (New York: Cambridge University Press, 2007), 172–74.
68. Bowser, *The African Slave in Colonial Peru, 1524–1650*, 27, 22; Ilona Katzew, *Casta Painting: Images of Race in Eighteenth-Century Mexico* (New Haven: Yale University Press, 2005), 46; Andrew B. Fisher and Matthew D. O'Hara, *Imperial Subjects: Race and Identity in Colonial Latin America (Latin America Otherwise)* (Durham, NC: Duke University Press, 2009), 146.
69. Bowser, *The African Slave in Colonial Peru, 1524–1650*, 27.

[Spaniards], in an orderly manner, seek for his salvation and tranquility."[70] Black slaves appeared as foreign imports; conquered Indians were new and untutored residents of the Spanish kingdom. But this alone does not explain the differential treatment indigenous and African-descended people received.

Iberian Christians paradoxically began to ignore territorially specific religious differences among Africans precisely because they held an increasingly territorial understanding of Christian supremacy and identity. European slaveownership had already begun to reduce African-ness to a body type, even before the symbolic year of 1492. Thus, while the Spanish classified both indigenous and black people according to their "territorial lineage," they perceived each lineage differently. They named indigenous peoples by their belonging to a certain land, the Indies, but they named imported slaves not *africanos*, but *negros*, that is, blacks.[71] In an infinitely regressing cycle of cause and effect, blackness justified enslavement because it signaled African descent while Africa qualified as a land suitable for conquest because it produced a race fit for enslavement.[72]

Put another way, originally, Iberian Christians had captured people as slaves because they hailed from certain places and professed certain faiths; now black people would be held as slaves because they possessed certain bodies.[73] It would not matter which religion she professed or which sort of moral character she expressed: blackness alone delineated the boundary between free and slave. White supremacy emerged in the Americas as a result of European imperial relations to space: Africans were incorporated into these American empires as intransigent outsiders while Indians were incorporated as docile insiders. As it had in fifteenth-century Europe, race in the Americas would not simply represent place, it would serve to reconfigure it in accordance with the prerogatives of racialized European imperial power. Black and indigenous peoples did not represent two interchangeable types of nonwhite peoples. Indigenous people, like other nonblack peoples, received immunity from enslavement, even as they suffered another form of racial oppression. Africans were enslaved

70. Edgar F. Love, "Legal Restrictions on Afro-Indian Relations in Colonial Mexico," *Journal of Negro History* 55, no. 2 (April 1970): 132.
71. Proctor, *Damned Notions of Liberty*, 42; W. E. B. Du Bois, *The Negro*, 1st edition 1915 (Reprint New York: Cosimo Classics, 2010), 6.
72. Bryant, *Rivers of Gold, Lives of Bondage*, 10, 56.
73. Ibid., 11, 49.

by Iberian masters because of not their nonwhiteness, but their blackness.

Just as white supremacy violently dominated black and indigenous peoples in different ways and for different reasons, so antiblackness supremacy empowered different classes of whites in different ways. Sometimes white people's interests conflicted. For example, while non-royal Spanish elites sought to use black slaves to maximize their profit, elevate their social status, and wage revolution against royal officials who displeased them, the Spanish Crown in turn deployed black slavery as a way to claim territory, display royal power, and to "govern owners and the enslaved alike."[74] In these ways, white people used black people as a weapon of intraracial combat. But even in using black people against each other in these ways, these differently situated whites still derived their shared racial power at black expense.

Only now can we begin to understand why Spanish colonizers did all they could to maintain racial separation between not just whites and nonwhites but black and indigenous people too.[75] The ideological and material underpinnings of Spanish imperial presence in the Americas depended upon more than just the preservation of the supremacy of Spanish, Catholic whiteness. It also required the continued existence of both enslaveable blackness and conquered indigeneity. If the distinction between blackness and indigeneity had disappeared, so would the logic and structures of Spanish colonialism. For this reason, the Crown prohibited Africans from living in Indian villages, donning indigenous styles of dress, or engaging in any manner of "trade, commerce, or communication" with Indians.[76] In order to prevent its subjects from escaping race through interracial sex, the Crown extended racially exclusive tributes and duties to their mixed-race children.[77] To this same end, in 1526 King Carlos decreed that African men would remain slaves even after marrying a free woman.[78] Contemporary scholars oversimplify the logic of Iberian conquest when they classify Spanish desires for racial separation as a strategy of mere divide and conquer.

In keeping indigenous and African-descended people completely separate, the Spanish Crown ultimately failed. But, so-called race

74. Ibid., 12, 35.

75. Ibid., 282.

76. Edgar F. Love, "Legal Restrictions on Afro-Indian Relations in Colonial Mexico." *The Journal of Negro History* 55, no. 2 (April 1970): 133.

77. Bowser, *The African Slave in Colonial Peru, 1524–1650*, 303.

78. Love, "Legal Restrictions on Afro-Indian Relations in Colonial Mexico," 135.

mixing neither subverted nor upended processes of white supremacist racialization; it merely made white supremacist racialization more complex and intricate.[79] It provided new ways of not just resisting racial hierarchy, but enforcing it as well. Even less did race mixing alleviate the stigmatizing link between enslavement and blackness.[80] For example, while the word for a person of mixed Spanish and indigenous descent means "mixed," the term mulatto "derives from the term *mulo* (mule), the sterile offspring of a horse and a donkey."[81] Mestizaje and *mulatez* did not signify equivalent versions of partial whiteness. According to historian Ben Proctor, "the Spanish believed mestizos suffered from 'diluted but not polluted blood,' whereas they thought that African ancestry 'permanently corrupted' Indian and Spanish blood."[82] Even partially African-descended Spanish Americans suffered dishonor for their criminalized bloodlines in a way that differently oppressed people of indigenous descent did not.

THE ESTABLISHMENT OF ANTIBLACKNESS SUPREMACY IN ANGLO NORTH AMERICA

As it had with the Spanish and Portuguese, English expansion into the Americas occurred in fulfillment of and in accordance with preexisting ideologies and mechanisms of dominion over land. Just as Iberian ideologies of Christian supremacy over Jews but especially Muslims propelled them into the Americas, the English initially came to Virginia not just to reap economic profit but to liberate the inhabitants of the New World from the "papist tyranny" wrought by Spanish imperial rule.[83] And likewise, just as the Christian kingdoms of Portugal and Spain expelled the Muslims and Jews who resided within the peninsula's newly reconquered lands during the fifteenth century, England's emerging bourgeoisie class began to enclose the commons in the sixteenth and seventeenth centuries, forcing peasants off the land and into the factories.[84] And finally just as early Spanish colonizers of the Americas considered the Taínos a type of Canary

79. Ibid., 286.
80. Michel-Rolph Trouillot, *Silencing the Past: Power and the Production of History* (Boston: Beacon, 1997), 77.
81. Proctor, *Damned Notions of Liberty*, 42.
82. Ibid.
83. Ibid., 7.
84. Ibid., 14–17.

Islander, the English compared the Indians they encountered in North America to Irish people whom they perceived as savages. The Englishman Hugh Peter observed upon his 1641 return from Massachusetts, "the wild Irish and the Indian do not much differ." Like the Irish, "the Indian" wore his hair long,[85] did not "plant any gardens or orchards," refused to "enclose or improve their lands," "live together in settled villages or towns," or "make any provision for prosperity."[86] In the English imagination, the Indian, like "the wild Irish . . . could become good, that is, civil and Christian, only by submission."[87]

But these imperial projects also had some substantial differences. While Spain and Portugal expelled the Muslims and Jews it had absorbed, the English still had access to the labor of both the "wild Irish" and the displaced English peasantry.[88] In the seventeenth century, Irish political prisoners as well as unwanted members of England's landless peasantry—vagrant children, jobless proletarians, and convicted felons—were shipped to the shores of Virginia, Maryland, and Carolina to labor, voluntarily as well as involuntarily, planting tobacco and picking colonial corn.[89] Although the English failed to exploit indigenous labor in a systematic fashion for even a short time as the Spanish had, they were not without a pool of subjugated laborers.

But despite the obstinately papist, purportedly cannibalistic and sexually immoral character of the undomesticated Irish, the English would not seek to transform them into a race of slaves. England's reliance upon involuntary Irish labor in their overseas colonies would prove just as fleeting and unsystematic as Christian Iberia's experiments in Indian and Jewish slavery.[90] Nor would England's proto-capitalist class reduce the English proletariat they so disdained to a state of slavery. In fact, the first English colonizers of the Americas did not rely on slavery of any kind.[91] Even after the Treaty of Breda

85. Christian F. Feest, *Indians and Europe: An Interdisciplinary Collection of Essays* (Lincoln: University of Nebraska Press, 1987), 136.

86. John Huxtable Elliott, *Empires of the Atlantic World: Britain and Spain in America, 1492-1830* (New Haven: Yale University Press, 2007), 79.

87. Edmund S. Morgan, *American Slavery, American Freedom* (New York: W. W. Norton, 2003), 20.

88. Theodore W. Allen, *The Invention of the White Race, Volume Two: The Origins of Racial Oppression in Anglo-America* (London: Verso, 1997), 4.

89. Allen, *The Invention of the White Race*, 54, 65, 121.

90. Allen, *The Invention of the White Race, Vol. Two,* 206.

91. A. Leon Higginbotham Jr., *In the Matter of Color: Race and the American Legal Process. The Colonial Period*, vol. 1 (Oxford: Oxford University Press, 1980), 19.

granted English planters access to African slaves, European-born and European-descended people would comprise the majority of the colonies' servants for the bulk of the seventeenth century.[92] As they had in Ireland, English elites seemingly believed they could colonize and capitalize without enslaving either foreign savages or domestic vagrants. What compelled these English planters to amend their criteria of enslavement and introduce the black body as a new title of enslavement as their Iberian predecessors had?

The English took racial inspiration from their Iberian predecessors; due to their example, the English associated blackness with slave status even before they arrived in the Americas. As Tamara E. Lewis chronicles, in early sixteenth century England, "African" captives "were known by a range of new terms borrowed from Iberian languages," including "'negroes,' 'blacks,' 'moors,' or 'blackamoors.'"[93] Evidencing the extent to which this linguistic framework shaped the English imagination, in the waning decades of that century, English parish records frequently would classify African slaves who were baptized or buried as "Blackamoors."[94] Queen Elizabeth would authorize her 1601 Edict for the Expulsion of Negroes on the grounds that "most of [the blacks residing in England] are infidels, having no understanding of Christ or his Gospel." As such, "said kind of people should be with all speed avoided and discharged out of this Her Majesty's dominions."[95] As late as 1677, an English judge ruled that "the Negroes were infidels, and the subjects of an infidel [African] prince, and are usually bought and sold in America as Merchandise." These naming practices substantiate Lewis's argument that "Catholic interpretations of humanity based on religious status were adopted by Protestant English secular legal and political jurisdictions to classify Africans as enslaved property."[96] As it had in Spain and Portugal, the English brand of antiblackness supremacy also possessed an anti-Islamic underbelly.[97]

Unsurprisingly, then, in the latter half of the seventeenth century,

92. Ibid., 154.

93. Tamara Elisabeth Lewis, *"To Wash a Blackamoor White:" The Rise of Black Ethnic Religious Rhetoric in Early Modern England*. Diss. Vanderbilt University, 2014, 8.

94. Tamara E Lewis, "'Like Devils out of Hell': Reassessing the African Presence in Early Modern England," *Black Theology* 14, no. 2 (2016): 112–13.

95. Lewis, "Like Devils Out of Hell," 115.

96. Ibid., 117.

97. For more on this history, see Grimes, "'Birtherism' and Antiblackness: The Anti-Islamic Ante-Life of Africanized Slavery" in *Political Theology*, forthcoming.

English planters would begin to justify the uniquely black character of slavery by referencing African origin. In this way, in 1670, the Virginia Assembly classified all "non-Christians imported into Virginia by sea" as slaves. This same act sentenced Indians, referred to as "non-Christians imported into Virginia by land," to a twelve-year stint of indentured servitude.[98] Although indigenous and black peoples were denigrated as equally non-Christian, only black people came from Africa and therefore only black people could be held as slaves for life.[99]

As in Spain and Portugal, although differences in religious identity initially made race possible, race ultimately made differences in religious identity irrelevant. Thus, even though enslaved Africans' non-Christian status made them enslavable, conversion to Christianity would not set them free. Due to a 1667 act assuring fretful slave-owners that "baptism of slaves doth not exempt them from bondage," imported Africans would remain enslaved even after they received the sacrament of baptism. Around this same time, the Virginia Assembly overturned laws that treated Irish servants more harshly than English ones and accorded them equal protection on account of their birth in "Christian nation."[100] While birth in "any Christian nation whatsoever" secured for the Irish woman a reprieve from prolonged bondage, birth in a purportedly non-Christian nation condemned the African woman to unending enslavement.

But this midcentury emergence of white privilege alone did not transform whiteness into an identity of difference from and power over blackness.[101] Why? Although they were privileged relative to black people, non slave-owning whites did not yet exercise power over them. Scholars typically point to Bacon's Rebellion of 1676 as the turning point of black-white relations. Prior to this event,

98. Morgan, *American Slavery, American Freedom*, 329.

99. English planters treated African slaves differently from Indian slaves largely because they could. Even captive Indians still had families nearby; they could be rescued or avenged. In contrast, African slaves were separated from their loved ones and communities of origin by an ocean; they could be enslaved for life with relative ease. But even this spatial distinction does not fully explain the Africanization of slavery: after all, deported Irish rebels had also been separated from their loved ones by the same ocean.

100. Virginia and William Waller Hening, *The Statutes at Large: Being a Collection of All the Laws of Virginia, from the First Session of the Legislature, in the Year 1619: Published Pursuant to an Act of the General Assembly of Virginia, Passed on the Fifth Day of February One Thousand Eight Hundred and Eight . . .*, 1823, 539.

101. Kenneth Morgan, *Slavery and the British Empire: From Africa to America* (New York: Oxford University Press, USA, 2008), 22.

upper class whites could not keep black and white people apart. Even after white people received immunity from enslavement, many of them still sided with black people. Denied the legal right to marry, bond laborers formed families anyways; faced with double the penalty for fornicating with African-American men, European-American women "would do so anyways."[102] African and European slaves would run away and plot rebellion together just as free laborers would side with their bonded counterparts.[103] This would change after Bacon's Rebellion.

Many scholars characterize the increasing Africanization of slavery in the wake of Bacon's Rebellion as an epiphenomenon of class relations. As historian Edmund Morgan argues, seventeenth-century planters in Virginia invented racism as a way of pacifying lower-class whites and preventing them from allying with lower-class blacks in class disputes.[104] Put another way, colonial elites would win a class war by fomenting a class war.[105] But the history of antiblackness supremacy complicates the arguments of scholars who describe the emergence of so-called racism as merely a by-product of class struggle. White investment in black slavery arises from neither the invention of white privilege nor the foolish gullibility of lower-class whites, but for the sake of the world-creating structural antagonism between slave and free. Put another way, lower-class whites were not tricked into antiblackness supremacy; they were empowered by it.[106] And since slavery is unique, so is the power it provides. After Bacon, even the poorest whites could act like masters to even free blacks.

I critique what I term the class warfare theory of racism's creation for the following reasons.[107] First, while European bond-laborers had long enjoyed certain privileges that African bond-laborers lacked, such as, since 1661, immunity from lifetime slavery, they did not

102. Ibid., 158.

103. Ibid., 154.

104. Morgan, *American Slavery, American Freedom* (New York: W. W. Norton, 2003), 297, 309, 320, 324, 344, 381. For similar arguments, see Theodore W. Allen, *The Invention of the White Race, Volume 1: Racial Oppression and Social Control* (London: Verso, 1994), 23, 70, 134–35, 185; David Roediger, *The Wages of Whiteness: Race and the Making of the American Working Class* (London: Verso, 1991), 12, 13.

105. Morgan, *American Slavery, American Freedom*, 381.

106. Wilderson, *Red, White, & Black*, 29, 31.

107. Matthew Frye Jacobson also critiques what he terms "rigid economic" explanations for racial oppression, arguing that "economics alone . . . cannot explain" the rise of whiteness. *Whiteness of a Different Color: European Immigrants and the Alchemy of Race* (Cambridge, MA: Harvard University Press, 1998), 16–20.

yet receive these privileges because Africans were denied them. But after Bacon, this changed.[108] Whites profited from laws prohibiting black slaves from owning property, as cattle owned illegally by black slaves would be seized and sold. The proceeds would be sent "to aid the colony's [white] poor." Skyrocketing revenues amassed on the backs of slaves also allowed colonial officials to shift the tax burden away from the economic activities of ordinary Virginians and onto the importation of African slaves and the exportation of tobacco. White men similarly organized into "special militia detachments" aimed at "dispersing all unusual concourse of negroes, or other slaves, and for preventing any dangerous combinations which may be made among them at such meetings."[109] An eighteenth-century statute in the nearby colony of Carolina required "every owner of a plantation" to employ one white man for every "ten negro men . . . possessed" as slaves.[110] Trusted to supervise slaves deemed untrustworthy and dangerous, lower-class white masculinity acquired social prestige and honor.

Second, the white ruling class shrewdly extended many of the pleasures of slaveownership to lower-class whites who lacked the resources to personally own slaves. In 1680, the Virginia Assembly made it an offense for black slaves to "lift his hand in opposition" not just against his master, but "against any Christian," and set as punishment for this offense a whipping of "thirty lashes on bare back";[111] and in 1705, the Assembly extended to all whites the impunity it had previously reserved only for those wealthy enough to own black slaves, declaring it lawful "for any person or persons whatsoever, to kill and destroy [runaway] slaves by such ways and means as he, she, or they shall think fit, without accusation or impeachment of any crime." Making the Assembly's intentions clear, the statute specifically identified "dismemberment" as an acceptable means of correct-

108. Saidiya V. Hartman, *Scenes of Subjection: Terror, Slavery, and Self-Making in Nineteenth-Century America*, 1st ed. (New York: Oxford University Press, 1997), 25.

109. Although I agree with Allen that Bacon's Rebellion was in many ways a turning point in the history of racism, I disagree with his interpretation of its significance. Allen, *The Invention of the White Race*, 252.

110. South Carolina, *The Statutes at Large of South Carolina: Containing the Acts from 1716, Exclusive, to 1752, Inclusive, Arranged Chronologically. Id., 1838. Xxxi, 814 p* (A. S. Johnston, 1838), 272.

111. Virginia and Hening, *The Statutes at Large*, 481.

ing the "incorrigible" and "terrifying" other white people's slaves into obedience.[112]

At the same time, the legislature extended to white servants protections from the degradations and indignities of such unchecked violence. While disobedient black slaves could endure dismemberment at the hands of "any person . . . whatsoever," a 1682 statute ensured that a master cannot "whip a Christian white servant naked without an order from the justice of the peace."[113] If any such master were to whip his white Christian servant in such a fashion, he shall pay the offended servant forty shillings. Once it was perceived as the ultimate expression of nonblackness, even servile whiteness would be considered worthy of protection, especially from public acts of corporal punishment and degradation.

In addition to stigmatizing and disempowering free black people, the Africanization of slavery accorded honor and power to poor whites, religiously other whites, and white women. Even if poor whites could not financially profit from black slavery to the same degree as more elite whites could, they could still indulge in the pleasures and power(s) of slaveownership. Whites of both sexes could beat a black slave like a master could; they could amass honor from the black slave's dishonor like slaveowners did; they could demand deference like a master could and punish insubordination like a master could; they could extract sex from slaves of both sexes like a master could.[114] Misidentifying slavery's essence in the extraction of financial profit, we overlook its operation both as a relation of extreme power and a source of pleasure and honor.[115] Privilege similarly misses the point. The Africanization of slavery in Virginia did not institute an armistice in the intraracial war between rich and poor or Catholic and Protestant; it instead transformed whites of all social classes into bearers of a humanity brought into being by black people's violent expulsion from it.[116]

Once Africanized, slavery had to remain as such. Why? Paradoxically, as white mastery over black people intensified, so did white people's fear of them. Black slavery did not make white people feel

112. Higginbotham Jr., *In the Matter of Color*, 56–57.

113. Virginia and Hening, *The Statutes at Large*, 448.

114. Thavolia Glymph, *Out of the House of Bondage: The Transformation of the Plantation Household* (New York: Cambridge University Press, 2003), 3–7.

115. Hartman, *Scenes of Subjection*, 24.

116. Hartman and Wilderson, "The Position of the Unthought," 187.

safe; to the contrary, it made them feel existentially imperiled. The more direct violence whites inflicted upon black people, the more terrifying black people seemed to them.[117] Locked in a self-intensifying cycle, white attempts to quell insurrection only amplified their fear of it. When enslaved black people pursued freedom, they appeared not human, but dangerous. Unsurprisingly, then, all black people were treated like white criminals: they could not hold public office, they could not marry whites, and they were not allowed to move about or assemble without white permission and oversight.[118] The fear of black power never fully vanquished, white Virginians would seek to keep free black people from living within their borders, ordering any slaveowner who set a slave free to be able to pay for that slave's transport out of the colony.[119] Throughout the eighteenth century, the white Virginian's hunger for control over the bodies of black people would prove insatiable.

Even whites who came to hate slavery still feared both blackness and black people. In the first half of the nineteenth century, many Midwestern whites perceived slavery less as an injustice imposed upon the black slave from without and more as a type of contagion that black women and men carried with them wherever they went.[120] Iowa, Michigan, and Indiana passed a series of laws that imbued local judges with the power to personally expel black immigrants from the state. Other Midwestern states required black immigrants to post expensive bonds for each member of their family before entering the state.[121] Many whites throughout the North urged that the federal government should relocate emancipated slaves not to the American North but to Africa.[122] In the early years of the Civil War, President Lincoln and many members of Congress agreed, framing colonization to Africa as the proper response to emancipation, but then then take up residence elsewhere. The whites of New England also generally desired that black people receive emancipation, but reside elsewhere.[123]

117. For more on the way in which white attempts to quell insurrection only increased white people's fear of black slaves, see Alan Taylor, *The Internal Enemy: Slavery and War in Virginia, 1772-1832* (New York: W. W. Norton, 2013), 1–12.
118. Higginbotham Jr., *In the Matter of Color*, 45.
119. Ibid., 48.
120. Ibid., 84.
121. Leslie A. Schwalm, *Emancipation's Diaspora: Race and Reconstruction in the Upper Midwest* (Chapel Hill: University of North Carolina Press, 2009), 28–34.
122. Ibid., 27, 82.
123. Ibid., 31.

CARIBBEAN CONTEXTS OF ANTIBLACKNESS SUPREMACY

Historians and social theorists alike also fail to distinguish Africanized slavery and its afterlife from both colonization and the injustice inflicted on the marginalized and sometimes racialized nonblack immigrant. In order to correct these unintended misapprehensions, I turn to the undertheorized history of the Caribbean Irish. In addition to illuminating the structural dissimilarity between the nonblack immigrant of any kind and the native-born or slave-descended black person, the Caribbean Irish also provide a type of prototype by which marginalized outsiders, even those originally deemed nonwhite, utilize antiblackness supremacy.

After the Protestant Reformation, the Irish were slurred as not just wild, but "papist." They also refused to submit to English rule. Enemies of both the Protestant faith and the English Crown, they also violated the natural law, purportedly engaging in cannibalism and sexual perversion. As such, they were unfit for self-rule. For this reason, when Irishmen waged a war of rebellion against English rule in the 1640s, for example, Oliver Cromwell deported them to the English Caribbean colonies of Montserrat and Barbados as imprisoned indentured servants. Neither slave nor free, these kidnapped Irishmen initially both "were and were not white."[124] Today, racially conservative whites often cite this history so as to strip black history of its moral authority: white people were slaves too, they insist.[125] But unlike the Caribbean's black slaves, in time, Irish Catholics would qualify "as privileged members of the white community."[126] How did this happen?

The Irish person's voyage from whipped servant and despised enemy of the Crown to junior partner in English colonization projects occurred in quintessentially American fashion: the Irish acted as allies to English masters of black slaves. One struggles to determine which fact proves more incredible: that the English ended up entrust-

124. Jenny Shaw, *Everyday Life in the Early English Caribbean: Irish, Africans, and the Construction of Difference* (Athens: University of Georgia Press, 2013), 2.

125. Southern Poverty Law Center, "How the Myth of the 'Irish Slaves' Became a Favorite Meme of Racists Online," April 19, 2016, https://www.splcenter.org/hatewatch/2016/04/19/how-myth-irish-slaves-became-favorite-meme-racists-online. Accessed January 2, 2017.

126. Kristen Block and Jenny Shaw, "Subjects Without an Empire: The Irish in the Early Modern Caribbean," *Past & Present* 210, no. 1 (2011): 50.

ing the Irish with police powers over their black slaves or that the Irish sided with the very men who had dispossessed and deported them against black Caribbean women and men who had not harmed them at all.

Simple class analysis cannot adequately account for this: the English could have preferred the African-descended as junior partners in the project of Irish slavery. Plus, if the importation of African slaves to the foreign shores of the Caribbean proved profitable, would not the deployment of Irish slaves in Ireland prove equally so? In light of these factors, we ought to ask, why did the Irish people's "whiteness" come to matter more than their non-Protestant status, alleged savagery, or purportedly treasonous violence against the Crown? These questions prove especially pressing given that the Irish servants shipped to the Anglo-Caribbean proved much more belligerent than their counterparts in colonial Virginia.[127]

Further highlighting the inadequacy of simple class analysis, the English distinguished the Irish and the African-descended differently even before the Irish began to display their loyalty to either English sovereignty over the Caribbean or the English system of black slave-ownership. Common lore notwithstanding, Irish indentured servitude, though brutally unjust, differed from black slavery in several key ways. For example, the Irish were not assigned new names. And, although they were sold as chattel, they could not be separated from wife or child; nor were their spouses taken as sexual property of their master. In 1661 the Barbados Assembly in fact passed a series of laws in order "to ensure that there was no confusion about the differences between servitude and slavery."[128] Despite the many evils perpetrated by the English upon the Irish, they were never reduced to slavery.

In the Americas, the Irish have always endured situational, rather than structural, oppression. When rebelling against Cromwell, for example, they were considered servile enemies; when resisting colonization, they were deemed vile savages; however, when placed in spatial juxtaposition to enslaved black people, they transformed into junior partners in the English colonization project; and when petitioning Iberian Catholic monarchs for aid against the English, they became persecuted victims of a common Protestant enemy.[129] But blackness, regardless of its intersections with religious identity,

127. Allen, *The Invention of the White Race, Volume Two*, 226.
128. Shaw, *Everyday Life in the Early English Caribbean*, 15.
129. Block and Shaw, "Subjects Without an Empire," 34.

class status, or country of origin, remained forever fixed in place by its association with enslaveability. While the Irish exchanged status when they exchanged one island for another, black people's embodied and therefore un-severable association with Africa held them in place. As the history of the Caribbean Irish suggest, processes of racialization unfolded less for the sake of the preservation of whiteness, however defined, than for the perpetuation of antiblackness and the supremacy it provided.

For this reason, racial hierarchy required neither that all white people owned slaves nor that only white people owned slaves. It insisted only that all slaves were black. We may be tempted to dismissively describe cases in which significant numbers of black people owned black slaves as troubling and tragic exceptions to a nonetheless undisturbed rule of white supremacy. In this way, for example, scholars rightly point out that, in many places, such as Louisiana, free people of color owned black slaves not to exercise mastery over them, but to rescue loved ones from slavery.[130] But, even there, this was not always the case. Sometimes black people did own black slaves for purely base reasons.[131] The historical fact of black slaveownership illuminates the inner logic of Africanized slavery and its ongoing afterlife: white supremacy results from antiblackness supremacy much more than antiblackness supremacy results from white supremacy. Put another way, white people would concede black mastership in order to preserve black slavery, but they never would have conceded black slavery in order to preserve exclusively white mastership. White people need all slaves to be black much more than they need all masters to be white.

Especially on Caribbean islands with relatively large black populations, whites paradoxically maintained racialized power by extending slaveownership to a small minority of black women and men.[132] For example, white masters on the Danish-controlled islands of St. Thomas, St. John, and St. Croix (now the U.S. Virgin Islands) sometimes deeded black slaves to their black concubines and mulatto children in their wills.[133] In the Caribbean, black people also acquired black slaves independently. In St. Croix, for example, black people

130. Rebecca J. Scott, *Degrees of Freedom: Louisiana and Cuba after Slavery* (Cambridge, MA: Belknap, 2008), 27.
131. Ibid., 15.
132. Morgan, *Slavery and the British Empire*, 47.
133. Neville A. T. Hall, *Slave Society in the Danish West Indies: St Thomas, St John and St Croix* (Mona, Jamaica: Aarhus University Press, 1992), 143.

owned some of the island's largest plantations.[134] On these islands, antiblackness supremacy paved even black people's avenues to power.

But because slavery was not merely for black people only, but Africanized, these unenslaved black people could not escape slavery's stigma.[135] A Danish West Indian law required all freedmen to wear the cockade, a visibly prominent badge, in order to "identify doubtful claimants to free status."[136] Perceived blackness made one a slave by default. A black person was assumed enslaved until proven free: one had to visually opt out. But even faithful wearing of the cockade did not protect free black people from the violence of white subjugation. Free men could be beaten by white officers simply upon "a directive from the governor general to the Chief of Police, his assistant, or one of the freemen 'Captains.'" More than simply beaten like slaves could be, free black people were presumed criminals in the same way that enslaved people were. Routinely refused bail, freedmen frequently endured imprisonment without a trial for even minor offenses. Free black people were deprived of common markers of honor and sexual dignity. They could not apply for a public loan nor could they dance with whites without both receiving permission from the police and submitting to supervision by them.[137]

Sometimes antiblackness supremacy treated free black women and men like slaves precisely by differentiating them from their enslaved counterparts. For example, Danish colonial law compelled free black people to hunt and recapture black slaves who had run away from their white masters. If these free men refused to obey this injunction, they faced "mandatory corporal punishment and solitary confinement on bread and water."[138] Here whites exercised their power to act as masters to free black women and men.

Black people could not escape the stigma of slavery even by inflicting direct violence on other black people. For example, as in other parts of the Americas, including the United States, Caribbean masters enlisted black slaves as overseers or slave discipliners.[139] But while the lower-class white person who inflicts violence upon the slave shares

134. Ibid., 174.

135. Hartman, *Scenes of Subjection*, 25.

136. Hall, *Slave Society in the Danish West Indies*, 165.

137. Ibid., 173.

138. Ibid., 172.

139. Robert S. Starobin, "Privileged Bondsmen and the Process of Accommodation: The Role of Houseservants and Drivers as Seen in Their Own Letters," *Journal of Social History* 5, no. 1 (1971): 58.

in the honor of slaveownership, the black overseer ultimately affirms his own enslaveability. Even though a black overseer often received certain privileges that were denied to other black people, he still remained enslaved.[140] As such, he snapped the whip against another black slave's back not as an expression of his own will but as a fungible extension of his master's personhood. Free black islanders aspiring to higher social status similarly attempted to performatively distance themselves from slave positionality by "treating slaves as harshly or more harshly than did whites."[141] A black person who acts violently toward another black person does not acquire honor in the way a nonblack person does. He instead validates a moral order that deems the black body uniquely dangerous, dishonorable, undisciplined, and in need of violent correction.

***

More than an attitude inhering within individuals or a structure existing within society, antiblackness supremacy instead structures both the individual and society; we cannot pull the thread of antiblackness without unraveling the entire world. In this way, it establishes the rule that all human beings are encouraged to follow. But in contrast to nonblack people, black people's attempts to access the supremacy and honor that antiblackness supplies simultaneously work against them.

The preceding historical overview suggests that Africanized slavery was more antiblack than white supremacist. It further suggests that Africanized slavery would have empowered non-slaveowning whites more than it would have empowered slaveowning blacks. Configuring the black body as the body of a slave, antiblackness subjects black people not necessarily to poverty, but to heightened surveillance and vulnerability to direct violence. When antiblackness supremacy impoverishes black people, it does so as a means to a very specific end: to uphold the association between blackness and servile degradation. This helps to fulfill an arguably even more precious goal. Uniquely dishonored as slaves, even free black people can be abused like them. These insights better position us to begin sorting out the much-disputed relationship between race and class. White poverty and black poverty therefore differ not just in degree or prevalence.

140. Ibid., 67.

141. Hall, *Slave Society in the Danish West Indies*, 163.

Poor white people surely are deprived and often looked down upon, but only black poverty signals servility and enslaveability. Poverty ultimately makes black people fungible and killable in a way that it never has white people.

2.

The Nearly Global Afterlife of Black Slavery

As historian and literature scholar Saidiya Hartman notes, today, we inhabit not the aftermath of black slavery, but its afterlife.[1] Rather than trivializing the difference between pre-abolition and post-abolition forms of antiblackness supremacy, Hartman's formulation enables us to perceive historical continuities within antiblackness more clearly. Antiblackness supremacy possesses an adaptive, concessionary dynamism that enables it to withstand a wide array of circumstances. For this reason, antiblackness supremacy continues to exist as a contextually specific but ultimately consistent racial habitat throughout the Americas. Just as we cannot understand the operation of antiblackness supremacy in the contemporary United States without tracking its development over time, so must we attend to its movement within space.

In addition to more expertly outlining the afterlife of slavery in the post–Black Civil Rights U.S., this pan-American approach also positions us to more adeptly assess the racial impact of two much-discussed phenomena: the rise in the country's multiracial population and the arrival of large numbers of nonwhite immigrants from Asia, Latin America, and Africa and. When we mistakenly draw a sharp line between Anglo preoccupation with the preservation of pure-whiteness and Latin American embrace of mestizaje, the rise in the country's nonwhite population appears to signal the dawn of a new racial era. But this view in fact confuses one particular iteration of

1. Saidiya V. Hartman, *Lose Your Mother: A Journey Along the Atlantic Slave Route* (New York: Macmillan, 2008), 6.

racial domination, that which reigned in the U.S. American South during Jim Crow, with racial domination itself. While blackness, like whiteness, may be defined differently in each region, both Latin- and Anglo-America inhabit a world structured by the afterlife of slavery.[2] The demographic changes that have occurred since the end of the Black Civil Rights Movement will continue to alter antiblackness supremacy, but they will not end it.

The so-called "Latin Americanization of race in the United States" signals not a break with the country's racial past, but a new way of being what it has always been: antiblack.[3] The increasing nonwhiteness, both real and perceived, of the United States in fact promises to affirm white supremacy's unique dependence upon the stigmatizing association between blackness and slave status. Further dampening racial optimism, the spatially variegated character of antiblackness arms it with a wide array of strategies and methods by which to adapt to new racial circumstances. In order to appreciate the increasingly globalized operation of the afterlife of black slavery, this chapter compares the U.S.-American afterlife of slavery with the afterlives of slavery in the Latin American countries from which it has received the most immigrants: Cuba, Puerto Rico, the Dominican Republic, and Mexico. This approach further substantiates the argument that the link between antiblackness and chattel slavery makes antiblackness supremacy a particularly embodied and an incomparably unique form of oppression.

THE CUBAN AFTERLIFE OF SLAVERY

Beginning in the early nineteenth century, the Spanish Crown turned the previously marginal island of Cuba into a booming sugar colony by encouraging the immigration of slaveowning Spaniards and arranging the importation of more enslaved Africans.[4] But as the island's slave population increased, so did planters' fears of Haiti-style

2. Néstor Medina, *Mestizaje: Remapping Race, Culture, and Faith in Latina/o Catholicism* (Maryknoll, NY: Orbis, 2009), 48.

3. Eduardo Bonilla-Silva and Karen S. Glover, "We Are All Americans": The Latin Americanization of Race Relations in the United States," *The Changing Terrain of Race and Ethnicity* (2004): 149–83.

4. Christopher Schmidt-Nowara, *Slavery, Freedom, and Abolition in Latin America and the Atlantic World* (Albuquerque: University of New Mexico Press, 2011), 84, 128–29.

insurrection.[5] Royal agents managed to exploit these fears of "another Haiti" to weaken support for emancipation and successfully forestall abolition until the relatively late year of 1888.[6] Even when pursuing an abolitionist agenda, the island's revolutionaries would have to performatively distance themselves from any resemblance to Haiti's founding mothers and fathers.[7]

These habits of negrophobic perception and performance rooted themselves deep within Cuba's national body, outlasting both abolition and independence. Often, black Cubans could claim the rights and privileges of Cuban citizenship only to the extent that they relinquished a collectively black political identity. To many, corporate expressions of and mobilization around blackness appeared a singular "threat [to] the cause of Cuban national unity."[8] Evidencing this perception, early Cuban nationalists treated the island's *Partido de Independiente de Color* as a dangerous negro insurgency rather than a political party formed in order to "demand real, [rather than symbolic], equality for Afro-Cubans."[9] After arresting the party's leaders along with dozens of its members, the Island's mostly white government officials prosecuted them "for allegedly conspiring to impose a black dictatorship in Cuba," in the purported style of Haiti's black revolutionaries.[10] Despite their acquittal, the Cuban government rendered the party an illegal organization.

But these Afro-Cubans who resided mostly on the eastern part of the island would not surrender their claim to a collectively black political identity so easily.[11] In response, they waged an armed protest aimed at achieving "the re-legalization of their party." The Cuban government sent troops and volunteer soldiers to kill the assembled protestors. But they did not stop there. Perhaps seeking to prove that Cuba could detach itself from Spain without thereby surrendering to

5. Lisa Yun, *The Coolie Speaks: Chinese Indentured Laborers and African Slaves in Cuba* (Philadelphia: Temple University Press, 2009), 11.

6. Ada Ferrer, *Freedom's Mirror: Cuba and Haiti in the Age of Revolution* (New York: Cambridge University Press, 2014), 337–38.

7. Aline Helg, "Race and Black Mobilization in Colonial and Early Independent Cuba: A Comparative Perspective," *Ethnohistory* 44, no. 1 (January 1, 1997): 56; Rebecca J. Scott, *Degrees of Freedom: Louisiana and Cuba after Slavery* (Cambridge, MA: Belknap, 2008), 103.

8. Vera M. Kutzinski, *Sugar's Secrets: Race and the Erotics of Cuban Nationalism* (Charlottesville: University Press of Virginia, 1993), 5.

9. Helg, "Race and Black Mobilization in Colonial and Early Independent Cuba," 60.

10. Ibid., 63.

11. Ileana M. Rodríguez-Silva, *Silencing Race: Disentangling Blackness, Colonialism, and National Identities in Puerto Rico* (New York: Palgrave Macmillan, 2012), 194.

Africanity, this squad of assassins massacred thousands of Afro-Cuban men, women, and children with no connection to the political movement.[12] The slaughter proved successful: from this point on, Afro-Cubans would participate in Cuban politics only as individuals acting through "white-controlled parties."[13]

More than simply seeking to neutralize the threat of Haitian invasion, Cuba's founding generation suppressed blackness to disassociate itself from its slaveholding past.[14] They did this not so much to undo the effects of black slavery but to avoid having to take responsibility for them. As historian Rebecca J. Scott explains, "public discourse in Cuba . . . rarely addressed the question of what might be thought to be owed, and by whom, to those whose forced labor as slaves had built much of the nation's wealth."[15] If there are no black people, then there is no one to whom reparations are owed; if there are no black people, then there is no one to whom racial harm can be done. And if there can be no racial harm, then the country does not need to devise specific mechanisms to redress it. Cuba's racially inclusive ideology of citizenship paradoxically promoted a type of antiblackness. Cuba would attempt to eradicate not racial hierarchy, but racial difference.[16]

In truth, not even Cuba's racially inclusive concept of citizenship could undo the aftereffects of slavery. In the twentieth century, nonblack Cubans continued to treat Afro-Cubans "as former slaves, unfit for democracy and predisposed to crime."[17] Despite the absence of laws mandating segregation, "many social clubs, places of entertainment, hotels, private schools, and barbershops excluded blacks." Unofficial practices of antiblackness also barred black people from certain high-status occupations while confining a disproportionate share of them to positions that lacked prestige.[18] Africanity appeared a threat to Cuban identity while Spanish-ness seemed to strengthen it. While Cuba attempted to repel Afro-Caribbean immigration in general and Haitian immigration in particular, it simultaneously strove

12. Helg, "Race and Black Mobilization in Colonial and Early Independent Cuba," 63.

13. Ibid.

14. Jorge Aquino, *"Ni Blanquitos, ni negritos": Race, nation, and identity in United States Latino/a theology* (PhD diss., Graduate Theological Union, 2006), 8–9.

15. Scott, *Degrees of Freedom*, 215.

16. Gonzalez also covers this post-independence history in *Afro-Cuban Theology*, 66–69.

17. Helg, "Race and Black Mobilization in Colonial and Early Independent Cuba," 65.

18. Aline Helg, "Black Men, Racial Stereotyping, and Violence in the U.S. South and Cuba at the Turn of the Century," *Comparative Studies in Society and History* 42, no. 3 (July 1, 2000): 585.

to attract European immigrants in pursuit of an explicit policy of whitening.[19] As they did in the United States, these European immigrants to Cuba assimilated into a society structured by the afterlife of slavery.[20] Their post-abolition arrival does not make them innocent of antiblackness supremacy.[21]

THE AFTERLIFE OF BLACK SLAVERY IN PUERTO RICO

Puerto Rican nationalism styles itself "the fusion of three races." But this celebration of non-whiteness does not signal the absence of antiblackness nor has it severed the stigmatizing association between blackness and slave status. For example, shortly after abolition, Governor Don Segundo de la Portilla imagined that emancipated black people would respond to "complete freedom" by "abandoning their jobs at the plantations in an attempt to finally enjoy the freedom they so much desired." If allowed to "spread around the various towns of this Province," the Governor predicted, these ill-mannered and overly passionate blacks would "endanger our moral and material interests and threaten the public order."[22]

Seeking to keep black people in their purported place, government officials ordered newly free black Puerto Ricans to remain in the labor contracts they signed with their former owners when they were denied the ability to purchase land of their own.[23] They also stipulated that free black people could not move to a new location without the permission of both their employer and the *Protector de Libertos*. Placing black people under surveillance, these laws compelled *libertos* to "carry at all times a *cedula* (an identification form) that contained all personal and employment information."[24] Lighter-skinned Puerto Ricans typically feared black people when they could not control them.

These laws represent more than desperate attempts at planter class self-preservation. Lighter-skinned urban whites, who did not directly benefit from the subjugation of the black labor class as their rural

19. Scott, *Degrees of Freedom*, 231; Helg, "Black Men, Racial Stereotyping," 590.

20. Aquino, *Ni Blanquitos, ni negritos,* 115.

21. Scott, *Degrees of Freedom*, 115.

22. Rodríguez-Silva, *Silencing Race*, 27.

23. Luis A. Figueroa, *Sugar, Slavery, and Freedom in Nineteenth-Century Puerto Rico*, 1st ed. (Chapel Hill: University of North Carolina Press, 2005), 146, 152.

24. Rodríguez-Silva, *Silencing Race*, 44.

counterparts did, also sought to control the movements of the newly freed black body. For example, in the last decade of the nineteenth century, the white residents of Ponce, the island's wealthiest and most culturally refined city, perceived the recently emancipated black and mulatto women and men who migrated there as not pioneers of liberty fleeing plantation servility, but "*los indesables*," who "embodied vagrancy and criminality because they lacked stable wage jobs."[25] Like their U.S.-American counterparts, Puerto Rican urbanites spoke colorblindness in order to perform antiblackness.[26] City elites established new institutions—reform schools, hospitals, asylums, and charity organizations—in order to police these formerly enslaved Puerto Rican black and mulatto people.[27] Further entrapped by racially biased vagrancy laws, black and mulatto men of working age comprised the overwhelming majority of Ponce residents accused of committing crimes in between 1870 and 1890, despite constituting only about ten percent of the city's population.[28]

While plantation owners strove to keep the unenslaved black person residentially close, the urban elite attempted to keep the unsubdued black body residentially distant.[29] Seeking to keep black and mulatto residents spatially contained, city elites deployed housing codes justified by a disingenuous concern for poor sanitation as a pretext by which to relocate the black and mulatto poor to the city's fringes. In order to accelerate this segregation, whites automated it. City administrators divided the city into three circular zones radiating outward from the city center—buildings in the center were to be built with expensive rubble masonry while those in the outermost ring were to be built with wood. Purportedly organizing the city according to a purely class-based aesthetics, this policy preserved the "heart of the city" as the "domain of upper-class whites."[30]

Antiblackness was not a mere strategy of class oppression. Puerto Rican officials across the island sought to bring black performances of the distinctly Afro-Puerto Rican *bailes de bomba* under their control.[31] For example, in Guayama, an area with one of the highest concentrations of formerly enslaved black Puerto Ricans, the town's

25. Ibid., 95, 97.
26. Ibid., 95.
27. Ibid., 98.
28. Ibid., 98–99.
29. Figueroa, *Sugar, Slavery, and Freedom in Nineteenth-Century Puerto Rico*, 41.
30. Rodríguez-Silva, *Silencing Race*, 102.
31. Figueroa, *Sugar, Slavery, and Freedom in Nineteenth-Century Puerto Rico*, 181.

municipal council banned the dance altogether.[32] But they did so not for a disdain of public dancing. For example, approximately twenty years later, the municipal council would "allow the celebration of other musical expressions . . . of more 'Hispanic' origin, such as *parrandas* and *serentas*."[33] Even after abolition, the *bailes de bomba* still threatened fugitivity and insubordination in the minds of whites afraid of black freedom.[34]

In addition to lacking the capacity to bring the afterlife of Puerto Rican slavery to an end, Puerto Rican mythologies of national mestizaje have "often precluded Afro-Puerto Ricans from speaking as one to collectively denounce and defy [their] discrimination and marginalization" even as it accords visibly African-descended Puerto Ricans opportunities unavailable to black people in the Jim Crow–style of antiblackness supremacy.[35] But although this origin story acknowledges that these three races have never been separate, it surely does not position them as equals.[36] When creating personal histories, for example, Puerto Rican elites typically emphasize both Spanish and indigenous ancestries while downplaying their Africanitiy.

Because it celebrates racial impurity, mestizaje does achieve a certain ideological distance from whiteness. But in truth, it denigrates blackness much more than it disrupts whiteness. In the afterlife of slavery, ideologies of racial fusion position whiteness as normative, unifying, and stabilizing and blackness as abnormal, divisive, and disruptive. As Rodríguez-Silva explains, Puerto Rico's "dominant classes have persistently underscored the white, Hispanic experience as the main thread that provides coherence to the history of the Puerto Rican people" while Puerto Ricans of all classes generally reserve the term "negro" for other Caribbean islanders, particularly those from the West Indies, or U.S. African Americans.[37] Even when visibly African-descended, Puerto Ricans typically call themselves not *negro/a* but members of *la raza de color*. If blackness is not named, then perhaps it does not exist. In so doing, they identify as nonblack by calling themselves nonwhite.[38]

32. Ibid., 182.
33. Ibid., 183.
34. Hartman, *Scenes of Subjection*, 63.
35. Rodríguez-Silva, *Silencing Race*, 10.
36. Figueroa, *Sugar, Slavery, and Freedom in Nineteenth-Century Puerto Rico*, 5.
37. Rodríguez-Silva, *Silencing Race*, 5.
38. Ibid., 6.

The afterlife of slavery still structures life in contemporary Puerto Rico. Recently, intellectuals and activists have called attention to the fact that Puerto Ricans have "associated blackness with diminished intellectual abilities and negative aesthetic images."[39] Although these racialized notions simultaneously arise from and refer back to the island's slave past, prevailing habits of racial silencing conspire to conceal the operation of antiblackness in Puerto Rico.[40] Ideologies of racial fusion deny blackness much more than they defeat antiblackness.

Ultimately, the racial systems that arose in Cuba and Puerto Rico in the wake of independence resembled and anticipated the style of racial domination that has emerged in the United States in reaction to the Black Civil Rights Movement of the mid-twentieth century.[41] This ideology of colorblindness contains three key features: first, it maintains that accusations of racism or assertions of (black) racial identity serve to divide and distract us from what we hold in common as citizens, humans, or some other form of identity. Second, this ideology trumpets the moral and strategic superiority of racially neutral political movements and policies over those that seek to implement racially specific solutions or organize around an explicitly racial identity. And third, this ideology insists upon a general disavowal of racial responsibility: since there are no racists, there can be no victims of racism. The afterlife of black slavery can operate through racially explicit laws and discourses as well as regimes of colorblindness.[42]

THE AFTERLIFE OF AFRICANIZED SLAVERY IN THE DOMINICAN REPUBLIC

Perhaps no country better demonstrates the centrality of antiblackness to American systems of racial classification than the Dominican Republic. Although many people in the Dominican Republic would qualify as "black" according to U.S. standards, "Dominican

39. Ibid., 2.

40. Ibid., 217.

41. As Gary Dorrien explains, although "the name 'civil rights movement' is usually reserved for the movement of the 1950s and 1960s," black civil rights activism actually began in 1884 and has "three historic phases." Dorrien, *The New Abolition: W.E.B. Du Bois and the Black Social Gospel* (New Haven: Yale University Press, 2015), 1.

42. Eduardo Bonilla-Silva, *Racism without Racists: Color-Blind Racism and the Persistence of Racial Inequality in America*, 3rd ed. (Lanham, MD: Rowman & Littlefield, 2009).

nationalism has been . . . centered on a rejection of African ancestry and blackness."[43] Dominican antiblackness especially contrasts black, African, and purportedly non-Christian Haiti with its own white, Hispanic, and Catholic character. As elsewhere, Dominican antipathy for Haiti expresses a deeply rooted fear of the unenslaved and defiantly African-identified black woman or man.

While slaveholders throughout the Atlantic world anxiously sought to forestall the spread of Haitian-style slave revolt to their part of the world, only Dominican masters of black flesh shared an island with these triumphant revolutionaries. Their fears proved well founded. In 1822 the Haitian army overpowered Spanish colonial troops and governed the Dominican Republic for the next twenty-two years. Abolishing slavery and encouraging former slaves from the United States to immigrate to the temporarily united island, these black rulers initially were resisted by the predominately white Dominican master class and welcomed by the "impoverished mulatto and black masses."[44] But Haitian rule brought the Dominican side of the island more than freedom from slavery. Forced to order its economic life toward paying the government of France usurious reparations for the slaves the Haitian revolution stole from them, Haitian rule eventually proved unpopular even with the newly emancipated black and mulatto masses. Ultimately, many black and mulatto Dominicans would come to believe Haiti was "antithetical to all things Dominican."[45]

This perception reflects more than economic self-interest or national pride. Citizens of the Dominican Republic sought distance from Haiti because it broke nearly all the rules of American antiblackness.[46] While other American countries sought to extend the life of black slavery, Haiti would violently abolish it. While other American countries drew their life from the social death they imposed upon black slaves, black Haitian revolutionaries declared "death to all whites."[47] While many other American countries would whiten their population by soliciting European immigration, Haiti would blacken

43. David Howard, *Coloring the Nation: Race and Ethnicity in the Dominican Republic* (Oxford, UK, and Boulder, CO: Lynne Rienner, 2001), 1–2.

44. Ginetta E. B. Candelario, *Black behind the Ears: Dominican Racial Identity from Museums to Beauty Shops* (Durham, NC: Duke University Press, 2007), 37.

45. Ibid., 259.

46. Ibid.

47. Laurent Dubois, *Avengers of the New World: The Story of the Haitian Revolution* (Cambridge, MA: Harvard University Press, 2009), 116.

its population by welcoming survivors of black slavery as refugees. Other American countries upheld violent territorial expansion as the unique prerogative of European sovereigns and those who claimed descent from them while Haiti would claim this right for itself too. Every other American country founded its revolutionary identity on some iteration of nonblackness, whether white, mestizo, or indigenous, while Haiti alone declared itself black from the start. Other American nations celebrated an ideology of white or race-less citizenship while the Haitian Constitution declared all its citizens, even the German and Polish men who took up arms alongside the island's black revolutionaries, black. The triumph of Haiti threatened not just to abolish black slavery across the Americas, but also to incorporate nonblack Americans into blackness.

Dominican hostility to African Haiti has persisted into the present day. For example, the mid-twentieth-century dictator, Rafael Leonidas Trujillo, invited Europeans, including Eastern European Jews, to settle on the island and as a type of human fortification on the country's Haitian border. Seemingly because these recruits appeared white in contrast to black-skinned Haitians, their Jewishness did not seem a threat to Catholic *Dominicanidad* in the way that Haitian voodoo did. Put another way, just as Dominican racial ideology denigrates and seeks distance from not just nonwhiteness in general but blackness in particular, so it defends not just Catholicism in particular but white religiosity in general. In Europe, these Jewish people were victims of increasingly racialized mistreatment. But in the Dominican Republic, they were nonblack if not white. As a result, these Jewish immigrants paradoxically appeared to strengthen the Dominican Catholic character while Catholic black Haitians endangered it.

A Dominican textbook used in the waning years of Trujillo's dictatorship indoctrinated a generation of children in this anti-Haitian ideology. In contrast to black "Haiti [which] is inhabited by a mob of savage Africans," it explained, "we Dominicans should be in debt to our blood," which has rescued us from the horrors of undiluted blackness. Because "the Haitian is an enemy . . . incapable of evolution and progress," this textbook instructs its young readers that "Haitians should be transferred to French Guyana or to Africa. The Dominican race and civilization are superior to that of Haiti. Haiti has no importance in the world." To this end, Trujillo characterized his 1937 slaughter of between nine and twenty thousand Haitian people who inhabited the island's borderlands as an "attempt to 'save' the Dominican nation from 'Africanization' and the 'illegal' entry of Haitian immigrants."[48] In addition to repelling the Haitian blackness without, Trujillo sought to eradicate the non-Haitian blackness within. To this end, he applied skin-lightening cosmetic powders on his own visibly African-descended body and commissioned biographies that declared him of purely Spanish and French ancestry.[49] Refusing to inherit his grandparents' blackness, Trujillo transferred his own performatively acquired whiteness back to them.

This Dominican fear of contaminating black Haitian invasion persists today. During the frenzied weeks between November 1996 and January 1997, Dominican officials deported 15,000 Haitians. In 2015, the Dominican Republic again purged itself of thousands of black, Dominican-born children of Haitian immigrants.[50] Dominican spatial practices have kept blackness at bay in another way: the underpaid Haitian immigrants who work in the country's sugar fields remain confined within what David Howard identifies as "ethnic ghettoes."[51]

The intensity of anti-Haitian sentiment may seem to suggest that Dominicans denigrate Haiti not for its blackness, but for its foreignness. But this oversimplifies. Dominican ideology targets Haiti precisely because its foreignness epitomizes both blackness and the threat of incorporation into it.[52] Further evidencing this nation's negrophobic mindset, contemporary Dominicans categorize themselves as not black or mulatto, but wheat-colored, rosy, fair, or ashen.[53] Adhering to a complex, but decidedly antiblack aesthetics, Dominican banks rarely employ dark-skinned women and men as tellers or cashiers.[54] In general, citizens of the Dominican Republic seek distance from and superiority over even Dominican blackness.

Dominican racial beliefs and practices suggest that the one-drop rule represents not an essential component of antiblackness supremacy, but merely one possible strategy of it. To this end,

48. Howard, *Coloring the Nation*, 29.

49. Ibid., 9.

50. Daniel José Older, "Why U.S. Latinos Need to Get Loud About the Dominican Republic," *BuzzFeed*, accessed June 19, 2015, http://www.buzzfeed.com/danieljoseolder/us-latinos-need-to-get-loud-about-the-dominican-republic.

51. Howard, *Coloring the Nation*, 30.

52. Ibid.

53. Candelario, *Black Behind the Ears*, 38; Kelly, Zahira @bad_dominicana: "sigh. being dominican is havin ya black dad be the king of black cool & style in his youth while talkin of black ppl as outside of himself." 10:37 am, June 29, 2015. Tweet.

54. Howard, *Coloring the Nation*, 8.

contemporary Dominicans seemingly believe racial identity is not so much about how one looks or from whom one descends, but what one wishes to claim. For example, as David Howard reports in his survey of residents of the Dominican city of Gazcue, "more respondents described themselves as *blanco/a* than would have been apparent at first sight." Government clerks issuing *cedulas* similarly assign Dominican citizens racial identity not by assessing their perceived phenotype, but out of respect for their social status. As a result, "*blanco* and *indio* accounted for 86 percent of the *cedulas* issued to upper, upper middle, and middle class interviewees" while "*indio* was the most popular term for the *cedulas* of lower class interviewees." Ultimately, Howard concludes, "the issuing clerk automatically assumes that an affluent Dominican would be considered as *blanco* rather than *indio claro*."

Dominican racial beliefs and practices also illuminate whiteness's unique dependence on antiblackness. While African descent, even when visible, does not make one automatically black, in the Dominican Republic, European descent, even if imperceptible, does secure a person's whiteness. One resident of Gazcue explains that "my parents are Spanish, so even though I look like a *mulata*, I'm definitely *blanca*."[55] Dominicans similarly utilize what many U.S.-Americans would consider an impossibly expansive notion of whiteness: as one interviewee explains, Dominicans define "the *raza blanca* [as] a mixture—Jews, *blancos*, Arabs, Chinese."[56] Whiteness operates not as a signifier of purely European appearance or ancestry but more specifically as a mode of nonblackness.[57]

Dominican ideologies of mestizaje also uphold antiblackness supremacy. Consider the speech that former Dominican President Dr. Joaquin Balaguer gave at the 1992 Ibero-American summit in Madrid. Further evidencing the way in which Dominican ideology of mestizaje perpetrates antiblackness more than it overturns white supremacy, he defined *el mestizaje* as "the violent alloy of two heroic metals which are mixed in the blood of our indigines and the descendants of those who arrived with Columbus from the other side of the Atlantic." In describing mestizaje as "the fusion of two cultures, or one could say, two civilizations," Belaguer not so subtly implies that

55. Ibid., 43.
56. Ibid., 17.
57. Ibid., 14.

"Africa" lacks both culture and civilization.[58] This perception perhaps helps to explain why, despite the rapid genocidal destruction of the island's original, indigenous population, many Dominicans describe themselves as "*indio*."[59] In attaching themselves to the Indies, they sever stigmatizing association with Africa.

In the Dominican Republic, race represents not so much a perceived phenotype, but an embodied performance of preconceived notions of Africanity and Hispanic Catholicism. In addition to associating certain negative characteristics with those perceived as visibly African-descended, this strategy simultaneously attaches Africanity to certain negative characteristics. The Dominican Republic's status as a Catholic, Hispanic, civilized, and racially mixed country automatically verifies that it has outgrown its Africanity. Given the country's demographics, Dominicans can cling to this un-African self-image only by defining their dark-skinned citizens as something other than black. In the Dominican Republic as elsewhere, antiblackness unfolds as a form of ancestral vindication—a way to affirm, even if unconsciously, that their ancestors had been right about Haiti and by extension blackness all along.

MESTIZAJE AND THE AFTERLIFE OF MEXICAN SLAVERY

Even though Mexico was one of the few American countries whose black slave population was outnumbered by both indigenous people and free black and mulatto people, black slavery still burrowed itself within the structures of Mexican life in key ways.[60] Between 1521 and 1639, approximately half of all Africans shipped to the Indies ended up in New Spain. Still more than a century and a half later, in 1793, the mostly free, but still racialized descendants of these black slaves—whether categorized as *pardo*, mulatto, *moreno*, or *morisco*—comprised nearly 10 percent of the colony's total population. As in other American countries, many nonblack Mexicans endeavored to retain the stigmatizing association between blackness and

58. Ibid., 46.
59. Ibid., 15.
60. Proctor, *Damned Notions of Liberty*, 2–3.

slavery, even after abolition.[61] Racially motivated vagrancy laws required that free Afro-Mexicans submit to positions of servile labor. Considered unfit for freedom, these Afro-Mexicans were monitored by curfew laws and compelled to reside in the domicile of their employers. Sumptuary laws limited the amount of luxury goods they could purchase and the amount of extravagance they could display. They could not occupy any office of prestige nor could they utilize Indians as laborers.[62]

Although Mexico abolished slavery, it did not dismantle the world it brought into existence: because Mexican slavery was Africanized, mestizo Mexico still lives in the afterlife of black slavery. Like other American countries, Mexico is not organized according to a simple white supremacist hierarchy that devalues all nonwhiteness in the same way and to the same degree. It instead is animated by two non-parallel and therefore incomparable structural positions, the genocidal incorporation of indigenous peoples into the Spanish kingdom as free vassals, and its extensive and prolonged reliance on black slavery. In this, Mexico qualifies as quintessentially American.

Due to the dual legacies of anti-indigenous and antiblack racisms, today, indigenous and black Mexicans occupy two distinct positions within Mexican society and endure two distinct forms of oppression, regulation, and ideological representation. For example, seeking to distinguish themselves from the Spanish colonial project they sought to dismantle, nineteenth-century Mexican revolutionaries of all shades celebrated indigenousness. In contrast, blackness appeared to these same individuals "as antithetical to national ambitions" due to its association with degraded and socially dead slaves.[63] While contemporary indigenous Mexicans remain marginalized in the present, their glorified past paradoxically supplies "the ideological foundation of Mexico."[64] Purportedly lacking a biological link to the indigenous past that authorizes Mexican belonging, Afro-Mexicans appear

61. Ben Vinson III, *Bearing Arms for His Majesty: The Free-Colored Militia in Colonial Mexico*, 1st ed. (Stanford, CA: Stanford University Press, 2003), 3.

62. Herman L. Bennett, *Africans in Colonial Mexico: Absolutism, Christianity, and Afro-Creole Consciousness, 1570–1640* (Bloomington, IN: University of Indiana Press, 2003), 62.

63. Bobby Vaughn and Ben Vinson III, "Unfinished Migrations: From the Mexican South to the American South—Impressions on Afro-Mexican Migration to North Carolina," in *Beyond Slavery: The Multilayered Legacy of Africans in Latin America and the Caribbean*, ed. Darién J. Davis (Lanham, MD: Rowman & Littlefield, 2005), 225.

64. Bobby Vaughn, "Blacks, Indígenas, Politics, and the Greater Diaspora," in *Neither Enemies Nor Friends: Latinos, Blacks, Afro-Latinos*, ed. Anani Dzidzienyo and Suzanne Oboler (New York: Palgrave Macmillan, 2005), 122.

insufficiently Mexican.[65] White supremacy alone cannot explain these founding actors' differential perception of indigeneity and Africanity. Would not simple white supremacy deem both black and indigenous people equally incompatible with or marginal to the life of the liberal republic?

Unlike indigenous and mestizo Mexicans, Afro-Mexicans descend from the socially dead and the natally alienated. For this reason, contemporary Afro-Mexicans are thought to differ from other Mexicans not for their distinct culture, but for their presumed lack of it. While Mexicans have "recognized that indigenous people possessed particular ways of living, dressing, celebrating, [and] worshipping," slave-descended Afro-Mexicans "speak only Spanish [and] dress in mestizo clothes."[66] Positioned as inheritors of social death, Afro-Mexican culture appears not as a form of life, but a lack of it.

Because the socially dead are believed incapable of giving life to a new nation, indigenous ancestry can be claimed in a way that blackness cannot. Erased from Mexico's origin story and relegated to enclaves on the country's coastal margins, blackness appears a purely foreign property. For this reason, Mexico could welcome small numbers of U.S. American and West Indian black people as agricultural and industrial laborers in the second half of the nineteenth century, even as it strove to deny its black heritage.[67] Because they were not Mexican, they could be black in Mexico. According to this view, the Mexican brand of blackness had been completely erased by unvariegated processes of mestizaje. Blackness was Mexico's past, not its heritage.

Rather than describing objective demographic reality, influential Mexican intellectuals expressed their desire for a nonblack future. In this way, for example, José Vasconcelos denigrated blackness "as a negative stain on racial progress" that "would vanish from the Mexican social body."[68] As if attempting to turn Vasconcelos's hope for a de-Africanized *raza cosmica* into a material reality, Mexican officials recruited European immigrants in order to execute a program of unabashed national whitening.[69] Rather than seeking to confine

65. Tryon Woods, "The Fact of Anti-Blackness: Decolonization in Chiapas and the Niger River Delta," *Human Architecture: Journal of the Sociology of Self-Knowledge* 5, no. 3 (June 21, 2007): 326.

66. Vaughn, "Blacks, Indígenas, and Politics," 121.

67. Vaughn and Vinson, "Unfinished Migrations," 225.

68. Ibid., 226.

69. Irene A. Vasquez, "The Longue Durée of Africans in Mexico: The Historiography of

individuals to blackness as in the pre-Black Civil Rights Movement United States, Mexican antiblackness supremacy encouraged Mexicans to bury their blackness.[70]

Of course, as in nearly every other American slaveholding country, these purportedly socially dead slaves and their descendants in fact contributed to the creation of many of the cultural forms that most epitomize the identity of the mestizo country that seeks to erase them. Indeed, mariachi, fandango, and *jarocho* music along with instruments like the marimba, *jarana*, *cajon*, and *tarima* all sprout from African roots.[71] Despite this, Mexico did not officially acknowledge its Africanity until 1992.[72] And only at the tail end of 2015 would the government of Mexico recognize Afromexicanos as a measurable population group.[73]

THE U.S.-AMERICAN AFTERLIFE OF SLAVERY

This comparative approach to racial history does not fashion Latin America in the image of an Anglo-American racial prototype. Although each Latin American country enacts a spatially specific form of antiblackness supremacy, the United States can fully describe its racial character only by accepting what it shares with the rest of America. As the history of Irish immigration demonstrates, even in the United States, antiblackness determines who qualifies as white more than white supremacy does. Just as they did in the English colonies of Virginia and the Caribbean in the seventeenth century, in the nineteenth century Irish immigrants to the United States would model immigrant incorporation by antiblackness supremacy and reveal white supremacy's true character.

Irish Catholics began trickling into Northern cities in the late 1820s, fleeing the economic deprivation and social indignities produced by Great Britain's imperial stranglehold on their country. In

Racialization, Acculturation, and Afro-Mexican Subjectivity," *Journal of African American History* 95, no. 2 (April 1, 2010): 190.

70. Proctor, *Damned Notions of Liberty*, 44.

71. Pancho McFarland, "Chicano Rap Roots: Black-Brown Cultural Exchange and the Making of a Genre," *Callaloo* 29, no. 3 (2006): 389.

72. Miriam Jiménez Román and Juan Flores, eds., *The Afro-Latin@ Reader: History and Culture in the United States* (Durham, NC: Duke University Press, 2010), 387.

73. Blanca Juárez, "Habitan 1.4 Millones de Afromexicanos En El País: Inegi," *La Jornada*, December 9, 2015, accessed December 17, 2015, http://www.jornada.unam.mx/ultimas/2015/12/09/habitan-1-4-millones-de-afromexicanos-en-el-pais-inegi-7219.html.

the late 1840s, immigration accelerated as years of Great Famine in a dying Ireland sent them to the Northern United States by the boat-load. In Ireland, the Irish acted as abolitionists and anti-imperialists. Upon their immigration to the United States, however, they adopted the habits of antiblack animus almost instantaneously. Incredibly, Irish Catholic immigrants preferred solidarity with English Protestants to alliance with oppressed African Americans. How did this happen?

Although Irish Catholic immigrants were undoubtedly disparaged by native-born whites, they were easily seen as better than native-born black people.[74] Unlike even the most affluent and erudite antebellum Northern blacks, the ragged and illiterate mass of famished Irish immigrants could performatively prove that they possessed a white body. Here I complicate Noel Ignatiev's argument for how the Irish became white in three ways. First, the Irish became white not over time, as Ignatiev famously argues, but through embodied encounter with space. Second, while Ignatiev rightly portrays the Irish's whiteness as a performative achievement, he unfortunately accords insufficient attention to the way in which this performance was carried on in, through, and for the sake of the body. Third, in engaging in antiblack actions, the Irish did not become white as Ignatiev contends; Irish-Americans were always white. They instead helped to preserve whiteness's operation as an identity of supremacist antiblackness.

From the moment of their typically un-chosen arrival in colonial Virginia, the Irish could make a performative argument about the whiteness of their bodies. Then, their birth in a Christianized country both spared Irish Catholics from slavery and ensured that they would be held as servants only temporarily. Birthplace verified and produced phenotype; Irish Catholics would be treated differently than so-called black people. In subsequent centuries, the markers of whiteness would change, but remain no less embedded in and displayed through the body. This fact changes the way we interpret the racial consequences of nineteenth-century Irish immigration to the United States. Not even their illiteracy, Catholicism, and purportedly culturally backward character could obscure their whiteness.

Ignatiev's interpretation of nineteenth century Irish antiblackness echoes Morgan's interpretation of colonial-era lower class white

74. Ibid., v.

antiblackness: these newer Irish exchanged solidarity with the black proletariat for alliance with white capitalists. They "became white" in order to acquire a class advantage: according to Ignatiev, only if they were accepted as could they sell their labor rather than be sold as slaves.[75] But there is no evidence that Irish immigrants were ever in danger of becoming enslaved. If English colonizers did not enslave them in Ireland, why would their Anglo-American cousins do so in the United States? Ignatiev overlooks the essence of antiblackness: Irish immigrants acted violently against black people not just because they feared being associated with black people, but also because they wished to act as masters over them.

Africanized slavery makes white power and black freedom antagonists. As in the colonial era, nineteenth century Irish immigrants did not simply enjoy racial privilege relative to black people; they extracted racial power from the servile subordination of black folks. For this reason, Irish immigrants were threatened by black freedom.[76] Between the American Revolution and 1830, free black people living in Northern cities achieved tremendous economic advancement, climbing the ranks from slaves to apprentices to independent artisans. But the Irish did not greet black people as fellow workers or co-victims of Anglo Protestant oppressors. As Ignatiev recognizes, predominately Irish immigrant mobs from Baltimore to Brooklyn rioted against free black workers several times in the early nineteenth century. For example, in 1828, in Cincinnati, during a three-day spree of violence, Irish men drove the city's 2,000 black residents to flee for the relative racial safety of Canada.[77] These collective Irish actions garnered great success: kept out of relatively high-paying positions of unskilled labor, Northern black workers were forced to toil as servile bootblacks and chimneysweeps.[78] These riots ensured that later waves of Irish immigrants entered cities where antiblackness supremacist violence had made black servitude seem natural and God-given.

Here, I amend Ignatiev's thesis. Rather than the events that established their whiteness, the antiblack actions of Irish mobs and minstrel performers helped to freeze the meaning of whiteness and blackness. Believing themselves bearers of nonblack bodies, nineteenth-century

75. Ibid., 3.

76. Noel Ignatiev, *How the Irish Became White* (New York: Routledge, 2009), 115.

77. Stephen J. Ochs, *Desegregating the Altar: The Josephites and the Struggle for Black Priests, 1871-1960* (Baton Rouge: Louisiana State University Press, 1993), 16–17.

78. Ibid., 115.

Irish Catholic mobs acted out of entitlement, not aspiration.[79] They perceived a demonstrative difference between their bodies and the bodies of those African-descended Americans held in slavery. Though Catholic, and colonized by England, the bodies of Irish immigrants made them appear more akin to native-born Anglo Protestants than to black people. For this reason, the Irish collectively demanded access to supremacist antiblackness from the moment they stepped onto U.S.-American soil. Holding the country's color lines in place, they helped to preserve the association between blackness and slave status. Irish Catholics did not *become* white; they remained as such.

Ignatiev misidentifies Irish immigration as a journey from non-whiteness to whiteness in part because he overlooks the specificity of antiblackness supremacy. Like other scholars, Ignatiev insists on defining slavery as a class relation; for this reason, he contends that, due to "caste oppression and a system of landlordism…the material conditions of the Irish peasant [were] comparable to those of an American slave."[80] Similarly deploying an overly broad account of racial evil, Ignatiev argues that "eighteenth-century Ireland presents a classic case of racial oppression."[81] Ignatiev is right that English colonizers racialized their Irish victims. But he is wrong that this racialization necessarily made the Irish not-white. After all, until the middle of the twentieth century, mainstream Western opinion recognized the existence of several "white" races. Ignatiev further errs by assuming that Irish people's racial otherness somehow made them similar to black people. Even if the Irish had been considered "nonwhite," simply because they possessed "nonblack" bodies, they were never treated like black people.

Ignatiev points to early nineteenth-century appellations like "smoked Irish," a name sometimes assigned to blacks, and "niggers turned inside out," a descriptive title occasionally placed upon Irish immigrants, as evidence of initial Irish unwhiteness.[82] Yet even these attempts to bring black and Irish people together only emphasized

79. Catherine M. Eagan, "'White,' if 'Not Quite': Irish Whiteness in the Nineteenth-Century Irish-American Novel (1)," *Eire-Ireland: A Journal of Irish Studies* (March 22, 2001): 66.

80. Ignatiev, *How the Irish Became White*, 2. Ignatiev also portrays the proletariat and the slave as nearly identical when he suggests that "the only essential distinction between the free worker and the slave" is that the former has "the right to choose among masters." *How the Irish Became White*, 100.

81. Ibid., 42.

82. Ignatiev, *How the Irish Became White*, 39, 41.

their embodied racial difference. Rather than establishing a similarity between Irish immigrants and African Americans, these phrases in fact reinscribe the color contrast between black and Irish bodies. Irish immigrants further held the meaning of the white body in place by avoiding interracial procreation. Although they lived in cities not yet racially segregated, the Irish did not widely intermarry with African Americans; nor did they display steady solidarity with them. Antiblackness supremacy's performative argument about the body triumphed over interruptive possibilities.

Predominately Catholic, Irish immigrants also performatively argued their embodied difference from blacks on the midcentury minstrel stage. In recent years, scholars have argued that the minstrel show played a central role in shoring up the whiteness of the Irish. Comprising a significant chunk of minstrel show audiences and performers, the Irish drew attention to their embodied whiteness on the minstrel stage. Paradoxically, by "blacking up," Irish minstrel performers emphasized not their similarity to but their difference from African Americans.[83] In contrasting their skin color with that of blacks, they proved they had the right body. In so doing, they responded to native-born whites' attempt to challenge the whiteness of Irish immigrants' bodies by caricaturing them as creatures with dark skin. Against this, Irish immigrants answered back, performatively arguing the whiteness of their skin. Unlike the black people they imitatively embodied, the Irish could wipe blackness off their pale faces.[84]

In addition to allowing Irish immigrants to make a performative argument about the whiteness of their bodies, blackface minstrelsy also allowed them to make a performative argument for the compatibility of Irish and U.S-American identity.[85] Paradoxically, the perceived "blackness" of the American minstrel show helped both to differentiate it from its English antecessors and to elevate it in the minds of midcentury Americans who lauded it as the fledgling nation's first original cultural form. Because the American minstrel show was also heavily Irish, it helped make Irish-ness seem truly American.[86] Irish immigrants dominated the minstrel stage, and Irish

83. Robert Nowatzki, "Paddy Jumps Jim Crow: Irish-Americans and Blackface Minstrelsy," *Éire-Ireland* 41, no. 3 (2006): 173.
84. Ibid., 173.
85. Ibid., 163.
86. Nowatzki, "Paddy Jumps Jim Crow," 163.

culture infused the minstrel show. Minstrel performers mixed Irish jigs and reels played by Irish fiddle with African American styles of dance and African instruments like the banjo.[87] In songs such as "Old Susannah," "Ol' Folks at Home," and "Darkey's Lament," displaced Irish immigrants expressed their nostalgia for Ireland as nostalgia for the slaveocracy of the agrarian South.[88] These songs helped assimilate Irish immigrants into America at the expense of black people, as the often-Irish white minstrel performer spoke through the black body as a ventriloquist.[89]

This brief survey of the all-American afterlife of black slavery enables us to recognize the special relation between white supremacy and antiblackness supremacy. Scholars of race have traced the historically specific and contextually adaptive character of whiteness. But they have paid less attention to the way in which antiblackness also strategically seeks to expand or contract the parameters of blackness. This overview further defuses any optimism that we can defeat antiblackness simply by addressing whiteness. If Anglo-America most feared black contamination of pure whiteness, Latin America most feared undiluted Africanity.[90] Rather than representing real alternatives to each other, these regions' contrasting stances on miscegenation paradoxically operate as complementary strategies of antiblackness supremacy.

87. Eric Lott, *Love and Theft: Blackface Minstrelsy and the American Working Class* (New York: Oxford University Press, 1993), 94.
88. Margaret Greaves, "Slave Ships and Coffin Ships: Transatlantic Exchanges in Irish-American Blackface Minstrelsy," *Comparative American Studies* 10, no. 1 (2012): 78–94.
89. Ibid., 92.
90. Helg, "Race and Black Mobilization in Colonial and Early Independent Cuba," 55.

3.

The Spatial Afterlife of Slavery in the Contemporary United States

Despite the triumphs of the Black Civil Rights Movement, whites have retained their ability to exercise spatialized power over black people.[1] Aided mightily by the black prison-ghetto, in the contemporary United States, antiblackness supremacy takes place by making racially segregated space. But just as we often fail to distinguish slavery from other forms of domination, so we misunderstand how the ghetto differs from other forms of spatial organization. The term "ghetto" does not stand in for any neighborhood in which either poor people live or members of the same racial or ethnic group cluster. It instead specifies "a historically determinate, spatially-based concatenation of mechanisms of ethno-racial closure and control."[2] As with slavery, purely economic explanations for the ghetto's existence fall short: its inhabitants are not necessarily poor. Compared to other residential patterns, the ghetto serves a unique purpose and tends toward a unique goal. While other enclosed residential spaces like the gated community protect its inhabitants by keeping the world out, the ghetto protects larger society by keeping its inhabitants in.[3] While the ethnic enclave helps incorporate its inhabitants into the

1. St. Clair Drake and Horace R. Cayton, *Black Metropolis: A Study of Negro Life in a Northern City* (1945) (Chicago: University of Chicago Press, 2015), 101.
2. Loïc J. D. Wacquant, "Three Pernicious Premises in the Study of the American Ghetto," *International Journal of Urban and Regional Research* 21, no. 2 (December 16, 2002): 343.
3. Bob Blauner, *Racial Oppression in America* (New York: Harper & Row, 1972), 83–89.

larger society, the ghetto forcibly excludes them from it. The means by which the ghetto entraps and encloses may change, but its ultimate end does not.

Contrary to common narratives of immigrant struggle, white ethnics never lived in complete social isolation as ghettoized black people did. They may have endured various forms of residential mistreatment, but they were never placed into ghettos. For example, even in the early twentieth century, the Chicago neighborhood designated as Little Italy counted "435 Italians, 362 Germans, and 99 Irish" residents. Nor did the vast majority of ethnic whites reside in ethnic enclaves: while only 61 percent of Polish Chicagoans inhabited heavily Polish enclaves, 93 percent of Chicago's black population remained within the walls of the city's black ghetto.[4] Further distinguishing ethnic enclave from black ghetto, white people gathered into ethnic clusters much more voluntarily than black people resided inside of ghettos, and they could leave much more easily. Nativists did not burn their newly purchased houses or devise legal instruments to keep them in their place.

The ghetto perhaps most differs from other types of residential clustering in the way it recapitulates slavery by hyper-stigmatizing those confined within it. As the spatial ghetto's human embodiment, ghettoized black people appear deservedly confined. The ghetto justifies itself by transferring its ignominy onto its black residents. Thusly fooled by their own spatial tricks, the antiblackness supremacist social body imagines that, if allowed to roam around, these people will simply carry the ghetto with them. Throughout the twentieth century, the ghetto protected white people from contaminating contact with black people while ensuring that blackness survived as a stigmatized identity beyond the confines of Jim Crow.[5]

It is not enough to describe the ghetto correctly. We must also reckon with how it came into existence. Rather than something that happened to black people, the ghetto qualifies as something that whites did to them. White practices of spatial violence built the black ghetto. More than simply fearing black people in accordance with

4. Douglas Massey and Nancy Denton, *American Apartheid: Segregation and the Making of the Underclass* (Cambridge, MA: Harvard University Press, 1993), 33.

5. L. Wacquant, "A Janus-Faced Institution of Ethnoracial Closure: A Sociological Specification of the Ghetto," in *The Ghetto: Contemporary Global Issues and Controversies*, ed. Ray Hutchison and Bruce D. Haynes (New York: Avon, 2012), 11.

their preconceived racial notions, whites constructed the ghetto to provide themselves a reason to continue fearing black people. Whites needed the spatial delusion that the ghetto supplied. As in previous iterations of the afterlife of slavery, nonblacks have attempted to spatialize race so as to preserve the association between blackness and slave status.[6]

In recounting the history of white spatial violence, we admittedly risk turning antiblackness supremacy into what Saidiya Hartman terms a "benumbing spectacle."[7] As sociologist Tamara K. Nopper and educator-activist Mariame Kaba explain, "one gets the sense that the only way to generate a modicum of concern or empathy for black people is to raise the stakes and to emphasize the extraordinary nature of the violations and the suffering" they endure. But more than simply failing to "garner the response desired or needed," this strategy "leaves black people in the position of having to ratchet up the excess in order to get anyone to care of pay attention."[8] It also makes the "routinized violence" inflicted upon black people appear not just normal, but perfectly just. In response, they lift up Hartman's scholarship for the way it aims to "illuminate the terror of the mundane and quotidian rather than exploit the shocking spectacle."[9] This chapter implements Hartman's approach, revealing the shocking spectacle of the white mob and quotidian terror of the white subdivision as interwoven components of a seamless garment of racial vice.

The history of the spatial afterlife of slavery also dispels convenient myths of what so-called racism looks like. In the past, antiblackness supremacy flourished by not appearing as evil; today, it survives by seeming not to exist. This ideology of colorblindness strategically confuses advances against antiblackness with its complete defeat. As a type of racial orthodoxy, the ideology of colorblindness counters a system of white supremacy long since discredited while preventing us from seeing or speaking about its contemporary workings.[10] We turn

6. Richard Rothstein, *The Color of Law: A Forgotten History of How Our Government Segregated America* (New York: W.W. Norton & Co., 2017), ix–x.

7. Saidiya V. Hartman, *Scenes of Subjection: Terror, Slavery, and Self-Making in Nineteenth-Century America*, 1st ed. (New York: Oxford University Press, 1997), 4.

8. Tamara K. Nopper and Mariame Kaba, "Itemizing Atrocity," *Jacobin*, accessed May 20, 2016, https://www.jacobinmag.com/2014/08/itemizing-atrocity/.

9. Hartman, *Scenes of Subjection*, 4.

10. E. Bonilla-Silva, "New Racism, Color-Blind Racism, and the Future of Whiteness in America," *White Out: The Continuing Significance of Racism* (Lanham, MD: Rowman & Littlefield, 2003), 271–84.

the past into a straw boogeyman, remembering it however we need to, so that we appear self-improved and comparatively innocent.

Correcting this, the history of racial segregation in the Northern United States reveals surprising continuities between our admittedly racist past and a purportedly postracial present. Whites have striven to portray racial inequality as the result of something other than the violence of white power. Antiquated theories of "biological racism" and the contemporary affirmations of colorblindness, cultures of poverty, and class reductionism all share a common need to cloak white racial preferences in the neutrality of objective fact. Just as "biological racism" fabricates racial inequality as natural and therefore binding, economic and cultural explanations similarly cast racial separation as an inviolable and reasonable law whites merely obey rather than invent. In disguising the power behind antiblackness supremacy, whites can play-act powerlessness. If whites did not create racial inequality, then they do not have to eradicate it. Delusions of white powerlessness provide whites the means of retaining their racial power. If there are no racists, then there can be no racism.

PHASE ONE (1890–1933): FROM THE GREAT MIGRATION TO THE GREAT DEPRESSION

In the first few decades after emancipation, the Northern black population remained relatively small, and Northern cities did not enforce notably high levels of racial segregation. But when the pace of black migration to cities both North and South picked up around 1890, it triggered in whites a need to redraw the lines between white and black.[11] Whites could no longer rely upon Jim Crow to keep black people in their place. Unable to exclude Southern black people from cities, whites began to deliberately exclude them from white neighborhoods.[12] In the postwar era, white practices of strategic spatial distancing from black people also began to enclose African Americans within a burgeoning ghetto.[13] By building the black ghetto, whites

11. Kenneth L. Kusmer, *A Ghetto Takes Shape: Black Cleveland, 1870-1930* (Champaign: University of Illinois Press, 1978), 35.
12. David M. P. Freund, *Colored Property: State Policy and White Racial Politics in Suburban America* (Chicago: University of Chicago Press, 2010), 14.
13. Kusmer, *A Ghetto Takes Shape*, 172.

could tap the "industrial reserve" the black labor force provided without either ceding whiteness or according blackness honor.[14]

Antiblackness supremacy set the terms by which European immigrants could assimilate. In the late nineteenth century, in certain cities, U.S.-born Northern whites sought residential distance from Eastern and Southern European immigrants at least as much and sometimes more than they did from native-born black people.[15] But the black population boom made these native-born whites change their mind about even swarthy European foreigners. Seeking to shore up their dominating difference over and against black people, Northern native-born whites began to see formerly disparaged European immigrants as kin. European immigrants began to reside increasingly close to native-born whites while moving ever farther away from native-born black people.[16] Place remade race: a pan-European form of whiteness began to take shape.[17]

These spatial practices helped to ensure that the new immigrants streaming ashore from Southern and Eastern Europe also would perceive black people as their common racial enemy. In incorporating these immigrants into the spatialized white social body, racial segregation froze the meaning of race in place; whiteness would continue to mean distance from and dominance over purportedly culturally inferior black people. Differences among whites—religion, national origin, and even language—would not matter as much as their constructed racial similarity. Even in an era of patriotic fervor, English-speaking native-born whites identified with non-English-speaking European immigrants more steadfastly than with similarly English-speaking native-born black people.

Playing a central role in promoting "the racial theory of property value," white real estate agents insisted not just that whites should be allowed to live apart from black people (they did not consider the residential preferences of black people), but that the government had the duty to encourage and facilitate such separation.[18] White real estate agents refused to show prospective black homebuyers properties located in all-white neighborhoods, and real estate boards

14. Ibid., 158.
15. Ibid., 38.
16. Ibid., 43.
17. Ibid., 160–65.
18. Carl H. Nightingale, *Segregation: A Global History of Divided Cities* (Chicago: University of Chicago Press, 2012), 321.

"expelled agents who violated the color line."[19] Spatially conditioned to believe black in-migration a dire threat, the entrance of even one black person would scare the vast majority of white residents away and incite them to sell their homes at discounted prices. Capitalizing on this, profit-seeking blockbusters of both races would stage scenes of conspicuous black entrance into a previously all-white neighborhood.[20] Invariably, these staged "minstrel shows" prompted panicked whites to flee and sell their homes for cheap.[21] White real estate agents would then turn around and sell these same homes to housing-starved black people for wildly inflated prices, gaining a tremendous profit. When black homeowners unsurprisingly defaulted, white realtors kept both the money and the house. Because black housing demand far outstripped supply, these realtors could pull this scheme on a seemingly endless succession of housing-hungry African Americans.[22] In this way, blockbusting destabilized neighborhoods, causing homes to lie vacant for months while also depriving homeowners of the money required for upkeep.[23]

Despite these coordinated efforts, more African Americans managed to purchase homes in urban, white neighborhoods in the late nineteen-teens and early twenties than ever before. The overwhelming majority of white people could not yet simply flee the city. Throughout the 1920s and 1930s, the high cost of homeownership and transportation technologies like the automobile ensured that only the most affluent whites would be able to preserve racial isolation by moving to the suburbs.[24] Those left behind relied upon much more racially explicit tactics such as the racially restrictive covenant to erect and then defend urban color lines.[25] As they had in previous eras of U.S. history, besieged whites answered with an unprecedented wave of terroristic violence against black pioneers. Whites would rather

19. Ibid., 37.

20. Massey and Denton, *American Apartheid*, 38.

21. Nightingale, *Segregation*, 310.

22. For a more in-depth look at how these predatory schemes played out in Chicago, see Beryl Satter, *Family Properties: How the Struggle over Race and Real Estate Transformed Chicago and Urban America*, 1st ed. (New York: Picador, 2010).

23. Massey and Denton, *American Apartheid*, 39.

24. Martha A. Lees, "Preserving Property Values—Preserving Proper Homes—Preserving Privilege: The Pre-Euclid Debate over Zoning for Exclusively Private Residential Areas, 1916-1926," *University of Pittsburgh Law Review* 56 (1995–1994): 377.

25. Ta-Nehesi Coates, "Terrorism Is Politics by Other Means," *The Atlantic*, February 25, 2013, http://www.theatlantic.com/national/archive/2013/02/terrorism-is-politics-by-other-means/273469/.

blow up a house than let black people reside in it: between 1917 and 1921, Northern whites detonated dynamite under the floors of black-owned homes on fifty-eight occasions. White mobs on the east side of Detroit attacked integrating black residents five times during the first six months of 1925. Nearly without exception, these acts of white terrorism went unpunished.[26]

PHASE TWO (1933–1945): SUBSIDIZING SEGREGATION—THE FEDERAL GOVERNMENT AS AGENT OF ANTIBLACKNESS SUPREMACY

The second phase of the United States' segregationist century spans from 1933, when the federal government began insuring mortgages, until 1945, when the United States declared victory in Europe. If, in the first decades of the Great Migration, the federal government accorded Northern whites permission to enact racial segregation, in the depths of the Great Depression, the federal government began to subsidize it. The federal government switched from simply permitting white practices of segregation, to actively subsidizing, encouraging, and institutionalizing them.

When the stock market crashed, so did the private housing market.[27] In response, President Franklin D. Roosevelt established the Home Owners Loan Corporation (HOLC) in order to refinance at-risk mortgages "at below-market rates." The HOLC distributed mortgage insurance according to the preexisting "racial theory of property values," which placed racial and national groups on a "spectrum of comparative desirability." Appraisers insured long-term mortgages for the native-born whites slotted into group A. Groups B and C tended to contain the risky foreign races, listed here in descending order: Scandinavians, North Italians, Bohemians or Czechs, Poles, Lithuanians, Greeks, Russian Jews, and South Italians.[28] Clinging to fading but still operative early-twentieth-century notions of race, they provided these groups only twenty- or ten-year loans. But these assessors unsurprisingly considered most black

26. Freund, *Colored Property*, 1–2.

27. Nightingale, *Segregation*, 343.

28. Jennifer S. Light, "Nationality and Neighborhood Risk at the Origins of FHA Underwriting," *Journal of Urban History* 36, no. 5 (September 1, 2010): 637.

people, regardless of class status or occupation, completely uninsurable and therefore consigned them to Group D.[29]

While these officials preferred that less-desirable nonblack groups not reside alongside native-born whites, they did not deny them loans in native-born white neighborhoods. They completely refused to insure mortgages only on black-owned properties located in all-white spaces, regardless of class status or national origin.[30] Black people remained trapped, especially in the North: they could receive federal money neither by staying in the all-black spaces to which white racism had confined them nor by leaving them.[31] Lacking access to federally subsidized housing loans, more black people moved into the Northern ghetto than were allowed to leave it.[32]

More than simply slowing black people's entrance into white spaces, federal money allowed middle- and lower-class whites more easily to escape residential spaces that had been penetrated by black people.[33] In ceding city blocks to space-starved black buyers, expansionist whites triggered a federal policy of scorched-earth disinvestment.[34] Though black pioneers who first integrated white neighborhoods typically were richer and better educated than their new white neighbors, federal reluctance to lend black people money ensured that even relatively high-income African American homeowners had less money to spend on housing repair than their less well-off white counterparts.[35] Antiblackness supremacy operated as self-fulfilling prophecy: lending money according to racialized conceptions of risk, the federal government helped transform white racial myth into structural reality. The decay of all-black spaces provided biased whites proof that they had been right about black people all along.[36]

Racialized residential spaces functioned as extensions of the racialized body. Onto black spaces, whites projected their fears about black people, believing black neighborhoods seething with danger, crumbling with physical decay, ridden by chaos, and pulsing with

29. Ibid., 647.

30. Ibid., 640.

31. Freund, *Colored Property*, 130.

32. Arnold R. Hirsch, *Making the Second Ghetto: Race and Housing in Chicago 1940-1960* (Chicago: University of Chicago Press, 1998), 5.

33. Nightingale, *Segregation*, 329.

34. Freund, *Colored Property*, 6.

35. Kevin M. Kruse, *White Flight: Atlanta and the Making of Modern Conservatism* (Princeton: Princeton University Press, 2007), 73.

36. Freund, *Colored Property*, 359.

sexual disorder. White neighborhoods similarly embodied whiteness. As such, whites considered them clean, orderly, safe, beautiful, and sexually virtuous.[37] Whites no longer needed to make explicit reference to black people to preserve white power; they need only refer to black neighborhoods. The black neighborhood was the black body.

Federal programs also allowed whites to continue believing that their affluence resulted from not racialized power, but the uncoerced workings of a free market.[38] In promoting HOLC and FHA racialized lending practices, federal spokesmen accorded prevailing ideologies of race and property further credibility. Now, not just private citizens but "state sanctioned . . . housing experts" insisted on the importance of protecting white spaces from both blackness and black people.[39] Whites hid even from themselves the power animating racial inequality. In so doing, they continued to disavow their responsibility for it.

PHASE THREE (1946–1968): THE SUBURB AS SEGREGATIONIST REFUGE

The third phase of the United States' segregationist century encompasses the twenty-two years between the end of World War II and the end of the Civil Rights Movement. Although the federal government would outlaw certain segregationist mechanisms, such as the racially restrictive housing covenant and the all-white lunch counter, it empowered or left undisturbed many others, such as the racialized home loan. And, through its support of the suburb, the federal government would promote racial residential segregation more effectively than ever before. Remembered as an era of increasing racial equality, the postwar era instead marks the period when residential segregation by race acquired structural permanence.[40]

When President Roosevelt signed the G.I. Bill in 1944, he authorized the Veterans' Administration to provide returning soldiers mortgage loans carrying terms even more favorable than those handed out by the FHA in the late 1930s.[41] The VA adopted the FHA's white supremacist system of risk-assessment, providing

37. Ibid., 364.
38. Ibid., 9.
39. Ibid., 115, 142.
40. Massey and Denton, *American Apartheid*, 46.
41. Freund, *Colored Property*, 177, 180–81.

prospective white homebuyers handouts from two federal agencies.[42] As Richard Rothstein chronicles, "many African American World War II veterans did not apply for government-guaranteed mortgages for suburban purchases because they knew that the [VA] would reject them on account of their race.[43] Despite their valor, black veterans remained "redlined."[44]

But the Second World War had not left whiteness completely unchanged. Embarrassed perhaps by the similarities between the anti-Semitic rhetoric of Nazis and the antiblack speech of ordinary U.S.-Americans, in 1947 federal bureaucrats removed explicitly racial language from appraisal manuals.[45] But this change in semantics did not alter the impact of federal lending practices. When these "colorblind" guidelines insisted it "necessary to recognize the presence of any adverse influences which lessen or destroy desirability, utility, or value, or the absence of safeguards intended to protect against declines in value or desirability"; or when they identified "nuisances or inharmonious uses of any kind" as among the characteristics rendering a property too risky to insure, they still complied with regnant ideologies of white supremacy that deemed black residents contaminating and incompetent.[46] Since whites had long thought of race in the code of property and place, they did not need to speak the phrase "black people" in order to perpetuate the practices that excluded them. Terms like "homeowner," "desirable," and "value" already operated as synonyms for white just as "nuisance," "undesirable," and "apartment" served as synonyms for black.[47]

In fact, during this era, the federal government would promote spatialized antiblackness more effectively than ever before. In addition to spending so much money subsidizing white homeownership that it became cheaper to build a new home than to refurbish an old one, the federal government allotted nearly all of its mortgage money to the construction of white-owned homes in suburbs.[48] In the decades following World War II, African Americans garnered

42. Ibid., 186.

43. Rothstein, *The Color of Law*, xi.

44. For more on the ways in which "there was no greater instrument for widening an already huge racial gap in postwar America than the GI Bill" see Ira Katznelson, *When Affirmative Action Was White: An Untold History of Racial Inequality in Twentieth-Century America* (New York: W. W. Norton, 2006), 113–41.

45. Ibid., 5, 208.

46. Freund, *Colored Property*, 209.

47. Ibid.

48. Massey and Denton, *American Apartheid*, 53.

increasingly high incomes, allowing them to enter white neighborhoods that had previously lain economically out of reach.[49] Suburbanization allowed whites to flee this rising tide of black power.[50]

Even momentous civil rights victories like the Supreme Court's 1948 decision declaring racially restrictive covenants unconstitutional could not slow the pace of the country's quickening spatial separation.[51] This ruling deprived whites of the ability only to prevent other whites from selling their homes to black people *if they so desired.* White people could continue discriminating against black homebuyers for another twenty years.[52] Above all, this case failed to slow racial segregation's acceleration because the suburb excluded black people much more effectively than the racially restrictive covenant ever had.[53] As Dearborn, Michigan mayor, Orville Hubbard, boasted to an audience of sympathetic white Southerners in the late 1950s, "Negroes can't get in here. . . . Every time we hear of a Negro moving in, we respond quicker than you do to a fire."[54] As before, suburban exclusionary zoning ideology proceeded as a type of class-coded aesthetics of racial threat. Zoning sought to exclude not just black-colored skin, but all that blackness signified to them: poverty, domestic disorder, violence, ugliness, indecency, and, increasingly, urbanness. Zoning's proponents did not need to name the enemy they described.

Although most whites fled the newly central city, they did not stop thinking of it as theirs. Translating economic power into political clout, suburbanized whites reorganized the city so that it better fulfilled their desires. When black neighborhoods stood in the way of white access to coveted city spaces, either recreational or economic, for example, whites simply had them leveled.[55] The federal government similarly spent billions building for suburban whites' wide highways connecting them to their central-city places

49. Hirsch, *Making the Second Ghetto*, 29.

50. Ibid., 16. This is not to say that there were no black residents of the suburbs. Beginning in 1925 around cities like New York and Chicago, black people settled in very small isolated suburban enclaves. Bruce D. Haynes, *Red Lines, Black Spaces: The Politics of Race and Space in a Black Middle-Class Suburb* (New Haven: Yale University Press, 2001), xxi.

51. Nightingale, *Segregation*, 356.

52. Freund, *Colored Property*, 210.

53. Ibid., 94.

54. Isabel Wilkerson, *The Warmth of Other Suns: The Epic Story of America's Great Migration* (New York: Vintage, 2011), 378.

55. Massey and Denton, *American Apartheid*, 56.

of employment. Often, these highways were placed inside the spines of black neighborhoods, tearing them in two.[56]

Federal spending practices also accorded white power much-needed ideological camouflage. In the Cold War era, whites needed to believe themselves not only not "racist" but also not "communist." Authorities assured them that federal meddling in the mortgage market represented not a violation of free market principles but their illumination. Rather than the gift that enabled their affluence, whites considered government housing subsidies a type of reward they earned by being hard-working winners. As if recapitulating the ideology that animated racialized slave mastership, whites believed both that they deserved these interventions but that they did not need them. They conversely imagined black people as those who did not deserve but greatly needed federal aid.[57] As whites, they had rights and well-earned rewards while slave-descended black folks had already been given more than they deserved. Black people were owed nothing and deserved nothing; white people had been given nothing and deserved everything they had.

Homeownership provided a new way of embodying both whiteness and citizenship. In contrast to the imperial era when "Christian" operated as synonym for "white," in the era of highly subsidized private housing, "advocates of racial exclusion regularly used the terms 'homeowner,' 'citizen,' 'voter,' and 'white' interchangeably."[58] Just as whiteness made federally subsidized homeownership appear capitalistic and therefore truly "American," so would suburban homeownership make European immigrants appear fully white, and therefore truly "American." Reversing trends of early-century suspicion of eastern and southern European immigrants, postwar native whites welcomed European immigrants into suburban whiteness whole-

56. George Lipsitz, *The Possessive Investment in Whiteness: How White People Profit from Identity Politics*, revised and expanded ed. (Philadelphia: Temple University Press, 2006), 8; Raymond A. Mohl, "Stop the Road Freeway Revolts in American Cities," *Journal of Urban History* 30, no. 5 (July 1, 2004): 674–706; Ronald H. Bayor, "Urban Renewal, Public Housing and the Racial Shaping of Atlanta," *Journal of Policy History* 1, no. 4 (1989): 419–39; Nicholas Lemann, "The Myth of Community Development," *New York Times*, January 9, 1994, accessed April 4, 2013, http://www.nytimes.com/1994/01/09/magazine/the-myth-of-community-development.html?pagewanted=all&src=pm; Laura Yuen, "Central Corridor: In the Shadow of Rondo," Minnesota Public Radio News, April 29, 2010, accessed April 4, 2013, http://minnesota.publicradio.org/display/web/2010/04/20/centcorridor3-rondo.

57. Freund, *Colored Property*, 328, 331–33, 360, 376.

58. Ibid., 376.

heartedly.[59] In this way, for example, immigrants and their children comprised nearly 30 percent of residents in Detroit's postwar suburbs.[60]

Whiteness had always defined itself in relation to power over racialized property. But twentieth-century whiteness increasingly would operate and understand itself not as mastery of black slaves but as deserving ownership of houses.[61] This growing association of whiteness with homeownership would also change the meaning of blackness. Once considered legal property, black people now appeared unfit to own it. As a white resident of a Detroit suburb proclaimed in 1956, "no matter where the negro has lived the property is hurt."[62] In the postwar era, embodied ideologies of whiteness continued to both shape and be shaped by operative notions of citizenship and freedom. Whiteness seemed neither prejudiced nor power-hungry, but the epitome of patriotic freedom.

This ideological camouflage also put whites in a good position to deflect the moral challenge of the swelling Black Civil Rights Movement. Whites did not oppose the civil rights of black people, they insisted, they were just defending their own rights.[63] As a white female resident of Dearborn fumed: "the whole Negro situation is getting ridiculous. All I hear about [is] the rights of Negroes. What about our rights?"[64] Turning structural reality upside down, whites portrayed themselves to be just as imperiled as black people. Such beliefs of course denied the relational character between white power and black: if whites could choose only white neighbors, then black people could not live wherever they wanted.

Even before a single piece of civil rights legislation was signed into law, many whites therefore believed themselves victimized by black freedom and consequently waged "urban guerilla warfare" against integrationists: in Chicago between "May 1944 [and] July 1946, forty-six black residences were assaulted," and, "beginning in January 1945, there was at least one attack per month (save for March 1946) and twenty-nine of the onslaughts were arson-bombings."[65] Over the next five years, white mega-mobs violently would repel attempts by

59. Ibid., 56–57.
60. Ibid., 282.
61. Ibid., 38.
62. Ibid., 335.
63. Ibid., 18, 377.
64. Ibid., 376.
65. Freund, *Colored Property*, 338; Hirsch, *Making the Second Ghetto*, 41.

black homeowners to integrate Chicago neighborhoods.[66] In contrast to their Southern counterparts, Northern whites did not need to hang "whites only" signs to preserve the whiteness of cherished municipal spaces. They could avoid interracial intimacy simply by staying in place. Losing neither power nor the appearance of innocence, Northern whites could carry on as though nothing had ever happened: 1968 looked little different than 1940.

PHASE FOUR (1969–1983): THE FEDERAL GOVERNMENT FAILS TO ENFORCE CIVIL RIGHTS LAW

The fourth phase of spatialized antiblackness supremacy opens in 1968, the year of Martin Luther King's assassination and ends in 1982, the year President Ronald Reagan reissued President Nixon's declaration of a war on drugs. Initially, the triumphs of the Civil Rights Movement seemed to signal the end of antiblack racial segregation. But in truth, the United States never did desegregate.[67] The persistence of racial segregation cannot be dismissed as an unfortunate but racially neutral by-product of class differentials. African Americans continued to experience high levels of segregation regardless of income.[68] How did residential segregation of black from white survive the Civil Rights Movement?

As it had during Reconstruction, the federal government failed to strip white people of the power to impose their will on the world. It also declined to repair the racial damage it had wrought over the previous six decades or so.[69] Ultimately, those who aimed to discriminate possessed more power than those who wished to resist it. Although the Fair Housing Act of 1968 outlawed discriminatory practices like racial steering and blockbusting, segregationist legislators had stripped it of adequate enforcement provisions.[70] President Nixon shut down Housing and Urban Development secretary George Romney's plan to comply with the law by "ordering HUD officials to reject applications for water, sewer, and highway projects from cities and states where local policies fostered segregated housing." Subsequent presidents shared Nixon's affinity for funding

66. Ibid., 53–55.
67. Massey and Denton, *American Apartheid*, 63.
68. Ibid., 85.
69. Rothstein, *The Color of Law*, xv.
70. Massey and Denton, *American Apartheid*, 195, 198.

segregation: over the course of the next forty years, the federal government would withhold money from communities who defied the Fair Housing Act on only two occasions.[71]

Whites also managed to overturn court-mandated programs of school integration. In protest of a federal busing order, a coalition of white mothers in Pontiac, Michigan carried placards proclaiming, "We're fighting for OUR civil rights now!" In addition to physically blocking the passage of buses carrying black children, they also chanted "nigger, nigger" at them as they drove by. One week before the commencement of the busing program, KKK-affiliated terrorists blew ten of the city's school buses to pieces.[72]

Whites also rolled back federal decisions that threatened to unite predominately white suburban school districts with overwhelmingly black urban ones. Within one week of one such a decision, ten thousand whites in one of Detroit's suburban counties had already formed an anti-busing organization. In nearby Oakland County, a white mother told a local newspaper, "I would never know if my children were safe. We pay high taxes for good schools and now they want to bus my children to an inner city school. No way. I'll fight first."[73] In 1971, these whites won the favor of the Supreme Court, who decried the lower court's decision as an occasion of improper federal meddling in the country's "deeply-rooted" tradition of "local control over the operation of schools."[74] Further preserving the suburb's antiblackness supremacist impact, in 1973, the Supreme Court ruled that "affluent suburbs bore no responsibility to share their property tax revenue with poorer districts in the city."[75] Northern school segregation occurred largely through the spatial separation of predominantly white suburbs from increasingly black central cities. In refusing to compel suburbs to share students or resources with

71. Nikole Hannah-Jones ProPublica et al., "Living Apart: How the Government Betrayed a Landmark Civil Rights Law," *ProPublica*, accessed June 24, 2015, http://www.propublica.org/article/living-apart-how-the-government-betrayed-a-landmark-civil-rights-law. For more on how the Fair Housing Act of 1968 failed to achieve desegregation, see Douglas S. Massey, "The Legacy of the 1968 Fair Housing Act," *Sociological Forum* 30, no. S1 (June 2015).

72. George Lipsitz, *How Racism Takes Place* (Philadelphia: Temple University Press, 2011), 27.

73. George R. Metcalf, *From Little Rock to Boston: The History of School Desegregation* (Westport, CT: Greenwood, 1983), 162.

74. Ibid., 188.

75. Kruse, *White Flight*, 257.

central cities, cross-district busing plans did not significantly desegregate Northern schools.[76]

Whites did not believe their anti-busing actions "racist." They opposed not school desegregation, they insisted, but only the forced busing of children from one part of town to another.[77] Tellingly, whites did not refuse prolonged daily car travel—largely due to rising rates of suburbanization, the average travel time of the daily work commute rose substantially throughout the 1970s.[78] This inconsistency indicates more than just irrationality. Unlike the long automotive commute of the suburban worker, busing circumvented the rules of residential segregation. When black people gained entrance to predominantly white schools by managing to purchase homes in the predominantly white neighborhoods that contained these schools, the overwhelming majority of whites believed their educational exclusion unjust.[79] Whites accepted the academic and residential legitimacy of black people who played by the rules because whites had so masterfully rigged these rules in their favor.[80] White flight served as a fail-safe: if more than a few black people ever succeeded in living in a predominantly all-white neighborhood at one time, the vast majority of whites would exit. The long commute preserved the hegemony of homeowning whiteness; busing threatened to upend it. For this reason, suburban whites accepted the long commute as an unavoidable means to a highly-desired end but resisted busing as an unnatural interference with their way of life.

Because white people remained in racially segregated places even after the Civil Rights Movement, so did their white supremacist habits. Constantly monitoring the racial makeup of their surroundings, white people left integrating neighborhoods lying close to black ghettos much more quickly than they fled integrating neighborhoods situated far away from them.[81] The farther away from black

76. John M. Jackson, "Remedy for Inner City Segregation in the Public Schools: The Necessary Inclusion of Suburbia," *Ohio State Law Journal* 55 (1994): 415.

77. Jane M. Hornburger, "Deep Are the Roots: Busing in Boston," *Journal of Negro Education* 45, no. 3 (1976): 242.

78. N. A. McGuckin and N. Srinivasan, "Journey to Work in the United States and Its Major Metropolitan Areas—1960–2000," Washington, DC, Federal Highway Administration, June 30, 2003.

79. David O. Sears and Harris M. Allen Jr., "The Trajectory of Local Desegregation Controversies and Whites' Opposition to Busing," *Groups in Contact: The Psychology of Desegregation* (1984): 148.

80. Kruse, *White Flight*, 258.

81. Massey and Denton, *American Apartheid*, 80.

neighborhoods whites moved, the more spatially secure they felt.[82] White people felt even safer in the suburbs. White people felt more racially secure in a suburb located less than five miles from a black neighborhood than they did in an urban area lying between ten and twenty miles away.[83]

Even in the purportedly egalitarian year of 1978, seventy two percent of whites admitted that they were unwilling to reside "in a neighborhood whose population was half black."[84] Turning the equity in homes purchased through the power of whiteness into the next home's down payment, whites paved themselves exit routes out of integrating suburbs.[85] When black people moved from the central city to the inner-ring suburb, whites simply fled to the outer-ring.[86] Comprising a clear numerical majority in every Northern metropolitan area, whites could easily outrun integration.

PHASE FIVE (1982–2016): "INSTEAD OF A WAR ON POVERTY, THEY GOT A WAR ON DRUGS SO THE POLICE CAN BOTHER ME."[87]

In the years since President Reagan's 1982 re-initiation of the "war on drugs," the black ghetto has changed in two major ways. First, the segregated black ghetto has become hyper-segregated; and second, the black ghetto has lost the jobs that had held it together. Hyper-segregation, uniquely inflicted upon black people, designates a condition in which African Americans experience at least four of the following five types of residential segregation: uneven distribution throughout a city; "rarely sharing a neighborhood with whites"; living in an enclave of contiguously clustered black neighborhoods; enduring "concentration within a very small area"; or experiencing "spatial centralization around an urban core." By 1980, "35 percent of the nation's black population and 41 percent of all blacks living in urban areas" lived in the hyper-segregated spaces of sixteen of

82. Ibid., 79.
83. Ibid.
84. Ibid., 92.
85. Nightingale, *Segregation*, 356.
86. Kruse, *White Flight*, 263–64.
87. 2PAC, *CHANGES [EXPLICIT]* (INTERSCOPE, 1998).

the nation's metropolitan areas, thirteen of which lay North of the Mason-Dixon line.[88]

Hit hardest by the country's accelerating transition from an industrial economy replete with high-paying manufacturing jobs to one offering its blue-collar workers low-wage and low-luster positions in the service and retail sectors, newly hyper-segregated Northern ghettos grew increasingly jobless, impoverished, and institutionally abandoned in the wake of the Civil Rights Movement.[89] Rising rates of spatially concentrated black joblessness also brought white supremacy's vestigial fears of the idle savage to the surface. African Americans inhabiting the ghetto could not be easily compelled to acquiesce to the lower-quality jobs left behind by manufacturing's flight.[90]

The black mass prison came to the rescue, levying institutional discipline upon the black ghetto by "warehousing" and thereby "physically neutralizing" the most rebellious members of the economically obsolete black proletariat.[91] Animated by the afterlife of slavery, the United States could not let the black inhabitants of the newly job-scarce and hyper-segregated black ghetto go free; it therefore began locking them up in an emerging black mass prison. The black mass prison reinforced the crumbling walls of the black ghetto.[92] The logic of Africanized slavery still structured the country's corporate perceptions. Although the federal government displayed a timid unwillingness to impose the full force of its will upon intransigent whites who violated newly passed anti-segregation laws, it felt no such trepidation about imposing its will on drug dealers who happened to be black. Even after the Fair Housing Act of 1968, white people continued to deny black people their right to fair housing with relative impunity. Those unlucky whites who were prosecuted were classified simply as civil offenders; they were sued and sometimes fined, but they remained free. Black people who sold and possessed drugs, on the other hand, were criminalized, captured, and physically detained.

In this way, the ghetto began to function as a "social prison" while

88. Massey and Denton, *American Apartheid*, 76–77.

89. Lincoln Quillian, "The Decline of Male Employment in Low-Income Black Neighborhoods, 1950-1990," *Social Science Research* 32, no. 2 (2003): 230–34.

90. Loïc Wacquant, *Punishing the Poor: The Neoliberal Government of Social Insecurity* (Durham, NC: Duke University Press, 2009), 208.

91. Ibid., xvi.

92. Ibid., 206.

the black prison came to operate as a "judicial ghetto."[93] The black mass prison gave a critical mass of black people a place to be so that they would remain hyper-visible symbolically while "disappeared" materially.[94] Despite nearly identical rates of illegal drug use and participation in the drug trade between black and white people, black people "constitute 80 to 90 percent of all drug offenders sent to prison."[95] Perhaps the war on drugs also punishes poorer black people for attempting to escape from the economic captivity of so-called "slave jobs."[96] Ultimately, because the illegal economic activities of ghettoized black people undermine the disciplining sovereignty of the black ghetto, they threaten the socio-symbolic order in a way the illegal economic activities of whites do not.[97] As a result, the average white person sees black people as spectacle—on the local eleven o'clock news trotted out in an orange jumpsuit and handcuffs, for example—more often than he encounters them as flesh-and-blood human beings.

The black mass prison also dignifies and revivifies lower-class whites, who also suffered job loss and plummeting wages as a result of economic deregulation.[98] While wages in other sectors plummeted, in many places the average salary of a prison employee rose dramatically.[99] During the era of chattel slavery, lower-class whites filled positions as overseers and militiamen; and, during the era of mass incarceration, they occupied high-paying slots as prison guard and parole officer when most prisons were placed in the small, rural towns these whites inhabited.[100] Even when the police officer or prison guard also has black skin, he confirms ideologies of antiblackness even more than he overturns them. As in the era of chattel slavery, in the afterlife of slavery, a black person who inflicts state-sanctioned violence on another black person does not acquire honor as a non-black person can. He instead validates a moral order that deems the black body uniquely dangerous, dishonorable, undisciplined, and in need of violent correction.

93. Ibid., 198.
94. Loïc Wacquant, *Deadly Symbiosis: Race and the Rise of the Penal State* (Cambridge: Polity, 2009), 97.
95. Michelle Alexander, *The New Jim Crow*, reprint (New York: New Press, 2012), 96.
96. Wacquant, *Punishing the Poor*, 196–97.
97. Ibid., 73.
98. Ibid., 55.
99. Ibid., 156.
100. Ibid., 157.

The spectacle of black mass incarceration also accords dignity and honor to all white people, even those harmed by economic restructuring. Under the regime of colonial white supremacy, the public whipping of black slaves rendered their "disobedience" ignoble; in the contemporary era of colorblind white supremacy, incarceration renders impoverished black men who disobediently seek economic profit illegally similarly ignoble. Through the prison, those who sought to escape precarious wage work by turning to highly profitable but illegal economic activities would be made an example of. Invigorating the afterlife of slavery, the black mass prison disciplines whites by physically punishing black people. The black mass prison goes further. In blackening physical punishment, whether carceral or extrajudicial, the black mass prison paradoxically accords honor even to those whites who find themselves locked inside of it.

The war on drugs further resembles chattel slavery in that it inflicts upon its subjects civic and social death.[101] Current as well as former prisoners are denied educational aids like Pell Grants, and, in an age of work insecurity, prisoners, already disproportionately poor, are "systematically excluded from social redistribution and public aid."[102] And, in almost every state, private employers can disproportionately deny black felons employment with impunity. They often can discriminate even against those who have been arrested but never convicted.[103]

The black mass prison also restores the three-fifths clause of the U.S. Constitution. Even though inmates cannot vote, they are counted as residents of the congressional districts in which they are imprisoned. These disproportionately black and ghettoized, disenfranchised persons accord disproportionately white and rural prison towns amplified political power. This same actuarial procedure transfers wealth from the disproportionately black central city to overwhelmingly white suburbs and towns.[104]

The prison-ghetto complex recapitulates black slavery most spectacularly in that it uniquely subjects black people to what Sexton and Martinique term "the ignorability of police impunity."[105] More

101. Wacquant, "Race as Civic Felony," *International Social Science Journal* 57, no. 183 (2005): 129–30.

102. Ibid., 130–31.

103. Alexander, *The New Jim Crow*, 146.

104. Wacquant, "Race as Civic Felony," 137–38.

105. Steve Martinot and Jared Sexton, "The Avant-Garde of White Supremacy," *Social Identities* 9, no. 2 (June 1, 2003): 172.

than simply denying black people the right to protect their person from ordinarily illegal searches, seizures, and detentions, the conspiracy between prison and ghetto portrays the black body as deserving of the most spectacular and therefore the most routine violence. Black people can become police property simply by breathing.[106] Because the Court allows police officers to use race as a factor in deciding whom to pull over, police departments disproportionately deploy these "pretext stops" against black drivers. As a result, the spectacle of black male motorists pressed up against their cars or being searched by police officers on the side of the country's highways or pressed face down on city sidewalks has become commonplace.[107]

Further sustaining the afterlife of slavery, incarceration renders the disproportionately black prisoner extremely vulnerable to routinized sexual humiliation, sexual abuse, and rape. A 2012 Justice Department study found that prison guards accounted for half of all sexual abuse inflicted upon the imprisoned.[108] In the year 2011–2012, more than 5 percent of men in some of our nation's prisons reported experiencing sexual misconduct at the hands of prison staff. In women's prisons, the yearly rates of prison guard sexual abuse surpassed 10 percent in several cases.[109] Like slavery, the black mass prison also rips black families apart: the state does not recognize an incarcerated person's full right to a family life. In recapitulating black slavery in these ways, the black mass prison preserves the association between blackness and slave status and extends to new generations of white people, both directly and vicariously, the powers and privileges of slave mastership.[110]

The black mass prison further resembles Africanized slavery in that it portrays itself as a response to blackness rather than a mechanism of antiblackness. Because the black mass prison "colored crime black" not just in the collective imagination, but also in the realm of material reality, whites have been able to posit a connection between blackness and criminality without seeming "racist."[111] They could claim to speak not in the subjective banter of racists but in accordance with

106. Alexander, *The New Jim Crow*, 105.

107. Ibid., 129, 131.

108. Liz Fields, "Half of Sexual Abuse Claims in American Prisons Involve Guards," ABC News, January 26, 2014, http://abcnews.go.com/US/half-sexual-abuse-claims-american-prisons-involve-guards/story?id=21892170.

109. U.S. Department of Justice, "Sexual Victimization in Prisons and Jails Reported by Inmates, 2011-12," 13. http://www.bjs.gov/content/pub/pdf/svpjri1112.pdf.

110. Alexander, *The New Jim Crow*, 6.

111. Loïc Wacquant, "From Slavery to Mass Incarceration," *New Left Review* 13 (2002): 387.

the authority of objective reality. As a result, the black mass prison has amplified white people's capacity to speak about black people in the code of space and place. To a linguistic arsenal already stocked with words like "ghetto," "wrong side of town," "dangerous area," and "inner-city," a self-servingly camouflaged whiteness added "prisoner," "thug," "crime," "gang banger," and "drug dealer."[112] This way of speaking is not just considered respectable; it often wins elections. For example, while promoting his smaller-government and lower-tax "Contract with America," Newt Gingrich described his suburban Georgia constituents as people who

> want safety, and . . . believe big cities have failed . . . people in Cobb County don't object to upper-middle-class neighbors who keep their lawn cut and move to the area to avoid crime. . . . What people worry about is the bus line gradually destroying one apartment complex after another, bringing people out for public housing who have no middle class values and whose kids as they become teenagers often are centers of robbery and where the schools collapse because the parents that live in the apartment complexes don't care that the kids don't do well and the whole school collapses.[113]

Gingrich deploys this coded antiblackness supremacist speech adroitly, never once mentioning the color either of the people wracked with fear or of those people purportedly destroying their publicly-funded apartments.

In treating black people as enemies who deserve not protection but punishment, the prison-ghetto complex counteracts the unprecedented post–Civil Rights social mobility and prestige enjoyed by the most affluent black people by intensifying its stigmatizing regulation of the most impoverished black people. As a result, regardless of social class or moral character, black people still do not receive the civic benefit of the doubt.[114] The war on drugs has refashioned the color-coded stigma of slavery for an age of purported color-blind racial egalitarianism.[115]

But what about black people who live outside the ghetto? In the post–Civil Rights era, class reductionism prevails: many whites

112. Nightingale, *Segregation*, 395; James W. Perkinson, *White Theology: Outing Supremacy in Modernity* (New York: Palgrave Macmillan, 2004), 162.
113. Ibid., 260–61.
114. Wacquant, "Race as Civic Felony," 137.
115. Ibid., 136–37.

across the political spectrum insist that, today, class accounts for racial inequality much more than race does. But this represents a case of wishful white thinking. (Indeed, we should question why so many white people are more comfortable attributing inequality to classism than to racism.) Largely due to racial segregation, African Americans typically experience middle-class status quite differently than their white counterparts do. Because middle-class black people must conduct their search for better housing within the confines of a segregated market, black middle-class neighborhoods often lie in close proximity to the impoverished places they sought to escape.[116] As a result, in 1995, scholars surmised that, measured by factors like exposure to crime, school performance, and income, "the 'worst' urban contexts in which whites reside are considerably better than the average context of black communities."[117]

Further undercutting attempts to reduce race to class, "the black middle class remains as segregated from whites as the black poor." While affluence slightly increases a black person's capacity to buy a home in a predominately white neighborhood, it does not enhance their capacity to keep their white neighbors from fleeing them.[118] This pattern holds despite the fact that, when middle-class black people manage to gain entrance in a predominately white neighborhood, they typically earn higher incomes than the whites they live alongside.[119] Nor does being poor increase a white person's odds of sharing a block with black neighbors of any class status.[120] Just as freeborn black people could not escape the stigma of slavery, so today even wealthy and impeccably law-abiding black people struggle to escape the stigma of the prison-ghetto complex.

Against the popular tendency to interpret the Black Civil Rights Movement as a definitive break with our country's antiblack past, I uncover continuity in whites' century-old commitment to sustaining segregation. Residential patterns established by a century of segregationist practices remain intact as the federal government continues to operate as an abettor of whites' racial preferences. More than whites

116. Mary Pattillo-McCoy, *Black Picket Fences: Privilege and Peril Among the Black Middle Class*, 1st ed. (Chicago: University of Chicago Press, 2000), 39.
117. Ibid., 29.
118. Lincoln Quillian, "Why Is Black-White Residential Segregation So Persistent?: Evidence on Three Theories from Migration Data," *Social Science Research* 31, no. 2 (June 2002): 220–21.
119. Richard D. Alba, John R. Logan, and Brian J. Stults, "How Segregated Are Middle-Class African Americans?," *Social Problems* 47, no. 4 (November 2000): 544.
120. Lipsitz, *How Racism Takes Place*, 36.

value justice, they insist on their own racial innocence. For this reason, they continue to believe the lies they have told themselves about black people. White racial power over black people appears both natural and necessary, a fact of life believed but not seen, embodied but unconfessed. Despite protestations of politically correct, postracial tolerance, contemporary whites act much like their "racist" forebears, pursuing the preservation of spatialized antiblackness by any means necessary.[121] Whites have yet to break their segregationist habits.

121. Eduardo Bonilla-Silva, *Racism without Racists: Color-Blind Racism and the Persistence of Racial Inequality in America*, 3rd ed. (Lanham, MD: Rowman & Littlefield, 2009), 25.

PART II

Diagnosing the Corporate Habits of Antiblackness Supremacy

More than just a structure of injustice, the spatialized U.S.-American afterlife of slavery functions as a habitat for vice. Offering an interdisciplinary description of these vicious antiblack racial habits, I attempt to overturn regnant notions of virtue and vice. I will do so by redirecting the moral gaze first from blacks to whites and then from the words of white folks to their bodies. First, because merely inhabiting the racially segregated space of the United States puts all nonblack people, but especially whites, on a trajectory of antiblack habituation, nonblack people both acquire and exercise the vice of antiblackness supremacy through their bodies. This vice does not simply reside in "the souls of white folks" as traditional accounts of Thomistic virtue theory would suggest.[1] Second, many scholars have debated the extent to which racial segregation has made black people behave badly; but they have generally failed to adequately describe the ways

1. W. E. B. Du Bois, *Darkwater: The Givens Collection* (New York: Washington Square Press, 2004).

in which nonblack people have been corrupted by their voluntary spatial isolation from black people.[2] This book aims to do just that.

2. Jamie T. Phelps, "Communion Ecclesiology and Black Liberation Theology," *Theological Studies* 61, no. 4 (2000): 673.

4.

Inverting Virtue

In recent decades, a good deal of scholarly attention has been accorded to assessing, justifying, and quantifying the alleged social pathologies of the black urban poor. On the right, Bell Curve proponents like Charles Murray depict black people as intellectually deficient and culturally backward and blame the welfare state for rewarding the bad habits of the black poor.[1] On the left, scholars like William Julius Wilson, Douglas Massey, and Nancy Denton disagree with their conservative counterparts not on whether black people behave badly but why they do so. While conservatives argue that black people are poor because they possess bad habits, these liberals believe they possess bad habits because they are poor. In this way, Wilson blames the alleged sexual irresponsibility and criminality of impoverished black people on the out-migration of jobs and middle-class black people from their residential spaces, and Massey and Denton similarly attribute black pathologies to their spatial separation from whites.[2]

But, instead of taking a side in the debate about "the culture of poverty," this book initiates a new conversation about virtue and vice.[3] According to traditional virtue theory, vices impede an

1. Richard J. Herrnstein and Charles Murray, *The Bell Curve: Intelligence and Class Structure in American Life* (New York: Simon & Schuster, 2010).

2. Douglas Massey and Nancy Denton, *American Apartheid: Segregation and the Making of the Underclass* (Cambridge, MA: Harvard University Press, 1993), 7–8.

3. William Julius Wilson, *When Work Disappears: The World of the New Urban Poor*, 1st ed. (New York: Vintage, 1997); Michael Harrington, *The Other America: Poverty in the United States* (New York: Scribner, 1997); O. Lewis, "The Culture of Poverty," *Society* 35, no. 2 (1998):

individual's capacity to pursue flourishing. But as moral philosopher Lisa Tessman demonstrates, vices of domination uniquely allow their bearers to amass power and privilege. In enacting white mastership, whites maldistribute flourishing and reinforce life-depriving color lines.[4] As detailed in the preceding chapter, whites have unleashed repeated racial violence against black people in order to preserve the segregationist status quo. Stretching back to the colonial era, when whites received permission to inflict violence on unruly black slaves with impunity, to the unpunished killing of unarmed black youth by police officers and their vigilante imitators, white racial violence comprises a deeply rooted racial habit. This chapter therefore urges ethicists and political scientists to spend significantly less time pondering why the urban black poor allegedly exhibit such high levels of social pathologies and much more time diagnosing the habits of antiblackness supremacy as "vices of domination." While even liberals like Massey and Denton perceive black people as singularly behaviorally impacted by their spatial isolation, this study uncovers white people as morally blighted by *their* strategic spatial isolation from and domination over black people.

This approach also shifts scholarly focus from white people's words to their bodies. Because the vices of antiblackness supremacy largely emerge from white and other nonblack people's embodied interaction with the spatial afterlife of slavery, we cannot adequately describe the moral life of racism if we do not accurately understand the role the body plays in racial habituation.

Like other forms of habituation, racial formation therefore occurs primarily through the ordinary place-based activities of daily life.[5] Human beings form habits through their bodies' daily and pre-rational encounter with the surrounding social and material environ-

7–9; Robert Rector, "The Poverty Solution: Marriage or Bust," *The National Review*, September 20, 2010, accessed June 20, 2017, http://www.nationalreview.com/corner/247138/poverty-solution-marriage-or-bust-robert-rector; Heather Mac Donald, "On Child Poverty, MSM Ignores the Basic Truth," *The National Review*, September 21, 2011, accessed June 20, 2017, http://www.nationalreview.com/corner/277977/child-poverty-msm-ignores-basic-truth-heather-mac-donald; Patricia Cohen, "Scholars Return to 'Culture of Poverty' Ideas," *New York Times*, October 17, 2010, http://www.nytimes.com/2010/10/18/us/18poverty.html.

4. Lisa Tessman, *Burdened Virtues: Virtue Ethics for Liberatory Struggles* (New York: Oxford University Press, 2005), 56–59.

5. Jane E. Goodman, "The Proverbial Bourdieu: Habitus and the Politics of Representation in the Ethnography of Kabylia," *American Anthropologist* 105, no. 4 (2003): 783.

ment.[6] As previously detailed, whites move into the least black neighborhoods possible, regardless of affordability, and they flee neighborhoods containing more than a token number of black people, even when these black residents are affluent. Whites avoid even fleeting entrance into predominately black neighborhoods, perceiving them as sites of danger and predation.

Antiblackness supremacy also relies upon automated and embodied habits of perception: antiblack forms of racial classification survive only if human beings learn to perceive human bodies in accordance with white supremacy's classificatory schema.[7] These perceptual habits do not just reflect reality; they serve to shape it. In addition to hating members of other racial groups because they look different, individuals also perceive members of other racial groups as different to the extent that they first hate them: scientists have found that people who harbor higher levels of pro-white bias, even when implicit, tend to exaggerate the physical differences between black and white faces.[8] In order to preserve the association between blackness and slave status, antiblackness strives to make black and white bodies appear more different than they are.

In addition to accruing through the body, the habits of antiblackness supremacy are expressed through them. Unsurprisingly, then, although whites frequently deny bias with their mouths, they consistently express aversion to blackness with their bodies. A turn-of-the-century study into the behavior and beliefs of whites illustrates the embodied character of white racial bias. While ninety-two percent of college students surveyed in the late 1990s expressed "no objection to" inviting a black friend over for dinner, nearly seventy percent of these students admitted they had not recently "invited a [single] black person for lunch or dinner."[9] Residential segregation and the racial habitus it generates make these statistics unsurprising: "only four of

6. Jeffrey J. Sallaz, "Talking Race, Marketing Culture: The Racial Habitus in and out of Apartheid," *Social Problems* 57, no. 2 (2010): 296.

7. Willy James Jennings, *The Christian Imagination: Theology and the Origins of Race* (New Haven: Yale University Press, 2011), 2011.

8. Tobias Brosch, Eyal Bar-David, and Elizabeth A. Phelps, "Implicit Race Bias Decreases the Similarity of Neural Representations of Black and White Faces," *Psychological Science* 24, no. 2 (February 1, 2013): 160.

9. Eduardo Bonilla-Silva, *Racism without Racists: Color-Blind Racism and the Persistence of Racial Inequality in America*, 3rd ed. (Lanham, MD: Rowman & Littlefield, 2009), 153, 157.

the college students interviewed reported having resided in neighborhoods with a significant black or minority presence."[10]

White people similarly feel race in their bodies even if they do not perceive it with their minds. When whites accidentally find themselves in black space, their bodies betray them. They may sweat, press down on the gas pedal, or clutch their purse.[11] White women feel afraid when black men walk towards them on the sidewalk; white motorists feel discomfort when lost in inner-city black neighborhoods.[12]

More than simply inhabiting and operating through our bodies, habits leave their mark on them. Habits of any kind imprint "neural maps" within the brain and help to determine the health, physical appearance, and comportment of human bodies.[13] This holds especially true in the case of the hyper-corporeal corporate vice of antiblackness supremacy. White people speak, walk, and dress in distinctively white ways. White bodies accrue heightened levels of comfort and health beginning *in utero*, and white babies survive infancy more often than black babies do.[14] Their adolescent bodies more frequently evade the disciplinary activities of an antiblackness supremacist judicial system: they are never stopped and frisked or followed at the mall; they are rarely shuffled from school to prison. They feel the press of handcuffs much less often than black men and women do. Since antiblackness supremacy operates primarily spatially, we become where we live. Whites acquire the vicious habits of antiblackness merely by inhabiting their bodies.

10. Bonilla-Silva, *Racism without Racists*, 341.

11. James W. Perkinson, *White Theology: Outing Supremacy in Modernity* (New York: Palgrave Macmillan, 2004), 177.

12. Kristen A. Myers, *Racetalk: Racism Hiding in Plain Sight* (Lanham, MD: Rowman & Littlefield, 2005), 48.

13. Elena Cuffari, "Habits of Transformation," *Hypatia* 26, no. 3 (2011): 535–36.

14. Anthony P. Polednak, "Trends in US Urban Black Infant Mortality, by Degree of Residential Segregation," *American Journal of Public Health* 86, no. 5 (1996): 723–26; James W. Collins Jr. and David K. Shay, "Prevalence of Low Birth Weight Among Hispanic Infants with United States-born and Foreign-born Mothers: The Effect of Urban Poverty," *American Journal of Epidemiology* 139, no. 2 (1994): 184–92; T. J. Mathews, M. F MacDorman, and National Center for Health Statistics (US), *Infant Mortality Statistics from the 2004 Period Linked Birth, Infant Death Data Set* (US Department of Health & Human Services, Centers for Disease Control and Prevention, National Center for Health Statistics, 2007).

THE EMBODIED VICE OF ANTIBLACKNESS SUPREMACY: AUTOMATIC, YET VOLUNTARY

Portraying the white body as a site of habituation into antiblackness supremacy might seem to exculpate whites. If whites acquire the vicious habits of antiblackness supremacy somewhat automatically and through their bodies, how can they be considered culpable when they act in accordance with their spatial conditioning? Indeed, the clear majority of whites have not consciously embarked upon a project of white supremacist conscientization as they would sign up for a session of music or dance lessons.[15] Partially for this reason, appeals to white innocence constitute a central rhetorical strategy of antiblackness supremacy. In this way, white people often disavow moral responsibility for whiteness by casting it as something unchosen, uninitiated, and given.[16]

But these fears rest on a misunderstanding of the character of Thomistic freedom and moral accountability. This defense seems credible only because we misplace the distinction between voluntary and involuntary actions. Following Aquinas, I describe white people as morally free not when we can make different racial choices, but because we do not want to make different racial choices. In truth, whites fail to recognize antiblackness supremacy not because they cannot, but because they do not want to.[17] In other words, we indulge in what Aquinas calls culpable ignorance. Cultivating culpable ignorance in order to perpetuate their moral delusions, we sin willfully.[18] White people have chosen ignorance.[19] The turn to the white body proposed in this chapter helps us hold ourselves accountable for racial vice.[20] While the white mind obfuscates, the white

15. Perkinson, *White Theology*, 164.

16. Elisabeth T. Vasko, *Beyond Apathy: A Theology for Bystanders* (Minneapolis: Fortress Press, 2015), 6.

17. Aquinas, *Summa Theologiae*, I–II.6.8.

18. Ibid., I–II.75.2.

19. M. Shawn Copeland, "Toward a Critical Christian Feminist Theology of Solidarity," in *Women & Theology*, ed. Mary Ann Hinsdale and Phyllis H. Kaminski, Annual Publication of the College Theology Society 40 (Maryknoll, NY: Orbis, 1994), 24.

20. Contemporary research into a phenomenon called "motivated reasoning" affirms Aquinas's contention that human beings believe what they want to believe. See for example Patrick W. Kraft, Milton Lodge, and Charles S. Taber, "Why People 'Don't Trust the Evidence': Motivated Reasoning and Scientific Beliefs," *The ANNALS of the American Academy of Political and Social Science* 658, no. 1 (March 1, 2015): 121–33.

body never lies. Hidden within a deeply habituated body, the habits of whiteness have become second nature.

White people are both conditioned by their encounter with spatialized antiblackness yet still culpable for the consequences of that conditioning. For Thomas, habits do not merely predispose us to perform a certain action; they also maximize our ability to move ourselves in the direction of a desired end.[21] They do not force individuals to act a certain way; they instead enable individuals to act more freely. But this freedom paradoxically carries a certain inertia. For example, LeBron James could choose to play basketball poorly if he so desired; it is hard to imagine him ever wanting to do so. We similarly would find it nearly unfathomable that a kind person would treat another person with cruelty. Although the virtuous possess both the positive freedom to act excellently and the negative freedom to choose, moral virtue nonetheless makes it difficult for the morally virtuous person to make sinful choices.[22] Acting badly inflicts pain on the virtuous just as committing a good act causes discomfort in the vicious.[23] For these reasons, habits are both voluntary and hard to break.

For Aquinas, habits need not be consciously acquired in order to qualify as voluntary.[24] Only when we are moved by something external, such as when we get pushed to the ground by a schoolyard bully, do our movements qualify as involuntary, that is, against or without the consent of our will.[25] Although some habits can happen to us, Aquinas rejects the view that we can ever be victims of our habits. Put another way, for Aquinas, human beings cannot acquire habits unless they want to.[26] Even if white people do not consciously choose to begin the process of habituation into whiteness, a Thomistic account of moral freedom depicts them as capable of voluntarily willing in alignment with the habits they did not deliberately decide to acquire. Though they are not entirely self-creating, they remain morally responsible.[27]

21. Craig Steven Titus, *Resilience and the Virtue of Fortitude: Aquinas in Dialogue with the Psychosocial Sciences* (Washington, DC: Catholic University of America Press, 2006), 120.

22. Bernard J. F. Lonergan, *Collected Works of Bernard Lonergan* (Toronto: University of Toronto Press, 2000), 96.

23. Aquinas, *Summa Theologiae*, II–II.59.2 ad 2.

24. Lonergan, *Collected Works of Bernard Lonergan*, 51.

25. Titus, *Resilience and the Virtue of Fortitude*, 119.

26. Aquinas, *Summa Theologiae*, I–II.55.4 ad 6.

27. Ibid., I–II.50.5.

Due to the nature of both vice in general and antiblackness supremacy in particular, white people's racial habituation has in fact increased their self-control and power. Antiblackness supremacy itself is empowering: formed in the shape of the master-slave relationship, the spatialized vice of antiblackness enhances the power of white wills precisely because and to the extent that it diminishes the power and freedom of black people. Vice of any kind similarly amplifies willpower. Like virtue, bearing the vices of antiblackness supremacy, white people act not like automatons, but as virtuosos of evil. As a form of embodied behavioral inertia, vice enables white people to persist in pursuit of their moral goals and aspirations. But vice, like virtue, produces not rigid repetition of the same narrow act but the drive, desire, and capacity to achieve a certain end.[28] The adaptability of vice empowers white people to replicate structures of antiblackness when possible but adjust them when necessary. They sometimes sustain antiblackness supremacy by changing it. White people can do what they will.

TOWARD A THOMISTIC UNDERSTANDING OF THE "EMBODIED VOLUNTARY"

But just as Thomas serves as a critical resource for contemporary antiracist scholarship, so has he acted as an unhelpful roadblock to it, especially in the field of Catholic theology. Indeed, partially because Thomistic anthropologies obscure the extent to which racial vice can enter the human person through the body, even antiracist Catholic scholars typically have underestimated white people's racial culpability. Too often, theologians and ethicists have portrayed white people as passively privileged or remotely complicit rather than actively engaged in racially evil acts. Put another way, we can spot the truck as it travels down the road; we can describe it and sometimes even chart its course, but we struggle to identify who is sitting behind the wheel. Moral culpability is spread too thin: scholars sketch pictures of suspects nobody can recognize.

In order to sharpen the diagnostic capacities of existing ethical frameworks, I illustrate how antiblackness supremacy often works

28. Servais Pinckaers, *The Pinckaers Reader: Renewing Thomistic Moral Theology* (Washington, DC: Catholic University of America Press, 2005), 299.

upon the body first.[29] In this way, it typically qualifies as a decision the body makes and the mind justifies. This claim does not simply repeat moral philosopher Martha Nussbaum's insights into the way in which the emotions participate in cognition. It takes one step further, arguing that the body also shapes cognition non-rationally through what I term the embodied voluntary.[30] In order to develop and defend this concept, this chapter brings a Thomistic account of habituation into conversation with contemporary neuroscientific insights. Just as Aquinas enables us to perceive truths obscured by our historical context, contemporary thinkers can help Aquinas overcome the epistemological shortcomings of his own time and place.

Rather than projecting contemporary ethical theories onto the historical Aquinas, this approach takes inspiration from him and offers a Thomistic critique of Thomas. Aquinas undoubtedly offers the most influential account of virtue theory in the Catholic theological tradition. But because Aquinas underestimates the extent to which vice can enter the soul through the body, his theory of virtue cannot capture the full scope of antiblackness supremacy's vicious operation.[31] Why? Identifying habits as the unique property of the sensitive, intellectual, and appetitive parts of the human soul, Aquinas credits habits with enabling an in-control soul to guide a compliant body. The body, Aquinas insists, "cannot be directly habituated": according to him, habits instill themselves only in the sensitive, intellectual, and appetitive parts of the human soul.[32] Here Thomas insufficiently appreciates the way in which habits can enter the soul by way of the body largely because he conceives of the relation between body and soul inaccurately.[33] Although Aquinas crafts a deeply embodied moral theology, he still sorts the soul from the body and identifies virtue and vice as activities of the former only.[34] For this reason, the legacy of Thomas's moral anthropology continues to limit the diagnostic

29. Perkinson, *White Theology*, 231.

30. Martha C. Nussbaum, *Upheavals of Thought: The Intelligence of Emotions* (Cambridge: Cambridge University Press, 2003).

31. Aquinas, *Summa Theologiae*, I–II.50.1; I–II.50.2; and I–II.50.3 ad 3.

32. Tom Sparrow and Adam Hutchinson, *A History of Habit: From Aristotle to Bourdieu* (Lanham, MD: Lexington Books, 2015), 71; ST I–II.50.

33. I agree with Herbert McCabe's claim that certain Thomists have been "unwittingly influenced by Cartesian principles," but, unlike McCabe, I place some of the blame for insufficiently embodied Thomisms on Aquinas himself. *The Good Life: Ethics and the Pursuit of Happiness* (London: Continuum Books, 2005), 2.

34. Aquinas, *Summa Theologiae*, I.75.4. Aquinas's anthropology can provide justification for what Kelly Brown Douglas identifies as "platonized Christianity" that has accorded white

powers of contemporary thinkers despite the fact that they admittedly define the difference between the soul and the body quite differently than Thomas—much of what we today would locate in the body Thomas places in the soul.[35]

Aquinas's moral anthropology qualifies as insufficiently embodied because, despite explicitly defining the soul as the form of the body, Aquinas sometimes conceives of the soul as incorporeal and internal to an external body. The "intellectual part" of the soul, Aquinas explains, is rightfully "called the 'inward' man" while the more intimately embodied "sensitive part" of the soul is "called the 'outward' man."[36] And while Aquinas believes that "the soul must be in the whole body, and in each part thereof," he cautions that it "is not a form merged in matter, or entirely embraced by [it]."[37] More than simply separating soul from body, Aquinas ranks the soul's powers according to their operational independence from the body.[38] The rational soul, for example, ranks highest precisely because it operates without the assistance of "any corporeal organ."[39] The sensitive soul, on the other hand, qualifies as more perfect than the purely physical aspects of the human person but less perfect than the less fleshly intellect and will. Needing the body only to register sensation, the sensitive soul acts "through a corporeal organ, but not through a corporeal quality."[40] While the rational soul commands the body, the sensitive soul merely uses it. For Aquinas, the body exists passively as a dead instrument; brought to life only at the mercy of the soul, it lacks a true capacity for knowing or initiating action.[41]

Aquinas's description of nonhuman animal behavior helps to corroborate this claim. According to Aquinas, because nonhuman animals lack a human soul, they can only be "trained through a combination of punishment and reward." A cow returns to a barn only if he is herded, for example. For this reason, nonhuman animals cannot have true habits because habits organize action internally.[42] A cow routinely returning to his owner's barn would qualify as a

supremacy theological credibility. *What's Faith Got to Do with It? Black Bodies/Christian Souls* (Maryknoll, NY: Orbis, 2005), 25.

35. Ibid., I.78.1.

36. Aquinas, *Summa Theologiae*, I.75.4 ad 1.

37. Ibid., I.76.6; I.76.1 ad 4.

38. Ibid., I.76.1.

39. Ibid., I.78.1.

40. Ibid., I.78.1.

41. Ibid., I.78.1.

42. Ibid., I–II.50.3 ad 2.

habit only if the cow performed this action on its own accord. But Aquinas is not fully satisfied with this assessment. Softening his argument, Aquinas concedes that nonhuman animals can become "disposed by a sort of custom to do things in this or that way." When they do, he acknowledges "to a certain extent, we can admit the existence of habits in dumb animals."[43] Aquinas seems to further blur the line between habits and customs when he argues that customs can become like "second nature" to human beings.[44] Aquinas seemingly wants habits, which require both reason and a free will, to sometimes operate like customs, and customs, which happen to "dumb animals" externally and therefore involuntarily, to sometimes operate like habits. Why?

Here we ought to read Aquinas as attempting to account for something similar to what I call the body's pre-rational role in habituation, that is, the embodied voluntary, without knowing how. Given his scientific, cultural, and philosophical context, Aquinas could not have admitted the body's role in habituation without losing the ability to describe habits as reasonable and human beings as distinct from brute beasts. But centuries of philosophical and scientific advances have rendered Aquinas's distinction between the commanding reason of the human soul and the passive instrumentality of the human body both unnecessary and untenable. Today, we can recognize that the sensitive, intellectual, and appetitive faculties do not simply operate in and through the body; they also are shaped by it. Nor is the rational soul the body's proper master.[45] As demonstrated by the operation of racial vice, sometimes, the body leads the way in Thomistic processes of habituation: for example, the white body does not merely enact the habits of antiblackness supremacy; it also helps to acquire them.[46]

The existence of the embodied voluntary seems counterintuitive to us for two reasons: first, we possess an overly verbal and interior account of both the will, especially as it occurs as intention, and reason; and second, we adhere, even if implicitly, to an excessively hierarchical anthropology of mind over body. Although we may cringe at Aristotelian or Thomistic anthropologies that describe the soul as ruling the body like a master rules the slave, we still tend to conceive

43. Ibid., I–II.50.3 ad 2.

44. Ibid., I–II.78.2.

45. Ibid., I–II.77.3.

46. Here I take inspiration from W. E. B. Du Bois. While he focuses on "the souls of white folk," I urge us to examine their bodies. W. E. B. Du Bois, *Darkwater: Voices from Within the Veil* (1920. Reprint. Mineola, NY: Dover, 1999), 17.

of the body as that which merely takes orders from the mind.[47] We locate the will entirely in the mind, that is, the bundle of conscious and self-moving cognitive faculties, and not in the body. And even when we situate the mind largely or entirely in the brain, we still distinguish it from the body and envision it as the human person's moral command center. Perceiving the reason and the will as in some way incorporeal or distinctly interior to the body, theologians typically imagine the body as receiving moral instruction but never offering it. We therefore classify actions initiated by the body as involuntary and therefore morally insignificant, like we would a twitch, spasm, or a sneeze.

But recent neuroscientific insights suggest that the mind does not rule the body, at least not as we have conventionally thought. The body does not simply execute the mind's decisions with varying degrees of success as would a perfectly obedient slave; it actually participates in moral judgment and helps to execute moral actions. Rather than a spark that triggers a particular action, "consciousness appears to be bound to a posteriori signals arising from the completion of the action itself."[48] For example, when making tea or tying our shoes, we acquire conscious awareness of each phase of these automated activities only when interrupted by something unexpected, a loose teapot handle, a knock at the door, the meow of a hungry cat, or a busted shoelace. But the post hoc character of consciousness does not make these actions unintended or involuntary. When I bring a pot of water to boil, I act in accordance with my intention, even when I am not consciously aware of my actions.

We further underestimate the embodied character of moral decision-making because we typically retain a "conscious sense of will" only for a short period of time.[49] While the embodied patterns of habitual action remain, the memory of conscious awareness almost always proves fleeting: as one study concludes, consciousness "lags behind the action execution process." We slam the brake and then become aware of having chosen to do so. Affirming this, other neuroscientific studies record electrical "changes in brain state" not just

47. Aristotle, *Politics*, Book 1, Chapter 5; Aquinas, *Summa Theologiae*, I.II.77 ad 3; Kevin White, "The Passions of the Soul," in *The Ethics of Aquinas*, ed. Stephen Pope (Washington, DC: Georgetown University Press, 2002), 105.

48. Marc Jeannerod, "Consciousness of Action as an Embodied Consciousness," in *Does Consciousness Cause Behavior?*, ed. Susan Pockett, William P. Banks, and Shaun Gallagher (Cambridge, MA: MIT Press, 2009), 36.

49. Ibid.

before "the execution of a . . . voluntary act" but even before "the subjects express awareness that they are about to move."[50] Neuroscientists Hakwan C. Lau, Robert D. Rogers, and Richard E. Passingale similarly "throw doubt on the commonsensical view that the experience of intention, including the experienced onset, is completely determined before an action." While "the commonsensical view is attractive," they explain, "when we assume that the main function of experience of intention is for the conscious control of action . . . the data suggest that the perceived onset of intention depends at least in part on neural activity that takes place after the execution of action, which could not, in principle, have any causal impact on the action itself."[51] In many cases, intentions arise in the body before they gather together in the mind. They represent not mental causes of actions but embodied characteristics of them.

These findings compel us to distinguish the will—that principle which makes an action intentional and voluntary—from our conscious awareness of the experience of willing. We can intend an action without realizing or remembering that we did so. Rather than existing solely in the mind as a discrete spot of consciousness as is commonly thought, our awareness of the embodied voluntary often emerges as a narrative construction. For example, in the aftermath of a near-miss car crash, I have asked myself, "Why did I slam the brakes?" My mind assesses the circumstances and travels back in time to recollect the answer: "to avoid ramming into the deer that unexpectedly dashed out before me." I either did not consciously command my foot to press the pedal or I did not retain the memory of having done so. I still acted voluntarily and as I intended to. This same mechanism makes it possible for us to genuinely wonder just ten seconds after leaving the house in a rush whether we unplugged the hairdryer, turned the burners off, or remembered to grab our cell phone. In this way, "humans know themselves by their actions, not by their thoughts."[52] Here the mind acts less like the body's master than its official biographer.

This post hoc quality of consciousness pertains even more to actions performed out of habit. A new driver, for example, is much more likely to consciously think about her actions before she executes

50. Walter Freeman, "Nonlinear Brain Dynamics and Intention According to Aquinas," *Mind and Matter* 6, no. 2 (2008): 228.
51. Ibid.
52. Ibid.

them. But this self-consciousness reflects the new driver's lack of skill and freedom. Precisely because she must consciously map her actions out in her head before she commits to switching on the ignition or flipping on her turn signal, she is actually less free than the seasoned driver who operates her vehicle attentively but relatively unreflectively. The best way to do something well is to do it so often that one does not have to think about it in advance. Put another way, the better one becomes at performing a certain action, the less she needs to consciously reflect upon or even acknowledge her performance of said action. This holds especially true for the vice of antiblackness supremacy, which enters and operates primarily through the body. The typically unconscious character of white people's performance of antiblackness therefore renders it both more effective and more voluntary than most actions that require conscious forethought.

The average white person's lack of conscious awareness of their racial actions renders them not innocent but perfectly habituated and entirely culpable. White people typically acquire awareness of and begin to consciously reflect upon their embodied habits only when something physically interrupts their performance of them. White people's spatial environment allows them to execute their embodied will nearly completely unimpeded: they do not possess an awareness of their voluntary actions because their environment does not interrupt them. They are like the person who bends down to tie her shoe while engaging in spirited conversation, or uses a knife and fork to feast on her favorite meal without thinking of anything at all.

The embodied character of both racial habituation and moral actions further underscores the difficulty of reforming the world within us without simultaneously reforming the world outside of us. Because they are at home in their racial habitat, white people typically experience their spatial circumstances as neither unpleasant nor unnatural, but comfortable and appropriate.[53] The claim that antiblackness supremacy enters through the body does not proclaim whites as innocent. White people will the habits their bodies have helped them acquire. Because the vices of antiblackness supremacy render white people inept at the practice of racial justice and skillfully adept at the pursuit of racial injustice, they accord white people the power to preserve and protect the spatial afterlife of slavery.[54] The

53. Aquinas, *Summa Theologiae*, I–II.75.1 ad 3; and I–II.75.2.

54. Lisa Tessman, *Burdened Virtues: Virtue Ethics for Liberatory Struggles* (New York: Oxford University Press, 2005), 56–59.

spatial afterlife of slavery in turn only strengthens the operation of the deeply embodied, vicious racial habits that keep it in motion. White people's wills have become conformed to the world's injustice; the world, in turn, has become uniquely conformed to white people's wills.

THE WHITE RACIAL HABITS OF ANTIBLACKNESS SUPREMACY IN ACTION

Armed with a Thomistic account of culpability, freedom, and what I term the embodied voluntary, we can perceive white people's participation in racial evil much more clearly. White people do not just passively receive privilege. They actively practice antiblackness and benefit from the supremacy it provides them. They flee integrating neighborhoods; they support policies that preserve the racial status quo; and they refuse to make amends for racial injustice.[55] In addition to avoiding black people, white people directly harm them.[56] They use the prison system as an instrument with which to discipline and punish black people; they accord impunity to law enforcement officers who kill unpacified black people; and they support the death penalty more than two and a half times as often as black people do, not despite its well-known bias against African American suspects, but precisely because of it.[57] White people are skilled at systems of violence.[58]

Hiding within white bodies shaped in the image of the antiblack society they inhabit, the habits of antiblackness supremacy have become second nature. Although whites differ from each other dramatically in terms of region, religion, politics, education, sexual orientation, gender identity, and wealth, they share residence in racially segregated space in common. Shining a spotlight on the white body, this book asks white people, "How does it feel to be a problem?"[59]

55. Yancey, *Who Is White?*, 78–80.

56. Andrew Prevot, "Beyond White Privilege: Toward an Uncensored, Subaltern, and Aporetic Theological Response to the Crises of Race and Racism," *Catholic Theological Society of America*, June 2014 Conference.

57. James D. Unnever and Francis T. Cullen, "The Racial Divide in Support for the Death Penalty: Does White Racism Matter?," *Social Forces* 85, no. 3 (March 1, 2007): 1281–1301.

58. Perkinson, *White Theology*, 150.

59. W. E. B. Du Bois, *The Souls of Black Folk*, 11. See also George Yancy, ed., *White Self-Criticality beyond Anti-racism: How Does It Feel to Be a White Problem?* (Lanham, MD: Lexington Books, 2014).

This focus on white bodies rather than white persons is intentional. As M. Shawn Copeland points out, in our antiblackness supremacist society, "the black body, over-determined, is every, all, any black."[60] More than ideologies of antiblackness supremacy need to be unlearned, the white body needs to be spatially repositioned—against its will if necessary.

This is not a call to violence against white people. Nor it is a proposal to forcibly relocate whites en masse. This exhortation instead uncovers embodied racial vice as a problem to which we do not yet know the solution. Indeed, all forms of rehabituation follow a path that cannot be set in advance. These caveats notwithstanding, our discomfort at the thought of coercive action against whites serves as an occasion for self-reflection. As earlier chapters have demonstrated, all levels of government have worked "to segregate America." And still today, the U.S. housing market already coercively constrains the choices of black renters and homebuyers in a unique way: only certain U.S.-Americans are truly free to live wherever they choose.[61] Do we value white people's freedom to segregate more than we do black people's freedom to reside in racially inclusive neighborhoods? Why does a legal and financial system that penalizes antiblackness supremacy seem so much more outrageous than one that penalizes both blackness and black people? This call for coercion acknowledges the antagonism that antiblackness supremacy maintains between black life and freedom and white power and mastery. In general, black people have become freer only by making white people less free: for example, black people escaped slavery only if white people could not recapture them; black people attained emancipation only because white people were legally prevented from owning them; black people could sit at the front of city buses only because white people were denied the freedom to sit exclusively among their own kind. If the antagonism between black and white freedom remains true in the case of contemporary residential segregation, it is only because white freedom continues to draw strength from black bondage. Or perhaps we ought to say that much of what white

60. M. Shawn Copeland, *Enfleshing Freedom: Body, Race, and Being* (Minneapolis: Fortress Press, 2009), 17. See also, Frantz Fanon, *Black Skin, White Masks* (New York: Grove, 2010), 93; George Yancy, *Black Bodies, White Gazes: The Continuing Significance of Race* (Lanham, MD: Rowman & Littlefield, 2008), 71.
61. Rothstein, *The Color of Law.*

people perceive and experience as freedom in fact qualifies as a form of mastership.

We cannot trust the words of whites for another reason: they deploy a sophisticated linguistic racial code that seeks to hide the moral truth their bodies tell. Depicting racial segregation as a state of affairs that requires no explanation, whites blame racial segregation on anything but their racial power and prejudice. Living almost entirely alongside other nonblacks, whites learn this ideology of colorblindness like a second language.[62] This discourse increases white racial power by denying it exists. If whites believe their actions are devoid of racist intent, they feel entitled to continue performing them, regardless of their racial outcomes.[63] Colorblindness serves as a shield and a sword. Declaring colorblindness, whites jettison antiblackness as an explicit ideology so as to maintain it as a structural fact.[64] Antiblackness supremacy has conceded the error of its old ways in order to defend the righteousness of its new ones. As a type of racial orthodoxy, the ideology of colorblindness counters a system of antiblackness supremacy long since discredited while preventing us from perceiving its contemporary workings.[65] If "colorblindness" provides the cure, then Jim Crow must supply the disease. In the past, antiblackness supremacy flourished by not appearing as evil; today, it survives by seeming not to exist. Whites further divert attention from their bodies by framing racism as a problem of premeditated, malicious intellectual intent. Habituated by their residence in racially segregated space, whites bear antiblackness supremacy in their bodies long before they acquire ideological strategies to defend and describe it. Besides, the moral truth of white life lies less in the words they speak than the ways their bodies occupy space. For this reason, white people ought to be not listened to, but watched.

62. Ibid., 75–76.

63. Bonilla-Silva, *Racism without Racists*, 76.

64. Howard Winant, *The World Is a Ghetto: Race and Democracy Since World War II* (New York: Basic Books, 2002), 170.

65. Eduardo Bonilla-Silva, "New Racism, Color-Blind Racism, and the Future of Whiteness in America," in *White Out: The Continuing Significance of Racism* (Lanham, MD: Rowman & Littlefield, 2003).

5.

The Catholic Corporate Habits of Antiblackness in the Era of Chattel Slavery

The insights outlined in the previous chapter about individual white bodies can be used to morally analyze the church's corporate body as well. Like the bodies of individual whites, the corporate body of the Catholic Church has been habituated by its encounter with the spatial afterlife of slavery.[1] For this reason, contemporary Thomists cannot scrutinize the moral dispositions of individuals alone. Without reducing the church to its corporate vices, this chapter nonetheless demonstrates their centrality to the church's corporate character. The Catholic Church has participated in and been habituated by every phase of this country's ever-shifting, ingeniously adaptive history of antiblackness supremacy. This history of the U.S. Catholic Church's habits of antiblackness supremacy surveys not just an aggregation of individual actions performed by white people who happened to be Catholic. It outlines the history of the Catholic Church's inherited corporate habits. In order to expose the history of corporate, Catholic habits, this chapter re-narrates the history of the Catholic Church and disturbs its inherited ecclesial self-understandings.[2]

The church comprises the graced, but historically embodied, body

1. Pierre Bourdieu, *The Weight of the World: Social Suffering in Contemporary Society* (Stanford, CA: Stanford University Press, 1999), 128.

2. Jay P. Dolan, *In Search of an American Catholicism: A History of Religion and Culture in Tension* (New York: Oxford University Press, 2003).

of Christ. This church is holy but not trans-historically perfect.[3] Although this chapter uncovers the church as animated by a corporate vice, it does not discount the church's internal diversity. Nor does it discredit the efforts of those mostly black Catholics who have attempted to re-habituate the church and instill in it new racial habits.[4] Rather than erasing the historical existence of black Catholics, the theory of corporate vice sheds light on the antiblackness supremacist patterns against which they have struggled so tirelessly. The forthcoming narrative therefore tracks how the performatively received, historically real body of Christ continues to exercise corporate habits of antiblackness supremacy and white supremacy despite the steady racial virtue of most of its black members.

Habits have a history. Just as personal habits have a personal history, so social habits have a social history.[5] The Catholic corporate habits of antiblackness supremacy are both inherited and transmitted. Carrying an accumulating inertia, they have survived from one era into the next. But like all traditions, the corporate habits of antiblackness supremacy do not stay in stasis. They exercise a vibrant dynamism, allowing them to adapt to ever-changing circumstances. Resilient yet flexible, these habits have infested the core of corporate U.S. Catholic identity. Once locked in, bad habits reinforce themselves relatively automatically. Habits comprise character just as character fuels habits.[6] These bad racial characters also insist on creating society in their own image. Unwilling to interrupt its habits of antiblackness supremacy, the church has retained its antiblack character. The church cannot surrender its antiblack vices while still attached to its antiblack character.

3. Jamie T. Phelps, "Joy Came in the Morning: Risking Death for Resurrection," in *A Troubling in My Soul: Womanist Perspectives on Suffering and Evil*, ed. Emilie Townes (Maryknoll, NY: Orbis, 1993), 53–54.

4. For more on the history of black Catholic resistance to ecclesial white supremacy, see Mary Shawn Copeland, LaReine-Marie Mosely, and Albert J. Raboteau, *Uncommon Faithfulness: The Black Catholic Experience* (Maryknoll, NY: Orbis, 2009).

5. This insight builds upon Jamie T. Phelps's argument that "the contemporary patterns of social segregation and exclusion of black men and women from participation in ministries and decision making within the church are grounded on historical patterns." "Joy Came in the Morning," in *A Troubling in My Soul: Womanist Perspectives on Suffering and Evil*, ed. Emilie Townes (Maryknoll, NY: Orbis, 1993), 57.

6. Aquinas, Summa Theologiae, I–II.52.3.

SLAVE OWNERSHIP AS A CORPORATE CATHOLIC HABIT

Perpetuated for centuries, the practice of African slavery would root itself deep within the corporate body of the Catholic Church. Catholic residence in the antiblackness supremacist space of the nineteenth-century United States affirmed and amplified this habit. Like the black slaves they owned, these habits were passed down intergenerationally: white Catholic children learned how to wield power over black people from their parents—the practices of white mastership were cultivated in the white home. Catholic children grew up in a culture in which white ownership appeared ordinary and mundane. They worshiped in a church undisturbed by chattel slavery. For example, the first bishop of the diocese of Natchez, Mississippi, John Joseph Chance, was born in 1795 to a wealthy white slaveowning family in Haiti. As a small child, his family fled its native country's war of black independence, seeking racial refuge in Baltimore. Chance's family moved from one white supremacist slaveocracy to another.[7] Patrick Nelsen Lynch, the third bishop of the diocese of Charleston, South Carolina, grew up in one of the most affluent slaveholding Catholic families in the state.[8]

Every aspect of the church's corporate life took place within the context of the United States' slaveocracy. It shaped bodies and society. For this reason, residence in the United States infused the habits of racialized power into the bodies even of European Catholic clerics originally unaccustomed to ownership of black women, children, and men. Whether born in Ireland, Italy, France, or England, immigrant clerics adopted the antiblackness supremacist customs of their adopted country. U.S.-American antiblackness shaped the Catholic Church at least as much as the church shaped the United States.

Importantly, Catholicism provided these missionary immigrants no reason to question and little desire to resist the habituating power of their adopted country's peculiar institution. When French missionaries arrived in the Southern United States in the first half of the nineteenth century, for example, they claimed to care not so much for the social standing of bodies but for the eternal salvation of souls.

7. Cathedral of Our Lady of Sorrows, *Sketch of the Catholic Church in the City of Natchez, Miss: On the Occasion of the Consecration of Its Cathedral, September 19, 1886*, 1886, 21.

8. David C. R. Heisser, "Bishop Lynch's People: Slaveholding by a South Carolina Prelate," *South Carolina Historical Magazine* 102, no. 3 (July 1, 2001): 238, 242.

Despite their best efforts and sincere intentions, Catholic priests could not participate in slavery in a Catholic way. Undermining their evangelizing mission, French priests often sold slaves to non-Catholic "heretics" who happened to have deep pockets.[9] French missionaries ultimately ministered not in body-blind fashion but in conformity with the embodied habits of antiblackness supremacy.[10]

Elevating "religious freedom" above "legal freedom," many Americanized French clerics insisted that the emancipation of the slave's soul rendered the liberation of his body unnecessary. For example, in the first public statement about slavery issued by a Louisiana cleric, Bishop Antoine Blanc in 1852 characterized "true liberty [as] the 'glorious liberty of the children of God' by which Christ has made us free 'when we were delivered from sin.'" "This liberty," he opined, "is the only foundation of all liberty." "Perfect freedom," he continued, could be found only in the Christianized soul.[11]

We may wish to defend these French missionaries by claiming that they acted out of an overriding commitment to enslaved people's salvation. Perhaps they simply valued enslaved people's souls more than their bodies. But, in truth, French missionaries could interact with and administer the sacraments to black slaves only with the permission of their white masters.[12] Black people were sacramentally neglected. Forced to choose between their duties to the de facto white parish church and the black plantation, Catholic priests tended to stay in parochial place.[13] Their racial habits grew deep roots. By the time Pope Gregory issued his conditional condemnation of slavery in 1839, these missionary priests had switched from simply tolerating slavery to defending it ardently. For example, expressing a widely shared belief, French missionary Stephen Rousselon insisted that abo-

9. Michael Pasquier, "'Though Their Skin Remains Brown, I Hope Their Souls Will Soon Be White': Slavery, French Missionaries, and the Roman Catholic Priesthood in the American South, 1789–1865," *Church History* 77, no. 2 (2008): 351–53.

10. Pasquier, "'Though Their Skin Remains Brown,'" 362; Kenneth J. Zanca, *American Catholics and Slavery, 1789-1866: An Anthology of Primary Documents* (Lanham, MD: University Press of America, 1994), 236.

11. Pasquier, "'Though Their Skin Remains Brown,'" 364.

12. Ibid., 362.

13. "Letter of William Henry Elder, Bishop of Natchez, to the Society for the Propagation of the Faith, in Which He Describes His Ministry to Slaves, 1858," in *"Stamped with the Image of God": African Americans as God's Image in Black,* ed. Cyprian Davis and Jamie Phelps (Maryknoll, NY: Orbis, 2003), 33.

lition would bring "the total destruction of the South."[14] Like many of his peers, Rousselon was much more dedicated to saving the white South than he was any black person's soul.

In addition to incorporating foreign-born French missionaries into distinctly American habits of living, antiblackness supremacy also enabled English Catholic colonists to support the project of American Independence. At first glance, this seems to contradict expectations. Many claimed that the United States' liberal celebration of individual freedom clashed with conservative Catholic regard for mutual obligations and social hierarchy.[15] Yet, the overwhelming majority of Catholics living in the British colonies supported revolution. How could this be so?

Much more than in the "freewheeling" North, the slaveholding South advanced a hierarchical ideology of rights and corresponding duties.[16] The slave owed her master obedience; the master in turn owed his slaves food, shelter, and moral guidance. In tempering individualism, racialized slavery made republicanism "more palatable" to the average eighteenth-century white Catholic colonist. U.S. Catholics could support rebellion in the name of a white supremacist social order founded upon racialized hierarchy and mutual obligation.[17] Largely for this reason, the only white Catholics who remained loyal to the British Crown lived in Pennsylvania, a non-slaveholding space.[18] Catholics seemed especially at home amidst hierarchy: while American independence prompted a small but significant minority of Protestant whites to set their black slaves free, Catholic masters retained their slaves even after the triumph of U.S.-American freedom.[19]

In the decades after Independence, chattel slavery would shape the corporate body of the Catholic Church quite literally. Until famished Irish immigrants flooded Northern cities in the late 1840s, the majority of the nation's Catholics lived in the slaveholding Southern states of Maryland, Kentucky, and Louisiana.[20] The economics of

14. Stephen J. Ochs, *A Black Patriot and a White Priest: Andre Cailloux and Claude Paschal Maistre in Civil War New Orleans* (Baton Rouge: Louisiana State University Press, 2006), 112.
15. Maura Jane Farrelly, "American Slavery, American Freedom, American Catholicism," *Early American Studies: An Interdisciplinary Journal* 10, no. 1 (2012): 85.
16. Farrelly, "American Slavery, American Freedom, American Catholicism," 86.
17. Ibid.
18. Ibid.
19. Ibid., 91–92.
20. Ibid., 84–85.

slavery dictated the demographics of Catholicism as Southern population centers were also centers of enslavement. For example, in 1789, the Catholic Church headquartered the United States' first and only diocese in the slaveholding city of Baltimore because it anchored the only region of the country to contain a large number of Catholic residents.[21]

Diocesan borders would expand as the practice of slavery did. Founded in 1793, the diocese of New Orleans held its headquarters in "the slave-trade capital of the United States."[22] This spatial overlap serves as no coincidence. The Catholic Church anchored the second diocese in the United States in the city of New Orleans and not some other city precisely because it served as a major population center. New Orleans amassed much of its wealth and identity as a result of its booming trade in black flesh; slave-related economic activity drew people to the city like a magnet.[23] This trade also created the context in which all other activities took place: in New Orleans, "slave auctions and Catholic churches shared the same blocks." Catholic New Orleanians became desensitized to the sight of the whip-scarred bodies of trafficked blacks.[24]

Catholic dioceses took the shape that slavery assigned them throughout the South. In 1808, the Catholic Church created the Kentucky diocese of Bardstown to meet the pastoral needs of wealthy Catholic, slaveowning planters from Maryland who had emigrated there in search of unexhausted soil.[25] In a few years, church officials would relocate Kentucky's diocesan to Louisville, a city that would soon act as one of the major northern ports in the country's emerging domestic slave trade. The church centered its diocesan bodies in other slave port cities: soon Lexington, St. Louis, and Natchez, Mississippi would also hold holy Sees. Domestically trafficked black slaves traveled from one diocesan city to another. Herded together in Lexing-

21. Jay P. Dolan, *In Search of an American Catholicism: A History of Religion and Culture in Tension* (New York: Oxford University Press, 2003), 14.

22. Pasquier, "'Though Their Skin Remains Brown,'" 351.

23. Edward E. Baptist, *The Half Has Never Been Told: Slavery and the Making of American Capitalism* (New York: Basic Books, 2014), 51–56, 82–83; William Boelhower, *New Orleans in the Atlantic World: Between Land and Sea* (New York: Routledge, 2013), 181–82; John Hugh O'Donnell, *The Catholic Hierarchy of the United States, 1790-1922* (Washington, DC: Catholic University of America Press, 1922), 50.

24. Walter Johnson, *Soul by Soul* (Cambridge, MA: Harvard University Press, 2009), 174.

25. Benjamin Lewis Fitzpatrick, *Negroes for Sale: The Slave Trade in Antebellum Kentucky* (BiblioBazaar, 2012), 17.

ton, they arrived in Natchez; stockpiled in St. Louis, they ended up in New Orleans.

All of these cities grew in size and power largely because their white merchants traded expertly in slaves. In these cities, slavery seemed not indecent but mundane. In adapting themselves to pre-established sociopolitical boundaries, dioceses in many ways ratified the social practices that created these boundaries. Catholic dioceses patterned themselves after chattel slavery. The Catholic diocese conformed to the habituating power of antiblackness supremacy; it did not disrupt it.

Given this spatial framing, it is not surprising that white Catholic participation in chattel slavery pervaded every facet of the church's corporate body. The first Catholic bishop of the United States, John Carroll of Baltimore, personally acted as master of black slaves. While Archbishop of St. Louis, Peter Richard Kenrick claimed several black people as his personal property. Bishop John Mary Odin, the Vicar Apostolic of Texas, held slaves at his Galveston Residence. On the eve of Civil War, the Archbishop of New Orleans and the Bishop of Natchitoches each owned two black human beings.[26]

Catholic religious communities also acted in accordance with their spatial conditioning. In Maryland and Louisiana, Capuchins and Jesuits held black people as chattel.[27] And just south of St. Louis, in Perry County, the Vincentians owned more slaves in 1830 than any other slaveholder in the area.[28] Sulpicians in both Baltimore and Bardstown, Kentucky kept black women and men in chains.[29] And women acted just like men. For example, ten of the twelve communities of women religious in the Old South held slaves. Even the Carmelite nuns who founded the first contemplative community in the United States in 1791 also pressed black flesh into slavery. Despite their renunciation of worldly pleasures, they retained the right to exercise the white prerogative to extract profit and pleasure from holding black slaves in captivity.[30]

26. Heisser, "Bishop Lynch's People," 240–41.

27. Stephen J. Ochs, *Desegregating the Altar: The Josephites and the Struggle for Black Priests, 1871-1960* (Baton Rouge: Louisiana State University Press, 1993), 13.

28. Cyprian Davis, *The History of Black Catholics in the United States* (New York: Crossroad, 1995), 38.

29. Ibid.

30. Black religious sisters provided a counterwitness to the white supremacy displayed by their white counterparts. See Cyprian Davis, O.S.B., "Henriette Delille: Servant of Slaves, Witness to the Poor," in *Uncommon Faithfulness: The Black Catholic Experience*, ed. M. Shawn Copeland, LaReine-Marie Mosely, and Albert J. Raboteau (Maryknoll, NY: Orbis, 2009).

Catholic dioceses also owned black slaves as a corporate body. Wealthy Catholic laymen often deeded black slaves to the body of Christ in their wills. One wealthy Kentucky planter donated a 650-acre plantation well stocked with slaves to the bishop of Lexington for the benefit of the diocese.[31] The diocese of Charleston, South Carolina also routinely received slaves upon the death of wealthy lay members. In other cases, bishops initiated diocesan slave-ownership. In this way, bishop Benedict Joseph Flaget of Bardstown obtained diocesan slaves and then deeded them to his successor, Martin John Spalding. While being trained for the priesthood, many young Catholic men also received training in antiblackness supremacy. For example, bishops Louis William DeBourg of New Orleans teamed up with Joseph Rosati of St. Louis to supply Missouri's St. Mary's Seminary with black slaves.[32] And in all the country's seminaries, future priests read from a moral manual penned by Bishop Kenrick that defended the practice of slavery as an opportunity to save the soul of the soteriologically imperiled African savage.[33]

The Southern white Catholic laity also embodied the place-produced habits of antiblackness supremacy. In fact, in Maryland, lay Catholics owned slaves at significantly higher rates than their non-Catholic counterparts and let their slaves go free at much lower rates than their Calvinist neighbors did.[34] In fact, half of the early-nineteenth-century Chesapeake Catholic pioneers to the newly cleared lands of central Kentucky owned slaves while only one third of Kentucky's overall white population did. When these Catholic slave-owners came to Kentucky, they brought their slaveowning habits with them. Kentucky's Catholics remained united: "unlike . . . the Kentucky Baptists, Methodists, and Presbyterians, Catholics never split over the issue of slavery." Nearly all of the so-called "Bluegrass Catholics" supported the practice of chattel slavery, regardless of their class status.[35]

Catholicism held slaveowners together in other ways. At the turn of the nineteenth century, the disproportionately Catholic cities and diocesan centers of Baltimore and New Orleans provided racial safe haven to thousands of predominately Catholic planters fleeing the

31. Heisser, "Bishop Lynch's People," 248.
32. Ibid., 240–41.
33. Davis, *The History of Black Catholics in the United States*, 48–49.
34. Farrelly, "American Slavery, American Freedom, American Catholicism," 90, 94.
35. C. Walker Gollar, "Catholic Slaves and Slaveholders in Kentucky," *The Catholic Historical Review* 84, no. 1 (January 1, 1998): 51.

Haitian revolution. In so doing, they helped both to extend the life of slaveocracy and to snatch freedom away from the thousands of black slaves these whites brought with them.[36]

Lying deeply rooted in the church's corporate body, the corporate Catholic habits of antiblackness supremacist slaveownership could not be dislodged by mere moral suasion, even when levied by papal authors.[37] Pope Gregory's 1839 antislavery tract did not inspire even a small minority of U.S. Catholics to abandon their slaveowning habits. His passionately argued missive arrived far too late, appearing approximately 339 years after the transatlantic slave trade's brutal inception. Southern bishops also interpreted Pope Gregory's letter in accordance with their wills rather than their reason, refusing to believe that it actually condemned the practice of chattel slavery as it existed in the United States.[38] Cognition conformed to embodied patterns of inhabiting space. They believed what they wanted to believe.

Some Catholic bishops ignored Gregory's letter, but others strenuously defended themselves against it. For example, Charleston bishop John England wrote a series of impassioned public letters to John Forsyth, Martin Van Buren's Secretary of State, in order to convince him that Gregory had not penned an abolitionist text.[39] Still unsatisfied, England also set about crafting a comprehensive and richly theological account of the compatibility between Catholicism and U.S.-American slavery.[40] Pope Gregory's denunciation ultimately galvanized pro-slavery Catholics against a common, newly energized, abolitionist enemy. Southern Catholic clerics also would continue holding slaves until they were forced by the Civil War to surrender them.[41] Even a Pope could not make white Catholic minds accept a truth their bodies could not bear.

Although the Civil War eventually took the slaves of white Catholics away from them, it could not fracture the corporate body

36. Diane Batts Morrow, *Persons of Color and Religious at the Same Time: The Oblate Sisters of Providence, 1828-1860* (Chapel Hill: University of North Carolina Press, 2002), 3–4.

37. Aquinas, *Summa Theologiae* I–II.51.2; and I–II.51.3.

38. Zanca, *American Catholics and Slavery, 1789-1866*, 192.

39. John F. Quinn, "'Three Cheers for the Abolitionist Pope!': American Reaction to Gregory XVI's Condemnation of the Slave Trade, 1840-1860," *The Catholic Historical Review* 90, no. 1 (2004): 78.

40. R. Frank Saunders Jr. and George A. Rogers, "Bishop John England of Charleston: Catholic Spokesman and Southern Intellectual, 1820-1842," *Journal of the Early Republic* 13, no. 3 (October 1, 1993): 319.

41. Heisser, "Bishop Lynch's People," 241.

of the Catholic Church in the U.S. South. The church publicly blessed the regimental flags of Confederate battalions in Catholic churches and held burials of slain Confederate soldiers, and every Southern bishop supported the Confederacy without exception.[42] Antiblackness supremacy gathered nonblack Southern Catholics into one body as Southern lay Catholics of all nationalities—French, Spanish, Italian, German, and Polish—enlisted as Confederate soldiers.[43] Southern white Catholic fidelity to the Confederacy also helped to overcome or at least curtail anti-Catholic prejudice among white Protestants; in becoming Confederates, white Southern Catholics became more thoroughly American.[44] Like other groups who have been perceived as foreign, white Southern Catholics staved off "outsider status" by joining the fight to defend antiblackness supremacy.[45] And while black slaves suffered spiritual neglect on far-flung Southern plantations, Southern bishops ensured that Catholic chaplains accompanied every white Catholic Confederate soldier to battlefields all over the South.[46]

THE CORPORATE CATHOLIC HABITS OF ANTIBLACKNESS SUPREMACY IN THE POST-EMANCIPATION SOUTH

Because antiblackness supremacy remained in place after Confederate surrender, so did the deeply intertwined corporate Catholic habits of white and antiblackness supremacy. The church's white supremacist habits adapted but survived, helping to build a new regime of white supremacy. During the course of the next century, Catholic parishes, religious communities, and institutions continued to take on the segregationist character of the places they inhabited.

Although slavery had ended, many white bishops still perceived black people as slave-like. They were not forced, either by their relatively well-intentioned Vatican supervisors or their own civil society,

42. Michael Pasquier, *Fathers on the Frontier: French Missionaries and the Roman Catholic Priesthood in the United States, 1789-1870* (New York: Oxford University Press, 2010), 168, 189–95.
43. Michael Pasquier, "Catholic Southerners, Catholic Soldiers: White Creoles, the Civil War, and the Lost Cause in New Orleans," *Dissertation* (September 10, 2003): 26.
44. Gracjan Kraszewski, *Dogma and Dixie: Roman Catholics and the Southern Confederacy during the American Civil War* (PhD diss., Mississippi State University, 2016), 7, 10–12.
45. Ibid., 7.
46. Ibid., 29.

to learn to perceive blacks differently. For example, in 1903, nearly fifty years after emancipation, a visitor to the South quoted a white bishop who believed "it . . . best for Negroes to labor. Let them remember their condition and stay in their place, like good Negroes of the past."[47] Informed by these residual beliefs, Catholic bishops granted black Catholics neither equality nor freedom. At the Second Plenary Council of 1866, Catholic bishops rejected a Vatican-backed proposal for the creation of a "prelate who would have jurisdiction on a national level for the apostolate of black Catholics."[48] The bishops' conference instead assigned black Catholics to the jurisdiction of individual white bishops. This decision left black Catholics subject to the power of white bishops who believed them unfit for freedom. Though released from formal slavery, black Catholics would remain subject to the power of white ecclesial masters. For example, while denying black Catholic requests for a black parish headed by a black priest, New Orleans Archbishop Odin acceded to Confederate soldiers' request for a special ecclesial community headed by their favorite wartime chaplain.[49]

Unable to form their own parishes, Southern black Catholics remained trapped in white-dominated parishes where they continued to be treated like servile subordinates. Insisting on disciplining the black body directly as they had during slavery, Southern white Catholics replicated racial hierarchy not by separating themselves from black Catholics but by keeping them close. Black Catholics were crammed into the often-broken-down back pews of white-dominated churches.[50] They could come forward to receive the Eucharist only after the last white communicant had returned to her seat; they were forbidden from assisting in church ceremonies, singing in church choirs, or joining parish societies.[51] And, in many places, black and white children made their First Communion during separate masses held on separate days.[52]

Notions of national identity informed notions of Catholic identity.

47. Cyprian Davis, "The Holy See and American Black Catholics: A Forgotten Chapter in the History of the American Church," *US Catholic Historian* 7, no. 2/3 (1988): 172.
48. Ibid., 157.
49. Pasquier, *Fathers on the Frontier*, 179.
50. Justin D. Poché, "The Catholic Citizens' Council: Religion and White Resistance in Post-War Louisiana," *US Catholic Historian* 24, no. 4 (2006): 50.
51. Rhonda D. Evans, Craig J. Forsyth, and Stephanie Bernard, "One Church or Two? Contemporary and Historical Views of Race Relations in One Catholic Diocese," *Sociological Spectrum* 22, no. 2 (2002): 228; Poché, "The Catholic Citizens' Council," 50.
52. Evans, Forsyth, and Bernard, "One Church or Two?," 228.

Because of their status as civil outsiders, black people were also deemed ecclesial outsiders. Lumping native-born black citizens with indigenous people who did not want to belong to the United States, in 1887, church officials founded the Commission for the Catholic Missions among the Colored People and the Indians. As lay black Catholic leader Wyatt Turner would explain several decades later, "blacks should not be placed under the same bureaucratic control as Indians who were separated onto reservations and not considered citizens."[53]

Further amplifying the whiteness of the church, white bishops refused to implement programs of evangelical outreach aimed at attracting unchurched black people, such as the preaching of Catholic revivals. Many white bishops justified their inaction by disparaging the moral character of black people. Natchez archbishop Elder argued that the "semi-barbaric" sexual incontinence of "unsettled" black women and men rendered them incapable of conforming to the church's code of sexual conduct based on monogamous marriage.[54] The U.S. bishops declined to tend to the pastoral care even of already-baptized black Catholics. During Reconstruction and its violent reversal, many of the remaining black Catholics joined Protestant denominations where they could enjoy a measure of equality.[55] Habitually apathetic to the well-being of their black sheep, Catholic bishops refused to implement policies that would intensify black Catholics' attachment to the church, such as the construction of parochial schools and hospitals that would accept black Catholics as students and patients.[56] In contrast, white bishops lavished arriving European immigrants with pastoral care, tending to their spiritual and material needs.[57] Episcopal neglect of the black soul reflected episcopal disdain for the black body.

These perceptual habits continued to operate within the white body for several decades. Decades later, Fr. John Burke, the white New York priest in charge of the Catholic Board for Negro Missions, would recite these beliefs in a letter to concerned Vatican officials. Rebuking Vatican suspicions that the U.S. church had neglected

53. Ibid., 219.

54. Ochs, *Desegregating the Altar*, 40.

55. Evans, Forsyth, and Bernard, "One Church or Two?" 228.

56. Davis, *The History of Black Catholics in the United States*, 208; Davis, "The Holy See and American Black Catholics," 173; Ochs, *Desegregating the Altar*, 39.

57. Davis, *The History of Black Catholics in the United States*, 121.

its pastoral duties to African Americans, Burke instead blamed the whiteness of the Catholic Church on the moral incompetence of black people. "One of the obstacles of evangelization" among black people, he wrote, was "low standards of morality." Many black people, he continued, "would be unable to comply with the marriage laws of the church."[58] As in the era of chattel slavery, beliefs about the body shaped beliefs about the soul. White Catholic bishops could not believe the souls of black folks suited for salvation as long as they believed their bodies unworthy of freedom. Animated by slavery's afterlife, they deemed black people unfit for and incapable of family life.

While European Catholic immigrants brought their priests over with them, the dislocations of the transatlantic slave trade and intergenerational chattel slavery had denied black people access to black priests. These white bishops could have committed to correcting the ecclesial distortions wrought by chattel slavery. They instead outsourced responsibility for the cultivation of a black priesthood onto a foreign shepherd, the Josephite Fathers of Mill Hill, England.[59] Antiblackness would prevent even these fathers from cultivating a black priesthood and forming truly good intentions. Like white Catholics in general, many Josephites believed that slavery had ruined black people's moral character. Tellingly, they did not consider the moral damage inflicted upon those white Catholics who owned slaves or fought for slavery's survival. Distrusting black capacity to exercise sexual virtue, for example, the Josephites allowed white men to enroll in their seminary at age twenty, but required that black men wait an additional ten years before beginning their priestly studies.[60] Further limiting the pool of potential black priests, in 1905, the Josephites began to admit to their seminary only the lightest-skinned mulattos.[61]

When the Josephites belatedly managed to ordain a very small number of black priests, white Catholic bishops typically blocked them from working within their dioceses. In 1907, the Archbishop of New Orleans, James Hubert Blenk, denied the Josephites' third black priest, Fr. John Plantevigne, permission to work within the diocese

58. Ibid., 201.
59. Davis, "The Holy See and American Black Catholics," 157.
60. Ibid., 70.
61. Ibid., 214.

because he did not want to upset segregationist whites.[62] Eight years later, bishop John B. Morris of Little Rock ordered the immediate removal of Fr. John Dorsey, the second black Josephite priest, from St. Peter's Parish in Pine Bluff, Arkansas.[63]

In minds molded by antiblackness, black flesh could not image an implicitly white Christ. White Catholics denied black men ordination because they deemed it both impossible to imagine and sacrilegious to allow a black male body to stand in persona Christi.[64] White Catholics further feared black priests for the threat they posed to the prevailing white supremacist social order. As one panicked priest exclaimed, "Do you mean to tell me that after you have admitted this negro thus to your . . . pulpits . . . wedding and funerals, you will still exclude him from your parlors and tables? Of course not! . . . This doctrine . . . means ultimately amalgamation."[65] The United States' aversion to interracial sexual intercourse between black men and white women had seeped into the church's ecclesiology. Although Catholic priests vowed celibacy, white Catholics feared the symbolic import even of priestly black penises. If Christ could be both imaged as black and symbolically married to an implicitly white ecclesial bride, then could not ordinary black men also take white women as wives?

Even as the afterlife of slavery impeded the ordination of men classified as black, so it made otherwise racially suspicious women and men seem certifiably white. In this way, ordination helped the partially African-descended brothers James, Augustine, Alexander Sherwood, and Patrick Francis Healy "seize a white identity."[66] Of course their comparatively light complexions made this act of clerical passing possible. But their lightness did not entirely obviate visible evidence of their African descent.[67] Priestly garments and comportment somehow made Sherwood "a black man who was, somehow, not a black man." Despite ministering to a parish teeming with racist

62. Ochs, *Desegregating the Altar*, 169.
63. Ibid., 158.
64. Ibid., 5.
65. Ibid., 52.
66. James M. O'Toole, *Passing for White: Race, Religion, and the Healy Family, 1820-1920* (Amherst: University of Massachusetts Press, 2003), 21–22, 131.
67. Ibid., 76.

whites, he was accepted by his Irish parishioners without incident.[68] They saw him not as a black man but as an ordinary priest.[69]

Lighter-skinned Augustine and Patrick passed into whiteness even more easily.[70] While head executive of Georgetown between 1873 and 1882, Patrick instructed Julia Gardiner Tyler, the widow of the aggressively pro-slavery Confederate congressman-elect and ex-U.S. President John Tyler, in Catholic doctrine.[71] Their status as celibate priests further hid their blackness by defusing the sexual threat it posed.[72] Crucially, each man's status as Catholic clerics rendered their blackness not acceptable but symbolically neutralized; they in turn downplayed their blackness, declining "publicly [to] identify with Afro-American causes."[73] These men reaffirmed their nonblackness by means of antiblackness: each believed themselves not just different from but better than black people.[74]

Upon the demise of Reconstruction, white Catholics began to impose racial power over their black co-religionists not by separating them within the white-dominated parish but by excluding them from it. Carved out as a space for black agency and self-affirmation, the creation of a black national parish in the city of New Orleans initially served as a victory for racial equality in the church.[75] But by the time the archbishop of New Orleans started opening black national parishes in rural Louisiana, the black national parish had begun to provide an excuse to exclude black Catholics from the territorial parish. Catholic dioceses across the South would follow in New Orleans' lead, confining black Catholics to separate parishes whether they liked it or not.[76]

Jim Crow reigned even outside the Catholic South.[77] Until the end

68. Ibid., 121.
69. Ibid., 227.
70. Ibid., 150.
71. Ibid., 157.
72. Ibid., 227.
73. Ochs, *Desegregating the Altar*, 10.
74. David W. Southern, *John Lafarge and the Limits of Catholic Interracialism, 1911–1963* (Baton Rouge, LA: Louisiana State University Press, 1996), 71.
75. Davis, *The History of Black Catholics in the United States*, 208–9.
76. Mark Newman, "The Catholic Church in Arkansas and Desegregation, 1946-1988," *The Arkansas Historical Quarterly* 66, no. 3 (2007): 296; Evans, Forsyth, and Bernard, "One Church or Two?," 226.
77. For more on the ways in which black Catholics responded to and resisted racial segregation, see Cecilia A. Moore, "Dealing with Desegregation: Black and White Responses to the Desegregation of Raleigh, North Carolina, 1953" and Katrina M. Sanders, "Black Catholic Clergy and the Struggle for Civil Rights," in *Uncommon Faithfulness: The Black Catholic Experience*, ed.

of the 1950s, Catholic sisters in far northwestern Seattle relegated nonwhite patients to separate hospital wards. While accepting white Protestants and Jews, all twenty-five of Midwestern Chicago's Catholic hospitals banned black people as patients until the middle of this decade.[78] When forced to admit black patients, Chicago's Catholic hospitals acted like Arkansans, stowing them in all-black floors or hiding them in private rooms.[79] And, although they refused to hire black people as physicians and only rarely accepted black people as nurses, they had no problem employing black people as nurses' aides, kitchen help, or laundrywomen. White people feared not intimacy with black people, but their non-servility. Nearly one hundred years after the end of chattel slavery, Midwestern white Catholics still believed blacks were their subordinates. Nor did antiblackness supremacist habits necessarily progressively diminish over time. Around the turn of the century, Catholic University stopped admitting black students, keeping their doors shut to black students until 1936.[80] The University of Notre Dame, located only ninety miles from Chicago, did not enroll its first black student until 1944.[81] And despite being located just outside Philadelphia, Villanova University did not graduate its first black student until 1950.[82]

The habits of slaveocracy proved hard to kick, living on in the church's corporate body long after the era of chattel slavery had ended. During the era of chattel slavery, intimacy with blacks provided whites the pleasures and power of slaveownership both directly and vicariously. For this reason, white people did all they could to keep black people from running away from them.[83] But Reconstruction threatened to transform racial intimacy into a mechanism of racial equality. Only then did white people begin striving to keep black people away from them. White Catholics, even the most sacra-

M. Shawn Copeland, LaReine-Marie Mosely, and Albert J. Raboteau (Maryknoll, NY: Orbis, 2009).

78. Barbra Mann Wall, *American Catholic Hospitals: A Century of Changing Markets and Missions* (New Brunswick, NJ: Rutgers University Press, 2011), 77, 84.

79. Poché, "The Catholic Citizens' Council," 59–60.

80. Davis, *The History of Black Catholics in the United States*, 234.

81. Charles H. Martin, *Benching Jim Crow: The Rise and Fall of the Color Line in Southern College Sports, 1890-1980* (Champaign: University of Illinois Press, 2010), 69.

82. Casey Gradisar, "The Race Game," *The Villanovan*, March 17, 2004, accessed August 9, 2013, http://www.villanovan.com/2.7323/the-race-game-1.1025139#.UgUt7D7wGkI.

83. For more on white aversion to black fugitivity and the way in which black fugitivity possesses a unique capacity to overturn slavery's afterlife, see Katie Walker Grimes, *Fugitive Saints: Catholicism and the Politics of Slavery* (Minneapolis, MN: Fortress Press, 2017).

mentally active, proved not just susceptible to, but happily constituted by, the habituating power of antiblackness. The white church was not coerced into adopting an antiblackness supremacist comportment; it accepted antiblackness supremacy voluntarily. Fearing black freedom much more than it ever hated slavery, the church neither struggled nor second-guessed itself.[84] It certainly did not regret.

84. Aquinas, *Summa Theologiae* I–II.53.1 ad 1.

6.

Racial Segregation as a Corporate Habit of Antiblackness Supremacy in the Body of Christ

Habits, Aquinas explains, "are difficult to change."[1] Just as the habits of slaveocracy persisted after slavery's abolition, the habits of Jim Crow would carry on even in the absence of formal policies of mandatory segregation. In continuing to animate the world, the afterlife of slavery has continued to habituate the church. New means to the highly desired and esteemed end of segregation were easy to find. Receiving its identity from the racially segregated space it inhabited, the Catholic parish became where it lived. Performing the habit-forming practices of antiblack racial segregation not sporadically, but as a corporate body, the Northern Catholic parish first resisted and then fled racial integration, escaping to the suburb only when it ran out of unintegrated urban space.

The territorial character of the Catholic parish would seem to have equipped it with the capacity to overturn or at least resists regnant patterns of antiblackness supremacist habituation. But, in truth, the spatially situated character of the church's parochial body rendered it highly susceptible to the place-produced and body-shaping character of antiblackness supremacy. In the opening decades of the twentieth century, "the Catholic world . . . was disciplined

1. Aquinas, *Summa Theologiae* I–II.49.2 ad 3.

and local."[2] And Catholic parishes were so disciplined largely because they were so local. Unlike the synagogue or Protestant parish, the Catholic parish existed only as a set of spatial boundaries; it could not be moved. For this reason, Catholic pastors encouraged homeownership among their parishioners; Catholics owned homes at higher rates than non-Catholic whites of similar class background.[3]

Due to its uniquely spatial character, the place-bound Catholic parish also helped to organize and shape the Northern city. Even non-Catholic urbanites referred to neighborhoods by the name of the parish that anchored it.[4] Especially after the turn of the twentieth century, the residentially dense Northern city began to manufacture social identity spatially, preserving racial difference through residential distance.[5] The Northern city became Catholic just as it became racially segregated. Rather than harming the Catholic parish, these spatially divisive practices bound white parishioners to its corporate body more tightly.[6] Spatialized antiblackness did not simply shape the church's corporate body; it strengthened it. As a result, white Catholic parishes did not simply desire racial purity; they came to rely upon it. They could comprise a corporate body only if they kept black people out. Catholic parochial participation in residential segregation represents both a betrayal of its territorially inclusive character and the unsurprising result of it.

GOD, COUNTRY, ANTIBLACKNESS: ETHNICITY AS INCORPORATION INTO ECCLESIAL LIFE

The spatialized Catholic parish helped to incorporate Catholics into spatialized antiblackness in three primary ways: by assimilating European immigrants into antiblack whiteness, by instilling in its white members the habits of homeowning whiteness, and by simply inhabiting racially segregated space. During the late nineteenth and early twentieth century, the Catholic parish operated as the "way-station

2. John T. McGreevy, *Parish Boundaries: The Catholic Encounter with Race in the Twentieth-Century Urban North* (Chicago: University of Chicago Press, 1998), 38.
3. McGreevy, *Parish Boundaries*, 19.
4. Ibid., 13.
5. Ibid., 5, 15.
6. Jamie T. Phelps, "Joy Came in the Morning: Risking Death for Resurrection," in *A Troubling in My Soul: Womanist Perspectives on Suffering and Evil*, ed. Emilie Townes (Maryknoll, NY: Orbis, 1993), 57.

of ethnicity and Americanization."[7] In order to demonstrate the way in which ethnicity, like American identity, has always portended antiblackness, this chapter first tracks the history of three Catholic immigrant groups, the Germans, the Italians, and the Polish. It then outlines the ways in which Catholic corporate patriotism also amplified Catholic antiblackness among white Catholics of all ethnic backgrounds.

Germans began arriving to the United States in significant numbers in the middle of the nineteenth century: they resisted cultural assimilation for several decades after their arrival. The Catholic parish assisted them in this project, helping German immigrants and their native-born children and grandchildren preserve a sense of German identity. To this end, German parochial schools taught class in German, and German national parishes said Mass in the language of the homeland.[8] The eruption of the First World War would mark a turning point in German-American self-understanding: nationalists burned German-language books, outlawed the use of the German language for any purpose, and lynched a German immigrant in Illinois.[9] In order to defend Germans against these violent outbursts, Catholic parishes attempted to performatively argue the compatibility between German and American identities. To this end, in 1919, one German national parish began its celebration of the feast of St. Boniface, the apostle of Germany, by singing the U.S. national anthem. Other German parishes knitted socks for American soldiers encamped in muddy trenches. Just as the German national parish first helped ethnic Germans remain German while living in America, so it helped them to refashion German-ness from a non-American identity to a type of American-ness.[10]

But American-ness has never been raceless. In becoming U.S.-Americans, German immigrants also became not just commonly white, but antiblack. Prior to the First World War, Germans living in the United States perceived themselves as racially German much more than they considered themselves members of a larger white

7. Stephen Joseph Shaw, *The Catholic Parish as a Way-Station of Ethnicity and Americanization: Chicago's Germans and Italians, 1903-1939*, (Brooklyn, NY: Carlson, 1991).
8. Ibid., 34, 38, 42, 46.
9. Nell Irvin Painter, *The History of White People*, reprint (New York: W. W. Norton, 2011), 317.
10. Shaw, *The Catholic Parish as a Way-Station*, 97.

race.[11] So did many U.S.-Americans. For example, in 1755, Benjamin Franklin identified the Russians, Swedes, and Germans, as generally possessing "what we call a swarthy Complexion" and therefore concluded that the "Saxons" and English alone comprise "the principal Body of White People on the Face of the Earth."[12] At the turn of the twentieth century, most observers no longer doubted that Germans were white; they instead considered Germans but one of several so-called "European races."[13] But soon even these intra-European racial differences would melt away: contrastive encounter with black people who streamed north during the era of Great Migration would solidify German national inclusion by allowing them to acquire forms of pan-European unity at black expense. While Germans mixed with other European groups in their parishes and neighborhoods, black migrants were shut out of both.[14] In sponsoring minstrel shows featuring Irish and German parishioners wearing blackface, Catholic parishes further enabled German-Americans to bond with other European whites through the spectacle of the hyper-visible but physically absented black body.[15]

Antiblackness supremacy would clear a path to common whiteness and shared citizenship for even Italian immigrants, who initially occupied a much more racially despised position than their German predecessors ever had.[16] During his 1920 testimony before the House Committee on Immigration, the editor of the influential *Saturday Evening Post* framed his opposition to Southern and Eastern European immigration as a "matter of race," insisting that "these alien peoples are temperamentally and racially unfitted for easy assimilation."[17] Another prominent magazine man feared the way in which the arrival of "damned half-negro Italians, half-Mongol Jews, and

11. Russell Andrew Kazal, *Becoming Old Stock: The Paradox of German-American Identity* (Princeton: Princeton University Press, 2004), 126.
12. Orm Øverland, "Becoming White in 1881: An Immigrant Acquires an American Identity," *Journal of American Ethnic History* 23, no. 4 (2004): 132.
13. Joseph Deniker, *The Races of Man: An Outline of Anthropology and Ethnography* (New York: Charles Scribner's Sons, 1906), 339.
14. Russell A. Kazal, "The Interwar Origins of the White Ethnic: Race, Residence, and German Philadelphia, 1917-1939," *Journal of American Ethnic History* 23, no. 4 (2004): 78–131.
15. Ibid., 111.
16. Peter G. Vellon, *A Great Conspiracy against Our Race: Italian Immigrant Newspapers and the Construction of Whiteness in the Early 20th Century* (New York: New York University Press, 2014), 5; John Higham, *Strangers in the Land: Patterns of American Nativism, 1860-1925* (New Brunswick, NJ: Rutgers University Press, 2002), 66.
17. Painter, *The History of White People*, 301.

thoroughly bastardized Greeks and Levantines" would spawn the creation of "a new composition race of people wholly different from the Americans of the present day." As such, immigration restriction represented "a matter of life or death for the American people."[18] Affirming these anti-Italian sentiments, nativist politicians passed a series of quotas in order to limit their immigration to the United States. Although they were never treated as poorly as black people were, racialized Italian immigrants endured lynching, terrorism by nativist mobs, and job discrimination.[19]

Despite being initially unwelcome, Italians became white Americans just like the Germans had—with the assistance of both spatialized antiblackness and the uniquely spatial Catholic parish. The rules of immigrant assimilation stipulate that, before these swarthy Southern European immigrants could be accepted as truly U.S.-American, they first had to swap their village-based affiliations for a collective Italian identity.[20] According them Italian national parishes and establishing Italian seminaries, bishops facilitated this transformation.[21] Further affirming a shared sense of national identity, parochial Italian societies gathered together in annual citywide banquets.[22] Even as it helped to instill a sense of pan-Italian nationalism, the Catholic parish helped them retain a spatial connection to their old village-based identities, organizing processions in celebration of the traditional *feste*.[23] Even these seemingly innocent processes entangled them in antiblackness as the Catholic parish re-created the Italian village within neighborhoods in which African Americans were not allowed to live.

The Catholic parish also helped unite them with other nonblacks. Even the Italian national parish contained high rates of white ethnic diversity; all white parishes, whether national or territorial, excluded black people. Italian immigrants received treatment in Catholic hospitals reserved for white patients only and assistance from settlement houses that refused to include black residents.[24] In so doing, the Catholic parish also helped elevate Italian-Americans above native-born black people. Italian-Americans would be slurred as "guineas" both for their purported corporeal resemblance to blacks and

18. Ibid., 303–4.
19. Higham, *Strangers in the Land*, 66, 91, 264.
20. McGreevy, *Parish Boundaries*, 28.
21. Shaw, *The Catholic Parish as a Way-Station*, 111.
22. Ibid., 112.
23. Ibid., 114.
24. Ibid., 52–53.

southern Italy's geographical proximity to black Africa.[25] But like the Irish before them, Italian-Americans used the minstrel stage to performatively disprove perceptions of blackishness. Hosting minstrel shows in which Italian immigrants performed in blackface before a nonblack audience, the Catholic parish helped even the swarthiest Italians demonstrate the un-Africanity of their bodies. Although Italian immigrants, especially darker-skinned Southern Italians, endured racialized mistreatment from racial nativists, they were reliably differentiated from and elevated above black people from the moment they stepped on U.S.-American soil.

Like other immigrant groups, Italian-Americans internalized these habits of antiblackness, using the Catholic parish to distance themselves from blackness. For example, the Italian-American pastor of Chicago's St. Philip's Italian national parish kept his church closed to black Catholics for nearly four decades.[26] Justifying his actions, he insisted that "blacks could not coexist with Americans or Sicilians." His Italian parishioners agreed with him. As African Americans began to move into St. Philip's parochial boundaries around the year 1928, Italians began to move out. The archdiocese of Chicago accommodated the white flight of all the city's Italians, building them replacement parishes across the city.[27] Like other immigrants to the Americas, Italian-Americans would escape their status as racially suspicious aliens through contrastive encounter with the absented black body.

Like the Irish, Germans, and Italians, Polish immigrants were also Americanized by their encounter with the spatial afterlife of slavery. While not slurred for nonwhiteness, Polish immigrants did incur a type of ethno-racial stigma based upon their purported rural backwardness. Initially, Polish immigrants generally resisted Irish Catholic attempts to recruit them as allies in the bloody antiblack rampages of 1919.[28] And as late as 1927, researchers in Buffalo described the attitude of Polish immigrants to the city's relatively small black population as one of "indifference."[29]

25. Richard Alba, "Whiteness Just Isn't Enough," *Sociological Forum* 22, no. 2. (Blackwell, 2007): 234.

26. Shaw, *The Catholic Parish as a Way-Station*, 108.

27. Ibid., 105–7.

28. James R. Barrett and David R. Roediger, "The Irish and the 'Americanization' of the 'New Immigrants' in the Streets and in the Churches of the Urban United States, 1900-1930," *Journal of American Ethnic History* 24, no. 4 (2005): 15.

29. Kazal, "The Interwar Origins of the White Ethnic," 80.

But spatialized antiblackness eventually overcame their racial apathy. Less than twenty years later, this same Buffalo Polish community would organize under the leadership of Monsignor Alexander Pitass to block the construction of a black housing project on that city's east side. Polish-Americans also changed their orientation toward antiblack violence. They enthusiastically participated in the numerous antiblack riots that rocked the industrial North during the Second World War and its immediate aftermath. In St. Louis, Polish Catholic incorporation into the spatial afterlife of slavery appears to have occurred even earlier as in 1916 that city's Polish-American Association helped enact an ordinance segregating blacks from whites.[30]

Despite significant differences in their immigrant experiences, these three cases point to a relation between immigrant incorporation and antiblackness supremacy. Ethnicity paradoxically emphasizes how certain groups differ from each other in order to accentuate how they all differ from black people. In cultivating an ethnicity, an individual declares herself the descendant not of black slaves but of immigrants. While ethnic otherness serves to incorporate immigrants into both the church and nation, antiblackness supremacy strives to keep black people excluded from and subordinated within them.

In addition to encouraging European-descended Catholics to cling to notions of ethnic belonging, the Catholic Church further attempted to bind parishioners together as Catholics by binding them together as Americans.[31] But notions of U.S. citizenship had always been linked to whiteness.[32] Given this, Catholic nationalism did not compel white Catholics to treat even black soldiers like brothers. To the contrary, in the aftermath of both World Wars, white Catholics rioted fiercely in order to ensure that black heroism did not undo the link between citizenship and white supremacy.[33] In 1968, segregationist Chicago priest Fr. Lawler told a crowd of 2,500 unsettled whites that "all of your work as soldiers, sailors, and marines to defend your country becomes meaningless if you cannot fight for your own backyard" by keeping black people out of it.[34] Rather than binding

30. Philippe Bourgeois, "If You're Not Black You're White: A History of Ethnic Relations in St. Louis," *City & Society* 3, no. 2 (1989): 122.

31. Shaw, *The Catholic Parish as a Way-Station*, 15, 25; James R. Barrett, *The Irish Way: Becoming American in the Multiethnic City* (London: Penguin, 2012), 74.

32. Barrett and Roediger, "The Irish and the 'Americanization' of the 'New Immigrants,'" 4.

33. Cameron McWhirter, *Red Summer: The Summer of 1919 and the Awakening of Black America* (New York: Henry Holt, 2011); McGreevy, *Parish Boundaries*, 91.

34. McGreevy, *Parish Boundaries,* 232.

them together with black people, patriotism convinced Catholics of their superiority to native-born black women and men.[35]

Corporate Catholic practices did not simply tolerate this association between whiteness and U.S. citizenship; they encouraged it. Brought into relief against the backdrop of nonblackness, these ethnic, immigrant Catholics continued to appear more authentically American than native-born black Catholics even when Catholic officials like Mundelein began to suppress ethnic self-identification in favor a common pan-Americanism. While European-descended Catholics would be funneled into ethnically undifferentiated territorial parishes, Northern black Catholics would remain isolated in all black parishes.[36] Catholic bishops refused to force white Catholics to admit black Catholics into their parishes.[37]

Further excluding black Catholics from his project of Americanization, in between the First and Second World War, Chicago Archbishop Mundelein encouraged European-descended Americans to mingle together in archdiocesan organizations and societies. Yet many of these societies, most notably the Knights of Columbus, remained closed to black men until the 1960s.[38] Further binding European Catholics together, Mundelein opened seminaries open to whites of all backgrounds but refused to either permit black entrance into existing archdiocesan seminaries or to open a separate seminary for black priests in training. Mundelein also kept already-ordained black priests out of Chicago's black parishes. In 1934, Mundelein refused to allow four black priests recently ordained by the Divine Word Missionaries to work in the black parishes located in the city's rapidly expanding Black Belt. In the North, Mundelein argued, black people transformed into a "new species of negro," marked by "constant agitation for social equality with whites." Casting Northern

35. Chicago's archbishop at the time, John Cody, attempted to stem the tide of his parishioners' antiblackness. For example, after meeting with Martin Luther King and the SCLC, Cody mandated that every Chicago parish hear an anti-segregationist message during their Sunday homilies. Because antiblackness supremacy operated as a corporate vice, however, these efforts to morally persuade, though laudable, were not enough to overturn it. John T. McGreevy, "Racial Justice and the People of God: The Second Vatican Council, the Civil Rights Movement, and American Catholics," *Religion and American Culture: A Journal of Interpretation* 2, no. 4 (Summer 1994): 234.

36. Barrett, *The Irish Way*, 73.

37. Karen J. Johnson, "The Universal Church in the Segregated City: Doing Catholic Interracialism in Chicago, 1915-1963" (PhD diss., Rice University, 2013), 46.

38. Mary J. Oates, *The Catholic Philanthropic Tradition in America* (Bloomington: Indiana University Press, 1995), 65.

blacks as "sassy niggers," he believed "black priests should remain in the South throughout their priestly careers."[39] Mundelein eventually managed to help convince the bishop of Lafayette, Louisiana to place the four Divine Word priests within his diocesan boundaries.[40] As intended, Southern customs kept these priests in their place. Subject to the supervision of a white priest and forbidden from ministering to white Catholics, they served under the strictures of Jim Crow. They could neither "offer a hand to shake on meeting white priests" nor attend functions at the diocesan's cathedral.[41]

Mundelein did not simply separate black Catholics within the church's corporate body; he excluded them from it. Even as Chicago's Black Belt continued to expand throughout the 1920s, Mundelein did not open more black national parishes.[42] Just as black Northerners would be crammed into overcrowded slums, so would they be consigned to undersized parochial space. While these black parishes were formally called "national parishes," in truth they operated much more like ghettoes. Descended from natally alienated slaves, black Catholics could neither claim belonging to a foreign nation nor fulfill Mundelein's definition of a group both worthy and capable of Americanization.

Although antiblackness supremacy would bring white ethnics closer together, in truth, even at their most divided, white ethnics were never as far apart from each other as they were from black people. Polish and Lithuanian Catholics resented Irish episcopal monopoly and bitterly resented Irish attempts to force them to use English in their national parochial schools.[43] Despite this, in the secular arena, Polish Catholics still sided with the Irish against black people.[44] National parishes also contained relatively high rates of ethnic intermixture. For example, in 1920, Philadelphia's German national parish of St. Ignatius counted a population nearly 25 percent non-German.[45] While European national parishes allowed the entrance of a significant minority of ethnic outsiders, they panicked at the presence of even one black body in their midst.[46] White Catholics were free to

39. Ochs, *Desegregating the Altar*, 326.
40. Ibid., 337–42.
41. Ibid., 341.
42. Johnson, *The Universal Church in the Segregated City*, 52.
43. Shaw, *The Catholic Parish as a Way-Station*, 27; McGreevy, *Parish Boundaries*, 12.
44. McGreevy, *Parish Boundaries*, 232.
45. Kazal, "The Interwar Origins of the White Ethnic," 110.
46. Ibid., 109.

come and go; black Catholics suffered confinement to parishes not of their choosing. While the Catholic parish brought whites of all national backgrounds together, it helped to keep white and black Catholics apart. And so did the ethnically mixed but racially segregated Catholic parochial school.[47] The parochial school separated black children from the body of Christ. In the United States, the Catholic parochial school has long played a vital role in incorporating individual Catholics into the body of Christ.[48] But parish schools remained largely for whites only for much of the twentieth century, and black Catholic children often were forced to enroll in public schools.[49]

Parochial patterns conformed to secular ones.[50] While white ethnics often gathered into residential clusters, they never lived in complete social isolation as ghettoized black people did; they always shared residential space with other ethnic groups. They also blended bodies. Myths of interethnic antagonism notwithstanding, whites in the 1940s married interethnically at higher rates than whites marry black people today. By the 1960s, the remaining barriers to inter-European amalgamation had fallen away: today, most U.S.-Americans classed as "white" count at least two, and often many more, European countries as ancestral homelands.[51] While almost every white Catholic qualifies as thoroughly amalgamated ethnically, the overwhelming majority of nonblack Catholics have managed to hang on to their immigrant ancestors' nonblackness.[52] Racial segregation kept white bodies white.

White Catholic allegiance with other white Catholics cannot be dismissed as mere Catholic chauvinism. White Catholics rejected even black Catholics. For example, in the 1920s, a Brooklyn pastor advocated for the founding of a St. Peter Claver church for black Catholics, arguing that "our people "do not want the negroes in their church, in their homes, or their neighborhood."[53] They will-

47. McGreevy, *Parish Boundaries*, 34.

48. Ibid., 57.

49. Davis, *The History of Black Catholics*, 206.

50. Phelps, "Joy Came in the Morning," 57.

51. Richard D. Alba, "The Twilight of Ethnicity Among American Catholics of European Ancestry," *Annals of the American Academy of Political and Social Science* 454 (March 1, 1981): 93.

52. Michael Hout and Joshua R. Goldstein, "How 4.5 Million Irish Immigrants Became 40 Million Irish Americans: Demographic and Subjective Aspects of the Ethnic Composition of White Americans," *American Sociological Review* (1994): 65.

53. McGreevy, *Parish Boundaries*, 55–56.

ingly accepted the bodies of white Protestants, and, to a lesser extent, white Jews. Despite the fact that white Protestants had been the sole group to inflict chauvinistic violence upon white Catholics, they did not organize collectively to evict these non-Catholic newcomers from their residential spaces; these Protestants appeared an annoyance rather than a mortal threat.[54] Even before the Second Vatican Council softened Catholic attitudes towards Protestants and Jews, World War II–era Catholics, who were overwhelmingly white, married non-Catholics four times as often as white people wed black people today.[55] Race not only trumped religion, it decided what shape religion would take.

THE CATHOLIC PARISH AND THE HABITS OF HOMEOWNING WHITENESS

The spatialized Catholic parish helped to incorporate Catholics into spatialized antiblackness supremacy in a second way. Because white Catholics tended to incorporate themselves into a parish by means of homeownership, parochial membership reinforced the habits of homeowning whiteness. Reflecting the spatially particular character of the territorial Catholic parish, white Catholics, even when lower middle class, owned homes at much higher rates than their non-Catholic counterparts.[56] But homeownership had always been uniquely biased against black people. Thus, when Catholics incorporated themselves into their parish through homeownership, they also intensified their indoctrination into a system of white supremacy founded upon antiblackness.

Like other whites, disproportionately homeowning white Catholics abided by the racial theory of property values. And since the parish and neighborhood occupied the same space, white Catholics feared that black people would destroy their neighborhoods as well as their parishes. As early as 1907, the predominately white residents of Gesu Parish in North Philadelphia felt threatened by the "small pockets of blacks" living in their midst. Many parish

54. Eileen M. McMahon, *What Parish Are You From?: A Chicago Irish Community and Race Relations* (Lexington: University Press of Kentucky, 1996), 117.

55. Richard D. Alba, "The Twilight of Ethnicity," 93; Roland G. Fryer, "Guess Who's Been Coming to Dinner? Trends in Interracial Marriage over the 20th Century," *Journal of Economic Perspectives* 21, no. 2 (May 2007): 71–90.

56. McGreevy, *Parish Boundaries*, 18.

members believed that "close proximity of a larger number of the colored people might injure the Gesu Church."[57] Four decades later, Gesu's whites continued to keep even Catholic black people out, commanding them to join all-black Our Lady of the Blessed Sacrament instead. Fr. Thomas Love, Gesu's Jesuit superior, justified parochial policy thusly: "We have nothing against negroes but we cannot stand by and see property which represents the life-savings of some of our oldest parishioners become almost valueless or go to ruin."[58]

Under the influence of the racial theory of property values, white Catholics mistook self-fulfilling prophecy for inevitable fact of life: in this way, St. Sabina's Fr. Riordan believed "when whites were [in a certain neighborhood], it was an old neighborhood, but a good neighborhood. And then [blacks] took it over and it was burned out . . . they were ghettos right away."[59] One Irish-American ex-parishioner of Southwest Chicago's St. Sabina's recalls, "when I got [to the parish] in 1963, the black movement was right at the border. There was one black family that lived in the parish at that time. So it was like a 'the barbarians are at our border! The Huns are at the wall!' kind of experience."[60]

The habits of homeowning whiteness also led white Catholics to believe themselves entirely self-made. Rather than recipients of racially biased federal assistance, white Catholic homeowners styled themselves independent, hardworking, and self-sacrificing. Culpably ignorant of their reliance on federal assistance, white Catholics tended to believe themselves victims of black progress. For example, in the wake of Martin Luther King Jr.'s mid-sixties visit to the city, Monsignor Edward Burke, former chancellor of the Archdiocese of Chicago and acting pastor of a northwest-side urban parish, wrote an article in his parish bulletin in which he cried,

> When we fight for the rights of the Negro, we cannot overlook the rights of the white person. He has been forced to support, unaided, himself and his family. If he owns property, he purchased it by the sweat of his brow and is a true Christian when he asks that his possessions be not disturbed.[61]

57. Ibid., 250.
58. Ibid., 252.
59. Ibid., 159.
60. McMahon, *What Parish Are You From?*, 157.
61. McGreevy, "Racial Justice and the People of God," 236.

White supremacist mythologies of unaided white triumph over a hardscrabble social past disguised white power as white victimhood.

Culpably ignorant of the coercive character of racially segregated housing patterns, many Catholic whites perceived the relatively moderate achievements of the Civil Rights Movement as brutal displays of violent power. In a letter written to the nationally renowned integrationist priest, a white Catholic from Philadelphia raged, "It is not fair to shove people of another race down our throats."[62] From Milwaukee, another white Catholic expressed bitterness, "I can remember the first Mass that was read in the new [formerly all-white] church. Even then it was a sacrifice. . . . They [whites] have [now] been chased out of their homes by negroes, and now they and you are desgrating [sic] the church they built."[63] Just as white Catholics denied their reliance on federal assistance, so they denied their power. They did not choose to flee integrating neighborhoods; they were forced to. In their eyes, integrating blacks, not segregationist whites, held the bulk of the racial power. Because Catholic whites performed segregationist practices in accordance with the promptings of deeply embodied racial habits, their residential flight probably did feel unchosen. Vicious habits are difficult to disrupt. Sitting within the human person like a second nature, they often operate at a level deeper than consciousness. They are nearly irresistible.

Third, and finally, the Catholic parish served to incorporate European-descended Catholics into antiblackness supremacy simply by obeying its spatial logic. The place-based Catholic parish spun exceptionally thick social connections among its members.[64] But because parochial boundaries also operated as racial barriers, white Catholics belonged to social communities marked for whites only. As Falls recognized in the 1930s, "the lack of unity" evidenced between black and white Catholics is "partially due to the fact that black Catholics [could] not fully participate in the geographical parishes in which they lived."[65] Collective Catholic practices affirmed and reified secular patterns of racialized living. Replanting place-based forms of European Catholicism in the increasingly segregated soil of the Northern city, the Catholic parish cultivated the habits

62. McGreevy, *Parish Boundaries*, 204.

63. McGreevy, "Racial Justice and the People of God," 242.

64. McGreevy, *Parish Boundaries*, 24, 26.

65. Johnson, "The Universal Church in the Segregated City," 111.

of antiblackness supremacy.[66] Encouraging the "new" immigrants to remain in parochial space, the Catholic parish helped to place them on a trajectory of antiblackness supremacist habituation.

ANTIBLACKNESS SUPREMACY AS A TRULY CORPORATE VICE

Whites did not simply belong to a parish; they acted as one, performing segregation in coordinated fashion, with bishops, priests, and laity synchronizing themselves hierarchically. The church pursued segregation as a synchronized body: bishops, priests, and lay Catholics fell in line. Only a very small minority of relatively powerless white Catholics questioned their church's segregationist habits; even fewer organized to disrupt them. The more removed Catholic officials stood from the everyday embodied practices of antiblackness supremacy, the sooner they denounced them, at least in the abstract. Vatican officials pressured U.S. bishops, albeit unsuccessfully, to do right by black Catholics as early as the late nineteenth century.

But just as U.S. bishops ignored papal condemnations of slavery, so did they dismiss papal concerns about racial injustice within the U.S.-American church.[67] In Chicago, they did not admit aspiring black priests to the diocese's seminaries until 1942. In the Deep South, they did not ordain a black man until 1952. They did not forbid the racial segregation of Eucharistic reception until 1942; they did not issue a pastoral letter condemning segregation as sinful until 1956.[68] They stayed silent in the face of the vicious antiblack riots of 1919 and they made no public statement condemning the many acts of collective antiblack violence that occurred following the Second World War. The bishops ousted a segregationist leader from the priesthood on only one occasion.[69] Lay white Catholics rightly interpreted episcopal silence as tacit approval. As a white participant in the Trumbull Home riots of 1953–1954 would exclaim, "we mean to get the jigs out, that's all. . . . I'm a Catholic . . . and a good one, I'd say. But

66. Barrett and Roediger, "The Irish and the 'Americanization' of the 'New Immigrants,'" 16.
67. R. Bentley Anderson, "Prelates, Protest, and Public Opinion: Catholic Opposition to Desegregation, 1947-1955," *Journal of Church and State* 46 (2004): 618.
68. Ibid., 643.
69. Megan Graydon, "Priest and Ex-Chicago Alderman Dies," *Chicago Tribune*, November 13, 2013, accessed July 22, 2015, http://articles.chicagotribune.com/2013-11-13/news/ct-met-francis-lawlor-obit-20131113_1_chicago-area-the-rev-lawlor.

the Church hasn't got a right to tell me who I should live next to. And the Church knows it too, because it hasn't said anything about Trumbull Park."[70]

In addition to permitting white acts of antiblackness, Catholic bishops sometimes actively stamped out even meager attempts by statistically anomalous white Catholic priests to make black Catholics feel welcome in their parishes. For example, in 1949, the pastor of St. Columbanus parish refused to extend a welcome to a newly arrived black Catholic couple, Mr. and Mrs. Roscoe Johnson, because "he'd talked to the Chancery Office and they said he shouldn't do it.'"[71] Nearly fifteen years later, in 1963, one Milwaukee priest similarly lamented, "we would love to join the march on Washington but the Chancery office has said that it is very 'rash and imprudent' and has forbidden all priests from participating in it."[72]

During the century after abolition, white Catholic priests promoted the church's segregationist habits with similar uniformity, engaging in pro-black action only rarely.[73] In the Catholic-dominated urban North, priests exercised ample power, shaping both urban politics and ecclesial affairs.[74] Habituated by long-term residence in racially segregated space, they often used this power to protect the segregated character of their place-bound Catholic parishes. During the 1940s, priests in Baltimore, Buffalo, St. Louis, and South Bend, Indiana led ecumenical protests against placing federally funded housing units for African Americans in white neighborhoods. In the late 1940s, Irish-American priest Fr. F. J. Quinn, of Chicago's St. Ambrose parish, often interlaced segregationist diatribes within Sunday homilies. For example, during mass one morning, Quinn sounded the following alarm: "The Niggers have taken over Corpus Christi Church, Holy Angels, and St. Ann's and they are now trying to take over this church." Reassuring the congregation he had just

70. Alan Paton, *The Negro in America Today: A Firsthand Report* (National Association for the Advancement of Colored People, 1954).

71. McGreevy, *Parish Boundaries*, 93.

72. Ibid., 197.

73. For a rare exception to the rule of clerical antiblackness, see Richard Gribble, "A Conservative Voice for Black Catholics: The Case of James Martin Gillis, C.S.P.," *The Catholic Historical Review* 85, no. 3 (July 1, 1999): 420–34. Despite their advocacy on behalf of black Catholics, well-known white priests like John LaFarge and William Markoe still adopted a paternalistic tone toward blacks. They promoted black ecclesial inclusion more much than they supported true racial equality. See David W. Southern, *John LaFarge and the Limits of Catholic Interracialism, 1911-1963* (Baton Rouge: Louisiana State University Press, 1996), 113, 134, 138, 141.

74. McGreevy, *Parish Boundaries*, 124.

roused to attention, he then promised, "if it's left to me, they will not" succeed in gaining entrance to their sacred white space. Identifying antiblackness as ethnic duty, he explained that "our forefathers from Ireland came over here and prepared the way for us in this church." For this reason, he concluded, "the Niggers are not going to run us out."[75] Monsignor Patrick Molloy of St. Leo's church in Chicago similarly acted to personally repel black people from his parish throughout the 1950s and 60s. In addition to "watching local real estate transactions" for signs of racial change, he barred black people from entering parochial space, either as schoolchildren or as churchgoers.[76]

The white Catholic laity also enacted segregation automatically and as a coordinated body, comprising a significant majority of participants in the antiblack riots that shook the urban North in the aftermath of the Second World War. In Chicago alone, white mobs laid siege to the residences of their new black neighbors on six occasions.[77] In 1951, a mob of 5,000 rallied against the arrival of just one black family in the majority Catholic Chicago suburb of Cicero. Members of the crowd wore their Catholicism on their bodies: "observers described . . . boys wearing letter sweaters from Catholic high schools and girls fingering crosses around their necks." A man in the crowd quipped, "I don't want those jigs sitting in the same pew with me."[78] Two years later, in another heavily Catholic Chicago suburb called South Deering, whites waged several years of guerilla warfare against the first black residents of the Trumbull Park Homes housing project.[79] White Catholics in Detroit violently protested the integration of a new housing project named after Sojourner Truth. In these riots, the corporately antiblack parochial body appears visible, organized, and cohesive.

Given this coordination among all sectors of the church's hierarchically arranged corporate body, segregationist Catholics believed church officials had their backs. As one frustrated Catholic Interracial Council staffer sighed in the late 1940s, "it seems that it has come to the point where Catholics believe our church condones and approves

75. Ibid., 93.
76. Ibid., 131.
77. N. Caroline Harney and James Charlton, "The Siege on South Peoria Street," *Chicago Reader*, January 13, 2000, accessed July 22, 2015, http://www.chicagoreader.com/chicago/the-siege-on-south-peoria-street/Content?oid=901207.
78. McGreevy, *Parish Boundaries*, 97.
79. Ibid., 98.

segregation."[80] Within the Catholic Church, these interracial organizations remained the exception and not the rule.[81] While many white Catholics participated in segregated church societies like the Knights of Columbus, only a few white Catholics ever committed themselves to the cause of interracial activism. But actions qualify as expressions of habits only when they proceed with regularity. Just as one venial sin does not unmake virtue, so sporadic displays of moral goodness do not unravel vice. A body is what it does most of the time.[82]

Catholic parishes enacted racial segregation not just as corporate bodies, but also for the sake of them. Recognizing the threat integration posed to the cohesion of the church's corporately white body, in the late 1950s, Chicago Archbishop Meyer asked "community organization to ensure that negroes do gain access to our communities, but not to the degree that we merely extend the boundaries of the racial ghetto."[83] Recognizing that white Catholics would corporately tolerate only token integration, Meyer strove to disperse black people in scattered fashion across a wide swatch of white neighborhoods. White Catholic parishes, he conceded, could exist only as predominately white bodies. The white Catholic laity trusted that clerical power would hold the church's white parochial body in place. During the early 1940s, a white mob in the heavily Irish Philadelphia neighborhood of Kensington mobilized to forestall the rumored move-in of a black family. Not even government officials or police officers could convince them of their racial safety. The crowd dispersed only when Fr. Charles Mallon, pastor of Ascension Parish, assured them that their neighborhood would remain unintegrated.[84]

The case of St. Agnes parish in Flint, Michigan, explicitly affirms white lay confidence in the white priesthood's ability to keep black people at bay. The late 1960s resignation of its longtime pastor incited hundreds of parish families to flee the city.[85] As one former parishioner recollects,

80. Ibid., 93.

81. For other exceptions, see Richard Gribble, "Cardinal Humberto Medeiros and the Desegregation of Boston's Public Schools, 1974-1976," *Journal of Church and State* 48, no. 2 (Spring 2006): 327–53.

82. Aquinas, *Summa Theologiae* I–II.53.1. ad 1; I–II.71.4.

83. McGreevy, *Parish Boundaries*, 118.

84. Ibid., 92.

85. Thomas C. Henthorn, "A Catholic Dilemma: White Flight in Northwest Flint," *The Michigan Historical Review* (2005): 18.

> Well, I knew that was it. With Fr. Olk gone, I knew we had to get out. Father Olk would have kept [African Americans] . . . in line if they did come. . . . I think I heard about his retirement in the spring and we had our house sold before the kids were back in school [in the fall].[86]

Given the crucial role that white priests played in holding the church's white supremacist corporate body together, lay Catholics often refused to accept black priests as parochial authorities. In 1959, the white parishioners of Boston's St. Francis de Sales "would not receive communion from a black West Indian priest who had been working there."[87] Even as the number of black priests began to rise during the 1940s, white bishops were reluctant to assign them to predominately white parishes, due both to their own biases and to their deep fear of lay white backlash.

Further evidencing the corporate character of the church's segregationist comportment, Catholic parishes fortified spatialized antiblackness supremacy simply by existing. As result, Catholic parishes acquired a well-deserved reputation for segregationist power and segregationists therefore saw the Catholic parish as an effective ally. For example, in Detroit, white businessmen from all religious backgrounds "appealed to the local archbishop to establish an Italian national parish in one area, hoping that 'an Italian Catholic church, and possibly a Catholic school, would keep away the Negroes.'"[88] In 1947, Motor City officials similarly drew attention to the way in which notoriously segregationist "improvement association" located on the city's still-white east side "conform to the bounds of Catholic parish lines rather than subdivisions."[89] African Americans in Pittsburgh also tracked an association between the percentage of a neighborhood's white Catholic population and the intensity of its opposition to black integration. Fearing the antiblack character of the Catholic Church's spatialized antiblackness, Chicago's few black real estate agents encouraged their black clients to seek housing in Jewish areas and to avoid the Catholic Southside.

White Catholics shared this belief. In 1966, the pastor of Chicago's St. Rita of Cacia parish assured his white congregants that "if they all remained united, the incoming, [pro-integration], housing

86. Ibid.

87. W. C. Leonard, "A Parish for the Black Catholics of Boston," *The Catholic Historical Review* 83, no. 1 1997: 44–68.

88. Ibid., 37.

89. Ibid., 103.

demonstrators could never break down their real estate codes."[90] White Catholics did not err in this assessment. Parochial space edified against integration.[91] For example, in Boston, African Americans gained a residential foothold on the margins of parochial boundaries much more easily than they entered what historian Gerald Gamm identifies as the parish's "institutional core," that is, the area immediately surrounding parish buildings like church, school, and rectory.[92]

Performed repeatedly and over a long stretch of time, antiblack practices cemented into vicious antiblack habits. The church became what it had learned to do well.[93] Vicious habituation enabled the church to practice antiblackness both more adeptly and with less effort; the church engaged in antiblackness more voluntarily precisely by growing more attached to it. The vice of antiblackness supremacy penetrated the church's corporate body because the church willed it.[94]

TAKING THE CORPORATELY WHITE, ANTIBLACK BODY APART IN ORDER TO PUT IT BACK TOGETHER AGAIN

Antiblackness supremacy proved so integral to the corporate identity of the Northern parishes that white Catholics typically preferred to abandon their long-cherished parochial space rather than share it with black people, even when Catholic. Enabling white attachment to their segregationist habits, church officials supplied whites with new parishes whenever they moved to an area of the city where a Catholic parish did not yet exist. While black Catholics struggled to convince Northern bishops to open an adequate number of black national parishes, the Catholic parish followed frightened whites wherever they went.[95] No one forced malformed whites to break their segregationist habits.

Collective white Catholic flight operated as a reflex of the corporately habituated Catholic body. As early as the late nineteen teens,

90. Sister Margaret Ellen Traxler, "American Catholics and Negroes," *Phylon (1960–)* 30, no. 4 (1969): 358.

91. Ibid., 79.

92. Gerald H. Gamm, *Urban Exodus: Why the Jews Left Boston and the Catholics Stayed* (Cambridge, MA: Harvard University Press, 2001), 90.

93. Aquinas, *Summa Theologiae* I–II.78.2.

94. Ibid., II–II.156.3.

95. Shaw, *The Catholic Parish as a Way-Station*, 107.

the predominately Irish whites of Chicago's St. Elizabeth parish moved to other parts of the city when African American Catholics begin moving into their neighborhoods. Abandoned by its Irish founders' grandchildren, a newly re-segregated St. Elizabeth's emerged as "Chicago's center for black Catholicism."[96] In Philadelphia, integration similarly atomized parochial bodies. In 1918, when the pastor of the German national parish St. Ignatius allowed a small number of black Catholics to worship there, he astutely anticipated resistance from his nonblack parishioners. As black people began to move into the area surrounding St. Ignatius three years later, white churchgoers decided to exit it. In the short span of six years, this church lost nearly two thirds of its pre-migration population, prompting the diocese to re-designate St. Ignatius as a "parish for the colored."[97]

After the Second World War, the pace of racial turnover accelerated as African Americans began to leave their overcrowded slums and acquire housing in less densely populated parts of the Northern city. A midcentury report reveals the pace of racial change on Chicago's Southside: "predominately Catholic communities . . . have disappeared overnight, to be replaced by overwhelmingly Protestant and non-Catholic populations" that were nearly entirely black.[98] Unlike white Protestants who responded to black residential expansion by fleeing the city altogether, Catholic whites initially attempted to stay in the city in the decades after the Second World War, relocating to one of a dwindling number of still all-white and increasingly Catholic urban spaces.

But soon even these initially remote urban neighborhoods would cease providing racial safety. Although white Catholics fought before they fled, they did eventually emulate their non-Catholic counterparts and flee the cities they once called home. White Catholics fled their new black neighbors with startling alacrity. Exemplifying this, the white South Chicago parish of St. Sabina lost two thousand white families between 1965 and 1966. By 1970, formerly all-white St. Sabina was predominately black.[99] These whites left the racially infiltrated space of urban St. Sabina's to establish new parishes like St.

96. Timothy B. Neary, "Black-Belt Catholic Space: African-American Parishes in Interwar Chicago," *US Catholic Historian* 18, no. 4 (2000): 79.

97. Kazal, "The Interwar Origins of the White Ethnic," 108–10.

98. McGreevy, *Parish Boundaries*, 119.

99. Ibid., 170.

Linus's, St. Catherine's, and St. Germaine's in suburban developments like Oak Lawn.[100] Even their unique attachment to the spatialized Catholic urban parish could not convince these whites to share residential space with even a small number of black people.

Throughout the country, suburbanization coincided with urban integration un-coincidentally.[101] Between 1944 and 1963, over fifteen hundred Catholic families relocated from the Philadelphia parishes of Most Blessed Sacrament, St. Francis de Sales, and Transfiguration to the suburban Delaware Country parish of St. Denis. And in cold Milwaukee, integration prompted white Catholics to pull their children from parochial schools. In like manner, historically Catholic St. Louis experienced unparalleled white flight from city to suburb.[102]

White Catholics would continue to exchange the cherished urban parishes founded by their ancestors for the racial safe haven of the still-white suburb even after the triumphs of the Black Civil Rights Movement. Beginning in 1971, white flight stripped a Flint, Michigan parish of more than eight hundred of its twelve hundred original families in just seven years.[103] The Catholic population of North Philadelphia plummeted from eighteen thousand in 1970 to under eight thousand just over twenty years later.[104] A short time later, this same force would reduce the size of Detroit's diocesan population by half in just over a decade.[105] The opening of the twenty-first century only intensified this trend as an additional forty thousand, overwhelmingly white, Catholics would flee the northeastern Ohio city of Youngstown.[106]

Throughout the North, African American children gained unprecedented access to Catholic parochial schools only after white Catholics lost interest in them.[107] Rather than sharing parochial space with black people, white Catholics ceded it to them. But this racial transfer did not inaugurate racial equality. In contrast to the relatively

100. McMahon, *What Parish Are You From?*, 176.

101. McGreevy, *Parish Boundaries*, 84.

102. Bourgeois, "If You're Not Black You're White," 108.

103. Henthorn, "A Catholic Dilemma," 1–42.

104. T. Rzeznik, "The Church in the Changing City: Parochial Restructuring in the Archdiocese of Philadelphia in Historical Perspective," *US Catholic Historian* 27, no. 4 (2009): 73–90.

105. Jeffrey C. Bridger and David R. Maines, "Narrative Structures and the Catholic Church Closings in Detroit," *Qualitative Sociology* 21, no. 3 (1998): 327.

106. Thomas G. Welsh, *Closing Chapters: Urban Change, Religious Reform, and the Decline of Youngstown's Catholic Elementary Schools, 1960-2006* (Lanham, MD: Lexington, 2011), 2.

107. McGreevy, *Parish Boundaries*, 241.

affluent students who attend the typical private school, the disproportionately black children who attended so-called "inner-city" Catholic elementary schools were some of the nation's poorest children. Further distinguishing the inner-city black Catholic parochial school experience from that enjoyed by early-twentieth-century European ethnics, the church would soon close most of its institutions dedicated to educating disproportionately poor and black girls and boys.[108]

But the church did not cut costs everywhere. Across the nation, suburban parish structures typically cost several times as much urban buildings did; the church built a duplicate version of the urban parish at double and triple the cost buildings did.[109] Redeploying the habituating power of the society that had shaped it, the growth of the suburban church fed off the urban church as a parasite. In the post–white flight diocese of Dayton, for example, the church would close three inner-city parochial schools but open five new ones in the suburbs.[110] Resembling other institutions like banks and big industry, the Catholic Church deserted the city it once had defined.

In the suburbs, the ethnic distinctions that bound European-Americans to their place-based urban parishes also faded away. For example, today, Italian-American suburbanites typically worship in the distinctly Irish-American style that typifies white, Anglo, U.S. Catholicism, and there are far fewer national parishes in the suburbs than there ever were in large cities.[111] Especially in the suburbs, the characteristics that differentiated one group of white ethnics from another no longer matter as much. Upon their arrival in the suburbs, white people no longer needed ethnicity to distance them from black people as they had when they still lived in ever-integrating central cities.

In relocating to the suburbs, the average Catholic parish retained its whiteness but ceded much of its cohesiveness. The suburban parish did not bind as the urban one had. Rather than seeking to remain in parochial space as their urban counterparts had, suburban Catholics have tended to shop around for a parish of their liking. During the era of suburbanization, Catholics lost touch with the church's parochial

108. Thomas C. Hunt, Ellis A. Joseph, and Ronald James Nuzzi, *Handbook of Research on Catholic Education* (Westport, CT: Greenwood, 2001), 167.

109. Joseph Watras, *Politics, Race, and Schools: Racial Integration, 1954–1994* (New York: Routledge, 1997), 85; McGreevy, *Parish Boundaries*, 85.

110. Watras, *Politics, Race, and Schools*, 234.

111. Shaw, *The Catholic Parish as a Way-Station*, 139–40.

body in other ways. In the 1950s, an estimated seventy percent of Detroit's Catholics attended mass weekly while sixty-one percent of Irish-Catholics and fifty percent of Italian-Catholics in New York City did the same.[112] But by the start of the twenty-first century, less than half of Catholics reported attending mass each Sunday. Even more tellingly, while a mere seventeen percent of Catholics raised in the era before widespread Catholic suburbanization no longer belong to any particular parish, around forty percent of those raised after the suburbanizing 1960s currently hold no parochial affiliation.[113] The era of Catholic suburbanization also witnessed a dramatic decline in both the size of the parochial school population and the number of religious vocations.[114] Racist suburbanization has unmade the church's corporate body at least as much as the upheavals of either the Second Vatican Council or sexual revolution.

Like whites of all faith backgrounds, white Catholics cultivate communal ignorance about the way that antiblackness supremacy shaped them. Marketing a distinctly Catholic brand of colorblindness, Catholic parishes do not remember the way that antiblackness supremacy shaped them. Even less do they remember the way that they shaped antiblackness supremacy.

112. John T. McGreevy, "Religious Roots," *Reviews in American History* 28, no. 3 (2000): 418.
113. Ibid., 419.
114. Margaret F. Brinig and Nicole Stelle Garnett, "Catholic Schools, Charter Schools, and Urban Neighborhoods," *University of Chicago Law Review* (2012): 35.

7.

Nonwhiteness Will Not Save Us: The Persistence of Antiblackness in the "Brown" Twenty-First Century

Perhaps the church and the world are already changing on their own. Many cite both the recent rise in both the size of the Asian-American and Latino/a population and rates of interracial marriage as signs of both whiteness and white supremacy's impending demise or enervation.[1] Yet such optimism rests upon a misunderstanding of both the geographical span of white supremacy and its essential relation to antiblackness. As demonstrated in chapter two, all the Americas inhabit and work to preserve the afterlife of slavery. For this reason, when people immigrate to the United States from Latin America, they do not arrive as racial innocents. Rather than defeating white supremacy, the immigration of Latin American people to the

1. For example, see Josh Sanburn, "U.S. Steps Closer to a Future Where Minorities Are the Majority," *Time Magazine*, June 25, 2015; Demetria Martinez, "The Future Is Mestizo, the Future Is Now," *National Catholic Reporter*, March 6, 2009, accessed January 12, 2017, https://www.ncronline.org/news/people/future-mestizo-future-now; Hua Hsu, "The End of White America?" *The Daily Beast*, January/February, 2009, accessed January 12, 2017, http://www.theatlantic.com/magazine/archive/2009/01/the-end-of-white-america/307208/; Brian Ross, "Trump's Toxicity & the Death Throes of White Power," *Huffington Post* August 4, 2016, accessed January 12, 2017, http://www.theatlantic.com/magazine/archive/2009/01/the-end-of-white-america/307208/; William H. Frey, "America's Getting Less White, and That Will Save It," *Newsweek*, December 6, 2014, accessed January 12, 2017, http://www.newsweek.com/americas-getting-less-white-and-will-save-it-289862.

United States catalyzes a collision between systems of antiblackness supremacy. Many Asian immigrants also bring their own brand of antiblackness with them since ideologies that portray black people as slave-like and bestial circulate throughout countries such as Japan and China.[2]

Ultimately, then, these demographic changes will alter reigning processes of racialization, but it will not overturn them. Whiteness has expanded its borders in order to consolidate itself against blackness in the past; there is no reason to believe it will not realign itself in this way again in the future.[3] Plus, not every Asian- or Latino-American who appears as nonwhite today will be considered as such over the course of their whole life. This holds true for their children as well. As sociologist Richard D. Alba chronicles, in the year 2013, "among infants with a Hispanic parent, about 30 percent also had a non-Hispanic parent—and for two-thirds of them, that parent was white." A similar pattern held with respect to infants born to Asian parents.[4] Children produced by nonblack interracial and interethnic pairings both identify with and are perceived as white much more often than those resulting from black-white unions.[5] Whether due to intermarriage or an amended concept of whiteness, many nonblack immigrants will have children who fit within the current parameters of whiteness.[6]

But the survival of antiblackness supremacy does not depend upon the majority of nonwhite immigrants becoming white. Debates about the future of whiteness remain important, but they can distract and mislead us. Even without the expansion of whiteness, nonblack people of color will continue to participate in and benefit from this country's uniquely spatialized antiblackness supremacy. Racialized xenophobia of course has prevented nonwhite immigrant groups

2. Howard, "Black in the Non-Black Imagination," 38–41; John Russell, "Race and Reflexivity: The Black Other in Contemporary Japanese Mass Culture," *Cultural Anthropology* 6, no. 1 (March 18, 2013): 3–25; Barry Sautman, "Anti-Black Racism in Post-Mao China," *The China Quarterly* 138 (June 1, 1994): 413–37.

3. Orlando Patterson, "Race by the Numbers," *The New York Times*, May 8, 2001, accessed July 15, 2015, http://www.nytimes.com/2001/05/08/opinion/08PATT.html.

4. Richard Alba, "The Myth of a White Minority," *New York Times*, June 11, 2015.

5. Jennifer Lee and Frank D. Bean, *The Diversity Paradox: Immigration and the Color Line in Twenty-First Century America* (New York: Russell Sage Foundation, 2010), 107–13.

6. Eduardo Bonilla-Silva, *Racism without Racists: Color-Blind Racism and the Persistence of Racial Inequality in America*, 3rd ed. (Lanham, MD: Rowman & Littlefield, 2009), 192.

from following the "European assimilation model" perfectly.[7] But like their ethnic, European, "old" immigrant predecessors, these "new" immigrants have been habituated and empowered by the particular mode of antiblackness supremacy that structures life in the United States. Just as the social reality of "white supremacy" requires us to lump all peoples of color together as "nonwhite," so the social reality of "antiblackness supremacy" similarly requires us to lump otherwise diverse groups of people together as "nonblack." The latter naming strategy disrespects group differences no less than the former does. Rather than dismissing the distinct racial identities and racialized experiences of those who identify as neither black nor white, the "antiblackness supremacy" approach to racial evil argues that one does not have to be white in order to practice antiblackness.[8]

RESIDENTIAL SEGREGATION AS DISTINCTLY ANTIBLACK

The spatial afterlife of black slavery possesses two core components: racial segregation and the mass prison. Both phenomena operate together and in mutually reinforcing fashion; they rely upon the black ghetto for material and symbolic support. The spatial afterlife of slavery does not require that all black people endure incarceration or residential segregation; the racialized character of slavery's afterlife instead enables these institutions to harm even those black people it cannot directly capture. Due to their relation to Africanized slavery, mass incarceration and hyper-segregation perpetuate antiblackness supremacy even more than they aid white supremacy. While nonblack people of color and immigrant groups have experienced certain forms of spatial regulation and residential mistreatment, they have not been crammed into ghettos as black people have. Nor have nonblack people of color been brutalized by the justice system to the same

7. For more on the ways in which racialized xenophobia has prevented Latinos from following the European assimilation model, see Arlene Dávila, *Latino Spin: Public Image and the Whitewashing of Race* (New York: New York University Press, 2008), 12.

8. Here, I respond to Gonzalez's argument that we should not construct racial identity as simply a black or white affair; the term "antiblackness supremacy" argues that nonblack people derive a similar power from antiblackness, even if they do so to different degrees. It does not make any claim about nonblack people's social identities. *Afro-Cuban Theology: Religion, Race, Culture, and Identity* (Gainesville: University Press of Florida, 2011), 40–41; see also Arlene Dávila, *Latino Spin: Public Image and the Whitewashing of Race* (New York: New York University Press, 2008), 12–13.

extent or to the same ends: antiblackness supremacy travels along a trajectory of its own.[9]

Let us consider the ghetto first. Just as slavery differs from other forms of domination, so the black ghetto differs from the ethnic enclave, even when it is nonwhite. The ghetto involuntarily encloses its inhabitants in a way the ethnic enclave does not.[10] While the black ghetto contains a population more or less forced to remain inside its spatial limits, the ethnic enclave supports a population whose residence there occurs much more voluntarily.[11] The nonwhite ethnic enclave resembles its white predecessors in another way: it protects and edifies its inhabitants and facilitates their assimilation. For this reason, nonblack people reside in ethnic enclaves temporarily and strategically; the black ghetto has persisted for nearly a century.[12] While ethnic enclaves, even when nonwhite, provide launching points and serve as cocoons, the black ghetto operates as a holding pen.[13]

But even outside the ghetto, residential patterns operate in a uniquely antiblackness supremacist fashion. Like their European ethnic, old-immigrant predecessors, new immigrants have not experienced anywhere near the degree of residential segregation that black people have. They have not endured even briefly what black people have suffered for an entire century. Consider what scholars call the dissimilarity index, which measures what percentage of a certain racial or ethnic group would have to move to other parts of a certain city in order to achieve a perfect and proportional demographic distribution. For example, if a city contains a population half black and half white, a dissimilarity score of zero would indicate that each of this city's neighborhoods were half black and half white. A score of ninety, however, would mean that ninety percent of the city's black residents would need to relocate to create racially balanced neighbor-

9. Rothstein, *The Color of Law*, xviii.

10. Ceri Peach, "Urbanization: Ethnic and Religious Segregation," in *The Encyclopedia of Global Human Migration* (Malden, MA: Blackwell, 2013), 43.

11. Camille Zubrinksy Charles, *Won't You Be My Neighbor: Race, Class, and Residence in Los Angeles* (New York: Russell Sage Foundation, 2006), 165.

12. John R. Logan, Wenquan Zhang, and Richard D. Alba, "Immigrant Enclaves and Ethnic Communities in New York and Los Angeles," *American Sociological Review* 67, no. 2 (2002): 301; Ceri Peach, "The Ghetto and the Ethnic Enclave," *Desegregating the City: Ghettos, Enclaves, and Inequality*, ed. David P. Varady (Albany: State University of New York Press, 2005), 31; Min Zhou, *Chinatown: The Socioeconomic Potential of an Urban Enclave* (Philadelphia: Temple University Press, 1992), 2.

13. Logan et al., "Immigrant Enclaves and Ethnic Communities," 300.

hoods. What story do racial dissimilarity indices tell? They unveil the spatial life of the United States as structured by not generalized white supremacy, but unmatched antiblackness supremacy.

For example, in 2010, Chicago carried an Asian-white dissimilarity index of fifty and a Hispanic-white dissimilarity index of just over sixty. In contrast, the city's black-white dissimilarity index stood at nearly ninety. Further distinguishing Hispanic and Asian segregation from black, these two groups live in increasing proximity to whites as they move up the economic ladder.[14] This is not true with respect to African Americans. In fact, in the metropolis of Los Angeles, "the poorest Hispanics were less segregated [from whites] than the most affluent blacks."[15] Further distinguishing spatialized antiblackness from other forms of spatial concentration, only black people experience high levels of the multifaceted form of segregation known as hyper-segregation. While one in four black urbanites endured hyper-segregation in the year 1980, their Hispanic counterparts experienced only "low to moderate levels of segregation . . . on all dimensions."[16] More than simply excluding blacks from nonblack neighborhoods, the spatially extensive and all-encompassing character of hyper-segregation ensures they do not come into any sort of contact—casual, occupational, or social—with nonblacks.

But even these measures understate the case, especially when comparing black and Hispanic, as black Hispanics experience higher levels of segregation from non-Hispanic whites than white Hispanics do.[17] This skin-color differential holds even among Latino/as with the same national origin and colonized status, as black Puerto Ricans experience levels of racial segregation that approximate those endured by non-Hispanic African Americans.[18] In only four metropolitan areas—Chicago, New York, Newark, and Paterson, New Jersey—do Hispanics endure high levels of as many as three types of residential segregation. These exceptions prove the rule: three of

14. Joe T. Darden and Sameh M. Kamel, "Black Residential Segregation in the City and Suburbs of Detroit: Does Socioeconomic Status Matter?," *Journal of Urban Affairs* 22, no. 1 (January 1, 2000): 1–13.
15. Douglas Massey and Nancy Denton, *American Apartheid: Segregation and the Making of the Underclass* (Cambridge, MA: Harvard University Press, 1993), 87.
16. Douglas S. Massey and Nancy A. Denton, "Hyper-segregation in U.S. Metropolitan Areas: Black and Hispanic Segregation along Five Dimensions," *Demography* 26, no. 3 (August 1, 1989): 382.
17. Massey and Denton, *American Apartheid*, 114.
18. Ibid., 151.

these cities contain a Hispanic population predominately comprised of visibly African-descended Puerto Ricans.[19]

Like the European ethnics before them, immigrants from Asia and Latin America experience steadily decreasing rates of residential segregation in each successive generation.[20] This holds true with respect to other measures of middle-class respectability such as homeownership, income level, educational attainment, and occupation, even in the case of Mexican-Americans, who have endured both racial injustice and an ongoing legacy of colonial domination.[21] Affirming expectations of progressive immigrant incorporation, English fluency, homeownership, and higher income increased Asian and nonblack Latino immigrants' residential proximity to native-born, non-Hispanic whites.[22] While time, especially trans-generational, ameliorates immigrant status, the stain of black slavery has proved much more ineradicable.

Antiblackness supremacy shapes residential patterns even more strongly than xenophobia does. Quite incredibly, native-born black people experience markedly higher rates of residential segregation from native-born whites than do foreign-born nonblacks of any race or nationality.[23] Antiblackness supremacy also afflicts foreign-born black people. Consider the following statistics: black immigrants have nearly the same amount of formal education as their Asian counterparts and nearly three times as much as Latino/a immigrants; they earn higher salaries than their Latino/a counterparts and suffer slightly lower rates of poverty than they do; and they are more likely to speak English than are immigrants from either Asia or Latin America.[24] Defying common-sense notions of assimilation and upward mobility,

19. Massey and Denton, "Hyper-segregation in U.S. Metropolitan Areas," 383.

20. Nancy A. Denton and Douglas S. Massey, "Residential Segregation of Blacks, Hispanics, and Asians by Socioeconomic Status and Generation," *Social Science Quarterly* 69, no. 4 (January 1988): 798.

21. Jody Agius Vallejo, *Barrios to Burbs: The Making of the Mexican American Middle Class* (Stanford, CA: Stanford University Press, 2012), 9.

22. John Iceland and Melissa Scopilliti, "Immigrant Residential Segregation in U.S. Metropolitan Areas, 1990–2000," *Demography* 45, no. 1 (February 1, 2008): 81, 87, 88.

23. Ibid., 87.

24. Juliana Morgan-Trostle and Kexin Zheng, "The State of Black Immigrants: Part I: A Statistical Portrait of Black Immigrants in the United States," *New York University Law School Immigrants' Rights Clinic*, 12.

black immigrants suffer substantially higher rates of residential segregation than all other immigrant groups.[25]

Due to the afterlife of slavery, black spaces are uniquely stigmatized, disempowered, and dishonored, regardless of the ethnicity, class status, or nativity of its residents. Consider the case of two predominately nonwhite neighborhoods in Chicago, black Bronzeville and Latino/a Pilsen. During the closing years of the twentieth century, activists, real estate agents, and business owners began to rebrand these previously blighted neighborhoods in the hopes of attracting wealthier customers, clients, and neighbors. In response, each community engaged in organized efforts to curb, or at least control, these oncoming waves of gentrification. Who won? Prevailing understandings of white supremacy and class inequality would predict that prospective disproportionately white, middle- and upper-middle-class gentrifiers to be equally attracted to and turned off by each neighborhood: although the residents of both areas were disproportionately poor and overwhelmingly nonwhite, both neighborhoods enjoyed similar proximity to downtown and boasted of similarly affordable and historic housing stocks. But, although both neighborhoods became more affluent, only Pilsen became more ethnically and racially diverse. Pilsen's middle- and upper-middle-class gentrifiers included sizeable numbers of non-Hispanic people, including non-Hispanic whites, while Bronzeville's middle- and upper-middle-class gentrifiers were exclusively black.[26]

Both white supremacy and class chauvinism fail to explain this result for a single reason: comparison with Pilsen suggests that affluent, nonblack gentrifiers avoided Bronzeville not because it was poor or nonwhite, but because it was black. Nonblack people continue both to perceive their black countrywomen and men through the lens of slavery and to attempt to transform this imagined association into material reality. To this end, they project onto black spaces the attributes of a slave: social death, natal alienation, insubordination, insurrectionary danger and disloyalty, and stigmatizing dishonor.[27] The afterlife of slavery fashions blackness and black people

25. John Iceland and Rima Wilkes, "Hypersegregation in the Twenty-First Century," *Demography* 41, no. 1 (2004): 23–36.

26. Matthew B. Anderson and Carolina Sternberg, "'Non-White' Gentrification in Chicago's Bronzeville and Pilsen: Racial Economy and the Intraurban Contingency of Urban Redevelopment," *Urban Affairs Review* (December 10, 2012): 443.

27. This claim does not deny that gentrification has harmed certain of Pilsen's residents. For

as uniquely "phobogenic."[28] As a result, Pilsen and Bronzeville do not represent two equally and uniformly stigmatized spaces of nonwhiteness; they instead occupy separate corners within Chicago's collective racial imagination.[29]

Evidencing this, a sample of the city's white, middle-class respondents imagined black neighborhoods as sites of death and danger to be avoided at all costs. As one white business owner explained in 2010, "I still have guests arrive from the airport where the cab driver warned them not to come down here [to Bronzeville], that they'll get mugged, shot . . . it scares them . . . and it's bad for business."[30] Another white respondent confessed, "when you think of blacks in Chicago the first thing that comes to mind is poverty [and] . . . kids getting killed by other kids."[31] Even though Bronzeville's "median income has skyrocketed [and] thousands of low-income residents have been displaced from public housing demolition and spiraling costs," white Chicagoans continued to avoid it.[32]

More than simply refusing to move into black Bronzeville, the city's whites also have declined to visit it. Despite pumping money into a revitalized Blues District, organizers and planners could not transform "Bronzeville into a tourist destination and site for 'ethnic consumption' on par with other Chicago neighborhoods such as Greek Town, Chinatown, and Pilsen." As one local resident expressed in 2011, "I never saw one white person down here, they're just not gonna come flocking down from the North side to experience the blues."[33] Many white people enjoy black music; Chicago's whites simply preferred to consume black music without having to encounter black spaces. Pilsen too once emanated spatial stigma due to its nonwhiteness. But Pilsen's developers could rebrand the area "as an authentic and vibrant Mexican 'ethnoscape' inhabited by a new racialized subject: the hardworking, professional, and civically reliable Mexican citizen." In addition to attracting a sizeable middle- and upper-middle-class white residential population, Pilsen now exists as

more on this, see John Betancur, "Gentrification and Community Fabric in Chicago," *Urban Studies* 48, no. 2 (2011): 383–406.

28. Saidiya V. Hartman, *Scenes of Subjection: Terror, Slavery, and Self-Making in Nineteenth-Century America*, 1st ed. (New York: Oxford University Press, 1997), 57.

29. Anderson and Sternberg, "'Non-White' Gentrification," 437.

30. Ibid., 447.

31. Ibid., 444.

32. Ibid., 449.

33. Ibid., 448.

a type of "Mexican Chinatown."[34] This transformation occurred not despite its residents' perceived immigrant status, but precisely because of it. Their perceived descent from immigrants distinguishes them from those recognized as the descendants of slaves.

Precisely due to their native-born status, black residents of black spaces are both disallowed ethnicity and believed to lack the social life it generates. Black people's loss is Mexican-American people's gain; the black ghetto's social death somehow makes immigrant spaces seem more alive. In contrast to the black ghetto, which menacingly threatens physical and social death, the Mexican barrio appears to pulse with cultural life.[35] Chicago newspapers celebrate Pilsen's "lively culture of the Mexican-American people [which] is now evident in restaurants, shops, and the Mexican Fine Arts Museum." In this vein, another city resident believes that "Mexicans [are] . . . more festive [than blacks]." Despite the incalculable contributions of black culture to literature, language, fashion, sports, and music—blues, jazz, R & B, Rock and Roll, funk, hip hop—one white Chicagoan amazingly perceives black people as uniquely "lacking . . . a distinct cultural identity."[36] Rather than the consequence of mere ignorance, this perception reflects the position of blackness in the afterlife of slavery. Deeming it to be slave-like, whites attempt to deny black culture any independent existence of its own. More than simply co-opted by white culture, black culture appears to be its extension and surrogate. Echoing the way in which a member of Mississippi's white gentry likely considered cotton picked by the hands of his black slaves his property, white Chicagoans cannot recognize black culture as a distinct form of life.

Nonblack Latino/as benefit from antiblackness supremacy in another way. While the ghetto warehouses the natally alienated, the Mexican barrio nurtures the family-oriented. A white Chicagoan explains that, although Latino/as are "not American . . . [they are] way more cohesive, support one another, they stick together . . . [and have] stronger families" than black U.S. Americans. Implicitly denying the city's slave-descended blacks of a heritage, one white respondent implicitly distinguishes Mexican-Americans from African-

34. Ibid., 452.

35. The belief that Latino culture is unusually life-giving is widespread. For more, see Dávila, *Latino Spin*, 2.

36. Anderson and Sternberg, "'Non-White' Gentrification," 453–55.

Americans by noting the former's "strong . . . family tradition."[37] Unstained by the mark of slavery, this neighborhood's Mexican residents, even when poor and foreign born, appear family-oriented and communally interconnected: the antithesis of the social death and natal alienation we impose upon black people. Chicagoans report that when they think of Pilsen, they "think of . . . pride"; the black ghetto in contrast conjures stigma and dishonor.

Although their immigrant status, both real and perceived, can disadvantage Mexican-Americans, it also can advantage them, especially in relation to native-born black people, due to the way it makes them appear akin to whites and entirely unlike slave-descended black people. Inheriting the legacy begun by Pilsen's German, Irish, and Czech immigrant antecessors, Pilsen's most recent wave of Mexican immigrants claim the neighborhood as their rightful property. As the heirs of these European immigrants, Pilsen's Mexican-Americans also share a family connection to them. To this end, neighborhood promoters frequently emphasize its "100 years of immigrant legacy."[38]

Another woman explains that Mexicans "also don't have a vendetta" like black people purportedly do. Like many whites, this respondent perceives slavery not as an egregious and uncompensated crime, but a type of petty grudge unjustly held against whites by blacks with bad attitudes. Mexican immigrants, on the other hand, "come here to improve their lives and really work hard . . . and just seem more well-mannered, almost more professional."[39] As immigrants rather than descendants of slaves, Mexicans have no unrepaired past to avenge. They belong to the country's future, not its past; especially outside of the colonized Southwest, they do not remind the United States of its past sins in the way that black people do. They may forebode cultural takeover to paranoid xenophobes, but they do not threaten slave insurrection.[40] Mexican immigrants may continue to change the world, but they cannot end it as black rebellion or fugitivity can.[41] Precisely because Mexican immigrants begin as outsiders, they can become insiders. But as the ultimate insiders, black descendants of slaves must remain penned in.

37. Ibid., 454–55.
38. Ibid., 456.
39. Ibid., 454–55.
40. For an overview of the history of discrimination against Mexican immigrants to the United States, see John J. Betancur, "The Settlement Experience of Latinos in Chicago: Segregation, Speculation, and the Ecology Model," *Social Forces* 74, no. 4 (June 1996): 1301–14.
41. Wilderson, *Red, White, and Black*, 45, 52.

NONWHITE HABITS OF SPATIALIZED ANTIBLACKNESS SUPREMACY

But nonblack people of color do not simply passively receive the benefits of native-born white people's antiblackness supremacy. In addition to reinforcing the antiblack perceptions of native-born whites, the nonblack immigrant enclave also habituates its residents into spatialized antiblackness.[42] Like white people, nonblack people become where they live. The case of Chicago's Little Village neighborhood, renowned as "the Heart of the Mexican Midwest," exemplifies this. Protesting overcrowded conditions, in 2001 a group of mothers and other activists waged a heroic hunger strike that compelled city officials to build a long-overdue new public school in that neighborhood. But when it opened, many residents became outraged when they learned that the city would require some of Little Village's students to continue attending school in the adjacent black neighborhood of North Lawndale in order to comply with desegregation laws. They further resented the fact that some black residents from this black ghetto to their north would get to enroll in the new high school in place of these Mexican-American students.

Like their European-American predecessors, many of these Mexican-Americans believed that black people posed a threat to the integrity of their corporately Mexican-American and nonblack residential body. As one resident tearfully exclaimed, "Why have they divided our children?" Elaborating upon this, another community mother lamented the way in which city officials "chose black people to the north," that is, North Lawndale, to attend the new high school rather than "the people who are supposed to be in the school . . . it's our school."[43] Even though it would reintroduce the overcrowded conditions that necessitated the school's construction in the first place, the neighborhood voted in favor of an advisory referendum that called on the city to redraw the school district so that it conformed to the neighborhood's racialized borders and excluded black students from attending the new school. The Mexican-American residents of

42. Lilia Fernández, *Brown in the Windy City: Mexicans and Puerto Ricans in Postwar Chicago* (Chicago: University of Chicago Press, 2012), 221.

43. Gabriel A. Cortez, *Education, Politics, and a Hunger Strike: A Popular Movement's Struggle for Education in Chicago's Little Village Community* (PhD diss., University of Illinois at Urbana-Champagne, 2008), 119.

La Villita believed blackness a greater educational threat than overcrowding.

As evidenced by neighborhood-wide mobilization against a nonprofit organization's 2014 proposal to repurpose an abandoned factory into subsidized mixed-income housing, the predominately Mexican-American community of Little Village continues to fear residential intimacy with native-born black people. Despite reassurances that this project was not affiliated with the racially ignominious Section 8 housing program, many in the community imagined it a grave threat. Espousing the racial theory of property values, many feared that the arrival of public housing tenants would depress property values and increase crime, prostitution, and gang activity. Like non-Hispanic whites, these Mexican-American activists spoke of black people in the objective and therefore seemingly innocent code of place and criminality. As one protestor summarized, "to me it's about safety and economics."[44] Implicitly distinguishing the Mexican-American residents of Little Village from the native-born black people who might invade their neighborhood, the executive director of the Little Village Community Council proclaimed "homeownership [as] the dream that every immigrant came with when he left Michoacán or his little town."[45] Unlike black people who are perceived to rely dishonorably upon public housing, one activist pronounces, "Mexicans are homeowners."[46] The habits of homeownership perpetuate antiblackness supremacy even when practiced by nonwhites.

Well-meaning community leaders could fight this negrophobia only by validating it. In this way, alderman Ricardo Munoz promised his constituents that this building project would shelter only "large families where grandma lives with the aunt, the uncle, and the

44. Adriana Cardona-Maguigad, "Little Village Affordable Housing Development Draws Criticism from Some Residents," *The Gate News: Chicago Community News for Back of the Yards and Surrounding Neighborhoods*, December 19, 2013, accessed June 22, 2015, http://www.thegatenewspaper.com/2013/12/little-village-affordable-housing-development-draws-criticism-from-some-residents/.

45. Jackie Serrato, "Little Village Leaders Differ on Vision for 26th and Kostner," *The Gate News: Chicago Community News for Back of the Yards and Surrounding Neighborhoods*, February 5, 2014, accessed June 22, 2015, http://www.chicagonow.com/el-arco-press/2014/03/little-village-leaders-differ-on-vision-for-26th-and-kostner/.

46. August Sallas, "The Hispanic Times.com: Where's Ricardo? Housing Matters, Public Housing Project in Little Village, Little Village Community Meeting, Vote 2014 TV Show, Endorsed Cook County Democrats, Job Fair, Movie Review," accessed June 22, 2015, http://www.thehispanictimes.com/2014/01/wheres-ricardo-housing-matters-public.html.

nephew." Family here operates as a racial code that signifies the imagined difference between nonblack, socially vibrant, Latino/as and native-born, socially dead black people with broken or perhaps even nonexistent families. When the neighborhood Community Oversight Council drew up its final agreement with the institution financing the building project, it explicitly restricted occupancy to those who already lived within the neighborhood.[47] Further fortifying the neighborhood against the widely feared threat of black invasion, the organization resolved to install "a very high tech security system" and to hire someone from Little Village to guard the project in order "to create a culture of 'eyes' on the site all the time."[48]

Mexican-American strategies of spatialized antiblackness supremacy also resemble those deployed by twentieth-century European-American urbanites in their reliance upon gang violence. Just as Irish-American gangs patrolled their neighborhoods in search of black trespassers, so members of Mexican-American gangs have expelled black residents from many of Southern Californian spaces.[49] A 2000 study found that, in areas of Los Angeles marked by high concentrations of hate crimes, "the perpetrators were typically members of Latino street gangs who were purposely targeting blacks."[50] These attacks have occurred throughout the environs of Los Angeles, in Harbor Gateway, Pacoima, San Bernardino, Canoga Park, Wilmington, and Pomona. In Highland Park and Compton, black people have been subjected to violent eviction on numerous occasions.[51] This antiblack violence has overflowed the metropolitan limits of Los Angeles and spilled into the Californian cities of Carlsbad and Fresno. In 2007, four nonblack Latinos shot a Panamanian-American security guard because he had black skin. Like twentieth-century

47. 26th and Kostner Community Oversight Council Community Benefits Agreement with Mercy Housing, https://26kostneroversightcouncil.files.wordpress.com/2014/09/26k-oc-cba-draft-english-update-august.pdf. Accessed June 20, 2015.

48. 26th and Kostner Oversight Committee, Meeting Notes, December 16, 2014. https://26kostneroversightcouncil.files.wordpress.com/2015/02/26k-oc-12-16-14-notes-english.pdf.

49. Carl H. Nightingale, *Segregation: A Global History of Divided Cities* (Chicago: University of Chicago Press, 2012), 315.

50. Brentin Mock, "Latino Gang Members in Southern California Are Terrorizing and Killing Blacks," *Southern Poverty Law Center Intelligence Report* 2006 Winter Issue, accessed June 22, 2015, http://www.splcenter.org/get-informed/intelligence-report/browse-all-issues/2006/winter/la-blackout.

51. Of course, nearly all gangs in this country are formed along racial lines and intergang violence is often interracial violence. For more on this, see John Hagedorn, *A World of Gangs: Armed Young Men and Gangsta Culture* (Minneapolis: University of Minnesota Press, 2008).

white Catholic rioters who attacked even Catholic black people, these nonblack Latino young men beat a black man even though he was Latino.[52] They also recited a familiar script of antiblackness, as one victim recalls his assailant shouting, "Niggers have no business living in Pomona because this is [our] territory."[53]

Although the overwhelming majority of nonblack Latino/as undoubtedly abhor these young men's tactics, they most likely share their aversion to residential intimacy with black people, regardless of ethnic background. Researchers have found that Latino/as, like Asian-Americans and non-Hispanic whites, perceive native-born black people as the least desirable neighbors. In fact, while nearly one-fifth of non-Hispanic whites in a 2000 survey "expressed integration preferences that exclude black people [from their neighborhood] entirely," approximately thirty percent of Latinos and forty percent of Asian-Americans harbored the same desire to live in a neighborhood entire free of visibly African-descended residents.[54] This statistic might seem to indict Asian-Americans and Latino/as as more racist than non-Hispanic whites. But in truth these groups most likely espouse antiblack sentiments more freely than non-Hispanic whites because they need spatial separation from black people more than non-Hispanic whites do.[55] Unjustly slurred as un-American outsiders, these groups can prove that they belong to this world largely by affirming that black people do not. African Americans, on the other hand, do not display a similar aversion to residential intimacy with any of these other racial and ethnic groups.[56]

Further discrediting common confidence in the healing power of a rising Latino population, the county of Miami-Dade practices spatialized antiblackness supremacy despite the fact that it is "one of the rare places in the U.S. where a national ethnic minority, white Cubans and their descendants, shares substantial control of socioeconomic,

52. Sam Quinones, "Attack on Family in Compton Latest Incident in Wave of Anti-Black Violence," *Los Angeles Times*, January 25, 2013, http://articles.latimes.com/2013/jan/25/local/la-me-0126-compton-20130126.

53. Mock, "Latino Gang Members in Southern California."

54. Camille Zubrinsky Charles, "Neighborhood Racial-Composition Preferences: Evidence from a Multiethnic Metropolis," *Social Problems* 47, no. 3 (August 1, 2000): 386.

55. For a striking example of Asian-Americans mobilizing against antiblackness, see Vanessa Hua, "Letters Home: Asian Americans in Support of Black Lives Matter," *San Francisco Chronicle*, accessed July 13, 2016, http://www.sfchronicle.com/entertainment/article/Letters-Home-Asian-Americans-in-Support-of-Black-8354454.php.

56. Charles, "Neighborhood Racial-Composition Preferences," 387.

symbolic, and political power with native-born white Americans."[57] There, disproportionately white Cuban refugees of the Castro regime perpetuated antiblackness first against the region's native-born black people and then against a rising tide of Haitian and Cuban *Marielitos* immigrants, whom one Cuban-American city official described as "mostly blacks and mulattoes of a color that I never saw or believed existed in Cuba." Like their native-born counterparts, these black immigrants were relegated to ethnically specific, black ghettoes.[58]

Like their European predecessors, this earlier wave of Cuban immigrants pronounced their racial innocence, downplayed their racial power, overlooked their reliance upon federal aid, and overestimated their oppression.[59] In this way, in 1993, the Cuban-American Federation of Hispanic Employees of Dade Country espoused antiblackness in an open letter to a local newspaper, which argued:

> it may be okay with Anglos [to refer to them as insensitive] since, historically they are guilty of enslaving and degrading blacks for centuries; they owe blacks. But, folks, we Hispanics owe Blacks nothing: what are we guilty of? Of hard work, not only as bankers and entrepreneurs, but also as humble laborers and peddlers?

Because they are immigrants, they believe themselves to be racially innocent. They bear responsibility for neither the United States' antiblack afterlife of slavery nor Cuba's. Clearly contrasting themselves with native-born black people, the author adds: "Keep it clear in your head that we have never coerced assistance from anyone . . . some folks should try this, it is hard work, but not bad."[60] Reiterating ideologies of unassisted and self-made white success, this editorial

57. Anani Dzidzienyo and Suzanne Oboler, eds., *Neither Enemies nor Friends: Latinos, Blacks, Afro-Latinos* (New York: Palgrave Macmillan, 2005), 11.

58. Louis Herns Marcelin, "Identity, Power, and Socioracial Hierarchies Among Haitian Immigrants in Florida," in Dzidzienyo and Oboler, eds., *Neither Enemies nor Friends*, 213–14. See also Ann Louise Bardach, "Marielitos and the Changing of Miami," *Los Angeles Times*, April 24, 2005, http://articles.latimes.com/2005/apr/24/books/bk-bardach24; Jon Nordheimer, Special to the New York Times, "Riots Discomfit the Cubans of Miami," *New York Times*, November 26, 1987, sec. U.S.

59. Importantly, as Gonzalez points out, these were not the first Cubans to claim residence in the United States: "The first Cubans to arrive in the United States settled in Key West, and a large Afro-Cuban community established itself in Ybor City in 1869." These Afro-Cubans, she explains, "were subject to the racist segregationist practices of the United States" even as they "had access to privileges and resources not available to native-born African-Americans" due to their immigrant and therefore non-natally alienated status. *Afro-Cuban Theology*, 65.

60. Howard, *Black in the Non-Black Imagination*, 74.

positioned Cuban immigrants as both unfairly victimized by native-born black people and morally superior to them.[61]

Native-born, non-Hispanic whites have tended to agree with them, preferring immigrant newcomers to their black, native-born fellow citizens. While they continued to malign black people as "criminals, lazy, and dependent on hand-outs," Miami's non-Hispanic whites celebrated the Cuban community "as having strong Hispanic family values, [and being] hardworking, industrious, independent, [and] self-reliant." As the model bootstrapping immigrant, they also exemplified American-ness. Welcomed into the homes in white neighborhoods that they bought with the assistance of racist federal mortgage programs, these Latino/as easily gained local power "and then systematically shut blacks out."[62]

The spatial afterlife of slavery also conditions racial perception in nonresidential matters. White owners of small businesses consider nonblack people of color more desirable as employees than they do black people.[63] And nonblack Latino/as, whether mestizo/a or white, experience much higher rates of social and sexual intimacy with established, non-Hispanic whites than those designated as black.[64] Though nearly approximate in size—Latina/os comprise 16.7 percent of the U.S. population and African Americans 13.1 percent—non-Hispanic whites are nearly three times as likely to marry a nonblack Latino/a person as an African American one. But antiblackness is not just for whites only. Asian-Americans and nonblack Latino/as also perceive black people as the least desirable marriage partners and avoid them accordingly. African Americans, however, do not rank spousal preferences according to race; they qualify as the most open-minded.[65] Racial segregation operates less as a scheme of generalized white supremacy or xenophobia, and more as a targeted mechanism of antiblackness supremacy.[66]

61. For more on the relative homogeneity of this wave of Cuban immigrants, see Dávila, *Latino Spin*, 37.

62. Howard, "Black in the Non-Black Imagination," 73.

63. Tamara K. Nopper, "Minority, Black and Non-Black People of Color: 'New' Color-Blind Racism and the US Small Business Administration's Approach to Minority Business Lending in the Post-Civil Rights Era," *Critical Sociology* 37, no. 5 (September 1, 2011): 661.

64. Miriam Jiménez Román and Juan Flores, *The Afro-Latin@ Reader: History and Culture in the United States* (Durham NC: Duke University Press, 2010), 476.

65. Yancey, *Who Is White?*, 70–71.

66. Helen B. Marrow, "New Immigrant Destinations and the American Colour Line," *Ethnic and Racial Studies* 32, no. 6 (July 1, 2009): 1038. Even John J. Betancur, who argues that Mexican-Americans and Puerto Ricans suffer more residential mistreatment than their European

THE IMMIGRANT ADVANTAGE: STATE PRACTICES OF ANTIBLACKNESS

These racialized sexual preferences both reflect and reinforce existing structural realities. The United States remains structurally aligned against its native-born black citizens in a way it is not against Asian-Americans, Arabs, or Latino/as, even when they are immigrants. For example, when applying for bank loans of any kind, nonwhite immigrants can draw upon long histories of credit-worthiness established in their countries of origin.[67] As descendants of slaves, African Americans cannot call upon another country to vouch for them. They come before potential creditors as residents of a country that believes them unfit for ownership of either capital or property.[68]

Nonblack people of color, even when immigrants, also benefit from the support of the state in a way native-born black people do not. For example, the federal government began extending loans to minority owners of small business in response to the Black Civil Rights Movement, but nonblack people of color receive a disproportionate share of this federal largesse.[69] In the year 2006, for example, the Small Business Administration accorded Asian-Americans twice the number of loans and more than six times as much capital than they did black people, while Latino/as obtained about one and a half times the number of loans and twice as much capital as African Americans. Here too "colorblindness" operates as a scheme of antiblackness. In collecting Latino/as, Asian-Americans, and African Americans into a single classificatory category, "minority," the federal government hides the fact that it treats these groups differently from each other.[70]

The tendency to lump all people of color into a single category of disadvantaged nonwhiteness often serves to obscure and thereby

immigrant predecessors, concedes that Latinos "are less segregated than blacks in the sense that they live interspersed with other groups, particularly in areas in transition." "The Settlement Experience of Latinos," 1312.

67. Nopper, "Minority, Black and Non-Black People of Color," 662.

68. Hartman, *Scenes of Subjection*, 103.

69. This is not the only way in which nonblack people have benefited, often disproportionately, from the efforts of the Black Civil Rights Movement. As Nikole Hannah-Jones explains, the white supremacist "immigration policy [that barred] non-European immigrants from entering the United States was changed by the Civil Rights Movement." Ayana D. Byrd, "Bridging the Gap: A Conversation on the Black Diaspora in America," *Essence* 46, no. 4 (August 2015): 92.

70. Nopper, "Minority, Black and Non-Black People of Color," 652, 662.

excuse the uniquely persistent character of antiblackness supremacy in other ways. For example, universities tout their improved population of nonwhite students by erroneously including white Hispanics in this category. Colleges and universities also hide the fact that black enrollment drastically lags behind that of other, minoritized groups.[71] Reporters similarly celebrate skyrocketing rates of interracial marriage, ignoring that rates of black and nonblack interracial marriage have risen much less impressively. The good intentions of individuals notwithstanding, the phrase "people of color" allows whites to disguise old patterns of antiblackness as a new commitment to racial diversity.

Nonblacks of all types similarly put on blackness in order to obscure their participation in antiblackness.[72] Here I divide nonblack, nonindigenous people into two categories: one, older immigrants from Europe and their descendants and two, the newer immigrants from Asia and Latin America and their descendants. While non-Hispanic whites make themselves seem like black people by exaggerating the hardships their immigrant ancestors faced, nonblack new immigrants engage in blackface by underestimating the hardships these Europeans endured. These groups reach the same destination by traveling in the opposite direction. The first story vindicates non-Hispanic whites by claiming that, although their immigrant ancestors suffered oppression just like black people did, unlike black people, they have managed to rise to the top due to their hard work and patience. The second story, in turn, exaggerates the similarities between African-American and new immigrant experiences of injustice by downplaying the similarities between the stories of older and newer immigrants. In attempting undermine white supremacist nativism, this strategy simultaneously affirms antiblackness supremacy. While the experiences of newer, often racialized, immigrant groups undoubtedly differ from those of their European predecessors, all nonblack immigrant groups have advanced in U.S.-American society by way of antiblackness supremacy. And although

71. This naming strategy also hides socially salient differences among Latino/as. In this way, for example, while "U.S. born Cubans and Central and South Americans meet or exceed the education levels of [non-Hispanic] Whites . . . even third-generation Mexican Americans have high school dropout rates double or triple those of Anglos." Frank D. Bean, Stephen J. Trejo, Randy Capps, and Michael Tyler, "The Latino Middle Class: Myth, Reality, and Potential" (*Tomás Rivera Policy Institute*, 2001), 2. http://trpi.org/wp-content/uploads/archives/midclass.pdf, accessed January 2, 2017.
72. Sexton, "People-of-Color-Blindness."

nonwhite immigrants surely have suffered white supremacist violence, both structural and interpersonal, they have not endured antiblackness supremacy in either the past or the present. For these reason, both types of pro-immigrant narratives obscure the uniquely vicious character of antiblack racism by crediting each group's success not to antiblackness supremacy, but to their hard work alone.[73] Black people therefore are portrayed as unique for the wrong reason. Rather than the victims of slavery and its afterlife, black Americans appear the only group unable, or perhaps unwilling, to pull themselves up by their bootstraps.

The complex racial reactions to the trial of George Zimmerman exemplify the way in which antiblackness supremacy structures the incorporation of nonblack immigrants and their descendants into social respectability and civic belonging. Many conservative commentators responded to the *New York Times*' calling Mr. Zimmerman a "white Hispanic" with outrage. Fox News contributor Bernard Goldberg believed it part of a larger conspiracy by delusional liberals to manufacture evidence of a racism that just doesn't exist. For this reason, he contends, the *Times* labeled Zimmerman a "white Hispanic" only "because they need the word 'white' to further the story line, which is, *White, probably racist vigilante shoots an unarmed black kid*."[74] A writer at the *National Review*, arguably the country's most popular politically conservative magazine, sarcastically agrees explaining that "[calling Mr. Zimmerman 'white'] is the way the blame for Martin's death belongs squarely at the feet of 'the system.' And 'the system' is a white thing, don't you know?"[75]

The mistaken belief that whiteness and Hispanic-ness cannot exist within the same human body animates these pro-Zimmerman protestations. In their minds, one is either white *or* Hispanic; one cannot be both. But, "Hispanic," as any diligent census worker knows, designates not a racial identity but an ethnic one. Despite this, U.S.-Americans of all political persuasions feel a strong need to

73. Dávila, *Latino Spin*, 7, 10.

74. Erik Wemple, "Why Did New York Times Call George Zimmerman 'white Hispanic'?," *The Washington Post*, March 28, 2012, http://www.washingtonpost.com/blogs/erik-wemple/post/why-did-new-york-times-call-george-zimmerman-white-hispanic/2012/03/28/gIQAW6fngS_blog.html.

75. Jonah Goldberg, "Playing the Race Card Again," *Los Angeles Times*, March 27, 2012, http://articles.latimes.com/2012/mar/27/opinion/la-oe-goldberg-trayvon-martin-race-20120327.

racialize Hispanic-ness so that it refers only to those who "look" phenotypically "*mestizo*."

But interestingly, even those who insist that Zimmerman's birth to a Peruvian-born mother disqualifies him for whiteness still place him above the blackness that Martin represents. In an online Fox News forum about the case, a post-er named "Josie" describes Zimmerman as a "human being who was violently being beaten down by 17 yo who was taller, more athletic, faster & on top of him, making it impossible to retreat!" In her eyes, only Martin's race matters and only Zimmerman exists as a human being. A woman operating under the appellation, "momsense1," speaks this ideology of conditional support for presumably nonblack *latinidad* explicitly: "Whatever he [Zimmerman] is—he's not a ghetto rat" like Martin. Others also believe Zimmerman's racial identity matters much less than Martin's. As another respondent named Barry fumes,

> I am certain that . . . Zimmerman's rights were violated as White/Hispanic. Had Zimmerman been black this never would have happened, meaning if he were black, Martin would never have turned on Zimmerman, attacked Zimmerman, started pounding Zimmerman's head into the concrete and since Zimmerman (as a black man) would never have felt threatened and feared for his life he would not have felt compelled to defend himself resulting in the shooting death of Martin.[76]

The imagined menace of the undisciplined black body brings otherwise opposed and isolated Anglo whites and nonblack Hispanics together. Although "whiteness" and "Hispanic-ness" remain separated by a hyphen, they operate in allegiance, standing united in self-defensive violence against the black male body.

Under other conditions, many of these whites would not treat Zimmerman so nicely. For example, what if George's name were Jorge? What if, rather than killing a black teenager, he became famous for sitting in an Arizona prison after being arrested for "looking like an undocumented immigrant"? What if he sang the national anthem before a major sporting event?[77] Would he qualify as

76. The Greta Van Susteren Show, "Is George Zimmerman Hispanic or White? He Checked Off Hispanic on His Voter Registration." Greta Wire, Fox News, July 15, 2013, accessed July 23, 2013, http://gretawire.foxnewsinsider.com/2013/07/15/is-george-zimmerman-hispanic-or-white-he-checked-off-hispanic-on-his-voter-registration/.

77. "After Twitter Criticism for Singing National Anthem, Marc Anthony Reminds People He's American," *Star Tribune*, accessed June 8, 2015, http://www.startribune.com/marc-anthony-reminds-people-he-s-american-too/216033741/; Cindy Y. Rodriguez, "Mexican-

"American" to them then? I doubt it. In these contexts, many non-Hispanic whites would perceive him as an intruder rather than an ally. But in placing his body so decisively against the body of a black person and being prosecuted for it, George Zimmerman appears aligned with whiteness and its supremacist designs. Although most pro-Zimmerman Anglo whites deny that he is white, in killing a black adolescent, he counts as one of them. And like them, he suffers victimization by the violent, fugitive, and unpredictably undisciplined black body.[78] For this reason, he too possesses the right to kill a black person with impunity.

In fact, the killing of Trayvon Martin by a Hispanic person verifies preexisting antiblack biases in a way that his killing by a white person would not have. Because Zimmerman identifies as a Hispanic, he accords claims about the criminal character of black masculinity an added objectivity.[79] Even Hispanics, this thinking goes, recognize the predatory savagery of black men. George Zimmerman makes certain white people feel like they were right about black men all along. Just as many whites align themselves with Zimmerman, a Hispanic of disputed racial identity, against Martin, who is black beyond a shadow of a doubt, Hispanics take the side of whites in their perception of this case. According to a 2012 poll, "more than 90 percent of blacks perceived that race played a role in the shooting, compared with 68 percent of whites and 74 percent of Hispanics." And, while "eighty-one percent of blacks said they believed Zimmerman would have been immediately arrested had Trayvon been white," only forty percent of whites and fifty one percent of Hispanics agreed.[80]

National reaction to Rachel Jeantel, the teenaged girl to whom Mr. Martin was speaking on the cell phone when he was killed,

American Boy's National Anthem Sparks Racist Comments," *CNN*, September 16, 2013, accessed June 8, 2015, http://www.cnn.com/2013/06/12/us/mexican-american-boy-sings-anthem/index.html.

78. Kelly Brown Douglas, *Stand Your Ground: Black Bodies and the Justice of God* (Maryknoll, NY: Orbis, 2015), 108–23.

79. White Anglo opponents of affirmative action recently have begun to "express concern that Asian Americans are harmed by affirmative action" for a similar reason. Conservative scholars and activists have adopted this strategy because "opposition to affirmative action seems less racist if affirmative action programs can be characterized as harmful to both white and Asian American people, rather than something that is good for everyone but white people." Nancy Leong, "The Misuse of Asian Americans in the Affirmative Action Debate," *UCLA Law Review* Disc. 90 (2016).

80. Gallup Poll, "Blacks, Nonblacks Hold Sharply Different Views of Martin Case." http://www.gallup.com/poll/153776/blacks-nonblacks-hold-sharply-different-views-martin-case.aspx.

illustrates the incorporative power of antiblackness even more emphatically. Like Zimmerman, her mother arrived in the United States as an immigrant from another part of the Americas. Like Zimmerman, she speaks both U.S.-American English and her mother's mother tongue, Haitian Creole. Like Zimmerman, Ms. Jeantel even speaks Spanish. But race causes us to see their immigrant ancestries quite differently. Although Haiti was once a colony of France, Ms. Jeantel is not considered culturally French in the way that those descended from residents of countries colonized by Spain are considered Hispanic.

This occurs primarily because, unlike Mr. Zimmerman, Rachel Jeantel bears a body we all agree is black. Even more, she is marked by her belonging to the most African nation in the Western Hemisphere, one that exploded into being through slave revolution. While Mr. Zimmerman seems to embody law and order, Ms. Jeantel signifies decay and disorder. For example, in response to her testimony, more than one white person tweeted that she represents everything that is wrong with Florida's school system. On the widely watched Megyn Kelly show, one guest quipped, "I don't think [Jeantel] came across as brutally honest; I think she comes across as brutally ignorant."[81] Unlike Zimmerman, who embodies the gun-toting bravado of the Wild (White) West, Jeantel embodies blackness; she therefore receives no benefit of the doubt.

THE WAR ON DRUGS: MORE ANTIBLACK THAN WHITE SUPREMACIST

Nonblack people of color also enjoy relative and in some cases near complete immunity from the mass prison. The mass prison oppresses not all nonwhites in general, but black people most severely. For example, with the exception of U.S.-Americans of Laotian and Cambodian descent, whose incarceration rates approximate that of white Anglos, Asian-Americans end up in prison at lower rates than all other racial and ethnic groups, including non-Hispanic whites.[82] What about Latino/as? It is widely believed that the war on drugs

81. "'Brutally Honest' Or 'Brutally Ignorant'? Fox Guests Take On Rachel Jeantel's Zimmerman Trial Testimony," accessed June 8, 2015, http://www.mediaite.com/tv/brutally-honest-or-brutally-ignorant-fox-guests-take-on-rachel-jeantels-zimmerman-trial-testimony/.
82. http://www.migrationpolicy.org/sites/default/files/source_charts/rumbaut-table1-jun06.cfm.

ravages Latino/as as much as it does black people.[83] The often-repeated claim that the war on drugs equally afflicts black and Latino/a people springs from two conceptual errors: first, it dismisses the fact that the federal immigration detention centers possess a different social function than the state prisons that house the vast majority of the nonviolent prisoners of the war on drugs. Put another way, Latino/as comprise a disproportionate share of the federal prison population for an entirely different reason than black people represent a disproportionate share of the nonviolent drug offenders housed in state and local prisons and regulated by extensive probation programs. Without denying the injustice and inhumanity of our nation's immigration laws, I simply differentiate them from the uniquely antiblack war on drugs: the immigrant detention system seeks to mark certain, but not all, Latino/a immigrants as invasive foreigners while the prison-ghetto complex seeks to brand black people with the stain of slavery.

Second, in identifying black and Latino/a people as victims of a similar form of racial oppression, scholars fail to attend to the racial and geographical diversity of the U.S. Latino population.[84] Yes, Mexican-Americans in Texas and California suffered de facto segregation and exclusion in the first half of the twentieth century, and yes, Puerto Ricans have been captured in the interrelated "carceral mesh" of the prison-ghetto complex.[85] But while Mexican-Americans and Puerto Ricans both qualify as Latino/as, they did not suffer these injustices because they were "Latino." White Anglos in the Southwest imposed segregation on Mexican-Americans to continue a history of conquest and colonization: Latino/as living in other parts of the United States did not experience this system of formal segregation.[86] And today, Mexican-American residents of the Midwest, for example, typically suffer structural violence to the extent that they are figured as racialized immigrants. Puerto Rican inhabitants of the continental U.S., on the other hand, who typically reside in the Northeastern United States, comprise a disproportionate share of occupants of the prison and the ghetto because many of them qualify as black by mainland standards: Mexicans, South Americans, white Cubans,

83. See, for example, Mikulich et al., *The Scandal of White Complicity*, 32.

84. Román and Flores, *The Afro-Latin@ Reader*, 323.

85. Ariela J. Gross, "'The Caucasian Cloak': Mexican Americans and the Politics of Whiteness in the Twentieth-Century Southwest," *Georgetown Law Journal* 95, no. 2 (January 2007): 339.

86. Ibid., 346, 351.

or Salvadorans in this region typically lack visible evidence of African descent and therefore do not suffer this fate. Latino/a groups have been oppressed for different reasons, in different ways, to different ends, and out of loyalty to different histories.

Those who identify Latino/as as co-equal victims of the war on drugs typically cite the fact that "by the late 1980s, three of every four inmates serving a sentence in the prisons of the entire state of New York came from only seven black and Latino neighborhoods of New York City."[87] But rather than evidencing anti-Latino injustice, this statistic only underscores the uniquely antiblack character of the war on drugs. Indeed, each of the neighborhoods specified in this statistic contain a population either native-born black, Dominican, or Puerto Rican. None of them contain a significant population of any substantially nonblack Latino group.[88] Further distinguishing the carceral treatment of black and nonblack Latino/as, no other part of the country locks its Latino/a residents up anywhere near as often as the city of New York does. Unsurprisingly, Latino/as are most over-incarcerated in states whose Latino/a population is the most visibly African-descended: Massachusetts, Connecticut, Pennsylvania, and New York.[89]

In truth, although the overall Hispanic male incarceration rate surpasses the non-Hispanic white incarceration rate by 2.6, the overall non-Hispanic black incarceration rate surpasses the Hispanic male rate by 2.7.[90] The gap only widens in the case of women: while Hispanic women are almost twice as likely to be incarcerated as white women, black women are imprisoned nearly two and a half times

87. Loïc Wacquant, *Deadly Symbiosis: Race and the Rise of the Penal State* (Cambridge: Polity, 2009), 114.

88. Román and Flores, *The Afro-Latin@ Reader*, 472.

89. Ashley Nellis, *The Color of Racial and Ethnic Disparity in State Prisons* (The Sentencing Project, June 14, 2016), 3. Accessed June 9, 2017, http://www.sentencingproject.org/publications/color-of-justice-racial-and-ethnic-disparity-in-state-prisons/. As the Pew Research Center explains, "half of the nation's Puerto Rican origin population lives in the Northeast" and they comprise 54.8% and 54.1% of all Hispanics in the states of Connecticut and Pennsylvania and are also the largest Hispanic group in Massachusetts, New Jersey, and New York. D'Vera Cohn, Eileen Patten, and Mark Hugo Lopez, *2014. "Puerto Rican Population Declines on Island, Grows on U.S. Mainland."* Washington, D.C.: Pew Research Center's Hispanic Trends Project, July, 7. Accessed June 9, 2017, http://www.pewhispanic.org/2014/08/11/chapter-1-puerto-ricans-on-the-u-s-mainland/#geographic-distribution.

90. Other studies report a much smaller gap between non-Hispanic white and Hispanic incarceration rates. According to her findings, Hispanics are incarcerated 1.4 times as often as non-Hispanic whites. Nellis, *The Color of Racial and Ethnic Disparity*, 3.

as often as Hispanic women.[91] In both cases, the gap between black and Hispanic incarceration rates matches or exceeds the gap between Hispanic and white rates. Even in the notoriously anti-Latino border state of Texas, the gap between black and Hispanic incarceration rates nearly doubles the gap between Hispanic and white incarceration rates.[92] If relative immunity from incarceration accords whites privilege over Hispanics, then this same immunity endows nonblack Hispanics with at least as much privilege over blacks.

But perhaps these statistics err by lumping all Latino subgroups together. However, even after disaggregating the data, the mass prison remains uniquely antiblackness supremacist. Nationwide, in 2000, the incarceration rate for native-born black men stood at 11.6 percent. In contrast, the rate for the following Latino groups measured: 0.68 percent for Salvadoran and Guatemalan men; 1.07 percent for all Colombian, Ecuadorian, and Peruvian men; 2.71 percent for Mexican and Mexican-American men; 2.76 percent for Dominican men; 3.01 percent for Cuban men; and 5.06 percent for Puerto Rican men. Perhaps these statistics still underestimate the effect of mass incarceration on native-born Latino/as given that immigrants, who are incarcerated less often than their native-born counterparts, comprise a larger percentage of the Latino/a population than the black. But even if we exclude immigrants from our calculation, the highest rate of incarceration for a single native-born Latino group belongs to Mexican-American men at 5.9 percent.[93] This represents less than half the rate faced by black men. Further vindicating the uniquely antiblackness supremacist character of the mass prison, the only group whose rate of incarceration even approaches that imposed upon non-Hispanic black men is Puerto Rican men who lack a high school diploma, at 10.48 percent.[94] Many of these men would be classified as black.

What about black immigrants? Because they enter the United

91. Mark T. Berg and Matt DeLisi, "The Correctional Melting Pot: Race, Ethnicity, Citizenship, and Prison Violence," *Journal of Criminal Justice* 34, no. 6 (November 2006): 632.
92. "Justice Policy Institute, Race and Imprisonment in Texas: The Disparate Incarceration of Latinos and African Americans in the Lone Star State." http://www.justicepolicy.org/images/upload/05-02_rep_txraceimprisonment_ac-rd.pdf.
93. http://www.migrationpolicy.org/sites/default/files/source_charts/rumbaut-table1-jun06.cfm.
94. Rubén G. Rumbaut et al., "Debunking the Myth of Immigrant Criminality: Imprisonment among First-and Second-Generation Young Men," *Migration Information Source*, 2006, http://www.fosterglobal.com/policy_papers/DebunkingTheMythOfImmigrantCriminality.pdf.

States as immigrants rather than slaves, they can distinguish themselves from their native-born counterparts. In this way, U.S. Americans typically perceive the children of African immigrants, for example, as possessing a "stronger . . . work ethic and interest in education" than those native-born black Americans who are descended from Africanized slaves.[95] But just as their immigrant status mitigates their association with the social death of slavery, so their perceived blackness positions them below all other immigrant groups.[96] For example, black immigrants spend time behind prison bars more than three times as often as Mexican immigrants do. Although black immigrants comprise only 5.4 percent of the United States' unauthorized residents, they represent more than 20 percent of those who "face deportation on criminal grounds."[97] For example, in the year 2013, "more than three quarters of Black immigrants were removed on criminal grounds" compared to "less than half of immigrants overall."[98] Black immigrants were also more likely "to be identified through interactions with local law enforcement, because of . . . racial profiling" than their nonblack counterparts. As with other measures, immigrant status advantages black people relative to their native-born black counterparts while disadvantaging them relative to their nonblack fellow immigrants.[99] How can we explain this? More than simply attempting to disempower both blackness and black people, antiblackness supremacy strives to preserve the association between blackness and slave status. Perhaps for this reason, "three times as many African immigrants were removed for an immigration charge as for a criminal charge" while "twice as many Caribbean immigrants were removed for a criminal charge than an immigration charge."[100] Immigrants from sub-Saharan Africa are perceived as black, but they are not necessarily figured as descendants of Africanized slaves in the way that Afro-Caribbean immigrants are.

95. Byrd, "Bridging the Gap," 91.

96. Christina M. Greer, *Black Ethnics: Race, Immigration, and the Pursuit of the American Dream* (New York: Oxford University Press, 2013), 7, 11–19.

97. Juliana Morgan-Trostle and Kexin Zheng, "The State of Black Immigrants: Part II: Black Immigrants in the Mass Criminalization System," *New York University Law School Immigrant Rights Clinic*, 19, accessed January 3, 2017, http://www.stateofblackimmigrants.com/assets/sobi-deportation-sept27.pdf.

98. Morgan-Trostle and Zheng, "The State of Black Immigrants: Part II," 21.

99. Yaa Gyasi, "I'm Ghanaian-American. Am I Black?," *New York Times*, June 18, 2016, accessed June 20, 2016, http://www.nytimes.com/2016/06/19/opinion/sunday/im-ghanaian-american-am-i-black.html.

100. Morgan-Trostle and Zheng, "The State of Black Immigrants: Part II," 21.

As national reaction to the presidency of Barack Obama demonstrates, black immigrants illustrate the rules of blackness and immigrant status by serving as the exception to both.[101] The son of an African immigrant father and a white, Midwestern mother, he appeared sufficiently different from other black candidates like Jesse Jackson, who descended from U.S.-American slaves. But just as his immigrant heritage tempered his blackness, his blackness transformed his immigrant heritage into a type of indelible stain: many U.S.-Americans imagined him not just foreign-born but invasively and secretly Muslim. In contrast, Cuban-American senators Marco Rubio and Ted Cruz, also the sons of immigrant fathers, did not trigger similar fears in the minds of native-born, non-Hispanic whites when they were running for president. As in the Danish slave islands of St. John, St. Croix, and St. Thomas, antiblackness supremacy at once provides both the rules by which black immigrants to the United States must play to keep from losing and the apparatus that makes it more difficult for them to actually win.

What about class? Perhaps the mass prison appears uniquely antiblack only due to a correlation between blackness and lower-class status. Class status undoubtedly affects incarceration rates, but not in the way many might think. For example, Mexican and Mexican-American men without a high school degree are incarcerated less than half as often as black men who have graduated from high school. Nor can class differentials explain why white men without high school diplomas go to prison almost twice as often as their similarly credentialed Mexican-American counterparts.[102] Lower-class immigrants experience the prison system differently than lower-class non-immigrants do. We do not need to choose between class- and race-based analyses: rather than obscuring the role that class status plays in mass incarceration, the antiblackness supremacy approach to the study of racial inequality helps clarify it. Class matters when making comparisons within racial and ethnic groups, but it means relatively little when assessing incarceration rates across racial and ethnic lines.

Further underscoring the uniquely antiblackness supremacist character of the mass prison, black people are victimized by police violence more than any other racial or ethnic group. Despite com-

101. For more on the racialized reaction to Obama's election, see Grimes, "'Birtherism and Antiblackness," *Political Theology,* forthcoming.

102. http://www.migrationpolicy.org/sites/default/files/source_charts/rumbaut-table1-jun06.cfm.

prising a little over thirty percent of the city's population, black Chicagoans comprised over seventy-eight percent of those incapacitated by currents of electric taser fire by Chicago police during the first six months of 2014.[103] The afterlife of slavery ensnares even black children: seventy-seven percent of juveniles arrested by Chicago police in the year 2011 had black skin. The city's Hispanic population, which comprised twenty-eight percent of the city's total population and only eighteen percent of juveniles taken into police custody, received much more proportionate treatment.[104]

A 2014 incident in Alabama illustrates the way in which the afterlife of slavery renders the black body uniquely vulnerable to violent correction. One morning, a local resident placed a nonemergency phone call to the police in which he reported a "skinny black guy" whom he had "never seen . . . before . . . just wandering around" and "walking close to the garage." Before hanging up, the caller expressed feeling "nervous" about leaving his wife at home while this black man was roaming around.[105] Minutes later, video captured the police officers who were dispatched to the scene body-slamming the suspicious prowler to the ground ferociously and paralyzing him. But unlike almost every other case of unwarranted police violence unleashed against black women, children, and men, this act did not go unpunished. The offending police officer was arrested and fired, and the victim's family received a prompt apology from the chief of police. What allowed for this stunning turn of events?

The body-slammed victim turned out to be not a "skinny black guy" but an Indian grandfather visiting his immigrant son. The police department so swiftly levied criminal charges on one of its own not because the offending officer body-slammed a human being without cause, but because he treated a nonblack person like a black person. He erred not because he paralyzed a man but because he confused the dark skin of a person from India with the dark skin of a person descended from enslaved Africans.[106] In contrast, in the north-

103. "We Charge Genocide UN Shadow Report," 6, accessed June 23, 2015, report.wechargegenocide.org/index.html.

104. Ibid., 9.

105. Peter Holley, Abby Phillip, and Abby Ohlheiser, "Alabama Police Officer Arrested after Indian Grandfather Left Partially Paralyzed," *The Washington Post*, February 12, 2015, accessed June 20, 2015, https://www.washingtonpost.com/news/morning-mix/wp/2015/02/11/alabama-cops-leave-a-grandfather-partially-paralyzed-after-frisk-goes-awry/?utm_term=.3bff06fbe2d8.

106. Holley, Phillip, and Ohlheiser, "Alabama Police Officer Arrested after Indian Grandfather Left Partially Paralyzed."

ern city of Cleveland, police shot a twelve-year-old black boy named Tamir Rice who was standing in an unoccupied park holding a toy gun without even speaking to him and have yet to face even minor professional sanction. His body lay for more than six months in a city morgue awaiting the completion of the Cuyahoga County Sheriff's Department's criminal investigation. The city charged Rice's mother seventy-five dollars for each day it held her son's body hostage. Worn down by a strategically delayed investigation, Samaria Rice had her young son's body cremated.[107]

Like prevailing patterns of racial segregation, the mass prison operates less as a scheme of white supremacy or economic exploitation and more as a system of targeted antiblackness supremacy. Just as the racial theory of property value considers a wide array of characteristics unappealing, but blackness especially so, the mass prison polices other groups—the mentally ill, the poor and homeless, sexual minorities—while judging blackness the most out of control. When theologians describe hyper-incarceration as white supremacist, they erroneously portray all people of color as collectively disadvantaged by the judicial system.[108] Rather than describing either segregation or the mass prison as driven by a generalized and uniform animus toward all peoples considered "not white," we ought to instead perceive them as historically specific displays of power and embodied memory rooted most firmly, but not exclusively, in "the afterlife of slavery."[109]

For this reason, the racial changes initiated by the so-called new immigrants from Latin America, Asia, and Africa represent not a new "Latin Americanization" of race, but a rather unsurprising continuation of shared patterns of assimilation and empowerment

107. Wesley Lowery, "Six Months after Shooting, Tamir Rice's Family Has Him Cremated," *The Washington Post*, May 13, 2015, http://www.washingtonpost.com/news/post-nation/wp/2015/05/13/six-months-after-shooting-tamir-rices-family-has-him-cremated/; Shaun King, "Why Tamir Rice Has Not Yet Been Buried Six Months after Being Shot and Killed by Cleveland Police," May 5, 2015, accessed June 8, 2015, http://www.dailykos.com/story/2015/05/05/1382668/-Why-Tamir-Rice-has-not-yet-been-buried-six-months-after-being-shot-and-killed-by-Cleveland-Police.

108. For example, Cassidy, Mikulich, and Pfeil describe those who are disproportionately subject to hyper-incarceration as "poor people of color," but as the preceding demonstrates, mass incarceration does not in fact target all poor people of color. See also *The Scandal of White Complicity*, 4, 10, 13, 14–20, 32.

109. Saidiya V. Hartman, *Lose Your Mother: A Journey along the Atlantic Slave Route* (New York: Farrar, Straus & Giroux, 2008), 45.

through antiblackness.[110] Rather than weakening white supremacy, the post-1960s influx of immigration from Latin America and Asia has granted whiteness new members as well as many more allies. Even when nonblack people of color rightly protest and mobilize against their victimization by white supremacy, their measured incorporation into antiblackness ensures that their presence in the United States helps white supremacy at least as much as it hurts it. More than anything, immigration from Latin America and Asia has exposed white supremacy's fundamental relationship to antiblackness.[111] While it has arguably softened the boundary between white and nonwhite in some places, it has not disturbed the line between black and nonblack. Even if the line between white and nonwhite continues to blur, it is entirely possible if not likely that the line between those defined as the black descendants of U.S.-American slaves and the rest of humanity will hold firm.[112]

110. Eduardo Bonilla-Silva, "From Bi-Racial to Tri-Racial: Towards a New System of Racial Stratification in the USA," *Ethnic and Racial Studies* 27, no. 6 (2004): 931–50.
111. Sexton, "People-of-Color-Blindness," 31–56.
112. Yancey, *Who Is White?*, 15.

8.

Toward a Theory of Corporate Virtue and Vice

More than simply overturning prevailing narratives of white Catholic innocence both corporate and individual, the history of the church's participation in antiblackness supremacy compels the creation of a new theory of corporate virtue and corporate vice. Evaluating the church's parochial life through the lens provided by virtue theory, this theory argues that all the church's practices contribute to a process of corporate habituation. In so doing, this theory of corporate virtue builds upon Dan Daly's recent argument for the existence of structures of virtue and structures of vice. While Daly's theory highlights the moral impact of social structures upon individuals, my theory of corporate virtue unmasks the operation of vice within corporate bodies.[1] Rather than simply acting upon bodies, antiblackness supremacy lives within them just as habits do.[2] White people do not simply cooperate with racial evil; we *have* it. It qualifies as a "quality of [our] person which admits of no existential distance from" us.[3] For this reason, we ought to describe it as a habit.[4] And in distinction

1. Daniel J. Daly, "Structures of Virtue and Vice," *New Blackfriars* 92, no. 1039 (2011): 341–57.
2. ST I–II, 49.1.
3. Dan J. Daly, *From Nature to Second Nature: The Relationship of Natural Law, Acquired Virtue, and Moral Precepts in Thomas Aquinas's Summa Theologiae* (PhD diss., Boston College, 2008), 84.
4. Although the second aspect of what Daly defines as "structures of virtue or vice"—"the socially rooted moral habits willingly internalized by moral agents that consistently prescribe sinful human acts, and produce human unhappiness"—resembles what I mean by "corporate virtue or vice," it is misleadingly described. Calling these phenomena "structures" is rhetorically

to Pfeil, Mikulich, and Cassidy, who have astutely called attention to the fact that white Catholics are "fully immersed in and socialized by white habitus," my theory of corporate virtue scrutinizes the racial habituation of not just individual but corporate bodies.[5] It also focuses our attention on bodies, both our own and Christ's.

In so doing, this corporate theory of virtue and vice better positions Catholic theologians to move beyond an overly individualized account of sin.[6] Catholic scholars of racism have attempted to uncover individual white people's relation to sinful structures.[7] Others have endeavored "to retrieve the [older], manualist category of cooperation with evil and applied it to social sin" as a way of figuring out "how we are complicit in evil we do not intend."[8] But this framing lets white people off the hook. The theory of embodied voluntary vices allows us to recognize that white people *do* intend antiblackness, even without consciously realizing it. These attempts to capture the social character of racism are further limited by what I term a moral epistemology of individual salvation. Scholars rely so heavily upon the language of white privilege in large part because they rightly wish to convince every white individual that she bears moral responsibility for racial injustice.[9] But as the history of the corporate Catholic habits of antiblackness supremacy demonstrates, human beings do not sin just as individuals. Nor are we saved as such. This holds particularly true with respect to the corporate vice of antiblackness supremacy. At one level, in a world structured by antiblackness supremacy, individuals do not exist; these forces attend only to the group identities imprinted on our bodies. The Latino police officer who slammed a black woman's head into the hard ground of a rural highway while citing her for a traffic violation did not care about the details that made her different from every other human being who has drawn oxygen into her lungs—where she went to college, what her favorite song is, how she has spent her life in service to others.[10] All that mattered in that moment was her unsubdued blackness.

confusing: How can a "structure" inhere within the human person? Daly, "Structures of Virtue and Vice," 355.

5. Alex Mikulich et al., *The Scandal of White Complicity in US Hyper-Incarceration: A Nonviolent Spirituality of White Resistance* (New York: Palgrave Macmillan, 2013), 182.

6. Ibid., 4.

7. Ibid., 33.

8. Ibid., 8.

9. See for example Mikulich et al., *The Scandal of White Complicity*, 9.

10. Stephen A. Crockett Jr., "Sandra Bland Drove to Texas to Start a New Job, so How Did She

Racial evil operates corporately and habitually as well as individually; our ethical theories ought to describe it as such.

THE RHETORICAL AND CONCEPTUAL PERILS OF DESCRIBING RACISM AS A "CULTURE"

My theory of corporate virtue and vice also critiques recent attempts to describe whiteness as a type of culture. For example, drawing upon Bernard Lonergan's concept of culture, Massingale defines racism as "the underlying 'set of meanings and values' attached to skin color, a way of interpreting skin color differences that pervades the collective convictions, and practices of American life."[11] And indeed so-called "racism" does act through culture. But the term culture encourages us to imagine racism as an entity that operates above and around bodies. In this framing, antiblackness appears more as an opinion about bodies than an entity that inhabits them. The concept of culture just does not explain how antiblackness gets into the body. My theory of corporate virtue and vice seeks to remedy this by providing a more rhetorically powerful and substantively secure scaffolding upon which to fashion an adequately embodied account of antiblackness supremacy. This task proves especially urgent given that the vices of antiblackness supremacy often blend into the background of every living. Accruing through mundane actions, antiblackness supremacist habits seem not vicious but invisible. As a result, the vicious habits of segregationist antiblackness supremacy operate unnoticed and uninterrupted in both the church and the world. In response, this theory of corporate virtue and vice encourages us to look less at what the church says about race and much more to how its corporate body occupies space.

Antiblackness supremacy also can distort conversations about the relation between theology and culture. In the spatial afterlife of slavery, relatively minor cultural distinctions acquire major racial significance and serve as obvious and emotionally charged markers of racial difference and incompatibility. For example, many of the white people who belonged to Chicago's St. Sabina's parish in the

End Up Dead in Jail?," *The Root*, July 16, 2015, http://www.theroot.com/articles/news/2015/07/sandra_bland_drove_to_texas_to_start_a_new_job_so_how_did_she_end_up_dead.html.

11. Bryan N. Massingale, *Racial Justice and the Catholic Church* (Maryknoll, NY: Orbis, 2014), 1–2.

middle of the twentieth century blamed cultural differences between their new black neighbors and them for their parish's failure to hold blacks and whites together. As one white ex-parishioner un-ironically explained, whites "listened to the Beatles and the Beach Boys, [two all-white groups that drew much of their inspiration from African American music] and even the Supremes and Smokey Robinson [two black musical acts], whereas blacks listened to music she could only describe as 'funky' and unfamiliar to whites." These Irish-Americans further contrasted their preferring to "drink . . . whiskey from a standing position," with black patrons' "tending to order a pint of whiskey and then sit at a table by themselves or with friends" as evidence of racial incommensurability.[12] But their attachment to a distinctly Irish-American cultural identity proved situational. To begin with, in the city, they had always lived in ethnically diverse neighborhoods. One wonders: What made the cultural differences of black neighbors so much more intolerable than those of Italians, Poles, or Russians? Second, even if these Chicagoans truly moved to the suburbs to protect their Irish-ness, they ultimately failed. Like Irish-Americans across the country, in moving to the suburbs, they would lose much of what distinguished them from other white ethnic groups.[13]

Rather than simply asking whether culture changes or if it should, we also ought to assess why it does. In a world structured by antiblackness supremacy, assertions of cultural difference can justify and obscure racialized power just as surely as its suppression can. Like twentieth-century instantiations of European ethnicity, contemporary versions of nonblack ethnicity likely will be at least partially shaped by forces of antiblackness. While also working against unjust cultural and ecclesial domination by native-born whites, scholars also must attend to the ways in which even these assertions of culturally differentiated Catholicism act to offer nonblack Catholic groups a place in the church and society at the expense of both blackness and black people.

Indeed, the corporately embodied character of the Catholic Church as the body of Christ—while conducive to cohesion—has nevertheless rendered it particularly susceptible to and compatible

12. Jensen, "'No Irish Need Apply': A Myth of Victimization," *Journal of Social History* 36, no. 2 (2002): 172.

13. James R. Barrett, *The Irish Way: Becoming American in the Multiethnic City*, 1st ed. (New York: Penguin, 2012), 287.

with antiblackness supremacy. Amplifying its susceptibility to the spatial afterlife of slavery, the Catholic parish incorporates its members not just performatively but territorially.[14] And, like all bodies, the church is shaped by its habitat. In the United States, the Catholic Church has performed its body-shaping practices in a habitat of antiblackness supremacy. White Catholics therefore bring their racialized bodies with them when they form a parish, ingest the Eucharist, or process into the streets in celebration of a patron saint's feast day.[15] Rather than reconditioning the racialized Catholic bodies, embodied Catholic practices of incorporation have tended to, at best, capitulate to, or, at worst, amplify and affirm the habituating power of antiblackness supremacy.

THE STUNNINGLY EMBODIED CHARACTER OF ANTIBLACKNESS SUPREMACY WREAKS HAVOC UPON THE STUNNINGLY EMBODIED PRACTICE OF CATHOLICISM

This theory of corporate virtue and vice calls attention to the body for another reason. Antiblackness supremacy, like Catholicism, works primarily in and upon the body.[16] People become Christian by an encounter with holy water and the hands of a priest; Christians receive Christ's body inside of their bodies. Catholic practices work primarily upon the body for the sake of incorporating its members into a larger body, Christ's.[17] And so does antiblackness supremacy. Shaping bodies materially and contouring our perception of them, it encourages certain bodies to cleave together and others to remain apart. It also disciplines bodies: in addition to rendering black people uniquely vulnerable to servile violence, it provides white people the power to inflict this violence with impunity. While Catholicism animates a distinct mode of bodily comportment in both the liturgy and

14. John T. McGreevy, *Parish Boundaries: The Catholic Encounter with Race in the Twentieth-Century Urban North* (Chicago: University of Chicago Press, 1998), 11.

15. McGreevy, *Parish Boundaries*, 11.

16. Bruce T. Morrill, Susan Rodgers, and Joanna E. Ziegler, eds., *Practicing Catholic: Ritual, Body, and Contestation in Catholic Faith* (New York: Palgrave Macmillan, 2006), 4.

17. Louis-Marie Chauvet, *Symbol and Sacrament: A Sacramental Reinterpretation of Christian Existence* (Collegeville, MN: Liturgical, 1995), 352–53.

beyond it, antiblackness supremacy conditions bodies to act, think, dress, walk, and occupy space in accordance with its prerogatives.[18]

Like nonblack Catholics in general and white Catholics in particular, the church becomes where it lives. For this reason, the vice of antiblackness supremacy is not an easily excisable blemish marring the surface of the church's otherwise racially spotless corporate body; it instead pervades the church's corporate body, pulsing within it like blood or bone marrow. As such, antiblackness supremacy cannot be extracted from a corporate body that remains otherwise the same. Racial rehabituation will require more than merely cosmetic surgery. The church can rid itself of antiblackness only by performatively acquiring a new racial character.[19]

But this will be quite difficult. As a corporate habit, antiblackness supremacy possesses a self-perpetuating momentum, instilling in the church's corporate body an appetite for racial stasis. But this does not exculpate the church. Although the church, like all bodies, was partially "constituted by forces beyond [its] control," the church still retains moral responsibility for its antiblackness supremacist character. An act or personal character qualifies as voluntary not so much based on whether one could have acted or become otherwise, but on whether one wishes to have done or to have become as they did.[20] Unlike the involuntarily malformed agent who regrets the person she had to become, the church remains unaware of and undisturbed by its antiblackness supremacist character.[21] Like all vices, the corporate vice of antiblackness supremacy took up residence within the body of Christ because it was invited in. As Aquinas reminds us, moral agents acquire habits only voluntarily.[22] The church is not a victim of its vices. But the church is not entirely self-creating either. As long as the church continues to perform its body-building practices while residing in the body-shaping habitat of antiblackness supremacy, it will retain its deeply embodied and corporately vicious racial character. It cannot reform itself from within. The church feels perfectly at home within the habitat it helped to build. It has the habits it desires.

18. Chauvet, *Symbol and Sacrament*, 341.
19. ST I–II.53.3.
20. Massingale, *Racial Justice and the Catholic Church*, 30.
21. Ibid.
22. Aquinas, *Summa Theologiae* I–II.55.4 ad 6; 75.3; II–II.59.2 ad 2.

A THEOLOGICAL NOTE: RACIAL VIRTUE IS ACQUIRED GRACE

This theory of corporate virtue and vice may seem to focus on what many Thomists would call "acquired virtue," those habits human beings build, while neglecting so-called "infused moral virtues," those habits that God gives us. For this reason, one may wonder whether this theory perceives human beings as capable of surmounting sin on their own: Has it left sufficient space for God to act on us and in the world? In response, I argue that this theory of corporate virtue and vice ultimately qualifies as deeply theological: it does not deny human beings' fundamental dependence on God's goodness. Echoing Protestant moral theologian Jennifer Herdt, I "underscore the graced character of *all* virtue acquisition" and affirm "a genuinely non-competitive account of human and divine agency."[23]

More than simply theologically defensible, this theory of corporate virtue and vice can help defend Thomas's moral theology by vindicating Thomistic confidence "that grace can work through ordinary processes of habituation" and refuting what Herdt identifies as "hyper-Augustinianism." Popularized by early modern reformers, this belief insists that

> if there is any room for habituation into the Christian life, it must be sharply distinct from habituation into natural "virtue." A pure will, a pure heart, must be first given by God in some way outside of, and discontinuous with, ordinary moral psychology.[24]

As a Thomist, I echo Herdt's critique of this view.[25] But I also blame Thomists for the way their insufficiently embodied accounts of moral habituation have made their confidence in the compatibility between human and divine agency unnecessarily difficult to understand, explain, and defend.

This failure proves particularly frustrating given that Aquinas recognizes the error in what Herdt identifies as the "hyper-Augustinian" position. As Herdt explains, even in the case of those virtues infused

23. Herdt, "Redeeming the Acquired Virtues," *Journal of Religious Ethics* 41, no. 4 (2013): 734.
24. Herdt, *Putting On Virtue: The Legacy of the Splendid Vices* (Chicago: University of Chicago Press, 2010), 3.
25. For more on the way in which Aquinas's ethical arguments are deeply theological, see Jean Porter, *Natural and Divine Law: Reclaiming the Tradition for Christian Ethics* (Grand Rapids, MI: Eerdmans, 1999), 53, 123, 164–80.

directly by the Holy Spirit, "Aquinas denies that the Holy Spirit moves a human being as a mere instrument."[26] Aquinas instead specifies that the human person "is so acted upon, by the Holy Ghost, that he also acts himself, in so far as he has a free-will."[27] Put another way, Aquinas rejects the notion that human beings are God's slaves. Aquinas therefore describes passions such as love, hate, fear, and desire as similarly unenslaved: for Aquinas, the reason and will command these other parts of the soul "not . . . by a despotic sovereignty, as a slave is moved by his master, but . . . as free men are ruled by their governor, and can nevertheless act counter to his commands."[28] In fact, for Aquinas, it is the soul's freedom, relative to both God and itself, that makes habits both necessary and possible. Because it is free, the soul can act rightly only if it cultivates good habits.[29] It cannot be forced; therefore it must learn how to choose.

Unfortunately, Aquinas empowers the "hyper-Augustinian" position he intends to refute when he fails to grant the human body this same freedom.[30] Describing slavery as essential to moral formation, he contends that the reason and will ought to rule the body as a master drives his slave.[31] Like enslaved people and domesticated beasts, the body ought to be moved to action externally. It is driven rather than self-directing. Recall Patterson's definition of slavery: it sheds light on the extent to which Aquinas figures the body as a slave. Like enslaved people, Aquinas believes that the body is not truly entitled to a life of its own; it instead should live through its master and in accordance with his will.[32] More than simply incapable of acquiring habits, the slave-like body does not need them.[33] It has no choice but to obey.[34] And, like human masters of human slaves, the will gains honor and power at the body's expense: the will demonstrates its freedom through not just what it can refuse and resist, but also what it

26. Herdt, *Putting On Virtue*, 91; ST I–II.68.3 ad 2.

27. As Orlando Patterson explains, slaves are "the ultimate human tools." *Slavery and Social Death: A Comparative Study*, 1st ed. (Cambridge, MA: Harvard University Press, 1985), 302.

28. ST I–II, 9.2 ad 3; ST I–II, 68.3 ad 2; Herdt, *Putting On Virtue*, 91.

29. ST I–II, 68.3 ad 2.

30. For more on Aquinas's describing the body as an "instrument" of the soul, see Robert Pasnau, *Thomas Aquinas on Human Nature: A Philosophical Study of Summa Theologiae* Ia 75–89 (Cambridge: Cambridge University Press, 2002), 47, 113, 433; Joseph Peter Wawrykow, *The Westminster Handbook to Thomas Aquinas* (Louisville: Westminster John Knox, 2005), 75.

31. ST I–II, 81.5 ad 2; ST I–II, 85.5.

32. ST I, 76.1; ST I–II, 50.2.

33. ST I–II, 50.1.

34. ST I, 21.1 ad 3.

can make the body do.[35] According to this view, the will is free partially because the body is its slave.[36] Aquinas's anthropology likely reflects the limitations of his intellectual context: he conceives of the body as a slave-like instrument largely because he believes corporeal matter as incapable of both reason and self-movement. Contemporary observers now know this simply is not true. We do not need to be partially incorporeal to be fully human.[37]

Even if we ought not to judge Aquinas too harshly, we cannot deny the harm his anthropology has caused. In describing the human person as comprised of a masterly soul and a servile body, Aquinas unwittingly sabotages his arguments for the compatibility between human and divine agency. How? For Aquinas, the reason and the will are more perfect than the body and the sensitive soul that houses the emotions because they are more incorporeal than them. After all, he believes that only incorporeal faculties can govern or engage in purposeful action. But this anthropology unfortunately portrays the Holy Spirit, who bestows infused virtues, and the soul, which cultivates acquired virtues, as two spiritual, or at least incorporeal, agents fighting for control over the otherwise inert human body.[38] Such a battle inevitably qualifies as zero-sum: a slave cannot serve two masters; a ship can have only one captain just as a train can have only one conductor. Aquinas therefore legitimizes a "hyper-Augustinian" view that positions the human and divine wills as rivals: a given action is caused either by God or by the human person.

Human and divine agency ultimately seem incompatible largely because we conceive of the body as a slave in need of a master. But because the hyper-corporeal theory of corporate virtue and vice offered in this book uncovers the will as thoroughly embodied, it can help us overturn anthropologies that conceive of the will as a command-center existing inside of or somehow distinct from the body.[39] This theory instead contends that the will does not exist prior to the

35. ST I–II, 10.4 ad 1; ST I–II, 17.2 ad 1; ST I–II, 17.8 ad 2; ST I–II, 17.9; ST I–II, 17.9 ad 1.
36. ST I, 21.1 ad 3. Aquinas believes that the reason also is ultimately free. ST I–II, 10.3 ad 2; I–II, 10.3 ad 3.
37. As theologian Nancey Murphy points out, we do not even need to posit the existence of an incorporeal soul or mind in order to uphold hope in the resurrection of the body. *Bodies and Souls, or Spirited Bodies?* (New York: Cambridge University Press, 2006).
38. ST I, 76.4 ad 2; ST I–II, 9.5.
39. Although Aquinas believes that "habit or disposition is . . . to be found in the body by reason of its relation to the soul," he concludes that "if we take habit in its relation to operation, it is chiefly thus that habits are found in the soul." In this way, "habits are in the soul in respect of its powers." ST I–II, 50.2.

actions it produces; it is best known through them. In so doing, it enables us to reject those theories in which the will uses the body as an infinitely fungible tool.[40] Put another way, my theory of corporate virtue and vice empowers us to envision the relation between mind or soul and body as something other than that between a master and her slave.

Insufficiently embodied moral anthropologies similarly misconstrue so-called infused and acquired virtues as incompatible forces: categorizing virtues as either acquired or infused, it denies that they can be both. In response, my theory of corporate virtue and vice reminds us that, although the Holy Spirit is incorporeal, She does not infuse grace into souls alone. Consider the Eucharist. As "the source and summit" of Christian life, the Eucharist models how God habituates human beings and communities.[41] God does not use our bodies as fungible instruments; God gives us God's own body as a gift. Just as the church must performatively receive its sacramental identity as the body of Christ, so must individual human beings performatively receive God's transformative grace.[42] What does this mean? Yes, the church receives Christ's body as a gift, but only if it performs certain human actions. For example, a priest must speak certain words and wear certain clothes; human beings must somehow take the Eucharist into their own bodies. Put simply, if one does not eat and drink Christ's body and blood, she cannot receive them. Each of these skills are learned from others and perfected only through practice. One becomes what one does, and this includes the body of Christ. The Eucharist, like all of God's gifts, is an acquired taste. As Herdt affirms, "we do well not to be overly confident in our delineations of what is merely acquired versus infused virtue."[43] Rather than pitting sacramentally infused graces against human-acquired aptitudes as "hyper-Augustinians" might, we ought to learn the lessons the sacraments teach. Besides, if God is our Father, then we are not his slaves. Assertions of human freedom seem to infringe upon God's freedom only because we still confuse freedom with mastership.

40. Here, I critique Aquinas's claim that God "works *inwardly* in every nature and in every will." ST I–II, 68.2. Emphasis mine.

41. Congregation of Rites, instruction, *Eucharisticum mysterium*, 6.

42. Chauvet, *Symbol and Sacrament*, 146, 414.

43. Herdt, "Redeeming the Acquired Virtues," 736.

PART III

Antiblackness Supremacy and the Sacraments of Initiation

The corporately vicious operation of antiblackness supremacy within the corporate body of the Catholic Church requires theologians to change the way they conceive of liturgy, ethics, and the relation between the two. While scholars increasingly describe the sacraments of baptism and Eucharist as partial solutions to the scourge of white supremacy, my research suggests that the sacraments of baptism and the Eucharist as practiced historically have lacked the power to disrupt the church's idolatrous attachment to antiblackness supremacy.[1] At times, these sacraments have even acted as rites of initiation into a world order structured by black slavery and its afterlife. Although black slaves used baptism as a means of pursuing rights and dignity otherwise denied, their ingenious spiritual resistance could not sever the alliance between baptism and slavery.[2] Rather than proposing

1. Bryan N. Massingale, *Racial Justice and the Catholic Church* (Maryknoll, NY: Orbis, 2014), 125; Amy Levad, *Redeeming a Prison Society: A Liturgical and Sacramental Response to Mass Incarceration* (Minneapolis: Fortress Press, 2014).

2. John D. Garrigus and Christopher Morris, *Assumed Identities: The Meanings of Race in the*

these sacraments as even partial antidotes to the racial injustices of a presumed external culture, this section chronicles the way in which these sacramental practices have been corrupted by it.[3]

Atlantic World (College Station: Texas A&M University Press, 2010), 68. M. Shawn Copeland provides a brief overview of the many ways in which enslaved black women resisted their captors, in *Enfleshing Freedom: Body, Race, and Being* (Minneapolis: Fortress Press, 2009), 43–46.

3. Levad, *Redeeming a Prison Society*, 84.

9.

Baptism and the Eucharist as Habits of Antiblackness Supremacy

The corporate vice of antiblackness supremacy has twisted more than just the church's extra-liturgical, parochial actions in its image. Because it pervades the church's corporate body, antiblackness supremacy permeates all its practices, no matter how sacred. The theory of corporate virtue and vice outlined in this book further helps to explain why this holds especially true in the case of baptism and the Eucharist, two of the church's sacraments of initiation. In calling attention to the church's truly corporate and fully embodied character, this theory enables us to perceive the church's body-building practices as neither automatic nor ahistorically static, but shaped by its habitat.

BAPTISM AND SLAVERY: ALLIES IN INCORPORATION

Let us consider baptism first. Although sacramentally baptism aimed to incorporate black and white Christians into Christian community for the sake of salvation and reconciliation, in practice it consolidated their respective places in the slaveocratic racial hierarchy that structured life in the Catholic Americas.[1] This assertion initially seems

1. Herman L. Bennett, *Africans in Colonial Mexico Absolutism, Christianity, and Afro-Creole Consciousness, 1570–1640* (Bloomington: Indiana University Press, 2003), 13.

counterintuitive if not libelous. Indeed, prevailing understandings portray baptism as a type of protest of, or at least protection against, the degradation inflicted by slavery. After all, baptism claims to incorporate individuals in order to liberate them and grant them new life while slavery captures its victims in order to deprive them of both freedom and true life. But, we misunderstand the relation between baptism and chattel slavery because we misapprehend the intimate relation between slavery and belonging.[2] We in turn fail to perceive the affinity between these two seemingly antagonistic conditions because we cling to overly generic conceptions of slavery. Slavery is not a form of marginalization; it operates as a perverse and often intimate form of violently enforced belonging. When we acknowledge this, we position ourselves to better appreciate the way in which slavery so easily turned baptism inside out.[3]

Slavery incorporates perversely precisely because it incorporates enslaved people so thoroughly and effectively. In a certain sense, a slave belongs to his master or mistress even more closely than husbands do to wives or children to their parents. But unlike spouses or children, enslaved people belong to their masters only because they are not allowed to truly belong to anyone else. Indeed, before a slave can be attached to her master, she has to be uprooted from her original social network. Why? Dislocated from ties of mutual obligation to a protective communal network, a slave owes nothing to anyone but her master. And to him she would owe everything.

In performatively enacting the natal alienation of the newly enslaved, baptism enhanced the power the slave's future master would wield over her.[4] Baptism helped force black people to die to their former, chosen life and rise to life in a state of unchosen social death. Kidnapped from various locations within the continent of Africa, captives were transported to one of the slave fortresses that lined the western coast of Africa. There, Portuguese priests turned these slave pens into baptisteries. While sprinkling holy water on shackled African captives, some of whom were already Catholic, these priests assigned them a Portuguese name.[5] Performed en masse, baptism

2. Orlando Patterson, *Slavery and Social Death: A Comparative Study*, 1st ed. (Cambridge, MA: Harvard University Press, 1985), 50.
3. Patterson, *Slavery and Social Death*, 13, 50.
4. Ibid., 5.
5. Ibid., 13, 55.

stripped Africans of their social identities as well as their individuality, helping to consolidate them into a single racial type.[6] Baptismal practices assisted slaveocracy in a further way. Ecclesiastical authorities also allowed the slave ship captains to baptize cargo in danger of dying before landfall. In so doing, they placed these kidnappers in charge of not just the bodies of their African captives, but their souls as well.[7]

Baptism's alliance with slavery persisted even after trafficked Africans arrived in the Americas. Incredibly, African-born women and men who had been stolen away from everyone they had ever loved somehow found the courage to form new communities on the other side of the ocean.[8] But just as slavery forced black women and men to belong to white masters, so it prevented them from truly belonging to one another. Enslaved mothers were routinely sold away from children for whom they would never stop looking and from nursing infants whose faces they would never forget. Slavery separated spouses or forced them to build a married life based upon weekly visits. Further undermining the sanctity of sexual relationships between enslaved women and men, not to mention the rights and dignity of enslaved individuals, slavery enabled white masters to sexually violate married men and women with impunity.[9] Even when baptism incorporated enslaved human beings into the new life of Christian community, it did not protect black Christians from the

6. Iberian opposition to this practice was practically nonexistent. The lone voice of opposition, Spanish Dominican friar Tomás de Mercado, critiqued not the de-individualizing and coerced practice of mass baptism, but what he perceived as the incompatibility between "reports of mass slave baptism at embarkation on the West African coast with the indignities to which these new Christians were subjected on arrival to Spain." A. J. R. Russell-Wood, "Iberian Expansion and the Issue of Black Slavery: Changing Portuguese Attitudes, 1440-1770," *The American Historical Review* 83, no. 1 (1978): 35.

7. My point is not to deny that church authorities issued these decrees with the salvation of enslaved people's souls in mind, but to point out the way in which antiblackness operated through genuine concern for conversion. Besides, although it was exceedingly rare, as the lone voice of Friar Bartolomé de Albornoz demonstrates, it was possible for Iberians to perceive the immorality of enslaving people in order to save their souls. Russell-Wood, "Iberian Expansion and the Issue of Black Slavery," 35.

8. M. Shawn Copeland, "Blackness Past, Blackness Future—and Theology," *South Atlantic Quarterly* 112, no. 4 (September 21, 2013): 637.

9. For more on the sexual abuse and forced surrogacy endured by female slaves see M. Shawn Copeland, *Enfleshing Freedom: Body, Race, and Being* (Minneapolis: Fortress Press, 2009), 48–51. For more on the sexual abuse of male slaves see Robert Richmond Ellis, "Reading through the Veil of Juan Francisco Manzano: From Homoerotic Violence to the Dream of a Homoracial Bond," *Publications of the Modern Language Association* 113, no. 3 (May 1, 1998): 422–35; Lee Michael Penyak, "Criminal Sexuality in Central Mexico, 1750-1850" (PhD diss., University of Connecticut, 1993), 275.

sting of social death. It could not hold together what slavery could tear asunder.

More than simply lacking the power to solidify slave-family ties, baptism sometimes helped to sever them. Baptism rebranded newly kidnapped Africans, signifying that they belonged no more to their families and communities of origin but only to the culture and kin group of their new masters. Baptismal practices also often deprived enslaved women and men of socially recognized custody of the children their own bodies had created. In so doing, they empowered prevailing forces of social death. For example, slave masters arranged the baptism of enslaved children without their parents' permission, and, when filling out baptismal certificates for the enslaved, priests in places like Louisiana usually identified the child's master as father, even when they knew he was not.[10]

Baptism certified black social death in yet another way. In Jamaica, slaves could take a family after receiving baptism and this in fact served as a major incentive for enslaved Jamaicans to receive the sacrament.[11] Especially if we forget Patterson's definition of slavery, this fact may appear to vindicate baptism. But rather than evidencing baptism's role as protector of the enslaved, this aspect of baptism only underscores its complicity in their enslavement. Why? In granting black slaves a surname, baptism gave them as a gift what should have been theirs as a right. White Jamaicans, on the other hand, received a surname simply by being born; they did not need to be baptized to acquire a family name. Here baptism enforced slavery's logic perfectly: black people receive life of all kinds—physical, social, and familial—not as a right they are owed, but as a gift that they can never deserve.

Baptism affirmed enslaved people's violently enforced dependence on white masters in a further way. Adult black slaves frequently lacked the power to resist the baptismal impulses of purportedly pious masters and royal sovereigns.[12] Like infants baptized as a result of their parents' actions, these adults were thought to lack a will of

10. Stephen J. Ochs, *A Black Patriot and a White Priest: Andre Cailloux and Claude Paschal Maistre in Civil War New Orleans* (Baton Rouge: Louisiana State University Press, 2006), 26.

11. Patterson, *Slavery and Social Death*, 57.

12. For example, in 1568, Prince Henrique, acting in his office as Archbishop of Lisbon, "removed the option of refusing baptism" from slaves regardless of age. Catholic France's 1685 *Code Noir* similarly mandated that all slaves receive Catholic baptism. Although this was not the first time Catholic authorities mandated baptism for a purportedly inferior group, this fact demonstrates how Catholic practices that pre-dated the invention of antiblackness proved eas-

their own.[13] Forcibly submerging enslaved people in its waters, baptism enacted enslaved people's dishonorable powerlessness before and infantilizing dependence upon their white masters. Because the slave master's honor fed off her slave's dishonor, these coercive baptismal practices also amplified the honor of slave masters who had their chattel baptized in this way. Even when priests asked newly arrived slaves for their permission before baptizing them, their status as kidnapped victims limited their capacity to consent.[14] Held in a position of almost complete powerlessness, these slaves felt their dependence on white power deep within their ocean-rocked bodies. In saying "no" to the "requests" of those who owned them, they risked further, more brutal, corporal punishment. Those who cannot say no cannot say yes.

In addition to lacking the freedom to decline this sacrament, black slaves were denied the freedom that ought to have issued from it.[15] Baptism would occasion the emancipation of black slaves only when white masters commanded. And they did not will this very often, even for their mulatto children.[16] The very few black slaves who were emancipated at baptism received freedom due to not the sacrament but white mercy. In giving freedom as a gift and not a right, baptism branded the black slave as a pardoned subject who lives in a state of utter dependence upon her master's will rather than one who deserves life and freedom on her own right. Because it secured freedom for nonblacks only, baptism helped to solidify the stigmatizing association between slave status and African descent. In so doing, it helped to make race. Baptism affirmed racialized standards of virtue. For white Catholics, slavery represented the consequences of sin; for black Catholics, slavery served as a precondition of piety. Put another way, white Catholics could be free as long as they were

ily amenable to it. Bennett, *Africans in Colonial Mexico*, 33; Ochs, *A Black Patriot and a White Priest*, 20.

13. Ibid., 63.

14. Angel Valtierra, *Peter Claver: Saint of the Slaves* (Westminster, MD: Newman, 1960), 111.

15. Although this link between baptism and emancipation was not present in the New Testament, later generations of Christians did believe freedom to be the proper consequence of baptism. For example, despite medieval-era lapses, colonial-era Christians initially had retained a belief that baptism ought to bring freedom to the enslaved. R. L. Winer, "Conscripting the Breast: Lactation, Slavery and Salvation in the Realms of Aragon and Kingdom of Majorca, c. 1250–1300," *Journal of Medieval History* 34, no. 2 (2008): 164–84 (167, 171, 172, 174).

16. James Patrick Kiernan, "Baptism and Manumission in Brazil: Paraty, 1789-1822," *Social Science History* 3, no. 1 (1978): 66; Lyman L. Johnson, "Manumission in Colonial Buenos Aires, 1776-1810," *The Hispanic American Historical Review* 59, no. 2 (May 1, 1979): 260.

good while black Catholics were thought to be good only as long as they remained enslaved.[17]

Baptism therefore unsurprisingly upheld and helped to create a moral order in which it was believed that slaves could enter God's kingdom only if they had accepted and acquiesced to their enslavement.[18] In the Capuchin-run parishes of the French Antilles, for example, those black slaves who had been both baptized and sacramentally married occupied the highest ranks in the liturgical strata. As a reward for their obedience and "as an incentive to other [slaves]," they were allowed to don both "cassock and surplice." To the other slaves, they acted as catechists and sat at the front of the church. The second sacramental slave caste included those who had been baptized but not yet experienced the purportedly civilizing power of marriage, while the third caste held the catechumens. But the lowest class numbered not those who had yet to be baptized but those women and men who resisted their enslavement, whether by stealing away, slipping poison into the food white masters ate, or aborting the enslaved life that stirred inside of them. These actions were classified as particularly serious sins for a simple reason. Unlike their outwardly compliant counterparts, a runaway slave refused to remain in his master's chains; a slave who poisoned her master refused to let her captor live; and a slave who aborted her fetus refused to let her body be used as a vessel for breeding new slaves.[19] Forced to kneel at the back of the church for a period of several months to a year, they endured corrective surveillance by highest-ranked slaves who had been sacramentally empowered to act as their overseers.

Despite scholarly claims to the contrary, baptism did not provide black Catholics even spiritual equality.[20] Ordinarily, baptism grants Christians access to the other sacraments.[21] But even free black people were deprived access to holy orders, and slaveowners often held the power to keep their baptized chattel from the altar and to prevent

17. The Protestant rulers of colonial Virginia also severed the connection between baptism and emancipation, but for blacks only, of course. For more on this, see Rebecca Anne Goetz, *The Baptism of Early Virginia: How Christianity Created Race* (Baltimore: Johns Hopkins University Press, 2012), 86–90.

18. Copeland, *Enfleshing Freedom*, 42.

19. Sue Peabody, "'A Dangerous Zeal': Catholic Missions to Slaves in the French Antilles, 1635-1800," *French Historical Studies* 25, no. 1 (2002): 85.

20. Ochs, *A Black Patriot and a White Priest*, 23; Bennett, *Africans in Colonial Mexico*, 35.

21. Catechism of the Catholic Church, 1213. This teaching was retained in the current Catechism from the Catechism of the Council of Trent.

spouses who lived on separate plantations from visiting one another.[22] Antiblackness supremacy ultimately blocked the pathway to ecclesial adulthood. As in society, enslaved Africans were treated like ecclesial children not because they were loved but so that they would remain disempoweringly dependent. As Patterson explains, "On the surface, the relationship [between slave and master] appears to be a straightforward adoption."[23] But unlike children, who eventually attain adulthood or legal majority and enjoy all the rights and obligations of membership in a family, a slave at best qualifies "either . . . as an illegitimate quasi-kinsman or as a permanent minor who never grew up."[24] Despite being encouraged to call themselves brothers and sisters to white Christians, black people were not treated like other members of God's family.

These historical snapshots lead to disturbing theological conclusions. Performed under conditions of antiblackness supremacy, baptism became perverse: it ushered slaves not out of bondage and into freedom, but from freedom and into bondage.[25] It brought slaves not out of death and into life, but from life and into death, both social and physical. Baptism ought to pronounce liberation and life to be kindred spirits, essentially connected.[26] But Africanized slavery severed this connection, keeping its victims alive only so that they may toil as slaves. Here, we do not anachronistically import contemporary notions back to an alien past. To the contrary, Africanized slavery pitted spiritual freedom against physical freedom in historically unprecedented fashion, as earlier generations of Christians had recognized that baptism ought to set human beings free from not just sin, but also physical slavery. Rather than inducting black slaves into the death that led to resurrected life, baptism stood guard at the tomb.[27]

22. Ochs, *A Black Patriot and a White Priest*, 21.

23. Patterson, *Slavery and Social Death*, 63.

24. Ibid., 63.

25. M. Shawn Copeland, "The (Black) Jesus: Reflections on Black Power and the (White) American Christ," in *Christology and Whiteness: What Would Jesus Do?* ed. George Yancy (New York: Routledge, 2012), 182.

26. Catechism of the Catholic Church, 1221.

27. For more on the relation between antiblackness supremacy and baptism, see Katie Walker Grimes, *Fugitive Saints: Catholicism and the Politics of Slavery* (Minneapolis: Fortress Press, 2017), 11–21.

FEASTING ON DEATH: THE EUCHARIST AND BLACK SLAVERY

Like baptism, the Eucharist also has served the ends of antiblackness supremacy. In addition to lacking the power to bind black and white Catholics together in defiance of antiblackness supremacy, the Eucharist also has helped to amplify the vicious operation of antiblackness supremacy both within and outside of the church. Black slaves were incorporated into Christ's body not so much by eating the body of Christ but by being eaten by it. This held true both because, like enslaved people everywhere, Africanized slaves were subjected to "a special form of human parasitism" and, as slaves in the Catholic Americas, they were relatively neglected sacramentally.[28] The slave trade effected a peculiar transubstantiation, "transforming [African-descended] women and men" from fully alive human beings "into dead matter." As such, they could serve as infinitely fungible, "enjoyable properties" that were used and consumed by white bodies.[29] Enslaved people recognized their status as food: As one English participant in the slave trade reported, "Europeans hold out as a general doctrine to their slaves that Europeans will kill and eat them." This doctrine, the officer confessed, "keeps the slaves in order."[30] As food, their death paradoxically kept others alive.

Just as metabolic processes turn food into not just fuel for bodies, but flesh, blood, and bone, so slavery turned black people into money, wealth, and land. Like all slaves, black people were "the ultimate human tools."[31] It is perhaps more precise to say that their humanity made them the ultimate tools. Surpassing all available inanimate objects in utility, they performed nearly every task and supplied masters with nearly every form of pleasure. Black social death pumped life through white people's veins; it sustained their social life. Black slaves, not Christ, served as the bread of white life. Rather than simply eating Christ's murdered flesh, black slaves were eaten as such.

Just as the church receives its corporately embodied life from the Eucharist, so slaveholding societies draw social life from slaves. In both cases, practitioners live by consuming the murdered bodies of

28. Patterson, *Slavery and Social Death*, 14.

29. Saidiya V. Hartman, *Lose Your Mother: A Journey Along the Atlantic Slave Route* (New York: Macmillan, 2008), 68.

30. Ibid., 113–14.

31. Patterson, *Slavery and Social Death*, 302.

human victims. This perhaps partially explains why slavery seemed not discordant but resonant with the deeply Eucharistic Catholic imagination. Slaves became one body with their masters just as surely as those who feast on the Eucharist become one with Christ.

Largely because we continue to misunderstand slavery, contemporary Christians continue to misunderstand the character and ethical requirements of belonging. Slaves differ from the unenslaved by not just their lack of freedom, but also the all-encompassing simplicity of their dependence. A slave, Patterson explains, "was powerless in relation to another precisely because he had to depend exclusively on another person for protection."[32] While the unenslaved belong to many people, enslaved human beings belong only and entirely to their masters. Slaves also differ from their unshackled counterparts in that they cannot make claims on other people. For example, non-enslaved husbands and wives may exercise property rights in their spouses; they also possess rights over their children and are allowed to fulfill obligations to kinfolk and other social relations. A slave, on the other hand, can never make demands or exercise rights: she cannot prevent her master from selling her son away, for example; he stays at her side only if her master allows him to. Nor can an enslaved person fulfill duties to anyone other than her master.

Especially in its perverse, albeit undeniable, historical affinity with Eucharistic practices, slavery rebukes those who celebrate Christian community uncritically.[33] Slavery teaches us that it matters not just whether human beings belong and depend but on whom and how they do so. Freedom consists not so much in independence, but in the right type of belonging. As Patterson summarizes, "a person departed from the condition of slavery to the degree that he was able to spread the source of his protection as wide as possible—without, at the same time, making it too diffuse."[34] Individuals similarly gain freedom to the extent that they can exercise countervailing rights over others. Just as one who claims rights but acknowledges few if any duties enacts mastership rather than freedom, so one who lacks rights and possesses only duties acts more servile than free. Romanticized encomiums for dependence therefore do not correct prevailing

32. Ibid., 28.

33. Stanley Hauerwas, *A Community of Character: Toward a Constructive Christian Social Ethic*, 1st ed. (Notre Dame: University of Notre Dame Press, 1991), 130.

34. Patterson, *Slavery and Social Death*, 28.

tendencies toward individualistic self-assertion.[35] If anything, these critiques only empower those who wish to disguise mastership as freedom. In so doing, their authors unwittingly ratify one of the Western world's worst conceptual errors: mistaking mastership for freedom. Slavery enlisted the Eucharist in its service so easily partially because belonging is ambivalent.

THE SACRAMENTS OF INITIATION IN THE AFTERLIFE OF SLAVERY

Slavery's afterlife continues to display the ambivalence of belonging. In the era of chattel slavery, baptism reified white power by helping to bind black slaves to their white masters. But in the period after slavery's abolition, baptism would reinforce this power by helping to keep blacks and whites apart. Again, baptism was both impotent and culpable. Rather than bringing racially segregated parochial spaces together, baptism solidified their separateness. Nor did baptism grant black Catholics access to white Catholic hospitals, universities, or religious orders. Ratifying a community's lines of belonging at least as much as it realigns them, baptism created a corporate body shaped by the spatial afterlife of slavery.

During slavery's afterlife, the Eucharist also has continued to strengthen habits of antiblackness supremacy. Despite high rates of Northern Catholic Eucharistic reception, white Catholics comprised a significant majority of the participants in the antiblack riots that shook the urban North in the aftermath of the Second World War. Northern white Catholics made no exception for Catholic blacks. At one all-white parish on the Southside of Chicago, white parishioners refused to sit in the same pews as the three African American women who attended mass there.[36] In addition to ostracizing these women, other residents would detonate homemade explosives outside of the church building all throughout mass in an attempt to scare them away. These whites could not become accustomed to this change.

35. For an example of an overly romanticized account of dependence as an antidote to individualistic self-assertion, see Stanley Hauerwas and John Swinton, *Critical Reflections on Stanley Hauerwas' Theology of Disability: Disabling Society, Enabling Theology* (New York: Routledge, 2004), 191–97.

36. McGreevy, *Parish Boundaries,* 98.

For over two years, area black Catholics could attend mass only under the protection of police escorts.[37]

In addition to lacking the power to bind black and white Catholics together in defiance of the prerogatives of antiblackness supremacy, the Eucharist has also amplified the vicious operation of antiblackness supremacy both within and outside of the church. For example, in 1942, the white Chicago parish of Visitation stood on high alert against the small black population that lived just outside its parish boundaries. One day, a white female parishioner saw eight black people visiting the home of a white labor organizer and feared that he had sold his house to them. Word of the impending invasion spread quickly. Crowds of nearly 10,000 whites gathered outside the white labor organizer's house for three consecutive nights. The corporately habituated Catholic parish helped to protect this white space: in order to root out troublemaking interlopers, white ringleaders would greet every unfamiliar figure with the angry question, "What parish are you from?"[38]

The Eucharist helped to cast black people as threats to not just white people's neighborhoods, but also the church's corporate body. Evidencing this, one white Catholic woman described integration as the undoing of the church's corporate body, lamenting the way in which black people "have . . . taken over all our parishes on the south side [of Chicago] . . . and [the way] the poor old white folks, who built these parishes from scratch had to give up everything and the parishioners are scattered all over."[39] In 1953, a white Catholic living in Detroit wrote an anguished letter to the editor of her diocesan newspaper lamenting the fact that "in the past few years we have seen the colored people almost take over a number of parishes." As a result, she explained, "where I grew up and where my family still lives, are on pins and needles, feeling that theirs will be the next parish to go."[40] And in the late year of 1968, white activist and Chicago resident Fr. Francis Lawlor wrote a letter to Cardinal Cody arguing that integration would lead to the steady "disintegration of white communities."[41]

These fears are racist, but not irrational: antiblackness supremacy

37. Ibid.
38. Ibid., 94–96.
39. Ibid., 171.
40. Ibid., 105.
41. Ibid., 232.

placed white parochial bodies in antagonistic relation to both blackness and black people. Unsurprisingly then, the entrance of black residents unmade corporately white, Eucharistically consolidated parochial bodies, thereby undoing the work of antiblackness supremacist incorporation performed over the years. Black people's penetrating white parochial space destroyed the Catholic parish's corporately white body, and, when the white neighborhood fell apart, so did the white parish. In the late 1950s, a powerful white priest in Cleveland sat in a "panic regarding the Negro question," wanting desperately "to be moved [to another parish] before the [integrating] parish [he currently served] collapsed."[42] Another white priest in Gary, Indiana anxiously fretted over the impact of a planned housing project upon his parish. Since this "new housing unit is being built two and a half miles from here," he assured himself that his parish would in fact be spared confrontation with the so-called "negro problem."

But not all white priests could find such racial safety: in Buffalo, one white parish priest sighed a lament of racial surrender: "The changes are bad," he confessed, "the colored people are coming in. Coming from St. Mary's, St. Ann's, St. Nicholas next door. That's the greatest change." Implicitly perceiving his parish as corporately white and therefore animated by antiblackness and the life-giving supremacy it offered, he recognized that "eventually, [integration will] ruin the parish. . . . I think it will have the same effect on the neighborhood. Don't know what can be done to stop it."[43] As these examples demonstrate, it is not that the Eucharist failed to bind Catholics into a truly corporate body; it simply did so in accordance with antiblackness supremacist modes of belonging. Nor was the Eucharist innocently impotent: rather than suffering as a victim of secular antiblackness, the Eucharist often acted as antiblackness supremacy's great ally.

Today, Christian modes of belonging remain largely in the service of white supremacy and the antiblackness supremacy that animates it. Neither baptism nor the Eucharist brings parochially segregated black and white Catholics together.[44] They do not incline white Catholics to share either power or space with their black co-religionists. White Catholics flee baptized black neighbors just as frequently

42. Ibid., 110.
43. Ibid.
44. Copeland, *Enfleshing Freedom*, 82.

as they flee those unwashed by the waters of baptism. Rather than providing a solution to the segregated Catholic parish's racial problems, these sacraments remain voluntarily corrupted by them.

HOLEY BODIES: POROSITY AND THE CORPORATE BODY OF CHRIST

Why have baptism and the Eucharist so consistently lacked the power to resist and overturn these antiblack modes of belonging? Because these sacraments of initiation bring individuals into a corporate body at once solid and porous, they build the body of Christ, but they do not seal it off from the world. For this reason, they cannot fortify the church's corporate body against penetrating exchange with the world it inhabits. This holds especially true in the case of contemporary racial habits: white Catholics, for example, bring their racialized bodies with them when they form a parish, ingest the Eucharist, or process into the streets in celebration of a patron saint's feast day. As Christ's necessarily porous body, the church remains inevitably open to the world and all its virtues and vices.

For this reason, the sacraments of baptism and Eucharist help to make the church a corporate body not magically but metabolically.[45] As a true body, the church changes its environment while simultaneously being changed by it. Bodies metabolize the substances that enter them differently depending both on the way in which they interact with the world they inhabit and on the character of their own constitution. Lungs charred by factory smoke will metabolize oxygen much less effectively than lungs allowed to breathe only the unpolluted air of the countryside. A weakened immune system can turn ordinarily innocuous bacterial visitors into murderous pillagers. Allergies can render otherwise healthful food poisonous. Yes, we become what we eat, but food also becomes what it is eaten by.

Just as the constitution of a body determines the impact of the particular food it ingests, so the character of the church's corporate body sets limits to the operation of the Eucharist. In situations of heightened habituation like spatialized antiblackness supremacy, the church's viciously habituated corporate body will assimilate the cultic meal to itself at least as much as it is assimilated by it. The world's

45. Monika Hellwig, *The Eucharist and the Hunger of the World* (Lanham, MD: Rowman & Littlefield, 1992), 1.

injustice almost always becomes the church's, even in the case of the Eucharist.

But porosity is not all bad. While porosity can imperil, the processes of breathing and eating unveil it as simultaneously life-giving. Bodies survive by a cycle of exchange in which the world outside the body is brought inside and then escorted back out again. This cycle of exchange translates stardust into sunlight and sunlight into photosynthesized plant life and photosynthesized plant life into the blood coursing through the veins of cattle and the blood coursing through the veins of cattle into the metabolizing cells of human beings. While bodies differ from the world around them, they also contain them. In a very real sense, we are sunlight and stardust and grazing animals and growing greenery. We are the nitrogen and phosphorus and carbon burst into being billions of years ago.[46] Perceptions of anthropomorphism notwithstanding, human beings exist not just as an end but also as a means. In breathing in oxygen, we breathe out the carbon dioxide that helps to keep all green things going. In ingesting food, we expel the waste that returns to the universe some of the nutrients we took.

While bodies must maintain a capacity to regulate what flows both in and out of them, a body that narrows its borders does not always become healthier. In fact, sometimes, good health and proper functioning depend upon a body's capacity to increase the number of outside substances that penetrate it. A world-class sprinter differs from a merely average athlete largely by her ability to admit and metabolize larger amounts of oxygen. A child who refuses to eat will suffer malnutrition and even death. Of course, a child who ingests too much food will also fall short of maximum vitality. As these examples show, it is not how much bodies let in but what they let in and how. The thoroughly embodied character of the church also ought to change the way we think about orthodoxy and dissent. Bodies thrive by biodiversity; they are not necessarily healthier when protected from contact with substances very much unlike them. It is not necessarily better to eat food derived from the bodies of special kin than from animals less closely related. Billions of bacteria swarm inside our intestines, making life possible. We could not be human without the assistance of the nonhumans living inside of us.[47] Only

46. Robert Ellsburg, *Thich Nhat Hanh: Essential Writings* (Maryknoll, NY: Orbis, 2001), 55.

47. Alan W. Walker and Julian Parkhill, "Fighting Obesity with Bacteria," *Science* 341, no. 6150 (September 6, 2013): 1069–70; Valerie Brown, "Bacteria Facts to Interest & Surprise You,"

sometimes, such as when matching for blood type in the case of blood transfusions, does difference itself imperil and poison. Porous bodies can be tortured, drowned, wounded, raped, and infected. But without porosity, bodies cannot eat, breathe, expel waste, have sex, or procreate. Indeed, a body that does not allow itself to be penetrated will soon die. If Christians ever succeeded in making the pores of Christ's body impenetrable, we would kill it.

Given the porosity of Christ's body, neither baptism nor the Eucharist can bring black and white Catholics together into one truly visible and politically viable body while they remain parochially and residentially segregated.[48] Even less can they strip whites of their deadly power. As long as the sacraments of initiation incorporate Catholics into racially segregated parishes, the church cannot sacramentally perform its way out of its habituation by antiblackness supremacy.[49] Rather than defying antiblackness supremacy, the sacraments of initiation leave both nonblack people and the racially segregated space that habituates them undisturbed.

The persistence of antiblackness supremacy compels us to shift our thinking and the terms of the current debate about the relationship between the church and the world. The history of antiblackness supremacy's corrupting influence on the church reveals that, rather than posing a threat to the church's distinctiveness as Stanley Hauerwas famously argues, justice in the world is a precondition for the church's identity as the visible body of Christ in history.[50] In contrast to theologians who expect the church to serve as an alternative to the sinful world, the lens of antiblackness supremacy reveals that the world's injustice almost always becomes that of the church. Instead of framing the issue as a choice between justice in the world and ecclesial integrity, the history of antiblackness supremacy suggests that injustice in the world is itself a threat to ecclesial integrity. Rather than seeking either to bridge the gap between liturgy and

accessed December 27, 2013, http://www.psmag.com/science/bacteria-r-us-23628/; Felisa Wolfe-Simon et al., "A Bacterium That Can Grow by Using Arsenic Instead of Phosphorus," *Science* 332, no. 6034 (June 3, 2011): 1163–66.

48. Copeland, *Enfleshing Freedom*, 82.

49. This argument echoes and builds upon Shawn Copeland's 1989 insight into the interrelationship between "change in the ecclesial mood" and "change in the social mood." Gayraud S. Wilmore, *African American Religious Studies: An Interdisciplinary Anthology* (Durham, NC: Duke University Press, 1989), 230.

50. For other worthy critiques of Hauerwas's suspicion of justice, see Jeffrey Stout, *Democracy and Tradition* (Princeton: Princeton University Press, 2004), 149–50; Nicholas Wolterstorff, *Justice: Rights and Wrongs* (Princeton: Princeton University Press, 2010), 97–98.

ethics or to replace one with the other, let us recognize them as interpenetratively co-constitutive. The church's sacramental practices help to comprise its ethical character just as the church's ethical character helps to shape its sacramental practices. Both are shaped by the habituating power of antiblackness supremacy. For these reasons, it is not enough to reform the church from within.

10.

Corporate Vices, Ecclesial Consequences: Poking Holes in the Ecclesiology of "Battened-Down Hatches"

The operation of the corporate vice of antiblackness supremacy in both the Catholic parish and in the sacraments of baptism and Eucharist requires us to critique the school of theological thought pioneered by Stanley Hauerwas and William Cavanaugh, whose innovative approach to the problems of postmodernity I call "sacramental optimism." I use the term "sacramental optimism" to refer to the belief that the church's practices, if enacted and understood properly, possess a demonstrable capacity to resist the atomizing individualism of the modern nation-state. Other scholars share their confidence, expressing similar optimism in the sacraments' ability to counteract racial division and injustice.[1] But such sacramental optimism is unwarranted, at least in the face of racial evil. Precisely because the church comprises a truly corporate body, Christians ought to enact not sacramental optimism but what I term *sacramental realism*. Just as we have failed to take the thoroughly embodied and fully corporate

1. See for example Amy Levad, who advocates what I term a modified sacramental optimism in that she foregrounds the ways in which the sacraments have colluded with injustice but still believes that they can performatively build the body of Christ on their own. Levad, *Redeeming a Prison Society*, 88–99. Bryan Massingale also subscribes to a modified sacramental optimism. See, for example, *Racial Justice and the Catholic Church*, 121, 126.

character of the human person seriously, so have we failed to do the same with respect to the body of Christ.

Despite significant differences among the scholars who express this sacramental optimism, I single out Hauerwas and Cavanaugh for extensive critique because each scholar's work intersects with mine even if we do not write on the same topics: Hauerwas retrieves the theo-ethical tradition of virtue theory as a resource for the contemporary church while Cavanaugh calls attention to the political power of the Eucharist. When we read Hauerwas and Cavanaugh, we drink in sacramental optimism as if from its source; they articulate exceptionally uncompromising arguments on behalf of a more robustly countercultural church. For this reason, in undermining the sacramental optimism of these great thinkers, I simultaneously uncover the often-unnoticed flaws afflicting much subtler expressions of sacramental optimism, which encourage us to look for racial solutions in the wrong places.

EXCOMMUNICATION AND MORTAL COMBAT: THE SACRAMENTAL OPTIMISM OF HAUERWAS AND CAVANAUGH

Cavanaugh uses the history of the Chilean church's initial capitulation to, but eventual triumph over, Pinochet's dictatorship to construct his Eucharistic political theology. Why? For Cavanaugh, the relation between the Eucharist and the torture that Pinochet deployed in Chile models the relation between the church and all nation-states, even those that do not torture. Just as torture unmakes individual bodies, so do nation-states unmake the corporate body of the church.[2] Initially, Cavanaugh admits, the Chilean church did not realize this. But eventually, the church's Eucharistic practices enabled Chilean Catholics to recognize and then resist the threat that both torture in particular and the Chilean nation-state in general posed to the church's identity as the body of Christ.

How? The church began to excommunicate torturers, barring them from the Eucharistic table and expelling them from the church's

2. Mary Doak, "The Politics of Radical Orthodoxy: A Catholic Critique," *Theological Studies* 68, no. 2 (May 1, 2007): 378–79.

corporate body.[3] The church also established a human rights organization called the *Vicaria de la Solidaridad* and participated in the Sebastían Acevedo Movement Against Torture. Cavanaugh acclaims these entities as "eucharistic" due to their ability to bind the church together as the Eucharist does. Because it can "provide the resources of a true counter-body or counter-discipline," he concludes, the Eucharist comprises a truly political response to worldly evil. Not content to just play defense, the church's newly invigorated body went on the offensive, as priests, nuns, and laypeople took to the streets in collective, public protest of torture. According to Cavanaugh, what the world unravels, the Eucharist can stitch back together.[4]

Cavanaugh seems to anticipate my approach to questions of embodiment when he presents these Eucharistic practices as providing a desperately needed alternative to what he terms "the cognitive approach to the liturgy." Cavanaugh laments this liturgical mentality for the way it mistakenly reduces the liturgy to mere "a place of formation," which individual Catholics then "leave behind [when they] graduate [to the pursuit of] justice in the 'real world.'"[5] For Cavanaugh, the case of the Chilean church proves that, when the church cedes the bodies of individual Christians to the disciplining power of the nation-state in this way, it unwittingly cedes their souls as well. As a result, Christians are conformed to the image not of Christ, but the state. But Cavanaugh's approach differs from mine due to the way in which he offers a sacramentally optimistic solution to this problem: when enforced by a selective process of excommunication and publicly corporate political action, Cavanaugh believes that the church's Eucharistic practices can reclaim Christian bodies from the disciplining power of the state, thereby building the church into a visible, public, politically efficacious, and ontologically unified body.

Hauerwas expresses an even more heightened sense of sacramental optimism. Hauerwas focuses on the atomizing and body-dissolving power of not torture, but liberal individualism. But Hauerwas shares Cavanaugh's confidence in the church's capacity to overcome this

3. William T. Cavanaugh, *Torture and Eucharist: Theology, Politics, and the Body of Christ* (Hoboken, NJ: Wiley, 1988), 248.
4. Ibid., 66, 71.
5. William T. Cavanaugh, "The Work of the People as Public Work: The Social Significance of the Liturgy," Institute of Liturgical Studies, Valparaiso University, April 2, 2008. http://scholar.valpo.edu/ils_papers/6/.

evil force, declaring that "there is no such unity in history other than that provided by the church."[6] Like Cavanaugh, who believes that the cultic Eucharist re-habituates bodies, Hauerwas contends that baptism "transfers . . . our citizenship . . . from one dominion to another." For this reason, he claims that even native-born white Christians live as "resident aliens" in the United States.[7] Rather than seeking to assimilate into this society, Hauerwas believes that Christians should remain distinct from it. In this vein, he denounces calls that Christians "be willing to suppress our peculiarities, join hands with whoever will join hands with us, and work for peace and justice."[8] Christian habits are necessarily countercultural: Christians belong to each other by alienating themselves from the world.[9] According to Hauerwas, the church serves as the world's sole school for virtue.

Cavanaugh and Hauerwas's sacramental optimism rests upon what I term an Augustinian cosmology of two cities: the worldly and essentially unredeemed City of Humanity versus the sacred and sharply countercultural City of God.[10] Their cosmology blames ecclesial dysfunction on despoiling contact with the outside world. According to Hauerwas, while the world "perverts [people] so terribly," the church alone "can get them straight" again.[11] For this reason, the church stumbles when it allows confusion between church and world to fester.

Cavanaugh and especially Hauerwas do not simply distinguish the church from the world; they perceive them as in competition with each other. Conveying his "sense of being embattled" as a Christian living in a liberal society, Hauerwas has compared his theological writings to "dispatches from the front" and described himself as trapped "behind enemy lines." For this reason, Hauerwas wants Christians not to passively withdraw from the liberal social order, but "to recognize that they are surrounded" and endangered by it. In his

6. Stanley Hauerwas, *The Hauerwas Reader* (Durham, NC: Duke University Press, 2001), 421.
7. Stanley Hauerwas and William H. Willimon, *Resident Aliens: A Provocative Christian Assessment of Culture and Ministry for People Who Know That Something Is Wrong*, 1st ed. (Nashville: Abingdon, 1989), 12.
8. Hauerwas and Willimon, *Resident Aliens*, 42. Here Hauerwas would also seem to be critiquing the view offered at the Second Vatican Council. See for example, Pope Paul VI, *Lumen Gentium: Dogmatic Constitution on the Church*, par. 34.
9. Ibid., 12.
10. William T. Cavanaugh, *Migrations of the Holy: God, State, and the Political Meaning of the Church* (Grand Rapids, MI: Eerdmans, 2011), 58–59; Hauerwas, *The Hauerwas Reader*, 39; Augustine, *The City of God* (Garden City, NY: Image Books, 1958), Book XV, Chapter 1.
11. Hauerwas and Willimon, *Resident Aliens*, 155.

view, Christians cannot participate in liberal society; they can only survive it.[12]

For this reason, rather than seeking to reform the world, the church ought to witness to it.[13] When the church pursues justice, he believes that it loses itself. Counseling Christians "to behave [as though] freedom [and] justice . . . are bad ideas," Hauerwas maintains that the church cannot transform the world without being consumed by it.[14] For Hauerwas, the church exists in the world as "a colony," which he compares to "a beachhead [or] an outpost."[15] Because it is besieged and outnumbered, it must fortify itself. The boundaries between church and world must remain clear, sharp, and self-protective.[16] Reflecting the militaristic spirit of Hauerwas's own language, I describe this ecclesiology as one of battened-down hatches.

MORE THAN ATOMIZATION: THE AMBIGUITY OF BELONGING

But this ecclesiology of battened-down hatches errs for two major reasons: one, it refuses to accept the necessarily porous character of Christ's body; and two, it fails to place the history of the church's vicious participation in white supremacy and antiblackness supremacy at the center of its analysis. Largely for these reasons, both Hauerwas and Cavanaugh overlook the ambiguity of embodied belonging and misidentify the atomizing individualism of modern liberalism in the case of Hauerwas and the nation-state in the case of Cavanaugh as the most urgent threats to the church's corporate identity as the body of Christ.[17]

12. Stanley Hauerwas, *Dispatches from the Front: Theological Engagements with the Secular* (Durham, NC: Duke University Press, 1995), 18.

13. Hauerwas therefore rejects what he terms the "transformationist approach" advocated by midcentury liberal theologian Reinhold Niebuhr. This approach promoted an "inclusive ecclesiology" aimed at making the world more just. But, Hauerwas contends, in calling for an "inclusive ecclesiology," Niebuhr "merely justifies what was already there—a church that had ceased to ask the right questions as it went about congratulating itself for transforming the world, not noticing, that in fact the world had tamed the church." Hauerwas and Willimon, *Resident Aliens*, 41.

14. Stanley Hauerwas, *After Christendom: How the Church Is to Behave If Freedom, Justice, and a Christian Nation Are Bad Ideas* (Nashville: Abingdon, 1991).

15. Hauerwas and Willimon, *Resident Aliens*, 12.

16. Ibid.

17. William T. Cavanaugh, "Dying for the Eucharist or Being Killed by It? Romero's Challenge to First-World Christians," *Theology Today* 58, no. 2 (July 1, 2001): 181.

To this end, Hauerwas quotes Alasdair McIntyre, who identifies the United States' "commitment to individualistic practices" as the major cause of "inequality and unfreedom."[18] But Hauerwas mistakes a national ideology of individualism for reality. In truth, the United States' deeply white supremacist character renders it only selectively committed to these so-called "individualistic practices." Even while espousing an ideology of individual rights, white people often have acted as a racial clique. Throughout the twentieth century, for example, the white parish in the urban North imposed inequality and spatial unfreedom on blacks not by emphasizing individualism, but by cultivating a fierce spatial communalism. Antiblackness turns to individualism as not an ideology, but a strategy; it rends human beings apart from each other in some circumstances but binds them together in others. McIntyre ignores the specificity of both slavery and antiblackness; after all, the single biggest cause of "unfreedom" in the United States is not "liberal individualism," but Africanized slavery. Besides, in the Americas, only black people can be said to truly lack "freedom" because they are the only group to have been subjected to slavery and its afterlife.

Against Hauerwas, I argue that, although some evils may issue from liberal modernity, the antiblackness born from the Africanization of slavery does not require a liberal nation-state in order to operate. It does not even need capitalism.[19] It has flourished in the very un-liberal, late-medieval Catholic monarchies of Spain and Portugal as well as in colonies controlled by the emerging bourgeoisie of Protestant Northern Europe. Raging against liberalism may loosen the grip that some evils have on us, but it will do very little to unsettle antiblackness supremacy. Antiblackness supremacy surely operates through liberal capitalism, but it does not rely upon it. Antiblackness supremacy made the modern world much more than it has resulted from it.

Hauerwas retains his sacramental optimism even in the face of racism. According to Hauerwas, once a person acknowledges "the absolute sovereignty of God . . . that person can no longer be a

18. Stanley Hauerwas, *A Better Hope: Resources for a Church Confronting Capitalism, Democracy, and Postmodernity* (Grand Rapids, MI: Brazos, 2000), 30.

19. This is not to deny, however, that antiblackness supremacy and capitalism have often been allies. For more on the relationship between antiblackness and capitalism, see Eric Eustace Williams, *Capitalism & Slavery* (Chapel Hill: University of North Carolina Press, 1944); Edward E. Baptist, *The Half Has Never Been Told: Slavery and the Making of American Capitalism* (New York: Basic Books, 2014).

racist."[20] History refutes this: Iberian Christians first Africanized slavery in fulfillment of their sincere belief in God's absolute sovereignty.[21] They violently subordinated indigenous people as Spanish vassals for this same reason.[22] Hauerwas perceives baptism with equal optimism: for him, "the categories of race, or the classification of people by color, do not exist in the new creation enacted in Jesus Christ."[23] Hauerwas's pronouncements notwithstanding, baptism has not erased racial evil. In fact, it has often intensified it.

For Hauerwas, the church can be a hero only if liberal modernity serves as the ultimate villain. For this reason, Hauerwas refuses to grant antiblackness supremacy a life of its own, insisting that "the modern nation-state . . . has been the primary agent for the categorization of people by race." In this same vein, he denies that "the race problem can be solved politically" and accuses those who claim otherwise of "confusing humanism with the gospel."[24] But it is Hauerwas who confuses his own ideology with historical truth: the so-called "modern nation-state" has neither created nor preserved white supremacy on its own. Christianity bears at least as much responsibility for Africanizing slavery and sustaining its afterlife as any secular power.[25] This history notwithstanding, abolishing the nation-state would not on its own ameliorate antiblackness: white people have dominated black people even, and sometimes especially, without the backing of state power.[26] In blaming the nation-state, Hauerwas perhaps unwittingly exonerates white individuals. Antiblackness supremacy does not simply operate through social structures; it inhabits white bodies as a vice. As long as white and other nonblack people continue to cling to these habits, they will attempt to twist any social, political, or ecclesial order into the shape of slavery's afterlife.

20. Stanley Hauerwas and Romand Coles, *Christianity, Democracy, and the Radical Ordinary: Conversations Between a Radical Democrat and a Christian* (Eugene, OR: Cascade, 2008), 98.

21. Katie Geneva Cannon, "Christian Imperialism and the Transatlantic Slave Trade," *Journal of Feminist Studies in Religion* 24, no. 1 (Spring 2008): 128–30.

22. For contemporary examples of how belief in God's sovereignty can feed racial injustice, see Elisabeth T. Vasko, *Beyond Apathy: A Theology for Bystanders* (Minneapolis: Fortress Press, 2015), 10, 101–2, 106.

23. Hauerwas and Coles, *Christianity, Democracy, and the Radical Ordinary*, 99.

24. Ibid.

25. George Yancy, "Introduction: Framing the Problem," in *Christology and Whiteness: What Would Jesus Do?* (New York: Routledge, 2012), 4; Cannon, "Christian Imperialism and the Transatlantic Slave Trade."

26. William T. Cavanaugh, "Killing for the Telephone Company: Why the Nation-State Is Not the Keeper of the Common Good," *Modern Theology* 20, no. 2 (April 1, 2004): 266–69; Doak, "The Politics of Radical Orthodoxy," 380, 383.

Hauerwas ultimately errs because, although he does mention the history of racialized Christianity, he does not allow his mind to be changed by it.[27] He instead deploys this history in order to vindicate positions he would have held anyway. Seeking to establish the church's capacity to build countercultural habits, he exalts the example of "black church congregations [that] continued to do the patient work of preparation necessary to create a people sufficient for the coming struggle."[28] But Hauerwas's self-defense backfires. In citing this example, Hauerwas concedes that the church's sacraments have bound Christians together not counterculturally, but within the parameters of belonging drawn by antiblackness racial segregation. Thus, if the black church succeeded in performatively receiving its identity as the body of Christ, then it did so due less to its Christianity than to its blackness.[29] Hauerwas guts the history of black Christianity like a fish, picking out the parts that look tasty but discarding the rest. In this way, Hauerwas seemingly ignores the fact that black Christians in general and black churches in particular have modeled the very form of Christian politics that Hauerwas has spent his career discrediting. More than simply attempting to survive a *truly* hostile social order, black Christians have deployed Christianity as an instrument of often-radical social reform and transformation.[30]

Cavanaugh similarly concedes that the Eucharist sometimes has acted "to reinforce a fixed social hierarchy within a certain location, and to exclude others, especially the Jews, from that space," but this fact does not shake his confidence in the cultic Eucharist's capacity to resist political evil as long as it is performed correctly.[31] In truth, however, the history of racial evil ought to make us pause: the church cannot impede habituation by corporate vice simply by clinging together more tightly. As the history of black slavery and its afterlife demonstrates, the church's corporate body has suffered enervating

27. For a longer narration of Hauerwas's theological autobiography of race and racism, see Hauerwas and Coles, *Christianity, Democracy, and the Radical Ordinary*, 87–100.

28. Stanley Hauerwas, *A Community of Character: Toward a Constructive Christian Social Ethic*, 1st ed. (Notre Dame: University of Notre Dame Press, 1991), 108. For another example, see Hauerwas, *A Better Hope*, 30.

29. For more on the black church's response to white racism, see James H. Cone, *For My People: Black Theology and the Black Church* (Maryknoll, NY: Orbis, 1984), 60–62.

30. See, for example, C. Eric Lincoln and Lawrence H. Mamiya, *The Black Church in the African American Experience* (Durham, NC: Duke University Press, 1990).

31. William T. Cavanaugh, "Theopolitical Imagination: Discovering the Liturgy as a Political Act in an Age of Global Consumerism," 2002, 116, http://works.bepress.com/william_cavanaugh/5/.

division not just by being bound together too loosely but also by being bound improperly, sometimes even too tightly. In the era of slavery, for example, these sacraments did not fail to incorporate disparate individuals into a cohesive body; they simply did so perversely, acting to consolidate systems of slaveocracy.

And even in the ongoing era of racial segregation, we oversimplify by offering a diagnosis of dissolution. Even as the sacraments of initiation fail to bring blacks and nonblacks together, they allow nonblacks, and especially whites, to be bound together too tightly. In fact, as demonstrated in previous chapters, the corporate body of the Catholic Church has been particularly susceptible to habituation by antiblackness precisely because it is conducive to cohesion. The flip side to cohesion is exclusion. In bringing certain bodies together, the Eucharist can also act to keep others apart. Nor can the church simply perform its corporate practices more meticulously: the Northern urban parish proves that the church has exercised the vicious habits of antiblackness supremacy even when it remained cohesively distinct from the world. The church was its most sacramentally active precisely when it was the most white supremacist. The interrelated vices of white supremacy and antiblackness supremacy have entered the church's corporate body not just when the church was acting in un-Catholic ways; the church acquired these vices even when being itself.

Sacramental optimism fails for a second reason. Because they wish to strengthen the unity and cohesiveness of the church's corporate body, Hauerwas and Cavanaugh perceive the porosity of Christ's body as an impediment rather than an ecclesial necessity. While they rightly stress the importance of cohesion, unity, and differentiation to the integrity of the church's corporate body, they overlook the fact that true bodies, whether social or individual, possess boundaries as well as pores. Unlike fortresses, corporate bodies cannot be walled off or sealed shut. Nor should they be. Possessing an essential porosity, bodies are not divided from the world; they interact with it. As a result, for example, when liberalism atomizes, it does so not because the church's corporate body intermingles too promiscuously with the secular body of the nation-state, but because the church's corporate body harbors an inevitable and essential porosity. In blaming the divided and enervated character of the body of Christ primarily on the atomizing individualism of the modern nation-state, these thinkers act like a homeowner who blames the rain for her leaky roof. No matter how eloquently the church explains itself or how expertly it performs its foundational sacraments, it cannot keep the world out.

The necessary porosity of all bodies, both our own and Christ's, also sobers Hauerwas's confidence in the church's capacity to school its members in the virtues. Opposing Kantian deontology, Hauerwas believes that "the story of Christ" alone provides "a truthful account of our existence." For Hauerwas, the particularity of the story supplies the answer to what he identifies as Christian ethics' captivity to Kantian categorical imperatives.[32] Implicitly eschewing natural law approaches to ethics, Hauerwas urges Christian ethicists to cease speculating about justice and instead derive all "principles and policies" from the story of God's "calling and forming a people to serve Him through Israel and the work of Christ."[33] Guided by this view, Hauerwas stipulates: "What is required is not that Christians always agree, but that their agreements and disagreements reflect theological convictions."[34]

But in describing "Christians [as those who] create the world by being a different people with different habits and practices from that of the world," Hauerwas tells only half the story.[35] Human beings do not simply have habits; they are also habituated by the world they inhabit. Unsurprisingly, then, the world's injustice leaves its mark even on our stories.[36] Just as Christians bring their racialized bodies with them when they receive the Eucharist, so they inhabit these bodies before they possess the power to learn Christian stories. When interpreted by minds shaped by white supremacy, scripture will always endorse white power. Nor did the church correct itself noncoercively as Hauerwas's analysis implies it could: Not theological narratives, but the deployment of power, brought Christian theological defense of chattel slavery to an end. Slaves fled the plantations; the Union army seized Atlanta. Only then did a theology of slaveownership become unthinkable. Although Hauerwas rightly critiques Kant for perceiving rationality as a force that purifies but

32. Miguel De La Torre, *Latina/o Social Ethics: Moving Beyond Eurocentric Moral Thinking* (Waco, TX: Baylor University Press, 2010), 21.

33. Stanley Hauerwas, "Reforming Christian Social Ethics: Ten Theses," in *The Hauerwas Reader*, 111.

34. Hauerwas, *A Community of Character*, 108.

35. Stanley Hauerwas, "Christianity: It's Not a Religion, It's an Adventure," in *The Hauerwas Reader*, 533–34.

36. De La Torre, *Latina/o Social Ethics*, 30.

does not itself need to be purified, he repeats this very mistake when speaking about storytelling. Sticking to a purely theological script will not bring Christians any closer to the truth that Hauerwas considers a criterion of good Christian living.[37]

Hauerwas and Cavanaugh are not sectarians, nor are they politically indifferent. Both thinkers simply want the church to inhabit the world more fully, engaging with society "on its own terms" rather than accepting the place that the state has assigned it.[38] But even when Hauerwas and Cavanaugh are right about liberal capitalism or the nation-state, they are wrong about the church. I do not advocate an ecclesiology of the porous body of Christ because I believe that the world is good or that the church can transform it. We ought to embrace this ecclesiology due to the character of not the world, but Christ's porous body.[39] Porosity represents not an incidental by-product of embodiment; it sits essentially at the center. Fleshy, Eucharistic bodies like the church can never exist in the world as a fortress does; they hold together because of their pores. Its holiness is holey. Hauerwas and Cavanaugh echo Augustine's belief that "there can be no justice and no common weal where God is not truly worshiped."[40] Yet the history of antiblackness supremacy suggests the opposite conclusion: God cannot be truly worshiped where there is no justice and no common weal.

GENDER TROUBLE IN THE BODY OF CHRIST

In implementing what I term an ecclesiology of the porous body of Christ, we also position ourselves to correct for the sexual distortions that inhere within ecclesiologies that figure the church, even if implicitly, as a virgin (and therefore sinless) mother.[41] For example, as theologian Steven Battin explains, when so-called *ressourcement*

37. As Dale Martin points out, "We are all socialized to read [scripture] in certain ways. . . . [we all] interpret texts according to assumptions and rules of interpretation they have internalized and that are reinforced by human society and culture." *Sex and the Single Savior: Gender and Sexuality in Biblical Interpretation* (Louisville: Westminster John Knox, 2006), 15.

38. Hauerwas, "It's an Adventure," 527.

39. De La Torre, *Latina/o Social Ethics*, 23.

40. William T. Cavanaugh, *Theopolitical Imagination: Christian Practices of Space and Time* (New York: T&T Clark, 2002), 15.

41. Rosemary Radford Ruether, "Mariology as Symbolic Ecclesiology: Repression or Liberation?" in *Sexism and God-Talk: Toward a Feminist Theology: With a New Introduction* (Boston: Beacon, 1993).

theologians "discuss the church in regard to its role in situations of violence, they tend to offer a rehearsal of general 'sins' or 'moral' shortcomings of the ecclesial community." In speaking this way, he continues, they depict "the church's fundamental constitution," what they often call "her countenance," as lying "somewhere or somehow 'above' the fray." According to this formulation, the church's feminine "holy chastity [remains] unscathed."[42]

This digression may appear tangential or even irrelevant to the arguments proposed earlier in this chapter. But the church is not unpenetrated like a virgin; it instead remains inevitably and essentially susceptible to penetration by outside forces of all types. So was Jesus. Even though we call the church "mother," it is also the male body of Christ.[43] And this male body of Jesus was also both porous and penetrated. For example, in his ministry, Jesus placed his body in contaminating intimacy with the penetrated bodies of prostitutes and let his body be touched and washed by the desperate hands of defiled women. On the cross, Jesus was penetrated by the swords of soldiers; his hands and feet were penetrated by nails. Stripped naked, he was subject to a violating sexual humiliation.[44] Like many prisoners throughout history, he perhaps even suffered the piercing violence of sexual assault.[45] But even if Jesus was not raped, his crucifixion was inherently rather than circumstantially sexually violent.[46]

We have further reason to emphasize the sexually violent character of Jesus's crucifixion due to the way in which crucifixion recapitulated many aspects of the experience of enslavement. Crucifixion made Jesus a slave, even if only for a day. Subjected to violent penetrations, torture, and stigmatizing public humiliation, Jesus was punished as though he were a disobedient slave.[47] Crucifixion also possessed a symbolic association with slavery as the Romans "first

42. Steven Battin, "The Praxis of Unity: A Postcolonial Perspective on the Unity of the Church" (PhD diss., University of Notre Dame), 17.

43. Gina Ingiosi, "Mystical 'Body': An Ecclesiology Informed by Judith Butler," in Kevin Ahern, *Visions of Hope: Emerging Theologians and the Future of the Church* (Maryknoll, NY: Orbis, 2013), 17.

44. David Tombs, "Crucifixion, State Terror, and Sexual Abuse," *Conflict Transformation*, 96, accessed January 6, 2014, http://www.conflicttransformation.ie/tombs/research/articles/crucifixion/.

45. Ibid., 104–7.

46. David Tombs, "Prisoner Abuse: From Abu Ghraib to *The Passion of the Christ*," in *Religion and the Politics of Peace and Conflict*, ed. Linda Hogan and Dylan Lee Lehrke (Eugene, OR: Wipf & Stock, 2009), 178.

47. Tombs, "Crucifixion, State Terror, and Sexual Abuse," 92.

adopted crucifixion . . . [in order] to humiliate and punish slaves," not necessarily to kill them. In time, they turned crucifixion into a form of execution and began to use it on rebellious noncitizens and criminals as well as slaves.[48] But this modification did not dilute crucifixion's unique association with servility: slaves qualify as the ultimate noncitizens, rebels, and criminals. Socially dead and natally alienated, slaves are typically thought unfit for citizenship; believed to be almost existentially rebellious against proper authority, slaves can never be punished too violently; often occurring as the consequence of crime or other wrongdoing, enslavement has always possessed a special material and symbolic kinship with criminality and imprisonment. The Romans explicitly articulated the symbolic resonance between crucifixion and slave status, as they "sometimes sarcastically referred to [slaves] as . . . 'cross bearers.'"[49] Crucifixion was inherently sexually humiliating and therefore violent because slavery was. Indeed, the power to sexually victimize slaves of any age or gender represents a central pleasure of slaveholding in all societies. Crucifixion, like slavery, operated as "a sexualized form of torture."[50]

Due to the way it treated Jesus like a slave in general and subjected him to sexual violence in particular, crucifixion therefore also emasculated Jesus.[51] Just as slavery rendered male slaves symbolically feminine by making them uniquely vulnerable to sexual abuse, so the sexually violent character crucifixion placed Jesus's naked body in a feminine position. Rather than penetrating women and male subordinates as true men ought, Jesus was the penetrated one. In this way, the condemned typically were crucified naked to heighten the humiliating contradiction between the spectacle of their unpenetrating penises and their violently penetrated bodies.

Crucifixion would have emasculated even if it had not been sexually violent. Like male slaves, crucified men are denied what is considered to be the uniquely masculine rights of bodily integrity and self-protection. In ancient Rome as in all slaveholding societies, only free males qualified as true men.[52] Although male slaves could procreate, they could not wield a phallus. Excised from ordinary chains of paternity and filiation, male slaves can neither inherit nor bequeath.

48. Tombs, "Prisoner Abuse," 178.

49. Frederick T. Zugibe, *The Crucifixion of Jesus: A Forensic Inquiry* (Lanham, MD: Rowman & Littlefield, 2005), 55.

50. Tombs, "Prisoner Abuse," 141.

51. Tombs, "Crucifixion, State Terror, and Sexual Abuse," 101.

52. Jennifer A. Glancy, *Slavery in Early Christianity* (Minneapolis: Fortress Press, 2006), 34.

For this reason, even in old age, male slaves remain like young boys.[53] In crucifying Jesus as slave, the Roman government dishonored him as one.

The church has tended to manage its anxieties about the penetrated and emasculated body of Christ by transferring the stigma of Jesus's penetration onto the bodies of women. In this way, the church remembers Mary, a symbol of the church itself, as an unpenetrated mother: not only did she never have sex, but, for much of the church's history, theologians insisted that she miraculously retained her hymen even after the experience of childbirth.[54] This cult of virgin maternity sometimes operates as a way for the church both to process and cover up the penetration experienced by Jesus on the cross. But the church ought not respond to the emasculating violation of Christ's body by policing the borders of its symbolically feminine body. In truth, in its identity as a human male and female mother, the porous and penetrated body of Christ reverses the procreative sexual experiences typical of each gender. Males ordinarily are thought to give life by penetrating and females by being penetrated. But, as a virgin mother, the church gives life without being penetrated, and, as the crucified male Christ, the church gives life by being penetrated. This depiction of the church as a penetrated and even despoiled body does not pile even more stigma onto women's hyper-sexualized bodies. It instead creates space for ecclesial honesty: the ecclesial body of Christ is penetrated because Jesus's body was.

The life-giving porosity of Christ's cruciform body provides further reason to discard Hauerwas's narrative approach to Christian ethics. Hauerwas places the cross at the center of his ethics, yet his ecclesiology of battened-down hatches overlooks the inevitably and necessarily penetrated character of Christ's cruciform body. Accepting it as an instrument of death, but not feminized dishonor, Hauerwas fashions the cross into a display of stereotypically masculine stoicism. In truth, however, Christ's body was entered, defiled, and emasculated. Desiring that the church enter the world without allowing the world to enter itself, Hauerwas implicitly and unwittingly

53. Ibid., 34–35.

54. As Gary Waller reports, "the Councils of Constantinople (553) and Lateran (640) . . . decreed that Mary's hymen remained intact before, during, and after Christ's birth." Theologians generally defended this assertion for the next one thousand years. *The Virgin Mary in Late Medieval and Early Modern English Literature and Popular Culture* (Cambridge: Cambridge University Press, 2011), 38.

figures the church as a type of unpenetrated penetrator.[55] But the church is not "a colony, a beachhead . . . [or] an outpost," as Hauerwas claims: an unpenetrated church can neither carry the cross nor comprise a true body. Nor can the church "serve the world on its own terms" as Hauerwas desires: a servant, by definition, cannot set the terms of her own service.[56] Not even free women and men engage with the world entirely on their own terms. The power that Hauerwas seemingly desires for the church belongs only to masters of slaves.

More than just a cause of his death, Jesus's feminized porosity made his ministry possible. Jesus's body possessed a feminized porosity even before he was nailed to the cross. Consider New Testament scholar Candida Moss's account of Jesus's encounter with the hemorrhaging woman in the Gospel of Mark. In this story, both the woman with the flow of blood and the twelve-year-old girl described as Jairus's daughter bear the stigmatized vulnerability placed upon feminized bodies. Their porosity models Israel's: the woman with the flow of blood has been leaking formerly life-giving fluid for twelve years while Jairus's daughter is twelve years old, the age that often signifies the onset of menstruation and the perils it brings. Moss spies a further connection. In this story, life-giving power flows out of Jesus just as uncontrollably as it flows out of the bleeding woman. Since leakiness paradoxically signaled both femininity and divinity, Moss suggests that Mark discloses Jesus as a God-man by imbuing him with a feminine flow of blood. Jesus's male body qualifies as fully human yet truly divine not despite, but partially because of, its porous femininity.[57]

The church exists most fundamentally not as a city or a society, but as a body.[58] As such, it will always be susceptible to the habituating power of the world it inhabits. In performing its body-shaping practices while residing within the spatial afterlife of slavery, the church becomes not only what it does, but also where it lives.[59] Place shapes habits, which in turn sculpt bodies. Exchanging an implicitly masculine ecclesiology of battened-down hatches for an ecclesiology of the

55. Stanley Hauerwas, "The Servant Community: Christian Social Ethics," in *The Hauerwas Reader*, 372.

56. Hauerwas, *A Community of Character*, 82.

57. Candida Moss, "The Man with the Flow of Power: Porous Bodies in Mark 5:25-34," *Journal of Biblical Literature* 129, no. 3 (September 1, 2010): 509.

58. *Lumen Gentium*, Dogmatic Constitution on the Church, 1964, par. 7–8, 30, 32.

59. Ingiosi, "Mystical 'Body,'" 17.

porous, penetrated, and unconventionally gendered body of Christ, we can recognize that in order to change the church's supremacist habits of antiblackness, we cannot merely change the way we inhabit space; we must also change the character of the places we inhabit. Rather than framing the issue as a choice between justice in the world and ecclesial integrity as Hauerwas often does, the history of antiblackness supremacy suggests that injustice in the world is itself a threat to ecclesial integrity.[60] What, then, can the sacraments do?

60. Bryan Massingale, "Response: The Challenge of Idolatry and Ecclesial Identity," 2012, 131, http://epublications.marquette.edu/cgi/viewcontent.cgi?article=1258&context=theo_fac.

PART IV

Re-habituating the Corporate Body of Christ

This critique of sacramental optimism advocates not sacramental pessimism, but what I call sacramental realism. Rather than blaming contaminating contact with the outside world for the church's failure to performatively receive its identity as the body of Christ in history as Cavanaugh and Hauerwas do, sacramental realism argues that the church's abandonment of the real Eucharistic meal in favor of the cultic one has stripped the Eucharist of much of its performative power. For this reason, it proposes a return to the real meal as modeled by Jesus in his practice of table fellowship.

In advocating for a return to the real meal, I continue my critique of Cavanaugh's confidence in the cultic Eucharist's capacity to provide a "body/soul discipline [that] produces actions, practices, habits that are visible in the world."[1] According to Cavanaugh, because the cultic Eucharist "arranges people into a certain order," it can counteract all sinful social orders. Because it does not simply work internally on and through human souls, but also "affects bodies externally," it can establish between Christians a bond that "is not merely a moral or psychological . . . but . . . ontological." Cavanaugh believes that the

1. William T. Cavanaugh, *Torture and Eucharist: Theology, Politics, and the Body of Christ* (Hoboken, NJ: Wiley, 1988), 196.

cultic Eucharist truly builds "a new kind of social body" that is not "left behind" but is visible, public, and politically efficacious.[2]

Perhaps the cultic Eucharist ought to act as Cavanaugh claims it does. But at least in its relation to antiblackness supremacy, it does not. Because it comprises a real meal only metaphorically, the cultic meal claims to discipline bodies by affecting souls. But as Cavanaugh himself points out, this is impossible. The Eucharist cannot reshape bodies it does not feed; it cannot unite bodies it does not bring spatially together. Such a Eucharist works in a very un-Catholic way: invisibly, immaterially, and incorporeally.

2. William T. Cavanaugh, "The Work of the People as Public Work: The Social Significance of the Liturgy." Institute of Liturgical Studies, Valparaiso University. April 2, 2008, http://www.valpo.edu/ils/assets/pdfs/cavanaugh_2008.pdf.

11.

Real Food for Real Bodies: From Sacramental Optimism to Sacramental Realism

In attempting to performatively receive its identity as Christ's real body by consuming a merely metaphorical meal, the church sends mixed signals about the body. On the one hand, the church identifies the Eucharist as the "source and summit" of Catholic faith because it comprises Christ's really present body.[1] But on the other hand, church leaders like Pope John Paul II partially locate the Eucharist's superiority to a "fraternal banquet" in the fact that it unites human beings along what he terms "an invisible dimension."[2] Pope John Paul II contends that the cultic Eucharist "superabundantly fulfills the yearning for fraternal unity deeply rooted in the human heart; at the same time it elevates the experience of fraternity present in our common sharing at the same Eucharistic table to a degree which far surpasses that of the simple human experience of sharing a meal."[3] Unlike ordinary meals, which unite only those seated at a single table, the Eucharist "unites heaven and earth" and "embraces and permeates all creation."[4] Like Aquinas who ranks human capacities according to their incorporeality, Pope John Paul II seemingly deems a feast sacred to the extent that it feeds invisible souls rather than material bodies.

1. John Paul II, *Ecclesia de Eucharistia*, par. 22.
2. Ibid., par. 35.
3. Ibid., par. 24.
4. Ibid., par. 5.

For Pope John Paul II, the cultic Eucharist does unite along a "visible dimension," but only with respect to "communion in the teaching of the Apostles, in the sacraments and in the Church's hierarchical order."[5] No wonder Catholics so often consider the church's body apolitically privatized. Rather than elevating the ordinary experiences of human life into occasions of grace as Jesus's table fellowship did, the cultic Eucharist renders them sacramentally irrelevant. The cultic Eucharist in fact encourages the ideology of privatizing separation of soul from body for which Cavanaugh blames the nation-state.[6] The cultic Eucharist does not "build a body" capable of holding together in the public sphere; the church's cultically constructed body enters the public arena only if individual Catholics take it there. Binding primarily "invisibly," the cultic Eucharist cedes Catholic bodies to the habit-forming power of antiblackness supremacy. Catholics bring their habituated bodies with them when they enter liturgical space and they leave that space with these bodies intact and largely undisturbed. The cultic Eucharist has tended to perform a body within the lines that antiblackness supremacy had already drawn on Catholic bodies.

According to the logic of the relatively standardized cultic Eucharist, a racially segregated parish seems just as sacramentally fitting as a parish aligned in defiance of antiblackness supremacy. Rather than enabling the church to performatively adjust the way its corporate body occupies racialized space, the cultic performance of the Eucharist assures us such comportment does not matter.[7] But meals just do not work this way. Place the same food on a different table or in front of different guests, and the meaning and function of the meal changes. For example, a meal at which invitees feast on food harvested by coercively employed migrant workers receiving below-subsistence wages performatively consolidates social injustice.[8] A meal at which a husband occupies the symbolic head of the table performatively upholds patriarchy. A meal at which white women and men are waited on by their abused black slaves performatively

5. Ibid., par. 35.

6. William T. Cavanaugh, *Torture and Eucharist: Theology, Politics, and the Body of Christ*, 1st ed. (Hoboken, NJ: Wiley, 1988), 149, 180.

7. Traci C. West, *Disruptive Christian Ethics: When Racism and Women's Lives Matter* (Louisville: Westminster John Knox, 2006), 125.

8. Enrique Dussel makes a similar point in "The Bread of the Eucharistic Celebration as a Sign of Justice in the Community," in *Can We Always Celebrate the Eucharist?*, ed. Mary Collins and David Power (Edinburgh: T&T Clark, 1982), 56–57, 61–63.

enforces antiblackness supremacy.[9] We cannot just eat the right food; we must eat the right food in the right way. Nor can we know exactly what food is until we know what it does.

Jesus's meals did not work this way. At the Last Supper, Jesus offered his body in the form of a real meal, which gave physical nourishment to human bodies; he engaged in conversation both ritualized and informal. In his ministry, Jesus "brought real food to the hungry" and "made himself seen to his disciples . . . in the context of a community meal."[10] Commemorating this, some of the earliest Christian communities ate Eucharistic meals not of bread and wine, but fish.[11] Through this food choice, they maintained the link between the consumption of real food and the performative reception of Christ's body that Jesus first forged over the course of his ministry and brought to a climax on the night before he died. The flattened-down sameness of contemporary Eucharistic space and substance in fact deprives it of the power to perform the body of Christ. Rather than "transgressing national boundaries and redefin[ing] who our fellow-citizens are" as Cavanaugh contends, the cultic character of the Eucharist actually diminishes its ability to overturn vicious spatial habitats.[12]

Consider Cavanaugh's description of the Salvadorian funeral of slain Spanish priest Rutilio Grande. The Sunday after Grande's assassination, he explains, Archbishop Oscar Romero canceled all masses except for Grande's funeral. Simulating physical proximity for those Salvadorians unable to travel to the cathedral, Romero broadcast the funeral Mass on public radio. Because it built a publicly visible and solidly unified corporate body, Cavanaugh celebrates Grande's funeral mass as a foretaste of "the day when rich and poor would feast together, of the day when the body of Christ would not be wounded by divisions."[13] Indeed, Grande's funeral did anticipate the eschaton. But his funeral defied regnant powers of social organization so effectively only because it brought people physically and materially together. As Romero recognized, Eucharistic celebrations unfolding

9. Alan Taylor, *The Internal Enemy: Slavery and War in Virginia, 1772–1832* (New York: W. W. Norton, 2013), 78–80.

10. Nathan Mitchell, *Real Presence: The Work of Eucharist*, expanded (Chicago: Liturgy Training Publications, 2007), 68–69.

11. Nathan D. Mitchell, *Eucharist as Sacrament of Initiation* (Chicago: Liturgy Training Publications, 1994), 102.

12. William T. Cavanaugh, *Theopolitical Imagination: Christian Practices of Space and Time* (New York: T&T Clark, 2002), 50.

13. William T. Cavanaugh, "Dying for the Eucharist or Being Killed by It? Romero's Challenge to First-World Christians," *Theology Today* 58, no. 2 (July 1, 2001): 185.

in separate liturgical spaces would not have clarified the body of Christ as adeptly as that singular celebration did. Romero changed the spatial circumstances of the Mass precisely because the cultic Eucharist lacked the body-performing power necessitated by the political moment. More than it affirms Cavanaugh's confidence in the cultic Eucharist, Grande's funeral suggests that the cultic Eucharist binds bodies together in defiance of social injustice not on its own, but only as a consequence of strategic interaction with its context.

RACIAL JUSTICE AS A COMPONENT OF SACRAMENTAL LICITY

To many, transforming the cultic Eucharist back into a real meal would seem to lessen its sacramental character. But those who think this way make the same mistake as Aquinas: substances do not become more holy by becoming less embodied. The eating of real bread and the sharing of real fellowship around a common table seems incommensurate with the real presence of the body of Christ only if one assigns to the soul a masterly superiority and autonomy not indicated by Jesus's practice of table fellowship. As Schillebeeckx reminds us, if "the son of God" can give "new meaning to the bread and wine" of the cultic meal, then he seems no less able to ascribe this meaning to the bread and wine of a real meal.[14] The bread and wine consumed during the Eucharist differ from ordinary bread and wine not because they look different than them, but because they function differently; they alone can transform the church into the body of Christ.[15] Put another way, the Eucharist exists not as a static substance, but an action that communities perform more or less adeptly: as liturgical scholar Nathan Mitchell points out, the New Testament uses the word "Eucharist" only as a verb and never as a noun.[16]

Sacramental theologian Louis-Marie Chauvet further affirms the performative character of the Eucharist when he reminds us that the sacraments do not possess "a kind of automatic efficacy that will assure the health of the soul, as a medicine procures that of the body."[17] Chauvet explains that they instead make visible a change that

14. Edward Schillebeeckx, *The Eucharist* (London: Sheed & Ward, 1968), 113.

15. Ibid., 131.

16. Mitchell, *Real Presence*, 66.

17. Louis-Marie Chauvet, *Symbol and Sacrament: A Sacramental Reinterpretation of Christian Existence* (Collegeville, MN: Liturgical, 1995), 407.

they themselves produce. Like recited wedding vows, the sacraments of baptism and Eucharist both bring about a new relationship and make a promise that cannot yet be fulfilled; they paradoxically make the church what it is while showing it what it still must become. Rather than rendering God's grace any less gratuitous, the performative character of the sacraments results from the fact that the sacraments, like all gifts, are not just given; they also must be received. Put another way, we do not suffer the sacraments passively like a slap in the face. We instead receive them by performing them; that is, we receive them only if we perform them. Given this, the church cannot performatively receive its identity as the body of Christ under just any condition.[18] In the Eucharist, we must "become what we receive." For this reason, if the church does not comprise the living sign of the body it celebrates, then it has not received the body of Christ.[19]

Rather than replacing overconfidence in the cultic meal with overconfidence in the real meal, this approach acknowledges the sacramental relevance of racial justice. Just as bread stolen from the hungry mouths of the poor "cannot become Eucharist," so liturgical spaces segregated for the sake of antiblackness supremacy cannot bring the body of Christ together.[20] When black and white people share neither parishes nor power, the Eucharist cannot build the body of Christ. When a class of people is baptized into the body of Christ as slaves, a salvific community of Christian kinship is not established. A corporate body bound together according to the prerogatives of antiblackness supremacy will always struggle to performatively receive its identity as the body of Christ.[21] For this reason, habits and practices that are usually considered to be extra-ecclesial or ecclesially irrelevant such as living in a predominantly white suburb, sending one's children to a predominantly white school, or simply being socialized into whiteness actually inhibit the effect and the reception of the sacraments, impede their functioning, and otherwise impair the church's ability to be the body of Christ in history.[22]

18. Amy Levad, *Redeeming a Prison Society: A Liturgical and Sacramental Response to Mass Incarceration* (Minneapolis: Fortress Press, 2014), 89.

19. M. Shawn Copeland, *Enfleshing Freedom: Body, Race, and Being* (Minneapolis: Fortress Press, 2009).

20. Chauvet, *Symbol and Sacrament*, 146; Dussel, "The Bread of the Eucharistic Celebration as a Sign of Justice," 63.

21. Copeland, *Enfleshing Freedom*.

22. As Gina Ingiosi points out, the Vatican II document, *Sacrosanctum Concilium* "implies that

This call for a return to the real meal does not repeat the heretical errors of Donatism, which hinged the validity and efficacy of a sacrament upon the moral purity of those who performed it. Sacramental realism instead recognizes the importance of expanding the boundaries of sacramental licity. Nor does it suggest that only the racially righteous be allowed to confect or receive the Eucharist; it does not turn to excommunication as a sacramental safeguard in the way that Cavanaugh does, for example. Precisely because it works *ex opere operato*, the efficacy of the real Eucharistic feast depends not on the moral character of the actors who perform or receive it, but how these inevitably morally imperfect persons perform and receive it.[23]

The cultic Eucharist's insufficiently embodied character has rendered it particularly amenable to the corporate vice of antiblackness supremacy. Why? More than simply enforcing structures of oppressive power, antiblackness supremacy attempts to make a performative argument about what the black body is like—how it ought to look and act and where it ought to be. In order to refute the performative argument about the body that antiblackness supremacy makes, the church must forward a different performative argument about the body. But it cannot do this while feeding souls alone. Because antiblackness supremacy brings certain bodies together and keeps other ones apart, so must the church's sacramental practices. And because antiblackness supremacy brings these bodies not just symbolically but materially together, so must the Eucharist.[24] Placing bodies in uncustomary positions, real meals realign our affections and help to reorient our wills in a way the cultic meal cannot. The church must eat a meal at least as real as antiblackness supremacy.

THE REAL MEAL AS A TOOL TO "DISCERN THE BODY"

Its superiority to sacramental optimism notwithstanding, sacramental realism cannot overcome the porosity of bodies, whether our own or

ecclesial action *can* occur outside of the liturgy." "Mystical 'Body': An Ecclesiology Informed by Judith Butler," in Kevin Ahern, *Visions of Hope: Emerging Theologians and the Future of the Church* (Maryknoll, NY: Orbis, 2013), 16.

23. Levad, *Redeeming a Prison Society*, 88.

24. Gérard Fourez similarly points out the importance of physical encounter with the poor during the Eucharist in his review of *Symbole et sacrament* by Louis-Marie Chauvet, *Revue théologique de Louvain* 20 (1989): 194–203. See also Timothy M. Brunk, *Liturgy and Life: The Unity of Sacrament and Ethics in the Theology of Louis-Marie Chauvet* (New York: Peter Lang, 2007), 185.

Christ's. Even if the church returned to the real meal, it still would lack the capacity to reform itself from within. Indeed, like cultic feasts, real meals can reinforce unjust social hierarchy just as they can improperly exclude. But, while the cultic meal easily obscures this interrelation between sacramental integrity and worldly justice, the real meal can illuminate it. Rather than realigning the church's corporate body automatically, a return to the real meal as advocated by the Apostle Paul enables us to more perspicaciously recognize when it is broken.

For Paul, Christian communities performatively received Christ's body not just by eating the right type of food, but also by eating the right food in the right way. Deeply committed to church unity, Paul chastised the affluent members of the community for impatiently eating before their lower-status fellows. Because they had paid for most of the food, they expected the honor of eating first. Bringing their habituated bodies with them to the Eucharistic table, these high-status early Christians turned the meal of Christian unity into a performative display of disunity.

As chastisement, Paul instructs them to "discern the body." This instruction reminds them of the connection between "the body of Christ crucified represented by the bread" and "the communal body of Christ represented by the gathered church."[25] Here Paul wants them to realize that they had not "become what they received." Largely because the church currently celebrates a merely cultic Eucharist, it typically interprets this counsel quite differently.[26] Paul's command to "discern the body" appears to prescribe introspective, individualized self-assessment. Rather than surveying the church's corporate body in order to assess its resemblance to the body of Christ, contemporary Catholics search their souls for the stain of mortal sin. Christians ought to examine their consciences. But we ought to interpret Paul as encouraging us to compare bodies. Unfortunately, however, the cultic Eucharist limits the ability of the church to recognize itself. The real meal, on the other hand, makes the body of Christ visible to itself in a way that the cultic meal cannot. While the cultic Eucharist obscures the damage corporate vice inflicts upon the body of Christ, the real meal brings the sacramental impact of these bad habits to the surface.

Despite the evaluative power of the real meal, the Eucharist did

25. Dale B. Martin, *The Corinthian Body* (New Haven: Yale University Press, 1995), 74.
26. This is a prime example of the principle, "lex orandi, lex credendi."

not operate on the early church like magic, rendering worldly justice sacramentally irrelevant. Even Paul's ability to recognize and therefore sacramentally overturn the habituating consequences of divisive social hierarchy ran up against sharp limits. While possessing a keen awareness of the way in which unevenly allotted social power among free women and men could impede a community's performative reception of Christ's body, he nonetheless carried the vicious habits of a slaveholding society deep within his body.[27] In both limiting sexual activity to marriage and insisting that the body of Christ ought neither to enter nor be entered by the defiled body of a prostitute, Paul espouses a sexual code of conduct that slaves would have struggled to follow. Subject to sexual abuse by their masters, slaves could save sex for marriage only if their masters permitted; pimped out by their masters as profitable prostitutes, slaves of both sexes were thereby declared inherently unworthy of membership in the body of Christ.[28] Even worse, while Paul excluded sexually violated slaves from Christ's body, he welcomed the masters who violated them. In a world structured according to the logic of slaveownership, sex with a slave did not count as an offense against chastity; after all, one cannot violate a body that one considers her or his own.[29]

Even when shepherded by saints and apostles, Christian communities need to subject themselves to the diagnostic capacities of the real meal.[30] Precisely because the real meal considers what takes place in, through, and among the human bodies it gathers together, the real meal positions us to discern this body more perspicaciously and therefore receive it more worthily. We are not only what, but how we eat. When we expect the sacraments to shape visible bodies rather than simply save invisible souls, we position ourselves to recognize the ways in which the church has failed to performatively receive its identity as the body of Christ. No matter how well we amend our sacramental performance, we will still bring our racialized bodies to the real meal. Rather than rendering us indifferent to this injustice,

27. While "Paul quotes a baptismal formula to remind his readers that their new identity in Christ abrogates other status markers" including those of slavery and freedom, he later "goes on to re-inscribe customary and legal distinctions between slave and free." Jennifer A. Glancy, *Slavery in Early Christianity* (Minneapolis: Fortress Press, 2006), 34–35.

28. Glancy, *Slavery in Early Christianity*, 50, 58.

29. Ibid., 63.

30. For more on the liturgical importance of communal discernment, see C. Vanessa White, "Keeping Current: Somebody's Calling: The Liturgy, Discernment, and Christian Discipleship," *New Theology Review* 20, no. 1 (2013): 74–75, http://newtheologyreview.com/index.php/ntr/article/viewFile/223/395.

a truly embodied Eucharist will make us ache for the eschatological coming of God's justice. A fully embodied Eucharist does not supersede justice; it uncovers its absence.

In purporting to operate more or less magically and medicinally, the cultic meal limits our capacity to assess the conditions of the Eucharist's necessarily contextual and strategic performance. Its licity confined to the narrow parameters of confectional propriety, the cultically consumed body of Christ can be sliced and diced without appearing to be damaged. As long as the priest bears valid ordination, recites the correct formula, and distributes the holy bread to hands unsoiled by mortal sin, we believe the sacrament efficacious. It does not seem to matter whether black people are barred, either explicitly or indirectly, from the Mass at which the Eucharist occurs; it does not seem to matter whether they receive Christ's body into their own as enslaved beings or as free women and men. The cultic Eucharist distracts from the performative character of Christ's body, both sacramental and ecclesial. When medieval theologians reversed longstanding precedent and began to identify the sacramental body of Christ as the real body and the church as his mystical body, they did not misinterpret the cultic Eucharist as Cavanaugh implies.[31] The cultic Eucharist itself has rendered the character of the church's corporate body increasingly irrelevant. According to the performative logic of the cultic Eucharist, only Christ's sacramental body must be real.

But, even in the case of a Eucharist that works *ex opere operato*, circumstances do matter. We cannot performatively receive our identity as the body of Christ under any circumstances. Nor can we expect merely metaphorically food to re-discipline racially habituated bodies. The church instead must eat as Jesus did. Recognizing that real meals can bind only bodies seated together at the same table, Jesus brought together people whom society would rather keep apart.[32] But Jesus did not simply unite the divided; he realigned them in defiance of life-depriving social hierarchy. As in all societies, Roman meals reflected Roman values. For this reason, Jesus sought to defy these imperial values by practicing table fellowship. Ministering in a deeply unequal society organized around notions of masculine honor

31. Cavanaugh, *Torture and Eucharist*, 211–15.

32. Nathan D. Mitchell, *Eucharist as Sacrament of Initiation* (Chicago: Liturgy Training Publications, 1994), 56.

and feminized shame, Jesus engaged in the intimate bodily activity of eating alongside purportedly despoiling prostitutes.[33]

In creating a table fellowship marked by socially strategic, open commensality, Jesus strove to create an inside with no outside; a clique open to all comers; a house with unlocked doors.[34] Rather than just a problem to be solved, the porosity of Christ's body proves theologically essential. In eating with both prostitutes and tax collectors, Jesus does not simply reject so-called unjust distinctions between the ritually clean rich and the ritually impure poor, he casts off even seemingly appropriate distinctions such as those between oppressively powerful tax collectors and their victims. Through his very odd and countercultural "willingness to eat anything with anyone at any time," Jesus performatively displayed the necessarily porous boundaries of his body.[35] Jesus did not rely upon excommunication as a sacramental safeguard: willingness and ability to eat alongside him were the only prerequisites to being included in the meal.

In insisting on the cultic meal, the church exhibits a selective sacramental literalism. Certain aspects of the Lord's Supper, such as Jesus's masculinity or the words he spoke, possess a seemingly self-evident inviolability.[36] Other elements, such as its truly fraternal character, on the other hand, not only can be discarded but also must be. Confected by hands attached to a woman's body, the sacramental host does not comprise Christ's body. Fake food possesses a power women's bodies are incapable of producing.[37] Women's bodies make Christ's body fake; fake food makes his body real.[38] Bodies matter, but only sometimes.

STRATEGIES FOR BUILDING NEW EUCHARISTIC HABITS

Today, U.S.-American Christians celebrate not an openly commensurate Eucharist strategically aligned against antiblackness supremacy, but a spatially racialized one. Because the corporately vicious

33. Mitchell, *Real Presence*, 60, 66.

34. John Dominic Crossan, *The Historical Jesus: The Life of a Mediterranean Jewish Peasant* (New York: HarperCollins, 2010), 261.

35. Mitchell, *Eucharist as Sacrament of Initiation*, 2.

36. John Paul II, *Ecclesia de Eucharistia*, par. 5.

37. Ibid., pars. 30–31.

38. John Paul II, *Ordinatio Sacerdotalis*, pars. 1, 2; CDF, *Inter Insignories*, par. 5.

operation of antiblackness supremacy shape-shifts through space and time, its impact upon the church's sacramental practices will vary. The criteria of sacramental licity therefore will differ under conditions of chattel slavery and under conditions of Jim Crow, for example. The church must balance continuity with strategic adaptation. It can only stand still by moving. As metabolic processes interacting with the porous bodies of both Christ and individual Christians, Eucharistic practices must operate strategically, contextually, and in fully embodied fashion. An openly commensurate, socially strategic, and real Eucharistic meal allows the church to regulate the body of Christ as Jesus did.

We must change the way we eat Christ's body in the following ways. First, the church must perform the Eucharist in the strategically spatially subversive fashion of Jesus. This requires accepting that Jesus is where he said he would be, in the bodies of the poor, the imprisoned, and the disinherited. The church must stop looking for Jesus where he does not reside.[39] In the era of the antiblack mass prison, Catholic bishops occasionally ought to allow the Mass to be said only inside the walls of disproportionately black penitentiaries. We similarly ought to reconsider the neutrality of parishes begun by white flight. Rather than believing these parishes sacramentally benign, we should consider them Eucharistically inhospitable. Rather than the place in which the body of Christ is brought into being, these parishes represent a means by which the body of Christ was rent apart.

Second, the church cannot expect the Eucharist to do "in the world" what it does not do during the liturgy. The Eucharist cannot bring black and white Catholics together into one body of Christ as long as they remain parochially and residentially segregated. In ingesting Eucharistically confected real bread while seated across from the real bodies of otherwise spatially separated co-religionists, Catholics are drawn into unity with Christ by being drawn into unity with racial others. A real meal would make the reconciliation required to ensure that "a true Eucharist takes place" not just possible but necessary.[40] Human beings find it almost impossible to continue hating someone with whom they habitually break bread.

But the Eucharist cannot bring white and black Catholics together into a body that performatively defies either antiblackness supremacy

39. Matt 28:6.

40. Cavanaugh, "Theopolitical Imagination," 52.

or white supremacy unless it unfolds as a display of black power and fugitivity. Black people must not simply sit at the table of Christian fellowship; they must occupy the head of it. Slaves, too, were considered "one body" with their masters since slavery's violence denied them a separate personhood. Eucharistic unity cannot prove an excuse for corporately white parishes to consume, metabolically make use of, and then excrete both blackness and black people: black people must eat rather than be eaten.

Third, when we expect the Eucharist to operate as "an embodied performance" of God's reign, we position ourselves to "discern the body."[41] For example, imagine if the archbishop of a diocese like Detroit allowed mass to be held only in the central city or in the surrounding suburbs. Every Sunday, the location of diocesan masses would switch: on the First and Third Sundays, the Eucharist could be found only inside the nearly all-black city. The disproportionately white denizens of the suburbs would have to travel to neighborhoods they ordinarily avoid in order to taste Christ's body on their tongue. On the Second and Fourth Sundays, the situation would reverse itself. Of course, current patterns of corporate habituation would prevent many white suburbanites from choosing to enter the central city while ensuring that the most impoverished black residents of Detroit would be unable to access the suburbs. But the sacramental impact of racial segregation could at least be felt. In order to amplify the sacrament's efficacy, Detroit's Catholics would need to work together as a corporate body to ensure that black and white bodies changed places. Perhaps the hassle of coordinating such sacramentally necessary travel would inspire the church to agitate for the expansion of public transit between inner city and outer suburb, for example. The sacramental impact of residential segregation nonetheless would remain at the surface.

Even if the church could never perfectly performatively receive its identity as the body of Christ, the diagnostic powers of the real meal would at least enable the church to feel the weight of its sin across every inch of its corporate body. Virtue theory recognizes that it is better to do evil knowing the truth about oneself than to commit this same evil believing it a moral good. In both cases, the sin is the same, but the chances for acquiring virtue are not. Those whose sin causes

41. Mitchell, *Eucharist as Sacrament of Initiation*, 7.

them true pain and discomfort have traveled further down the path of virtue than those who sin with ease or pleasure.[42]

This chapter charts a new course; it does not walk it all the way. Rather than absolving the field of theology of problems, it troubles it with new ones. In reconceiving the relationship between the sacraments and sin, this chapter introduces the unsettling possibility that we may never be able to fully receive Christ while residing this side of the eschaton. They must cast aside the easy answers of sacramental optimism and accept the hard truths of sacramental realism. Antiblackness supremacy has haunted the church's theology and its practices for centuries. Now the church must reckon with it.

42. Lisa Tessman, *Burdened Virtues: Virtue Ethics for Liberatory Struggles* (New York: Oxford University Press, 2005), 53–57.

12.

Dismantling Antiblackness Supremacy

Operating as a habit, antiblackness supremacy inclines nonblack people to certain actions. White people especially generally refuse to remain within or enter into racially integrated neighborhoods, to support policies that seek to compensate for the effects of racial segregation such as busing, the regional funding of school systems, or publicly funded healthcare. They almost always attend disproportionately white schools and belong to disproportionately and overwhelmingly white friend groups and families. And even more than whites avoid nonwhites, they specifically seek distance from black people.

Because habits are acquired by repeated actions, they must be unmade by actions that are equally repetitive yet entirely out of character. But human beings cling to their habits; they only rarely choose to unmake their habits voluntarily.[1] Habits unravel not by willpower alone but by concerted (and often coerced) counteraction.[2] This rehabituation proves even more difficult in the case of vices of domination like white supremacy and antiblackness supremacy. If human beings cling to habits that are bad for them, how much more will they cleave to patterns of actions that bring them comfort and pleasure like antiblackness supremacy does? Further impeding rehabituation, vices of domination accord people power over the groups

1. Jamie Phelps, "Joy Came in the Morning: Risking Death for Resurrection: Confronting the Evil of Social Sin and Socially Sinful Structures," in *A Troubling in My Soul: Womanist Perspectives on Evil and Suffering*, ed. Emilie M. Townes (Maryknoll, NY: Orbis, 1993), 56.

2. Aquinas, *Summa Theologiae*, I–II. 71.4; and I–II.75.4.

and individuals most harmed by them. White supremacy increases white people's ability to resist coercive measures of rehabituation.

But the vices of white supremacy and antiblackness supremacy do not infiltrate the bodies of individuals only; they also operate within corporate bodies, like the Catholic Church. In their corporate forms, these vices prove equally empowering and intransigent. White Catholics typically have changed their segregationist habits only when forced to by a higher power, as when bishops ordered the integration of parochial schools. Catholic corporate habits of white flight have allowed the church's corporate body to evade the rehabituating actions of integrationist church officials.

Because these vices operate corporately, the actions of a few good whites have never been enough to overturn them. The social and ecclesial revolutions of the 1960s admittedly did convince a liberal minority of white priests and laypeople of segregation's sinfulness. But these women and men ultimately failed to dislodge the church's corporate habits of spatialized antiblackness.[3] Lacking the power to disrupt regnant patterns of racial segregation in spheres both secular and sacred, this liberal minority could not rehabituate the church's corporate body.[4]

The deeply embodied and corporate character of these habits also helps to explain why moral suasion has proven relatively powerless against them. By the time Catholic leaders began publicly denouncing segregation as a sin in the years following the Second World War, the corporate habits of antiblackness supremacist segregation had already taken root within the corporate body of the Catholic Church.[5] Just as these habits remained mostly insensitive to magisterial condemnation, so they have continued to operate even without explicit episcopal encouragement. As embodied habits, the vices of antiblackness supremacy and white supremacy proceed from the church's spatially situated corporate body even if they no longer trickle down from its magisterial mind. A habituated body does not need to be explicitly directed in order to continue acting expertly.

Although the contemporary Catholic Church has more or less abandoned the explicit pursuit of parochial racial purity, it continues to inhabit and bear responsibility for survival of racially segregated

3. McGreevy, *Parish Boundaries*, 160, 169, 245.

4. Ibid., 176–77. Joseph Watras, "The Racial Desegregation of Dayton, Ohio, Public Schools, 1966–2008," *Ohio History* 117, no. 1 (2010): 93–107.

5. McGreevy, *Parish Boundaries*, 88.

places. When white Catholics fled the integrating city, they took their parishes with them. The suburb now provides both the non-black Catholic individuals and parishes the racial safety they could not find in the city. In the blackening central city, spatialized whiteness remained perpetually under siege. But in the suburbs, Catholic parishes have not needed to actively defend against blackness as they had before: the suburb does this work for them.

CATHOLIC SOCIAL TEACHING: FROM MORAL SUASION TO CORPORATE REHABITUATION

In changing our understanding of the problem, the theory of corporate virtue and vice can help to improve our understanding of its solution. The corporately vicious character of antiblackness supremacy suggests that, rather than providing moral exhortation premised on the existence of the goodwill of whites, Catholic magisterial teaching on racism ought to serve as an opportunity for reflecting upon and devising strategies of corporate rehabituation.[6] The antiblack practices of the church's corporate body do not simply proceed from deliberate choices; they also operate as automated reflexes of a deeply habituated body. As such, the church's segregationist habits often emanate from levels deeper than and prior to its self-reflective and deliberative consciousness. They cannot reliably be accessed by appeals to moral reason.[7] Because the church's participation in and performance of antiblackness supremacy is the result of corporate habituation, the church most needs new habits, not new teachings. In addition to adopting a more systemic and passionately articulated approach to racism as Bryan Massingale proposes, church leaders also ought to embrace the analysis of antiblackness described in these pages.

In order to model this new approach, I offer a constructive critique of arguably the most complete and systemic episcopal document on racism, the pastoral letter Cardinal George wrote for the Archdiocese of Chicago titled, *Dwell in My Love*. Created in accordance with the expert guidance of Sister Anita Baird, DHM, founding director of the archdiocesan Office of Racial Justice, George's letter represents the best of U.S. episcopal analysis of racism. George rightly

6. Massingale, *Racial Justice and the Catholic Church*, 43, 64, 74, 70, 71.

7. McGreevy, *Parish Boundaries*, 98.

recognizes the structural underpinnings of racial inequality, paying particular attention to what he calls "spatial racism," which "refers to patterns of metropolitan development in which some affluent whites create racially and economically segregated suburbs or gentrified areas of cities, leaving the poor—mainly African Americans, Hispanics and some newly arrived immigrants—isolated in deteriorating areas of the cities and older suburbs."[8] George even acknowledges that white Catholics also participated in spatial racism by "preventing the entrance of black people" into the neighborhoods they considered their own.[9] As Massingale notes, George's letter further surpasses other analyses in the way that it "espouses a wider range of responses to combat the social evil of racism."[10]

Despite these strengths, this historic document ultimately fails to offer an effective plan of antiracist action due to three interrelated conceptual errors. First, George does not grasp white supremacy's special relation to antiblackness supremacy. Second, he overlooks the corporately vicious character of both white supremacy and antiblackness supremacy. And third, he attempts to analyze racism without attending to the afterlife of slavery. Because George does not recognize the way in which the afterlife of slavery continues to structure life in the United States, he fails to differentiate antiblackness from other forms of racial and economic injustice. For example, George acknowledges the systemic character of racism. But, when specifying the correlation between spatial dynamics and social injustice, he does not mention race. Rather than attacking racial segregation, George here offers actions aimed at the eradication of poverty and economic segregation. Besides unhelpfully conflating economic oppression with racial oppression, this approach fuels the self-serving white belief that black people are segregated from whites only because (and when) they are poor, not because they are black and even if they are middle class.

Identifying racism as a systemic injustice but not also as a corporate vice, George makes the equally common mistake of believing that the Catholic Church can be reformed from within. For this reason, he encourages Catholics to change the internal dynamics of their corporate spaces, making the liturgy more aesthetically multicultural, encouraging more frequent preaching on racial justice, and cul-

8. Francis Cardinal George, *Dwell in My Love: A Pastoral Letter on Racism* (2001), 12.
9. Ibid., 8.
10. Massingale, *Racial Justice and the Catholic Church.*

tivating a more diverse teaching corps, for example.[11] These steps are important, but they are not enough. No matter what types of songs it sings during Mass, the church cannot operate as a force for racial justice as long as its schools and parishes remain racially segregated in the service of antiblackness supremacy. Catholics cannot merely change the way we inhabit space; we also must change the character of the places we inhabit.

In overlooking the uniqueness of antiblackness, George's endorsement of multiculturalism unwittingly promotes a type of people-of-color-blindness. For example, while white Catholics have inflicted racial harm on Asian-Americans, they have not perpetuated spatial evil on Asian-Americans in the way that they have black people. They have not locked Asian-American people up in prisons or ghettos.[12] In a similar way, the celebration of Our Lady of Guadalupe in a predominately Anglo parish does not atone for the exclusion of black people from nonblack Catholic spaces. Ultimately, multiculturalism can be good, but it is not always necessary. We would not chastise a predominately Irish-American Catholic parish for failing to celebrate Italian saints or to sing traditional German-language hymns. We sheepishly speak of "multiculturalism" because we are afraid and/or unwilling to admit the singular reality of antiblackness. Multiculturalism carries another danger. Given the United States' long history of black minstrelsy, the church should look suspiciously on the singing of black songs by white people, especially when unaccompanied by white submission to and intimacy with black people on a corporate scale. More than simply inadequate, white use of black culture possesses the power to paradoxically consolidate white difference from and power over black people.

Failing to recognize the racially segregated character of the archdiocese as a habitat for vice, George suggests that we ought to "engage schools, especially schools in the parish-sharing program, to do student cultural and academic exchanges."[13] Unacknowledged in this proposal is how and why students are separated. Bringing a token number of black Catholics temporarily into white Catholic space in a controlled fashion does not unsettle patterns of antiblackness supremacy. This proposal also implicitly places students from racially

11. Ibid.

12. Japanese-Americans were victimized by racist internment during the Second World War due not to their descent from or perceived similarly to slaves, but as foreign aliens.

13. George, *Dwell in My Love,* 8.

differentiated places in relation to each other as exchange students, not as neighbors or fellow parishioners. But in truth, black and white Catholics are not "foreigners" to each other; their spatial estrangement differs tremendously from the distance separating Swedes from Irishmen, for example. Here George portrays intra-diocesan spatial separation as innocent, harmless, and natural rather than a strategy of antiblackness supremacy.

George similarly proposes that we "continue to work for justice in funding Catholic schools in order to give all students the education necessary to experience personal success and contribute to the common good."[14] Does this refer to enhanced funding for programs like the Big Shoulders Fund, which raise money to subsidize tuition costs for students from low-income families? Or does it refer to the centralization and pooling of archdiocesan tuition money such that every school would receive equal funding? George's acceptance of the structural status quo in the years after this letter's release would seem to argue in favor of the former position. And so does his language elsewhere in the letter. For example, while George explicitly encourages Catholics to "promote tax-sharing policies between wealthy and poor communities," he does not mandate tuition sharing policies between wealthy and poor Catholic schools.[15]

Given the racially stratified character of Chicago's Catholic schools along with its decentralized funding system in which, for the most part, students receive whatever education their parents can afford, George's proposal here seems an argument for a type of "separate but equal" approach to Catholic schooling. Even when less affluent children receive a boost from the charitable funds doled out by the Big Shoulders Fund, they still typically attend schools that receive less funding and offer fewer opportunities than those typically attended by Chicago's white children.[16] As long as black children are allowed inside the church's corporate body, he seems to imply, it does not matter whether they exist within that body in positions that are either separate and/or unequal from their white counterparts.

In order to reverse its corporate habituation by antiblackness supremacy in the afterlife of slavery, the church ought to take the following actions. First, Catholic magisterial teaching ought to identify the spatial afterlife of slavery as a dire threat to the church's ecclesial

14. Ibid.
15. Ibid.
16. Big Shoulders Fund, http://www.bigshouldersfund.org/.

integrity. Since the prison and the ghetto work together to sustain this afterlife, the church ought to mobilize its institutional resources against the prison-ghetto complex with at least as much ferocity and single-mindedness as it currently pursues comprehensive immigration reform or seeks to overturn *Roe v. Wade*. In particular, the church ought to pressure the federal government to enforce fair housing laws both by withdrawing development funds from projects that carry a segregationist impact and by more effectively sanctioning individual landlords and real estate agents who violate these laws. The church must also empower and build partnerships with those organizations already working to dismantle regnant structures of segregation.

In addition to organizing against racialized enforcement of our nation's criminal code, the church also ought to strip incarceration of some of its stigma. To this end, it should call on states to return the franchise to all felons, even those still serving their sentences.[17] It should also mobilize against the bundle of unjust laws that deprive felons of eligibility for certain professional licenses, access to student loans and public assistance, and protection against job and housing discrimination.[18] The church must oppose these laws not just with its words but also with its corporate body, staging protests and engaging in acts of strategic civil disobedience against the prison system.

Second, the church ought to begin to reorganize parish boundaries. Rather than ratifying regnant patterns of antiblackness supremacist racial segregation, Catholic parishes ought to be placed in defiance of it. As suggested in the previous chapter, bishops also ought to consider closing those typically suburban parishes that provide whites racial safe-haven. Even if bishops cannot make lay whites share space and power with black people, they do not have to actively enable and sanctify their intransigence. Bishops have always granted their constituents' requests for new parishes selectively; they must begin to exercise their episcopal power in order to overturn established diocesan patterns of racial segregation rather than comply with them. As demonstrated by Bishop Terry Steib's unpopular decision to forego building new Catholic schools in Memphis's suburbs until predominantly black Catholic schools in Memphis's inner city were reopened, often bishops will have to pursue racial justice in their dioceses against the wishes of their white subjects.[19] They ought to care

17. Alexander, *The New Jim Crow*, 58.

18. Ibid., 53, 94, 144–48, 199.

19. David Waters, "First Students of Reopened Inner-City Catholic Schools Graduating, Head-

about black lives more than white feelings; they ought to promote black freedom before they attend to white comfort.

In calling for the development of strategies of parochial desegregation, I do not advocate for the abolition of predominately black Catholic parishes. Predominately black Catholic parishes do not represent the flip side of disproportionately white ones. Rather than serving as an instrument of oppression, the black Catholic parish allows its members to survive it. The black Catholic parish also helps prevent black Catholics from being swallowed up by, absorbed into, and dispersed throughout the white Catholic body. For these reasons, the church should give these parishes priority when divvying up limited institutional resources.

Similarly, the church ought to address and take responsibility for the way that its racially segregated primary and secondary school system promotes antiblackness supremacy. As with their public counterparts, Catholic primary and secondary schools in this country are also separate and deeply unequal.[20] Catholic secondary schools currently use admission tests to sort and rank prospective students, rejecting those students who fall below the academic standards they have selected for themselves. Combined with dramatic differentials in tuition costs, these tests act as racial gatekeepers and help to keep the "best" schools disproportionately white. Catholic schools should reconsider these admission tests; rather than accepting reigning U.S.-American notions of value and merit, Catholic schools should resist them when they perpetuate racial stratification. It is strange indeed for schools founded in the name of the messiah who welcomed the little children to turn those with low test scores away.[21]

Catholic primary and secondary schools also ought to reevaluate their recruiting strategies. Even those Catholic schools affiliated with a place-based parish typically rely on the outreach efforts of paid recruiters to replenish their pool of students. In the case of Catholic secondary schools, these recruiters visit Catholic seventh- and eighth-grade classrooms, coordinate "shadow days" during which

ing to College," *Memphis Commercial Appeal*, May 19, 2012, accessed July 24, 2012, http://www.commercialappeal.com/news/2012/may/19/jubilant-occasion/.

20. Jonathan Kozol, *The Shame of the Nation: The Restoration of Apartheid Schooling in America* (New York: Broadway, 2006); Dale McDonald, "United States Catholic Elementary and Secondary Schools, 2000-2001: The Annual Statistical Report on Schools, Enrollment and Staffing," 2001, http://www.eric.ed.gov/ERICWebPortal/contentdelivery/servlet/ERICServlet?accno=ED454614.

21. Matt 19:14.

prospective students spend a day attending class with a selected high school guide, and circulate marketing materials in churches, neighborhood centers, and online. It is not that these recruiting strategies are necessarily consciously racist. Nor should Catholic schools be uniform demographically, pedagogically, or spiritually. We must distinguish between the differences that uphold antiblackness and those that upend it. Context matters. Rather than critiquing those schools that educate racially oppressed populations, for example, we ought to direct our focus on predominately white Catholic primary and secondary schools. In addition to keeping white students at a social distance from black and brown ones, these schools also confer tremendous amounts of privilege and power. Their whiteness carries forward an ugly history of parochial, place-based vice.

If Catholic dioceses remain unwilling to pursue creative strategies of racial integration of schools under their jurisdiction, they could at least centralize school funding so that each school within a diocese receives relatively equal amounts of funding. Parents and guardians of Catholic schoolchildren would pay according to a sliding scale of financial capacity. This money would then be pooled and distributed based upon educational need.

Third, the church ought to initiate a racial segregation truth-telling commission at the diocesan and parochial level aimed at uncovering and then narrating the history of each parish and diocese's involvement in the maintenance of antiblackness supremacist racial segregation. This process ought to dramatize the way in which existing parish boundaries reflect and carry forward the prerogatives of antiblackness supremacy. Rather than using moral suasion as a replacement for rehabituation, this strategy deploys moral suasion as a means to the end of such rehabituation. It does not show whites what they need to do; it charts what needs to be done to them. Rather than waiting on whites to change their world, these truth-telling commissions uncover how the world of whites ought to be changed.

Institutions whether secular or sacred struggle to police themselves: non-Catholics equipped with relevant skill sets should play a substantial role in establishing, spearheading, and executing these commissions. Historians in particular can facilitate this process. Because this book chronicles the vicious operation of antiblackness supremacy in the Catholic Church's corporate body on a macro-level, it cannot capture all of antiblackness supremacy's details and local permutations. But the theoretical frameworks developed in this book can help historians and other scholars detail the workings of antiblackness supremacy in one parish or time period. In addition to advancing parochial self-understanding, these micro-histories will also help ethicists and church authorities to devise strategies of corporate rehabituation more expertly tailored to the particularities of their time and place. Anthropologists similarly ought to compile ethnographies of parochial whiteness as well as parochial antiblackness, which also will serve these ends. More than simply uncovering how the vices of antiblackness supremacy and white supremacy implanted themselves in Catholic bodies, these ethnographies also will determine how these vices continue to operate today.[22]

Fourth, scholars also ought to study the relation between white supremacy and the financial structure of the church. In my research, I repeatedly came across an organization called the Catholic Extension Society, which helped certain parishes fund church construction projects. Many historically white Catholic parishes mention the support they received from this society in their online histories, but I could find no evidence of this group lending money to black parishes. Without a sustained and thorough investigation, we cannot determine whether this information evidences a pattern of racialized lending practices by financial actors affiliated with the church or if it simply indicates the limitations of my rather small sample size. Given the antiblackness supremacist character of secular lending practices in combination with the church's own habits of antiblackness supremacy, we have ample reason to question the racial fairness of official lending practices.

Even if church organizations like the Catholic Extension Society did not lend money in white supremacist fashion, white parishes still benefited from the wealth of whites in ways that black parishes did not. Fledgling white parishes fleeing central cities often received land grants from rural white landowners; white parishes were also more likely to contain wealthy members capable of donating large sums of money to finance building projects. This racialized parochial wealth gap persists. Catholic scholars and officials ought to pursue strategies to counteract the financial effects of parochial racial and economic

22. For an example of the way ethnography can illuminate the inner workings of whiteness in a particular time and place, see Alison D. Goebel, "Small City Neighbors: Race, Space, and Class in Mansfield, Ohio" (University of Illinois at Urbana-Champaign, 2011), http://gradworks.umi.com/34/78/3478707.html.

segregation. The church ought to do more to redistribute wealth internally, reorganizing its financial structures in accordance with the preferential option for the poor.

Even today, the church's financial practices remain racialized. Founded in 1907, the Catholic Negro-American Mission Board aims "to build the Church in African-American communities."[23] Since 1980, this organization has belonged to the Black and Indian Mission Office in Washington, D.C., which raises money "to help communities build the church and preach the gospel of Jesus among the African-American, Native American, and Alaska Native people of God."[24] But as the early-twentieth-century black, lay Catholic activist Wyatt Turner explained when protesting the church's Commission for the Catholic Missions Among the Colored People and the Indians, "blacks should not be placed under the same bureaucratic control as Indians who were separated onto reservations and not considered citizens."[25] These missions also seem to rely upon the voluntary donations of individuals and institutions. In addition to positioning black people as outsiders to both church and nation-state, these missions seemingly lean too heavily on the unreliable largesse of whites habituated by antiblackness supremacy.

Fifth, the church should adopt a version of the National Football Association's "Rooney Rule."[26] Enacted in 2003, this rule required all NFL teams to interview at least one minority candidate when hiring new head coaches. Although this rule has not eliminated racial bias in hiring, it has reduced it significantly. In introducing predominately white owners and managers to black applicants they would not have considered before, this rule helped raise the number of black head coaches from two to seven in just four short years.[27] Catholic schools, universities, parishes, seminaries, and episcopal offices ought to enact a similar rule. In addition to forcing whites to hire outside of their

23. http://blackandindianmission.org/about-us/cnamb/.

24. http://blackandindianmission.org/.

25. Cyprian Davis, *The History of Black Catholics in the United States* (New York: Crossroad, 1995), 219.

26. For a more in-depth exploration of the Rooney Rule, see N. Jeremi Duru, *Advancing the Ball: Race, Reformation, and the Quest for Equal Coaching Opportunity in the NFL* (New York: Oxford University Press, 2012); Janice Fanning Madden and Matthew Ruther, "Has the NFL's Rooney Rule Efforts 'Leveled the Field' for African American Head Coach Candidates?," *Journal of Sports Economics* 12, no. 2 (April 1, 2011): 127.

27. Ashley Fox, "Rooney Rule Has Opened Doors for Minority Head-Coaching Candidates but It Could Do More," ESPN.com, May 19, 2015, http://espn.go.com/nfl/story/_/id/12867233.

preestablished and racially exclusive social networks, this rule would also put pressure on Catholic institutions to invest in the development of black religious sisters, priests, professors, and schoolteachers.

Sixth, the church must devise a new political agenda. The bishops' 2007 document evidences the shortcomings of the church's current political self-understanding. When the bishops decry "the destruction of unborn children through abortion," everyone knows exactly of what action they speak. But when the bishops insist that "racism . . . can never be justified," they refer to a sin much less well defined. The bishops condemn racism, but they provide no way of recognizing it. The church cannot effectively oppose a sin it does not accurately describe. Although they encourage Catholics to refrain from voting in alignment with pro-choice principles and to support "laws and policies to protect human life to the maximum degree possible, including constitutional protection for the unborn and legislative efforts to end abortion," the bishops fail to explain what proactive antiracist action would look like.

Without acquitting the Democratic Party of its complicity in the sins of either white supremacy or antiblackness supremacy, the Catholic bishops must confront the increasing whiteness of the Republican Party. This country's political parties have long operated in racialized fashion: during its first century, the GOP truly acted like "the Party of Lincoln," advocating abolition and sometimes even formal equality. The Democratic Party, on the other hand, represented the interests of racist white Southerners and working-class Northern whites. Postwar suburbanization prompted these working-class whites to switch sides, and President Johnson's signing of the Civil Rights Act lost the Democrats the white South for more than a generation. Completing this realignment, the Republican Ronald Reagan rose to the presidency on the wings of the "Southern Strategy." African Americans in turn abandoned the Party that abandoned them. The election of Barack Obama only intensified these trends: the Deep South currently sends only one white Democrat to the House of Representatives, and whites in all parts of the country identify with the Republican Party at higher rates than they did when the last Democrat held presidential office.[28]

28. Moni Basu, "Last White House Democratic Congressman in the Deep South Fights for Political Survival," *CNN* November 2, 2012, accessed March 25, 2014, http://inamerica.blogs.cnn.com/2012/11/02/last-white-house-democrat-in-the-deep-south-fights-for-political-survival/; Jeffrey M. Jones, "U.S. Whites More Solidly Republican in Recent Years:

Rather than pitting what are often caricatured as "the party of life" against "the party of social justice," I call on the bishops to interrogate the connections between whiteness and pro-life Republicanism. As tracked by Gallup in the year 2013, nonwhites were significantly more likely to identify as "pro-life" than whites: while fifty-one percent of nonwhites identified as "pro-life," only forty-six percent of whites did. A similar gap separates the races with respect to the label "pro-choice": while only thirty-seven percent of nonwhites call themselves "pro-choice," forty-eight percent of white respondents claim this title. These results produce a "net pro-choice score" of plus two for whites and negative fourteen for nonwhites.[29] But this heightened attachment to pro-life principles does not make nonwhites more likely to belong to the party that purportedly champions pro-life principles. For example, while 50.3 percent of non-Hispanic whites pledge allegiance to the Republican Party, only 21.2 percent of nonwhites do.[30] These data suggest that the whiteness of the Republican Party cannot be attributed to racial differences in support for abortion.

WHITE ANGLOS AND ECCLESIAL "MODEL MINORITIES"

Seventh, white Anglo Catholics must resist the temptation to treat Latino/a Catholics as what I call an "ecclesial model minority." Even when intended as a rebuke of xenophobic and often racist anti-immigrant sentiment, non-Hispanic white Catholic affirmation of Latino/a Catholics can reinforce pernicious patterns of antiblackness.[31] For example, when non-Hispanic white Catholics praise Latino/a Catholics for "refusing to identify as either Republican or Democrat," they implicitly denigrate African Americans, the group of U.S.-Americans most likely to identify with one party over the other, as divisive and polarizing. Echoing the afterlives of Cuban, Puerto Rican, and Dominican slavery, this claim portrays not

Party preferences more polarized by race and ethnicity under Obama," *Gallup Politics*, March 24, 2014, http://www.gallup.com/poll/168059/whites-solidly-republican-recent-years.aspx.

29. Lydia Saad, "Americans Misjudge U.S. Abortion Views: Perception that pro-choice position dominates contrasts with even split in actual views," *Gallup Politics*, May 15, 2013, http://www.gallup.com/poll/162548/americans-misjudge-abortion-views.aspx.

30. Jones, "U.S. Whites More Solidly Republican."

31. Dávila, *Latino Spin,* 3, 10.

antiblackness, but blackness itself as a threat to national unity. And when we celebrate Latino/as, whom we typically imagine as nonblack, for their purportedly moderate stance on legalized abortion, we implicitly affirm one of the vilest tropes of antiblackness, that black people are sexually promiscuous and irresponsible parents.[32] When we boast about U.S. Latino/as having "built a remarkable network of care for the needy," we cast native-born blacks as socially disconnected, dysfunctional, and lacking in family values.[33] These notions figure black people as voluntarily natally alienated. In so doing, these tropes implicitly but no less undeniably confuse antiblackness with the truth of black life.

Whether consciously or not, many white Anglos link the purportedly nonpolarized and therefore healing power of Latino/as to their embodiment of mestizaje as identity and way of life.[34] For example, Michael Baxter joins Cavanaugh in arguing that, because "Latinos in the U.S. have a sense for mestizaje . . . a sense that they can be both American and Mexican, for example," they can "stay in touch with their communities in Mexico" while simultaneously establishing exceptionally strong communal ties in their new U.S.-American homeland. According to Baxter and Cavanaugh, this ability to belong to two cultures at once in turn makes Latinos both more like Jesus, "who is both God and man, who forged a community from both Jew and gentile, who embraces all peoples regardless of—and indeed in spite of—the politics of nation-states."[35] Baxter and Cavanaugh are not alone: presenting her *mestiza* identity as an icon of continental unity, Pope John Paul II declared Our Lady of Guadalupe the patron saint of the Americas.[36]

Even if it were true that racial mixture somehow represented a

32. Charles C. Camosy, "How the Abortion Wars Will End—with a Truce, Not a Bang," *Los Angeles Times*, accessed June 21, 2015, http://www.latimes.com/opinion/op-ed/la-oe-0322-camosy-abortion-discourse-change-20150322-story.html.

33. Michael Baxter, "Reply to 'A View from Abroad' by Massimo Faggioli," *America Magazine*, March 31, 2014, accessed April 16, 2015, http://americamagazine.org/content/all-things/reply-view-abroad-massimo-faggioli.

34. Mike Jordan Laskey, "Life & Justice Lecture Presenter Charles Camosy," *Catholic Star Herald*, accessed June 24, 2015, http://catholicstarherald.org/life-justice-lecture-presenter-charles-camosy/.

35. Baxter, "Reply to 'A View from Abroad.'"

36. John Paul II, *Ecclesia in America*, Post-Synodal Apostolic Exhortation on the Encounter with the Living Jesus Christ: The Way to Conversion, Communion, and Solidarity in America, 1999, par. 11, http://w2.vatican.va/content/john-paul-ii/en/apost_exhortations/documents/hf_jp-ii_exh_22011999_ecclesia-in-america.html.

superior form of humanity, why have many Catholic scholars decided to call this process mestizaje as opposed to *mulatez*, especially given that the latter pre-dates the former historically and that the first Mexican settlers of present-day California were mulattoes, not mestizos?[37] The black roots of Mexican-America notwithstanding, what makes the mixture of Spanish with indigenous more universal and unifying than the mixture of European or indigenous with African?[38] Especially as defined by the one-drop rule, blackness already contains abundant "biological" racial mixture. In addition to denying the biological mixture within blackness, this rhetoric also overlooks the fact that black music, language, food, religion, fashion, and philosophy have been thoroughly and vibrantly "mixed" for over four hundred years. Black culture is a hybrid culture.[39]

For these reasons, blackness arguably includes and unifies even more adeptly than mestizaje. While mestizaje brings two cultures and races together, blackness can reconcile multiple racial identities within itself. For example, the child of a light-skinned African American parent (read: a person who most likely has more European ancestors than African ones) and a white, Asian, or mestizo/a parent will typically qualify as black in the eyes of black people. Blackness and black people have proved uniquely unifying in the cultural sphere as well. As novelist Daniel José Older reminds us, "almost every facet of Latino culture that has exploded as a global pop phenomenon—from tango to mambo, cha-cha-cha, and salsa to bachata and reggaeton—have been rooted in black culture, even if the faces we associate with them aren't usually black ones."[40] The Anglo-dominated United States has formed its musical identity through a similarly parasitic consumption of black cultural inventions.[41]

37. Martha Menchaca, *Recovering History, Constructing Race: The Indian, Black, and White Roots of Mexican Americans* (Austin: University of Texas Press, 2010), 170. For an example of this privileging, see Ruben Rosario Rodríguez, *Racism and God-Talk: A Latino/a Perspective* (New York: New York University Press, 2008). Like Rodríguez, most Latino/a theologians who privilege mestizaje typically claim that they do not intend to diminish antiblack racism, but as occurs with non-Latino white theologians such as Pfeil, they do not provide a theoretical framework that actually succeeds in doing this.

38. Kelly, Zahira @bad_dominicana. "Mestiza has come to mean white/native, noncaribbean nonblack latinamerican." 9am, June 23, 2015. Tweet.

39. John Thornton, *Africa and Africans in the Making of the Atlantic World, 1400–1800*, 2nd ed. (New York: Cambridge University Press, 1998), 8, 129–31.

40. Daniel José Older, "Why U.S. Latinos Need to Get Loud About the Dominican Republic," *Buzzfeed* June 18, 2015, http://www.buzzfeed.com/danieljoseolder/us-latinos-need-to-get-loud-about-the-dominican-republic#.st0OpE8g.

41. W. E. B. Du Bois, *The Souls of Black Folk* (CreateSpace, 2012), 11.

This elevation of mestizaje as supremely unifying also conspires to obscure the African identity of all the Americas in general and the United States in particular. Indeed, if all Mexicans, regardless of racial makeup, qualify as practitioners of mestizaje, as Baxter and Cavanaugh imply, then so all U.S.-Americans express an identity already intermixed with a blackness that is itself thoroughly hybridized in the aforementioned ways.[42] Like its music, U.S.-American fashion, language, political philosophy, religious practices, and athletics all evidence black people's openness to nonparasitic intermixture with other cultures.

This deployment of mestizaje also obscures the Africanity of Mexico itself: more than simply existing as a distinct cultural group within Mexico, scholars increasingly recognize the way in which "Afro-descendants served as cultural intermediaries between" Spanish and indigenous peoples. Black Mexicans played a central role in the creation of Mexican mestizaje.[43]

Inattention to the specificity and adaptability of antiblackness supremacy has led many racial observers astray. In particular, white, non-Hispanic promoters of the racially healing capacities of mestizaje often confuse an increasingly outdated ideology of U.S.-American whiteness with its lived reality: in addition to discounting the fact that U.S.-American blackness has always been multiracial, modern calls for multiculturalism often advance old strategies of pan-American antiblackness.[44] Even when explicitly positioned against ideologies of pure whiteness, this approach deploys recent nonblack heritage as a way to seek distance from and pronounce superiority over blackness. More than it liberates us from racism, this ideology seeks "freedom from . . . racial blackness."[45] In celebrating Latin American–style mestizaje, advocates of what Sexton terms "multiracial exceptionalism" increasingly confuse the suspension of the

42. Baxter, "Reply to 'A View from Abroad.'"

43. Frank T. Proctor, *Damned Notions of Liberty: Slavery, Culture, and Power in Colonial Mexico, 1640-1769* (Albuquerque: University of New Mexico Press, 2010), 45.

44. In a tribute to Virgilio Elizondo, the founder of U.S. Hispanic theology, John A. Coleman perhaps unwittingly admits the ways in which mestizaje can be used to seek distance from both blackness and black people when he argues that in describing the Christian past and the human future as mestizo, Elizondo "affirmed rootedness while destroying ghettoishness." "Virgilio Elizondo: Practical Theologian, Prophet, and Organic Intellectual," in *Beyond Borders: Writings of Virgilio Elizondo and Friends*, ed. Virgilio Elizondo and Timothy Matovina (Eugene, OR: Wipf & Stock, 2000), 239.

45. Jared Sexton, *Amalgamation Schemes: Antiblackness and the Critique of Multiracialism* (Minneapolis: University of Minnesota Press, 2008), 6.

one-drop rule with the eradication of racism itself.[46] Once a scheme of antiblackness supremacy, the one-drop rule now often operates on behalf of black power.

Besides, even during Jim Crow, whiteness ultimately acquired its coherence from parasitic consumption of the black body. This parasitism exists as a structural effect of the lingering association of blackness with slave status. Just as the slave exists not as herself but for her master, so white people relate to blackness not so much as a form of difference but as an instrument of nonblack self-creation and expression. Just as a master claims ownership over the body of his slave, so nonblack, but especially white, U.S.-Americans appropriate black cultural forms. We parasitically consume blackness like food, drawing life from it as we make it disappear.

Because blackness has never been allowed to belong to black people as *latinidad* has to Latino/as, nonblack U.S.-Americans struggle to recognize that they already inhabit a thoroughly mulatto culture.[47] Why? We cannot recognize intermixture with an entity that we believe exists as an extension of our own personhood. This parasitic relation between whiteness and blackness also makes it difficult for nonblack people to acknowledge their internal Africanity without slipping into a form of minstrelsy. In a sense, whiteness cannot recognize the full reality of blackness because it will not accord it the freedom to be truly other; whiteness instead seeks to prevent blackness from defining the terms of its own existence and difference from other groups.

This parasitism extends to the political sphere as well. As the founders of the Black Lives Matter Movement—Patrisse Cullors, Opal Tometi, and Alicia Garza—argue, not only do "non-black oppressed people in this country . . . benefit from anti-black racism," but also "Black Lives and struggles for Black liberation have played [a critical role] in inspiring and anchoring, through practice and theory, social movements for the liberation of all people." In this way, they continue, "the women's movement, the Chicano liberation movement, queer movements, and many more have adopted the strategies, tactics, and theory of the Black liberation movement."[48] White people

46. Ibid., 2.

47. Here, I do not deny that *latinidad* has been marginalized and denigrated in the United States. I simply claim that it has not been parasitically consumed as blackness has.

48. Black Lives Matter Movement: HerStory, accessed January 6, 2016, http://blacklivesmatter.com/herstory/.

have been similarly parasitic. During the colonial era, white and mestizo slaveowning American revolutionaries fed off black slavery when they positioned themselves as slaves of European monarchs.[49] In a sense, all Americans wear political blackface.

White Anglo Catholics who elevate mestizaje as uniquely universal and unifying most likely intend to upend white normativity by transferring the universality and teleological finality accorded it since the Enlightenment to specifically Latino mestizaje. But in so doing, they unwittingly turn mestizaje into a mechanism of racial supersessionism. Just as Christian supersessionism slanders Jewishness as clannish, these misuses of mestizaje implicitly position blackness as ontologically narrow and violently divisive.[50] In truth, blackness is both already thoroughly hybridized, biologically and culturally. Interacting with difference without expelling it from itself, blackness holds a culturally and racially diverse continent together. African Americans express more openness to egalitarian encounter and intimacy with nonblack people of all ethnicities, national origins, and racial backgrounds than any other U.S.-American group. Where the United States contains not just difference, but polarization and division, African Americans bear the least amount of blame.

THE CASE FOR ECCLESIAL REPARATIONS

Eighth, the church must agitate for reparations at all levels of government and for all African-descended inhabitants of the Americas.[51] The church must also provide to black Catholics ecclesial reparations. More than simply structuring the world, black slavery continues to pervade it. For this reason, the church ought to pursue reparations not to reform the pervasively antiblack world but to destroy it.[52] In a sense, the word "reparations" misleads. Slavery and its deadly afterlife cannot be repaired. Its injustice is immeasurable; the harm it caused is

49. Sexton, "People-of-Color-Blindness," 42.

50. For more on the relation between white supremacy and Christian supersessionism, see J. Kameron Carter, *Race: A Theological Account* (New York: Oxford University Press, 2008); Willie James Jennings, *The Christian Imagination: Theology and the Origins of Race* (New Haven: Yale University Press, 2010).

51. Brian Bantum, *Redeeming Mulatto: A Theology of Race and Christian Hybridity* (Waco, TX: Baylor University Press, 2010), 108.

52. Fred Moten, "Blackness and Nothingness (Mysticism in the Flesh)," *South Atlantic Quarterly* 112, no. 4 (September 21, 2013): 739.

incalculable.[53] But this does not excuse inaction. The church should pursue reparations not as a means of putting black slavery behind it, but a way of drawing the insufficiently lamented history of black slavery more deeply inside of itself.

To begin this process, the church ought to establish a commission charged with studying the effects of black slavery on all facets of its existence, including but not limited to its sacramental practices, theology, racial composition, distribution of financial resources, processes of canonization, structures of governance, and corporate politics.[54] Ecclesial reparations also will undoubtedly require making black Catholic parishes and ministries one of its financial priorities. In the United States, for example, the church ought to reopen shuttered black churches and parochial schools and accord them preferential funding. The church must do this even if it deprives some predominately white churches of financial oxygen.

Currently, the church counts only one American of African descent, the freeborn Peruvian Martín de Porres, as a saint. In comparison, the church has added eleven whites just from the United States to its official canon. The church must ask why it canonizes Catholics in a racially disproportionate fashion. It must investigate why its channels of saint-making have yet to recognize the saintliness of even one black American slave.[55] It also ought to ask, why, for example, is Peter Claver considered a saint for baptizing African captives in fulfillment of his self-image as "the slave of the slaves," but the actual slaves he sent to the docks of Cartagena to minister in his place for nearly two decades are not?[56]

Ecclesial reparations for black slavery will require a further revolution in the Catholic imagination. Christian theologians in the United States have written numerous works that do not simply respond to Germany's Shoah, but reconsider core Christian teachings in light of it.[57] In contrast, nonblack U.S.-Americans have yet to treat chattel

53. Stephen Best and Saidiya Hartman, "Fugitive Justice," *Representations* 92, no. 1 (Fall 2005): 1.

54. For a more in-depth study of the effect that antiblackness supremacy has had upon the church's hagiographical practices, see Grimes, *Fugitive Saints.*

55. Katie Grimes, "Racialized Humility: The White Supremacist Sainthood of Peter Claver, S.J.," *Horizons* 42, no. 02 (December 2015): 295–316.

56. Anna María Splendiani and Tulio Aristizabál, *Proceso de beatificación y canonización de San Pedro Claver* (Bogotá: Pontificia Universidad Javeriana, 2002), 114.

57. See for example, Donald J. Dietrich, *Christian Responses to the Holocaust: Moral and Ethical Issues* (Syracuse, NY: Syracuse University Press, 2003); Judith H. Banki and John T. Pawlikowski, *In the Shadow of the Holocaust: Christian and Jewish Perspectives* (Franklin, WI: Sheed &

slavery—an atrocity of our own context—with similar theological rigor.[58] Among contemporary nonblack theologians in general and white theologians in particular, black life continues to occupy "the position of the unthought."[59]

Attention to the afterlife of slavery poses a particular and heretofore unrecognized challenge to liberation and contextual theologies that identify history's victims as examples of "the poor." This descriptive approach may appear to accord liberation theology global relevance: as Jesus recognized, "the poor you will always have with you." But in truth a theory devised for the sake of class analysis cannot capture the full realities of racial oppression, especially in the case of antiblackness.[60] The African-descended peoples of the Americas suffer not from poverty, but the afterlife of slavery. This shift in analysis may prove quite difficult for Christian theology. While Christian scripture and tradition contain abundant support for the liberation of the poor, these sources barely speak about the liberation of actual slaves.[61] With few exceptions, Christian scripture and tradition seek to regulate slavery, not to abolish it.[62]

Admittedly, we cannot implement these strategies of corporate rehabituation without the compliance of Catholic bishops. Canon law and Catholic custom accord the bishops great power: in general, the laity cannot easily make their bishop act differently.[63] Just as they

Ward, 2001); Clark M. Williamson, *A Guest in the House of Israel: Post-Holocaust Church Theology* (Louisville: Westminster John Knox, 1993); James F. Moore, *Christian Theology After the Shoah: A Re-Interpretation of the Passion Narratives* (Lanham, MD: University Press of America, 1993); Elisabeth Schüssler Fiorenza and David Tracy, *Concilium 175: The Holocaust as Interruption* (New York: T&T Clark, 1984); R. Kendall Soulen, *The God of Israel and Christian Theology* (Minneapolis: Fortress Press, 1996) among several others.

58. James H. Cone, "Black Liberation Theology and Black Catholics: A Critical Conversation," *Theological Studies* 61 (2000): 737. For a rare exception to this rule, see Bernadette J. Brooten, ed., *Beyond Slavery: Overcoming Its Religious and Sexual Legacies* (New York: Palgrave Macmillan, 2010).

59. Saidiya V. Hartman and Frank B. Wilderson III, "The Position of the Unthought," *Qui Parle* 13, no. 2 (April 1, 2003): 185.

60. Jorge Aquino, *"Ni Blanquitos, ni negritos": Race, nation, and identity in United States Latino/a theology* (PhD diss., Graduate Theological Union, 2006), 5–6.

61. Jennifer A. Glancy, *Slavery as Moral Problem: In the Early Church and Today* (Minneapolis: Fortress Press, 2011), 12, 14.

62. Jennifer A. Glancy, *Slavery in Early Christianity* (Minneapolis: Fortress Press, 2006), 102; Glancy, *Slavery as Moral Problem*, 8–9; Patterson, *Slavery and Social Death*, 225.

63. This does not mean that the laity are entirely powerless or that they could not, under certain circumstances, change their bishop's behavior. See for example Aamer Madhani and Rudolph Bush, "Catholics Launch Donation Boycott: Archdiocese Urged to Adopt Reforms," *Chicago Tribune*, April 30, 2002. Accessed May 11, 2016.

represent a necessary part of any solution, the predominately white episcopacy comprises a part of the problem. These bishops embody the vicious habits of antiblackness supremacy just as surely as their lay white subjects do. They exercise the racialized habits of white supremacy and antiblackness supremacy and have become accustomed to the familiar contours of antiblack space. This country's bishops also will often have to be forced to "do the right thing."[64]

For these reasons, the church will need to be rehabituated with the help of outside pressure. Throughout the history of the United States, the church has made its most dramatic strides toward racial justice when coerced by more powerful forces. Slaveholding Southern Catholics did not set their slaves free until forced to by defeat. Many Catholic hospitals did not integrate without the threat of losing federal dollars. As these examples demonstrate, sometimes the church can be good only by being deprived of a certain measure of freedom. The Catholic Church ought to enjoy a certain amount of freedom from state regulation. But, especially in the case of antiblackness and the supremacy it accords, religious freedom qualifies as not a categorical good, but an occasional abettor of vice. Of course, antiblackness supremacy pervades the secular sphere just as it animates the sacred body of Christ. As demonstrated by the history of federally subsidized mortgage loans, for example, "big government" has acted as antiblackness supremacy's ally as well as its occasional enemy. The Catholic principle of subsidiarity proves helpful here: government involvement in the eradication of antiblackness supremacy should be "as small as possible, but [as] big . . . [as] necessary."[65] Although we should not expect Uncle Sam to come to the rescue, we cannot deny that we need him to.

Recognizing that antiblackness supremacy pervades all facets of our society, we should not expect the process of rehabituation to be easy. This book portrays antiblackness supremacy as a relation of power in

64. Gavin Edwards, "Fight the Power: Spike Lee on 'Do the Right Thing,'" *Rolling Stone*, June 2, 2014, accessed April 8, 2015, http://www.rollingstone.com/movies/news/fight-the-power-spike-lee-on-do-the-right-thing-20140620; Marianne Garvey, Brian Niemietz, and Oli Coleman, "Spike Lee Compares Garner's Death to 'Do the Right Thing,'" *NY Daily News*, December 10, 2014, accessed April 8, 2015, http://www.nydailynews.com/entertainment/gossip/confidential/scenes-spike-lee-film-eric-garner-death-article-1.2039895.

65. Pope Pius XI as quoted by Thomas Massaro, SJ in *Living Justice: Catholic Social Teaching in Action* (Lanham, MD: Rowman & Littlefield, 2011), 90; For a very astute explanation of the principle of subsidiarity, see Meghan Clark, "Subsidiarity Is a Two-Sided Coin," *Catholic Moral Theology blog*, March 8, 2012, accessed January 11, 2017, http://catholicmoraltheology.com/subsidiarity-is-a-two-sided-coin/.

order to convince readers of the role that power must play in tearing racial evil to pieces. We should feel pessimistic. But we ought not surrender to despair. History has changed; it can change again. The road ahead of us is long, but so is the one behind us. Besides, why would those of us who love justice ever stop fighting for it?

BLACK FREEDOM AND POWER ARE THE WAY

Rather than simply encouraging or compelling whites to "let" black people join them at white-made tables, we should instead strive to divest whites of their racial power. Rather than leaving Christians to their habits as Hauerwas proposes, white Christians need to be made to submit to spatial rehabituation.[66] Rather than distinguishing themselves from the world in order to serve and save it, white Christians need to be compelled to inhabit a world not of their making.[67] Rather than espousing a type of Pelagianism, this call to rehabituation exposes the narrow limits of white agency. White people cannot save themselves. The vice of antiblackness supremacy must be unmade by black power, which places black life and freedom first.[68] The church needs what Bryan Massingale recommends: sustained encounter with "the voice of Malcolm X" as "a valuable corrective for an overly-optimistic Catholic perspective" on the possibility of white racial solidarity with black people.[69] Theologians in turn must learn to care less about how to persuade whites to do the right thing and more on what they need to be made to do.

The church, including its theologians, must approach questions of racial mixture and diversity with great caution, resisting the temptation to automatically classify them as antidotes to racial evil. Although the "one-drop rule" originally emerged as a way to forestall black power by fortifying the boundary between white and black, today

66. Hauerwas perceives the church as a school of the virtues. His writings on this theme are extensive. In *After Christendom: How the Church Is to Behave if Freedom, Justice, and a Christian Nation Are Bad Ideas* (Nashville: Abingdon, 1991), Hauerwas wants to "recover the church as the locus of habits of speech to sustain our lives in service to the world."

67. In arguing that the "church must serve the world on its own terms," Hauerwas implies that the church can serve the world on its own terms. Hauerwas, *A Community of Character: Toward a Constructive Christian Social Ethic*, 1st ed. (Notre Dame: University of Notre Dame Press, 1991), 82.

68. James H. Cone, *Black Theology & Black Power* (Maryknoll, NY: Orbis, 1997), 6–8.

69. Bryan N. Massingale, "Vox Victimarum Vox Dei: Malcolm X as Neglected 'Classic' for Catholic Theological Reflection," *Proceedings of the Catholic Theological Society of America* 65 (2013): 83–84.

this expansive understanding of blackness often serves as not the ally of antiblackness but its enemy. We may aspire to "get beyond" whiteness, but let us never seek the same with respect to blackness.[70] In pursuing a "brown" or "beige" multiracial future, we do not overcome our sinful past; we bury the evidence of our crimes. The continued existence of bodies perceived as black sustains the memory of things others would rather forget; it restores enslaved ancestors to social life; it threatens their vindication.

The move to a multiracial or interracial future beyond not just whiteness, but also blackness is not without its theological proponents. In this way, theologian Kameron Carter considers what he terms "the blackness that whiteness created" as in conflict with a commitment to "receiving [one's] identity anew from Christ." Because he believes that blackness originally emerged as a response to the supremacist violence of whiteness, he concludes that "the settlement with blackness is a settlement with whiteness."[71] For this reason, rather than upending whiteness, he claims that blackness ends up imitating it, albeit less violently. Why? According to Carter, like whiteness, blackness defines itself by what it is against—in this case, whiteness—rather than by what it receives from God. Perceiving the establishment of binary identities as a root cause of violence, Carter calls for incessant destabilization of all identities; in clinging to any identity, we close ourselves off from both God and others.[72]

Another theologian, Brian Bantum, similarly casts all "racialized life . . . [as] an inherent trap" and contends that "the mere presence of mulatto/a bodies in the world frays an already unstable [racial] system."[73] But the history of antiblackness supremacy complicates this conclusion. While white supremacy may require the preservation of pure whiteness, antiblackness supremacy surely does not. Like other theologians, Carter and Bantum overestimate the interruptive power of racial mixture, indeterminacy, and so-called impurity because they identify white supremacy rather than antiblackness supremacy as the

70. For a more detailed critique of the desire to "get beyond" race, see Michael Omi, "Rethinking the Language of Race and Racism," *Asian Law Journal* 8 (2001): 161; Birgit Brander Rasmussen, *The Making and Unmaking of Whiteness* (Durham, NC: Duke University Press, 2001), 106, 109.

71. Carter, *Race*, 190. In this critique of blackness, Carter draws from the arguments of Victor Anderson, *Beyond Ontological Blackness: An Essay on African American Religious and Cultural Criticism* (New York: Continuum, 1995), 11.

72. Carter, *Race*, 192.

73. Ibid., 39, 112.

animating core of all racial evil. Both authors also freeze the mulatto body in time, imbuing it with an unconditionally disruptive essence. In so doing, they overlook the ways in which racial impurity sometimes strengthens antiblackness supremacy precisely by increasing the number of people considered not-white. In the contemporary United States, for example, so-called "biracial" identity sometimes serves as a way of proclaiming a certain individual half white rather than fully black.[74]

As with certain attempts to craft a mestizo theology, we can recognize the mulatto/a as a distinct—and distinctly disruptive—racial identity only because we believe blackness unmixed, both culturally and ancestrally.[75] But this perception confuses antiblackness with blackness. While antiblackness supremacy attempts to reduce blackness to an empty, uncommunicative opacity, black people always have resisted this. Black people have long possessed both a keen ability to remix cultures and an unsurpassed openness to "receiving those by 'nature' not in [their] family to be in its family [and] to carry on its bloodline," a capacity Carter believes all peoples except for the church lack. But blackness is not necessarily self-enclosed, either theologically or intercommunally, in the way that Carter claims. Newly enslaved Africans made new families with strangers after the Middle Passage just as their descendants raised children whose parents who had been sold away. Further unsettling prevailing assumptions about the essentially interruptive power of mulatto identity, black people sometimes have enacted this nonviolent receptivity not by overturning the racial binary, but by embracing it. For example, during the

74. Kerry Ann Rockquemore and Tracey A. Laszloffy, *Raising Biracial Children* (Lanham, MD: Rowman Altamira, 2005), 143; Kerry Rockquemore, David L. Brunsma, and Joe R. Feagin, *Beyond Black: Biracial Identity in America* (Lanham, MD: Rowman & Littlefield, 2008), 43; Council on Contemporary Families, "Dating Partners Don't Always Prefer 'Their Own Kind': Some Multiracial Daters Get Bonus Points in the Dating Game," July 1, 2015, accessed May 16, 2016, https://contemporaryfamilies.org/multiracial-dating-brief-report/; Lauren Loftus, "Want to Be Attractive to Online Daters? Be Biracial." *The Washington Post* July 1, 2015 accessed May 16, 2016, https://www.washingtonpost.com/news/soloish/wp/2015/07/01/want-to-be-attractive-to-online-daters-be-biracial/.

75. Further questioning the interruptive power of the mulatto body, Jared Sexton notes that "when black resistance is thought by the state and civil society to be effectively contained or neutralized, both practically and symbolically, the color line becomes considerably more fluid" whereas "when faced with the specter of violent black sexuality . . . white supremacy in the US has consistently conflated blacks and mulattos through retrenched enforcement of the one drop rule." If Sexton's reading of history is correct, it would suggest that the mulatto body appears "fluid" and boundary-busting only to the extent that the black body appears pacified. *Amalgamation Schemes*, 12.

long centuries of slavery, black people accepted mulatto/a children as their own, no matter how violent the circumstances of their conception.[76]

Carter and Bantum further underestimate the extent to which God redeems history by responding to it. As demonstrated by the wounded body of the resurrected Christ and the exodus of formerly enslaved Jews, the violence of crucifiers and enslavers does not have the last word. God does not save us from history; God saves us in it. Even if blackness originated as a crucifying wound, black people have transformed it into a mark of survival, a means of re-creation, and a pathway for new connection. Antiblackness supremacy attempts to impose a disempowering dishonor upon black people; black people repeatedly have striven to subvert this process. Sometimes, black people have resisted antiblackness supremacy not despite blackness, but through it. In this way, blackness can function like God's resurrecting redemption does: it turns death into life, and it builds new communities out of the shattered fragments of old families. Blackness represents not the tragic product of whiteness, but a dignifying and life-giving response to antiblackness supremacy.[77] In these ways, black people have modeled God's plan for resurrected bodies.

Blackness does not therefore mimic the logic of whiteness. While blackness helps to bring the dead back to life, whiteness lives only if others suffer death, both social and physical. Carter describes blackness as "the blackness that whiteness created." But what created whiteness? The history of antiblackness supremacy suggests that whiteness was created by antiblackness supremacy much more than it created blackness. Today whiteness continues to draw its existence largely from antiblackness supremacy. For this reason, whiteness will cede nearly everything else, arguably even itself, before it abandons antiblackness supremacy. Both whiteness and blackness define themselves in relation to the other. But only whiteness lives off blackness as a parasite does. In contrast to whiteness, which lives only if another group dies, black life possesses a unique capacity to live in death.[78]

76. For more on the history of rape and interracial procreation during chattel slavery, see Edward E. Baptist, "'Cuffy,' 'Fancy Maids,' and 'One-Eyed Men': Rape, Commodification, and the Domestic Slave Trade in the United States," *The American Historical Review* 106, no. 5 (2001): 1619–50; Copeland, *Enfleshing Freedom*.

77. Moten, "Blackness and Nothingness (Mysticism in the Flesh)," 738.

78. For an extended explanation of Patterson's argument for slavery "as a form of human parasitism," see *Slavery and Social Death*, 334–42.

Thus, as Moten suggests, if black death keeps the antiblackness supremacist world alive, then would not black life be the death of it?[79]

Other scholars attempt to solve the problem of race by not racial mixture, but so-called racial reconciliation. But this strategy often ends up downplaying or diluting blackness, no matter the intentions of its advocates.[80] Given persistent power discrepancies, racial reconciliation commonly occurs only on terms that viciously habituated whites can accept; it therefore remains within the lines of white comfort.[81] For this reason, it too often makes blackness disappear into or behind whiteness. Because blackness represents not a tragedy of an evil history, but a life-giving response to it, racial proximity does not necessarily provide the antidote to segregation aligned with antiblackness supremacy. As evidenced by chattel slavery, racial intimacy can serve the interests of antiblackness supremacy just as acutely as separation can. Any interracial relation, including one of intimacy or proximity, established according to the logic of antiblackness supremacy will be perverse. Nonblack people therefore ought to pass no judgment on those diverse but truly voluntary forms of black separation that seek to combat the evil of antiblackness supremacy, including but not limited to the black nationalism of Malcolm X or the heroic work of the historically black colleges and universities that survive today.[82] Black people are entitled to seek distance from nonblack people in general and white people in particular for the sake of their survival and psychological well-being.

Rather than selecting racial togetherness as our aim, we should strive for black freedom. Black freedom offers both an antidote to antiblackness supremacy and the surest sign of its defeat. Speaking in the depths of the Great Depression, a formerly enslaved, elderly North Carolina resident named Robert Falls breathes the outlines of this ethical project into being. Reflecting upon the immediate aftermath of emancipation, Falls recalls:

79. In a similar way, Jared Sexton asks, "Can one mount a critique of antiblackness without celebrating blackness?" "The Social Life of Social Death: On Afro-Pessimism and Black Optimism," *InTensions* 5 (2011).

80. For a more elaborate argument against what she calls "the reconciliation paradigm" and in favor of what she terms "the reparations paradigm," see Jennifer Harvey, *Dear White Christians: For Those Still Longing For Racial Reconciliation* (Grand Rapids, MI: Eerdmans, 2014), 158.

81. Amaryah Armstrong, "Refusing to Reconcile: Against Racial Reconciliation," *Women in Theology*, January 19, 2014, accessed May 10, 2016, https://womenintheology.org/2014/01/19/refusing-to-reconcile-against-racial-reconciliation/.

82. "Historically Black Colleges and Universities," National Center for Education Statistics http://nces.ed.gov/fastfacts/display.asp?id=667.

> I remember so well, how the roads was full of folks walking and walking along when the niggers were freed. Didn't know where they was going. Just going to see about something else somewhere else. Meet a body in the road and they ask, "Where you going?" "Don't know." "What you going to do?" "Don't know." And then sometimes we would meet a white man and he would say, "How you like to come work on my farm?" And we say, "I don't know." And then maybe he say, "If you come work for me on my farm, when the crops is in I give you five bushels of corn, five gallons of molasses, some ham-meat, and all your clothes and vitals whils you works for me." Alright! That's what I do . . . And I knowed then I could make a living for myself and I never had to be a slave no more.[83]

Falls links indeterminate uncertainty with freedom: the option to do and become something new delineates the difference between enslavement and freedom. Slaves always knew where they had to be: a bell sounded the start and end of the workday, and the crack of the whip kept their bodies in line. They could not stray outside the spatial limits their masters had set for them. But freedom set them loose. Once they were free, black women and men could make a new life quite unlike the one they had been living before. Unbound, they were making their way by walking. The black travelers Falls recalls were able to not know where they were going only because they had newly slipped the yoke of white power. Indeterminacy had made a new life possible.

Falls's account provides a parable for the contemporary church. Freedom empowered the black people whom Falls encountered on the post-emancipation road to walk wherever they desired and join up with whomever they choose. For this one brief moment, black women and men could decline the overtures of prospective white suitors. Community was not imposed upon them according to the prerogatives of white power. Able to say no, they could finally say yes, but only if they so desired. As this account illustrates, black freedom provides the means by which we can travel toward our ethical destination; it charts the course that vicious whites must be made to follow.[84] For this reason, it must come first. Counter-antiblackness supremacist community will be whatever comes next.

83. Federal Writers' Project, *Slave Narratives: A Folk History of Slavery in the United States From Interviews with Former Slaves*, Vol 15., Tennessee, 15–16. https://www.loc.gov/item/mesn150/

84. Jamie T. Phelps, "Moral Development in an African-American Catholic Context," *U.S. Catholic Historian* 7, no. 2/3 (1988): 335.

Vice, like the binding confinement of antiblackness supremacy, proves adaptive but predictable. It promises more of the same albeit in a different way. We always know where we are going. But the fugitive path of true freedom, like the path toward corporate racial virtue, brings the gift of uncertainty. Just as the church cannot know what racial virtue looks like until it acquires it, so we cannot know in advance where black freedom will lead us. Inspired by Falls, let us walk away from white vice even though we will not know where we are going until we get there.

Bibliography

26th and Kostner Community Oversight Council. "Community Benefits Agreement with Mercy Housing." https://26kostneroversightcouncil.files.wordpress.com/2014/09/26k-oc-cba-draft-english-update-august.pdf. Accessed June 20, 2015.

2Pac. *Changes [Explicit]* Interscope Records, 1998.

Abulafia, David. *The Discovery of Mankind: Atlantic Encounters in the Age of Columbus*. New Haven: Yale University Press, 2008.

———. "Stripped Assets: The Opening of the Atlantic and the Discovery of Mankind." *History Today* 58, no. 5 (May 1, 2008): 37.

Alba, Richard D. "The Myth of a White Minority." *New York Times*, June 11, 2015.

———. "The Twilight of Ethnicity Among American Catholics of European Ancestry." *Annals of the American Academy of Political and Social Science* 454 (March 1, 1981): 86–97.

———. "Whiteness just isn't enough." *Sociological Forum* 22, no. 2 (2007).

Alba, Richard D., John R. Logan, and Brian J. Stults. "How Segregated Are Middle-Class African Americans?" *Social Problems* 47, no. 4 (November 2000): 548–58.

Allen, Theodore W. *The Invention of the White Race, Volume One: Racial Oppression and Social Control.* London: Verso, 1994.

———. *The Invention of the White Race, Volume Two: The Origins of Racial Oppression in Anglo-America*. London: Verso, 1997.

Alexander, Michelle. *The New Jim Crow: Mass Incarceration in the Age of Colorblindness* reprint. New York: New Press, 2012.

Amend, Alex. "How the Myth of the 'Irish slaves' Became a Favorite Meme of Racists Online." April 19, 2016. *Southern Poverty Law Center: Hate*

Watch https://www.splcenter.org/hatewatch/2016/04/19/how-myth-irish-slaves-became-favorite-meme-racists-online. Accessed January 2, 2017.

Anderson, Bentley R. "Prelates, Protest, and Public Opinion: Catholic Opposition to Desegregation, 1947-1955." *Journal of Church and State* 46 (2004): 617–44.

Anderson, Matthew B., and Carolina Sternberg. "'Non-White' Gentrification in Chicago's Bronzeville and Pilsen: Racial Economy and the Intraurban Contingency of Urban Redevelopment." *Urban Affairs Review* 49, no. 3 (2013): 435–67.

Anderson, Victor. *Beyond Ontological Blackness: An Essay on African American Religious and Cultural Criticism*. New York: Continuum, 1995.

Aquinas, Thomas. Translated by Fathers of the English Dominican Province, *The Summa Theologica of St. Thomas Aquinas.* Grand Rapids, MI: Christian Classics, 1981.

Aquino, Jorge. *"Ni Blanquitos, ni negritos": Race, nation, and identity in United States Latino/a theology.* PhD diss., Graduate Theological Union, 2006.

Aristotle, *Politics.*

Armstrong, Amaryah. "Blackness and Value; Part 2: On Whiteness as Credit." Blog post, *Women in Theology*, February 11, 2015. http://womenintheology.org/2015/02/11/blackness-and-value-part-2-on-whiteness-as-credit/.

———. "On the Theo-Political Vision of Macklemore; Or, Why Proximity & Intimacy ≠ Solidarity." Blog post, *Women in Theology*, June 16, 2013. http://womenintheology.org/2013/06/16/on-the-theo-political-vision-of-macklemore-or-why-proximity-intimacy-%e2%89%a0-solidarity/.

———. "Refusing to Reconcile: Against Racial Reconciliation." Blog post, *Women in Theology.* Accessed May 10, 2016. https://womenintheology.org/2014/01/19/refusing-to-reconcile-against-racial-reconciliation/.

Associated Press. "Negroes Leaving Marion." *The Alliance Review and Leader (Alliance, Ohio)*, February 4, 1919.

Associated Press. "Quiet Night Follows Trouble of Monday: More Than 200 Negroes Leave the City." *The Marion Daily Star*, February 3, 1919.

Augustine. *The City of God*. Garden City, NY: Image Books, 1958.

"A War of Violence and Violations: the Consequences of Conquest: A Conversation with Antonia I. Castañeda." PBS. http://www.pbs.org/kera/usmexicanwar/aftermath/violence.html. Accessed July 25, 2016.

Bantum, Brian. *Redeeming Mulatto: A Theology of Race and Christian Hybridity*. Waco, TX: Baylor University Press, 2010.

Baptist, Edward E. "'Cuffy,' 'Fancy Maids,' and 'One-Eyed Men': Rape, Commodification, and the Domestic Slave Trade in the United States." *The American Historical Review* 106, no. 5 (2001): 1619–50.

———. *The Half Has Never Been Told: Slavery and the Making of American Capitalism*. New York: Basic Books, 2014.

Bardach, Ann Louise. "Marielitos and the Changing of Miami." *Los Angeles Times*, April 24, 2005. http://articles.latimes.com/2005/apr/24/books/bk-bardach24.

Barrett, James R. *The Irish Way: Becoming American in the Multiethnic City*. London: Penguin, 2012.

Barrett, James R., and David R. Roediger. "The Irish and the 'Americanization' of the 'New Immigrants' in the Streets and in the Churches of the Urban United States, 1900-1930." *Journal of American Ethnic History* 24, no. 4 (2005): 3–33.

Basu, Moni. "Last White House Democratic Congressman in the Deep South Fights for Political Survival." CNN, November 2, 2012. Accessed March 25, 2014. http://inamerica.blogs.cnn.com/2012/11/02/last-white-house-democrat-in-the-deep-south-fights-for-political-survival/.

Battin, Steven. *The Praxis of Unity: A Postcolonial Perspective on the Unity of the Church*. PhD diss., University of Notre Dame.

Baxter, Michael, and William T. Cavanaugh. "Reply to 'A View from Abroad' by Massimo Faggioli." *America Magazine*, March 31, 2014. Accessed April 16, 2015. http://americamagazine.org/content/all-things/reply-view-abroad-massimo-faggioli.

Bayor, Ronald H. "Urban Renewal, Public Housing and the Racial Shaping of Atlanta." *Journal of Policy History* 1, no. 4 (1989): 419–39.

Bean, Frank D., Stephen J. Trejo, Randy Capps, and Michael Tyler. "The Latino Middle Class: Myth, Reality, and Potential." *Tomás Rivera Policy Institute*, 2001. http://trpi.org/wp-content/uploads/archives/mid-class.pdf. Accessed January 2, 2017.

Bennett, Herman L. *Africans in Colonial Mexico Absolutism, Christianity, and Afro-Creole Consciousness, 1570-1640*. Bloomington: Indiana University Press, 2003.

Berg, Mark T., and Matt DeLisi. "The Correctional Melting Pot: Race, Ethnicity, Citizenship, and Prison Violence." *Journal of Criminal Justice* 34, no. 6 (November 2006): 631–42.

Best, Stephen, and Saidiya Hartman. "Fugitive Justice." *Representations* 92, no. 1 (Fall 2005): 1–15.

Betancur, John. "Gentrification and Community Fabric in Chicago." *Urban Studies* 48, no. 2 (2011): 383–406.

———. "The Settlement Experience of Latinos in Chicago: Segregation, Speculation, and the Ecology Model." *Social Forces* 74, no. 4 (June 1996): 1301–14.

Blauner, Bob. *Racial Oppression in America.* New York: Harper & Row, 1972.

Block, Kristen, and Jenny Shaw. "Subjects Without an Empire: The Irish in the Early Modern Caribbean." *Past & Present* 210, no. 1 (2011): 33–60.

Blumenthal, Debra. *Enemies and Familiars: Slavery and Mastery in Fifteenth-Century Valencia.* Ithaca, NY: Cornell University Press, 2009.

Boelhower, William. *New Orleans in the Atlantic World: Between Land and Sea.* London: Routledge, 2013.

Bonilla-Silva, Eduardo. "From Bi-Racial to Tri-Racial: Towards a New System of Racial Stratification in the USA." *Ethnic and Racial Studies* 27, no. 6 (2004): 931–50.

———. "New Racism, Color-Blind Racism, and the Future of Whiteness in America." In *White Out: The Continuing Significance of Racism.* Lanham, MD: Rowman & Littlefield, 2003.

———. *Racism without Racists: Color-Blind Racism and the Persistence of Racial Inequality in America,* 3rd ed. Lanham, MD: Rowman & Littlefield, 2009.

Bonilla-Silva, Eduardo, and Karen S. Glover. "'We are all Americans': The Latin Americanization of race relations in the United States." *The changing terrain of race and ethnicity* (2004): 149–83.

Bourgeois, Philippe. "If You're Not Black You're White: A History of Ethnic Relations in St. Louis." *City & Society* 3, no. 2 (1989): 106–31.

Bourdieu, Pierre. *The Weight of the World: Social Suffering in Contemporary Society.* Redwood City, CA: Stanford University Press, 1999.

Bowser, Frederick P. *The African Slave in Colonial Peru, 1524-1650.* Stanford, CA: Stanford University Press, 1974.

Bridger, Jeffrey C., and David R. Maines. "Narrative structures and the Catholic Church closings in Detroit." *Qualitative Sociology* 21, no. 3 (1998): 319–40.

Brinig, Margaret F., and Nicole Stelle Garnett. "Catholic Schools, Charter Schools, and Urban Neighborhoods." *The University of Chicago Law Review* (2012): 31–57.

Brosch, Tobias, Eyal Bar-David, and Elizabeth A. Phelps, "Implicit Race Bias

Decreases the Similarity of Neural Representations of Black and White Faces." *Psychological Science* 24, no. 2 (February 1, 2013): 160–66.

Brunk, Timothy M. *Liturgy and Life: The Unity of Sacrament and Ethics in the Theology of Louis-Marie Chauvet*. New York: Peter Lang, 2007.

Bryant, Sherwin K. *Rivers of Gold, Lives of Bondage: Governing through Slavery in Colonial Quito*. Chapel Hill: University of North Carolina Press Books, 2014.

Bulik, Mark. *The Sons of Molly Maguire: The Irish Roots of America's First Labor War*. Bronx, NY: Fordham University Press, 2015.

Buscaglia-Salgado, José F. *Undoing Empire: Race and Nation in the Mulatto Caribbean*. Minneapolis: University of Minnesota Press, 2003.

Byrd, Ayana D. "Bridging the Gap: A Conversation on the Black Diaspora in America." *Essence* (August 2015).

Camosy, Charles C. "How the Abortion Wars Will End—with a Truce, Not a Bang." *Los Angeles Times*, March 20, 2015. Accessed June 21, 2015. http://www.latimes.com/opinion/op-ed/la-oe-0322-camosy-abortion-discourse-change-20150322-story.html.

Candelario, Ginetta E. B. *Black behind the Ears: Dominican Racial Identity from Museums to Beauty Shops*. Durham, NC: Duke University Press, 2007.

Cannon, Katie Geneva. "Christian Imperialism and the Transatlantic Slave Trade." *Journal of Feminist Studies in Religion* 24, no. 1 (Spring 2008): 127–34.

———. *Katie's Canon: Womanism and the Soul of the Black Community*. New York: Continuum, 1995.

Cardona-Maguigad, Adriana. "Little Village Affordable Housing Development Draws Criticism from Some Residents." *The Gate Newspaper*, December 19, 2012. Accessed June 22, 2015. http://www.thegatenewspaper.com/2013/12/little-village-affordable-housing-development-draws-criticism-from-some-residents/.

Carter, Kameron J. *Race: A Theological Account*. New York: Oxford University Press, 2008.

Cassidy, Laurie M., and Alexander Mikulich. *Interrupting White Privilege: Catholic Theologians Break the Silence*. Maryknoll, NY: Orbis, 2007.

Catechism of the Catholic Church.

Cavanaugh, William T. "Dying for the Eucharist or Being Killed by It? Romero's Challenge to First-World Christians." *Theology Today* 58, no. 2 (July 1, 2001): 177–89.

———. "Killing for the Telephone Company: Why the Nation-State Is Not the Keeper of the Common Good." *Modern Theology* 20, no. 2 (April 1, 2004): 243–74.

———. *Migrations of the Holy: God, State, and the Political Meaning of the Church*. Grand Rapids, MI: Eerdmans, 2011.

———. *Theopolitical Imagination: Christian Practices of Space and Time*. New York: T&T Clark, 2002.

———. *Theopolitical Imagination: Discovering the Liturgy as a Political Act in an Age of Global Consumerism*. New York: T&T Clark, 2002.

———. *Torture and Eucharist: Theology, Politics, and the Body of Christ*. Hoboken, NJ: Wiley, 1988.

———. "The Work of the People as Public Work: The Social Significance of the Liturgy." Institute of Liturgical Studies, Valparaiso University. April 2, 2008.

Charles, Camille Zubrinksy. "Neighborhood Racial-Composition Preferences: Evidence from a Multiethnic Metropolis." *Social Problems* 47, no. 3 (August 1, 2000): 379–407.

———. *Won't You Be My Neighbor: Race, Class, and Residence in Los Angeles*. New York: Russell Sage Foundation, 2006.

Chauvet, Louie-Marie. *Symbol and Sacrament: A Sacramental Reinterpretation of Christian Existence*. Collegeville, MN: Liturgical, 1995.

Clark, Meghan. "Subsidiarity Is a Two-Sided Coin." *Catholic Moral Theology blog*, March 8, 2012. Accessed January 11, 2017. http://catholicmoraltheology.com/subsidiarity-is-a-two-sided-coin/.

Coates, Ta-Nehesi. "Terrorism Is Politics by Other Means." *The Atlantic*, February 25, 2013. Accessed January 1, 2015. http://www.theatlantic.com/national/archive/2013/02/terrorism-is-politics-by-other-means/273469/.

Cobb, Charles E. Jr. *This Nonviolent Stuff'll Get You Killed: How Guns Made the Civil Rights Movement Possible*. Philadelphia: Basic Books, 2014.

Cohen, Patricia. "Scholars Return to 'Culture of Poverty' Ideas." *New York Times*, October 17, 2010.

Colás, Yago. "A Desire Named Steph Curry." *Between the Lines* blog post. Accessed January 27, 2016. http://yagocolas.com/index.php/2015/06/16/a-desire-named-steph-curry/.

———. *Ball Don't Lie: Myth, Genealogy, and Invention in the Cultures of Basketball*. Philadelphia: Temple University Press, 2016.

Coleman, John A. "Virgilio Elizondo: Practical Theologian, Prophet, and Organic Intellectual." In Virgilio Elizondo and Timothy Matovina, eds.,

Beyond Borders: Writings of Virgilio Elizondo and Friends. Eugene, OR: Wipf & Stock, 2000.

Collins, James W. Jr., and David K. Shay. "Prevalence of Low Birth Weight Among Hispanic Infants with United States-born and Foreign-born Mothers: The Effect of Urban Poverty." *American Journal of Epidemiology* 139, no. 2 (1994): 184–92.

Cone, James. "Black Liberation Theology and Black Catholics: A Critical Conversation." *Theological Studies* 61 (2000): 731–47.

———. *Black Theology & Black Power.* Maryknoll, NY: Orbis, 1997.

———. *For My People: Black Theology and the Black Church.* Maryknoll, NY: Orbis, 1984.

———. *God of the Oppressed.* Maryknoll, NY: Orbis, 1997.

Congregation for the Doctrine of the Faith. *Inter Insigniores: On the Question of Admission of Women to the Ministerial Priesthood.* 1976. http://www.vatican.va/roman_curia/congregations/cfaith/documents/rc_con_cfaith_doc_19761015_inter-insigniores_en.html.

Congregation of Rites, *Eucharisticum mysterium.*

Cooper, Afua. *The Hanging of Angélique: The Untold Story of Canadian Slavery and the Burning of Old Montreal.* Athens: University of Georgia Press, 2007.

Cooper, Thomas, and David James McCord. *The Statutes at Large of South Carolina: Containing the Acts from 1716, Exclusive, to 1752, Inclusive, Arranged Chronologically. Id., 1838. Xxxi, 814 p.* A. S. Johnston, 1838.

Copeland, M. Shawn. "African American Catholics and Black Theology: An Interpretation." In Gayraud S. Wilmore, ed., *African American Religious Studies: An Interdisciplinary Anthology.* Durham, NC: Duke University Press, 1989.

———. "Blackness Past, Blackness Future—and Theology." *South Atlantic Quarterly* 112, no. 4 (September 21, 2013): 625–40.

———. "The (Black) Jesus: Reflections on Black Power and the (White) American Christ." In George Yancy, ed., *Christology and Whiteness: What Would Jesus Do?* New York: Routledge, 2012.

———. *Enfleshing Freedom: Body, Race, and Being.* Minneapolis: Fortress Press, 2009.

———. "Toward a Critical Christian Feminist Theology of Solidarity." In Mary Ann Hinsdale and Phyllis H. Kaminski, eds., *Women & Theology,* Annual Publication of the College Theology Society 40. Maryknoll, NY: Orbis, 1994.

———, ed. *Uncommon Faithfulness: The Black Catholic Experience*. Maryknoll, NY: Orbis, 2009.

Cortez, Gabriel A. *Education, Politics, and a Hunger Strike: A Popular Movement's Struggle for Education in Chicago's Little Village Community*. (PhD diss., University of Illinois at Urbana-Champagne, 2008).

Crenshaw, Kimberle. "Mapping the Margins: Intersectionality, Identity Politics, and Violence against Women of Color." *Stanford Law Review* 43, no. 6 (1991).

Crockett, Stephen A. Jr. "Sandra Bland Drove to Texas to Start a New Job, so How Did She End Up Dead in Jail?" *The Root*, July 16, 2015. http://www.theroot.com/sandra-bland-drove-to-texas-to-start-a-new-job-so-how-1790860528.

Crossan, John Dominic. *The Historical Jesus: The Life of a Mediterranean Jewish Peasant*. New York: HarperCollins, 2010.

Crowfoot, Silas Niobeh. *Community Development for a White City: Race Making, Improvementism, and the Cincinnati Race Riots and Anti-Abolition Riots of 1829, 1836, and 1841*. PhD diss., Portland State University, 2010.

Cuffari, Elena. "Habits of Transformation." *Hypatia* 26, no. 3 (2011): 535–53.

Daly, Daniel J. *From Nature to Second Nature: The Relationship of Natural Law, Acquired Virtue, and Moral Precepts in Thomas Aquinas's Summa Theologiae*. PhD diss., Boston College, 2008.

———. "Structures of Virtue and Vice." *New Blackfriars* 92, no. 1039 (2011): 341–57.

Darden, Joe T., and Sameh M. Kamel. "Black Residential Segregation in the City and Suburbs of Detroit: Does Socioeconomic Status Matter?" *Journal of Urban Affairs* 22, no. 1 (January 1, 2000): 1–13.

Dávila, Arlene. *Latino Spin: Public Image and the Whitewashing of Race*. New York: New York University Press, 2008.

Davis, Cyprian. *The History of Black Catholics in the United States*. New York: Crossroad, 1995.

———. "The Holy See and American Black Catholics: A Forgotten Chapter in the History of the American Church." *US Catholic Historian* 7, no. 2/3 (1988): 157–81.

Davis, Cyprian, and Diana L. Hayes, eds. *Taking Down Our Harps: Black Catholics in the United States*. Maryknoll, NY: Orbis, 1998.

Davis, Cyprian, and Jamie T. Phelps, eds. *"Stamped with the Image of God": African Americans as God's Image in Black*. Maryknoll, NY: Orbis, 2003.

De La Torre, Miguel. "Beyond machismo: A Cuban case study." *Annual of the Society of Christian Ethics* (1999): 213–33.

———. *Latina/o Social Ethics: Moving Beyond Eurocentric Moral Thinking.* Waco, TX: Baylor University Press, 2010.

———. "Masking Hispanic Racism: A Cuban Case Study." *Journal of Hispanic/Latino Theology* 6, no. 4 (1999): 57–73.

Deniker, Joseph. *The Races of Man: An Outline of Anthropology and Ethnography.* New York: Charles Scribner's Sons, 1906.

DePillis, Lydia. "Police Union: 'We Don't Believe It's an Issue of Race. We Believe It's an Issue of Poverty.'" *The Washington Post*, December 4, 2014. https://www.washingtonpost.com/news/storyline/wp/2014/12/04/police-union-on-brown-and-garner-we-dont-believe-its-an-issue-of-race-we-believe-its-an-issue-of-poverty/.

Doak, Mary C. "Cornel West's Challenge to the Catholic Evasion of Black Theology." *Theological Studies* 63, no. 1 (2002).

———. "The Politics of Radical Orthodoxy: A Catholic Critique." *Theological Studies* 68, no. 2 (May 1, 2007): 87–106.

Dolan, Jay P. *In Search of an American Catholicism: A History of Religion and Culture in Tension.* New York: Oxford University Press, 2003.

Dorrien, Gary. *The New Abolition: W.E.B. Du Bois and the Black Social Gospel.* New Haven: Yale University Press, 2015.

Douglas, Kelly Brown. *Stand Your Ground: Black Bodies and the Justice of God.* Maryknoll, NY: Orbis, 2015.

———. *What's Faith Got to Do with It? Black Bodies/Christian Souls.* Maryknoll, NY: Orbis, 2005.

Drake, St. Clair, and Horace R. Cayton. *Black Metropolis: A Study of Negro Life in a Northern City* (1945). Chicago: University of Chicago Press, 2015.

Dubois, Laurent. *Avengers of the New World: The Story of the Haitian Revolution.* Cambridge, MA: Harvard University Press, 2009.

Du Bois, W. E. B. *Darkwater: The Givens Collection.* New York: Washington Square Press, 2004.

———. *The Souls of Black Folk.* CreateSpace, 2012.

Duru, N. Jeremi. *Advancing the Ball: Race, Reformation, and the Quest for Equal Coaching Opportunity in the NFL.* New York: Oxford University Press, 2012.

Dussel, Enrique. "The Bread of the Eucharistic Celebration as a Sign of Justice in the Community." In Mary Collins and David Power, eds., *Can We Always Celebrate the Eucharist?* Edinburgh: T&T Clark, 1982.

Eagan, Catherine M. "'White,' If 'Not Quite': Irish Whiteness in the Nineteenth-Century Irish-American Novel (1)." *Eire-Ireland: A Journal of Irish Studies*, March 22, 2001.

Elliott, John Huxtable. *Empires of the Atlantic World: Britain and Spain in America, 1492-1830*. New Haven: Yale University Press, 2007.

Ellis, Robert Richmond. "Reading through the Veil of Juan Francisco Manzano: From Homoerotic Violence to the Dream of a Homoracial Bond." *Publications of the Modern Language Association* 113, no. 3 (May 1, 1998): 422–35.

Ellsburg, Robert. *Thich Nhat Hanh: Essential Writings*. Maryknoll, NY: Orbis, 2001.

Emmons, David M. *The Butte Irish: Class and Ethnicity in an American Mining Town, 1875-1925*. Champaign: University of Illinois Press, 1990.

Evans, Rhonda D., Craig J. Forsyth, and Stephanie Bernard. "One Church or Two? Contemporary and Historical Views of Race Relations in One Catholic Diocese." *Sociological Spectrum* 22, no. 2 (2002): 225–44.

Fanon, Frantz. *Black Skin, White Masks*. New York: Grove, 2010.

Farrelly, Maura Jane. "American Slavery, American Freedom, American Catholicism." *Early American Studies: An Interdisciplinary Journal* 10, no. 1 (2012): 69–100.

Federal Works Project. *Tennessee Slave Narratives: Slave Narratives from the Federal Writers' Project 1936-1938*. Carlisle, MA: Applewoods, 2006.

Feest, Christian F. *Indians and Europe: An Interdisciplinary Collection of Essays*. Lincoln: University of Nebraska Press, 1987.

Fernández, Lilia. *Brown in the Windy City: Mexicans and Puerto Ricans in Postwar Chicago*. Chicago: University of Chicago Press, 2012.

Ferrer, Ada. *Freedom's Mirror: Cuba and Haiti in the Age of Revolution*. New York: Cambridge University Press, 2014.

Fields, Liz. "Half of Sexual Abuse Claims in American Prisons Involve Guards." ABC News, January 26, 2014. http://abcnews.go.com/US/half-sexual-abuse-claims-american-prisons-involve-guards/story?id=21892170.

Figueroa, Luis A. *Sugar, Slavery, and Freedom in Nineteenth-Century Puerto Rico*, 1st ed. Chapel Hill: University of North Carolina Press, 2005.

Fisher, Andrew B., and Matthew D. O'Hara. *Imperial Subjects*: *Race and Iden-*

tity in Colonial Latin America (Latin America Otherwise). Durham, NC: Duke University Press, 2009.

Fitzpatrick, Benjamin Lewis. *Negroes for Sale: The Slave Trade in Antebellum Kentucky*. Notre Dame: University of Notre Dame Press, 2008.

Fourez, Gérard. "Symbole et Sacrement. A Propos de L'étude de L.-M. Chauvet." *Revue Théologique de Louvain* 20, no. 2 (1989): 194–203.

Fosmoe, Margaret, "1947 Saw First Black Notre Dame Grads." *South Bend Tribune*, February 26, 2009. http://articles.southbendtribune.com/2009-02-26/news/26729743_1_black-men-black-student-rotc.

Fox, Ashley. "Rooney Rule Has Opened Doors for Minority Head-Coaching Candidates but It Could Do More." ESPN.com, May 19, 2015. http://espn.go.com/nfl/story/_/id/12867233.

Fox Nation, "O'Reilly Clashes with Harvard Professor over Oprah: She's 'Indicting' America as a Racist Nation." FoxNation.com, January 18, 2016. http://nation.foxnews.com/2013/11/19/oreilly-clashes-harvard-professor-over-oprah-shes-indicting-america-racist-nation.

Freeman, Walter. "Nonlinear Brain Dynamics and Intention According to Aquinas." *Mind and Matter* 6, no. 2 (2008): 207–34.

Freund, David M. P. *Colored Property: State Policy and White Racial Politics in Suburban America*. Chicago: University of Chicago Press, 2010.

Frey, William H. "America's Getting Less White, and That Will Save It." *Newsweek*, December 6, 2014. Accessed January 12, 2017. http://www.newsweek.com/americas-getting-less-white-and-will-save-it-289862.

Fryer, Roland G. "Guess Who's Been Coming to Dinner? Trends in Interracial Marriage over the 20th Century." *Journal of Economic Perspectives* 21, no. 2 (May 2007): 71–90.

Gallay, Alan. *Indian Slavery in Colonial America*. Lincoln: University of Nebraska Press, 2009.

Gallup. "Blacks, Nonblacks Hold Sharply Different Views of Martin Case." Poll. http://www.gallup.com/poll/153776/blacks-nonblacks-hold-sharply-different-views-martin-case.aspx.

Gamm, Gerald H. *Urban Exodus: Why the Jews Left Boston and the Catholics Stayed*. Cambridge, MA: Harvard University Press, 2001.

Garrigus, John D., and Christopher Morris. *Assumed Identities: The Meanings of Race in the Atlantic World*. College Station: Texas A&M University Press, 2010.

Garza, Alicia, Patrisse Cullors, and Opal Tometti, "Black Lives Matter:

Founding Principles." Accessed January 6, 2016. http://blacklivesmatter.com/guiding-principles/.

———. "Black Lives Matter: HerStory." Accessed January 6, 2016. http://blacklivesmatter.com/herstory/.

George, Cardinal Francis. *Dwell in My Love: A Pastoral Letter on Racism* (2001).

Glancy, Jennifer A. *Slavery as Moral Problem: In the Early Church and Today*. Minneapolis: Fortress Press, 2011.

———. *Slavery in Early Christianity*. Minneapolis: Fortress Press, 2006.

Glymph, Thavolia. *Out of the House of Bondage: The Transformation of the Plantation Household*. New York: Cambridge University Press, 2003.

Goebel, Alison D. *Small City Neighbors: Race, Space, and Class in Mansfield, Ohio*. PhD diss., University of Illinois at Urbana-Champaign, 2011. http://gradworks.umi.com/34/78/3478707.html.

Goetz, Anne. *The Baptism of Early Virginia: How Christianity Created Race*. Baltimore: Johns Hopkins University Press, 2012.

Goldberg, Jonah. "Oprah, Obama, and the Racism Dodge." *National Review Online*, November 19, 2013. Accessed January 18, 2016. http://www.nationalreview.com/article/364359/oprah-obama-and-racism-dodge-jonah-goldberg.

———. "Playing the Race Card Again." *Los Angeles Times*, March 27, 2012.

Gollar, C. Walker. "Catholic Slaves and Slaveholders in Kentucky." *The Catholic Historical Review* 84, no. 1 (January 1, 1998): 42–62.

Goodman, Jane E. "The Proverbial Bourdieu: Habitus and the Politics of Representation in the Ethnography of Kabylia." *American Anthropologist* 105, no. 4 (2003): 782–93.

González, Michelle A. *Afro-Cuban Theology: Religion, Race, Culture, and Identity*. Gainesville: University Press of Florida, 2011.

Gradisar, Casey. "The Race Game: With visions of reforming 'Vanillanova,' six seniors present the Admissions office with a plan to increase diversity." *The Villanovan*, March 17, 2004.

Graydon, Megan. "The Rev. Francis X. Lawlor, 1917-2013: Catholic priest won term as alderman, drew controversy for efforts to slow black migration in 1960s and '70s." *Chicago Tribune*, November 13, 2013.

Greaves, Margaret. "Slave Ships and Coffin Ships: Transatlantic Exchanges in Irish-American Blackface Minstrelsy." *Comparative American Studies* 10, no. 1 (2012): 78–94.

Greer, Christina M. *Black Ethnics: Race, Immigration, and the Pursuit of the American Dream*. New York: Oxford University Press, 2013.

Gribble, Richard. "A Conservative Voice for Black Catholics: The Case of James Martin Gillis, C.S.P." *The Catholic Historical Review* 85, no. 3 (July 1, 1999): 420–34.

———. "Cardinal Humberto Medeiros and the Desegregation of Boston's Public Schools, 1974-1976." *Journal of Church and State* 48, no. 2 (Spring 2006): 327–53.

Grimes, Katie Walker. "Black Exceptionalism: Antiblackness Supremacy in the Afterlife of Slavery" in eds. Vincent W. Lloyd and Andrew Prevot *Antiblackness and Christian Ethics* Maryknoll, NY: Orbis Books, 2017.

———. "Breaking the body of Christ: the sacraments of initiation in a habitat of white supremacy." *Political Theology* (2017).

———. *Fugitive Saints: Catholicism and the Politics of Slavery*. Minneapolis: Fortress Press, 2017.

———. "Racialized Humility: The White Supremacist Sainthood of Peter Claver, S.J." *Horizons* 42, no. 2 (December 2015): 295–316.

Gross, Ariela J. "'The Caucasian Cloak': Mexican Americans and the Politics of Whiteness in the Twentieth-Century Southwest." *Georgetown Law Journal* 95, no. 2 (January 2007).

Gyasi, Yaa. "I'm Ghanaian-American. Am I Black?" *New York Times*, June 18, 2016. Accessed June 20, 2016. http://www.nytimes.com/2016/06/19/opinion/sunday/im-ghanaian-american-am-i-black.html.

Hagedorn, John. *A World of Gangs: Armed Young Men and Gangsta Culture*. Minneapolis: University of Minnesota Press, 2008.

Hall, Gwendolyn Midlo. *Slavery and African Ethnicities in the Americas: Restoring the Links*. Chapel Hill: University of North Carolina Press, 2009.

Hall, Neville A. T. *Slave Society in the Danish West Indies: St Thomas, St John and St Croix*. Mona, Jamaica: Aarhus University Press, 1992.

Hannah-Jones, Nikole. "Living Apart: How the Government Betrayed a Landmark Civil Rights Law." *ProPublica*. Accessed June 24, 2015. http://www.propublica.org/article/living-apart-how-the-government-betrayed-a-landmark-civil-rights-law.

Harrington, Michael. *The Other America: Poverty in the United States*. New York: Scribner, 1997.

Hartman, Saidiya V. *Lose Your Mother: A Journey Along the Atlantic Slave Route*. New York: Macmillan, 2008.

———. *Scenes of Subjection: Terror, Slavery, and Self-Making in Nineteenth-Century America*, 1st ed. New York: Oxford University Press, 1997.

Hartman, Saidiya V., and Frank B. Wilderson III. "The Position of the Unthought." *Qui Parle* 13, no. 2 (April 1, 2003): 183–201.

Harvey, Jennifer. *Dear White Christians: For Those Still Longing for Racial Reconciliation.* Grand Rapids, MI: Eerdmans, 2014.

———. *Whiteness and Morality: Pursuing Racial Justice Through Reparations and Sovereignty.* New York: Springer, 2007.

Hauerwas, Stanley. *A Better Hope: Resources for a Church Confronting Capitalism, Democracy, and Postmodernity.* Grand Rapids, MI: Brazos, 2000.

———. *A Community of Character: Toward a Constructive Christian Social Ethic*, 1st ed. Notre Dame: University of Notre Dame Press, 1991.

———. *After Christendom: How the Church Is to Behave if Freedom, Justice, and a Christian Nation Are Bad Ideas.* Nashville: Abingdon, 1991.

———. "Christianity: It's Not a Religion, It's an Adventure." In *The Hauerwas Reader.*

———. *Dispatches from the Front: Theological Engagements with the Secular.* Durham, NC: Duke University Press, 1995.

———. "How 'Christian Ethics' Came to Be." Originally published in 1997; republished in *The Hauerwas Reader*. Durham, NC: Duke University Press, 2001.

———. "Reforming Christian Social Ethics: Ten Theses." In *The Hauerwas Reader.*

———. "The Servant Community: Christian Social Ethics." In *The Hauerwas Reader.*

———. "Should War Be Eliminated: A Thought Experiment." Originally published in 1984; republished in *The Hauerwas Reader*. Durham, NC: Duke University Press, 2001.

Hauerwas, Stanley, and Romand Coles. *Christianity, Democracy, and the Radical Ordinary: Conversations Between a Radical Democrat and a Christian.* Eugene, OR: Cascade, 2008.

Hauerwas, Stanley, and William H. Willimon. *Resident Aliens: A Provocative Christian Assessment of Culture and Ministry for People Who Know That Something Is Wrong*, 1st ed. Nashville: Abingdon, 1989.

Haynes, Bruce D. *Red Lines, Black Spaces: The Politics of Race and Space in a Black Middle-Class Suburb.* New Haven: Yale University Press, 2001.

Helg, Aline. "Black Men, Racial Stereotyping, and Violence in the U.S.

South and Cuba at the Turn of the Century." *Comparative Studies in Society and History* 42, no. 3 (July 1, 2000):

———. "Race and Black Mobilization in Colonial and Early Independent Cuba: A Comparative Perspective." *Ethnohistory* 44, no. 1 (January 1, 1997): 576–604.

Hellwig, Monika. *The Eucharist and the Hunger of the World*. Lanham, MD: Rowman & Littlefield, 1992.

Hening, William Waller. *The Statutes at Large: Being a Collection of All the Laws of Virginia, from the First Session of the Legislature, in the Year 1619: Published Pursuant to an Act of the General Assembly of Virginia, Passed on the Fifth Day of February One Thousand Eight Hundred and Eight . . .*, 1823.

Henthorn, Thomas C. "A Catholic Dilemma: White Flight in Northwest Flint." *The Michigan Historical Review* (2005): 1–42.

Herdt, Jennifer A. *Putting On Virtue: The Legacy of the Splendid Vices*. Chicago: University of Chicago Press, 2010.

———. "Redeeming the Acquired Virtues." *Journal of Religious Ethics* 41, no. 4 (2013): 727–40.

Herrnstein, Richard J., and Charles Murray. *The Bell Curve: Intelligence and Class Structure in American Life*. New York: Simon & Schuster, 2010.

Heisser, David C. R. "Bishop Lynch's People: Slaveholding by a South Carolina Prelate." *South Carolina Historical Magazine* 102, no. 3 (July 1, 2001): 238–62.

Hester, Tom. "Willingboro: A half-century of suburbia." *New Jersey dot com*. October 12, 2008. Accessed July 25, 2016. http://www.nj.com/news/index.ssf/2008/10/willingboro_a_half_a_century_o.html.

Heywood, Linda M., and John K. Thornton. *Central Africans, Atlantic Creoles, and the Foundation of the Americas, 1585-1660*. New York: Cambridge University Press, 2007.

Higginbotham, A. Leon Jr. *In the Matter of Color: Race and the American Legal Process. The Colonial Period*. Vol. 1. Oxford: Oxford University Press, 1980.

Higham, John. *Strangers in the Land: Patterns of American Nativism, 1860-1925*. New Brunswick, NJ: Rutgers University Press, 2002.

Hirsch, Arnold R. *Making the Second Ghetto: Race and Housing in Chicago 1940-1960*. Chicago: University of Chicago Press, 1998.

Holley, Peter, Abby Phillip, and Abby Ohlheiser. "Alabama police officer arrested after Indian grandfather left partially paralyzed." *The Washington*

Post, February 12, 2015. Accessed June 20, 2015. https://www.washingtonpost.com/news/morning-mix/wp/2015/02/11/alabama-cops-leave-a-grandfather-partially-paralyzed-after-frisk-goes-awry/?utm_term=.3bff06fbe2d8.

Holton, Kimberly DaCosta. "Fado Historiograhy: Old Myths and New Frontiers." *Portuguese Cultural Studies*, no. 1 (2014): 1.

Hornburger, Jane M. "Deep Are the Roots: Busing in Boston." *Journal of Negro Education* 45, no. 3 (1976): 235–45.

Hout, Michael, and Joshua R. Goldstein. "How 4.5 Million Irish Immigrants Became 40 Million Irish Americans: Demographic and Subjective Aspects of the Ethnic Composition of White Americans." *American Sociological Review* (1994).

Howard, David. *Coloring the Nation: Race and Ethnicity in the Dominican Republic*. Oxford, UK and Boulder, CO: Lynne Rienner, 2001.

Howard, Natasha. "Black in the Non-Black Imagination: How Anti-Black Ideology Shapes Non-Black Racial Discourse." PhD diss., University of New Mexico, 2011.

Howell, Kellan. "Baltimore Riots Sparked Not by Race but by Class Tensions between Police, Poor." *Washington Times*, April 29, 2015. Accessed January 27, 2016. http://www.washingtontimes.com/news/2015/apr/29/baltimore-riots-sparked-not-by-race-but-by-class-t/?page=all.

Hsu, Hua. "The End of White America?" *The Daily Beast*, January/February, 2009. Accessed January 12, 2017. http://www.theatlantic.com/magazine/archive/2009/01/the-end-of-white-america/307208/.

Hua, Vanessa. "Letters Home: Asian Americans in Support of Black Lives Matter." *San Francisco Chronicle*, July 12, 2016. Accessed July 13, 2016. http://www.sfchronicle.com/entertainment/article/Letters-Home-Asian-Americans-in-Support-of-Black-8354454.php.

Hunt, Thomas C., Ellis A. Joseph, and Ronald James Nuzzi. *Handbook of Research on Catholic Education*. Westport, CT: Greenwood, 2001.

Iceland, John, and Melissa Scopilliti. "Immigrant Residential Separation in U.S. Metropolitan Areas, 1990-2000." *Demography* 45, no. 1 (February 1, 2008): 79–94.

Iceland, John, and Rima Wilkes. "Hypersegregation in the Twenty-First Century." *Demography* 41, no. 1 (2004): 23–36.

Ignatiev, Noel. *How the Irish Became White*. New York: Routledge, 2009.

Ingiosi, Gina. "Mystical 'Body': An Ecclesiology Informed by Judith Butler."

In Kevin Ahern, ed., *Visions of Hope: Emerging Theologians and the Future of the Church*. Maryknoll, NY: Orbis, 2013.

Jackson, John M. "Remedy for Inner City Segregation in the Public Schools: The Necessary Inclusion of Suburbia." *Ohio State Law Journal* 55 (1994): 415.

Jacobson, Matthew Frye. *Whiteness of a Different Color: European Immigrants and the Alchemy of Race*. Cambridge, MA: Harvard University Press, 1998.

Jacob Schoenlaub. *The History of Marion County, Ohio: Containing a History of the County, Its Townships, Towns, Churches, Schools, Etc; General and Local Statistics; Military Record; Portraits of Early Settlers and Prominent Men; History of the Northwest Territory; History of Ohio*. Marion, OH: Leggett, Conaway, 1883.

Jeannerod, Marc. "Consciousness of Action as an Embodied Consciousness." In Susan Pockett, William P. Banks, and Shaun Gallagher, eds., *Does Consciousness Cause Behavior?* Cambridge, MA: MIT Press, 2009.

Jennings, Willie James. *The Christian Imagination: Theology and the Origins of Race*. New Haven: Yale University Press, 2011.

Jensen, Richard J. "'No Irish need apply': A Myth of Victimization." *Journal of Social History* 36, no. 2 (2002): 405–29.

John Paul II, Pope. *Ecclesia de Eucharistia*. Encyclical. April 2003. Accessed January 31, 2017. http://www.vatican.va/holy_father/special_features/encyclicals/documents/hf_jp-ii_enc_20030417_ecclesia_eucharistia_en.html.

———. *Ordinatio Sacerdotalis*. Apostolic Letter. May 1994. Accessed January 31, 2017. https://w2.vatican.va/content/john-paul-ii/en/apost_letters/1994/documents/hf_jp-ii_apl_19940522_ordinatio-sacerdotalis.html.

Johnson, Cedric. "An Open Letter to Ta-Nehisi Coates and the Liberals Who Love Him." *Jacobin*, February 3, 2016. Accessed February 3, 2016. https://www.jacobinmag.com/2016/02/ta-nehisi-coates-case-for-reparations-bernie-sanders-racism/.

Johnson, Karen Joy. *The Universal Church in the Segregated City: Doing Catholic Interracialism in Chicago, 1915-1963*. PhD diss., Rice University, 2013.

Johnson, Lyman L. "Manumission in Colonial Buenos Aires, 1776-1810." *The Hispanic American Historical Review* 59, no. 2 (May 1, 1979): 258–79.

Johnson, Walter. *Soul by Soul*. Cambridge, MA: Harvard University Press, 2009.

Joseph, Mark. "No, Oprah, America Isn't Racist: Column." *USA TODAY*, November 24, 2103. Accessed January 18, 2016. http://www.usatoday.com/story/opinion/2013/11/24/oprah-obama-racist-bbc-freedom-medal-column/3693405/.

Katzew, Ilona. *Casta Painting: Images of Race in Eighteenth-Century Mexico*. New Haven: Yale University Press, 2005.

Katznelson, Ira. *When Affirmative Action Was White: An Untold History of Racial Inequality*. New York: W.W. Norton, 2005.

Kazal, Russell Andrew. *Becoming Old Stock: The Paradox of German-American Identity*. Princeton: Princeton University Press, 2004.

———. The Interwar Origins of the White Ethnic: Race, Residence, and German Philadelphia, 1917-1939." *Journal of American Ethnic History* 23, no. 4 (2004): 78–131.

Kiernan, James Patrick. "Baptism and Manumission in Brazil: Paraty, 1789-1822." *Social Science History* 3, no. 1 (1978): 56–71.

Klein, Herbert S. *The Atlantic Slave Trade*. New York: Cambridge University Press, 1999.

Kozol, Jonathan. *The Shame of the Nation: The Restoration of Apartheid Schooling in America*. New York: Broadway, 2006.

Kraft, Patrick W., Milton Lodge, and Charles S. Taber. "Why People 'Don't Trust the Evidence': Motivated Reasoning and Scientific Beliefs." *The ANNALS of the American Academy of Political and Social Science* 658, no. 1 (March 1, 2015): 121–33.

Kraszewski, Gracjan. *Dogma and Dixie: Roman Catholics and the Southern Confederacy during the American Civil War*. PhD diss., Mississippi State University, 2016.

Kruse, Kevin M. *White Flight: Atlanta and the Making of Modern Conservatism*. Princeton: Princeton University Press, 2007.

Kusmer, Kenneth L. *A Ghetto Takes Shape: Black Cleveland, 1870-1930*. Champaign: University of Illinois Press, 1978.

Kutzinski, Vera M. *Sugar's Secrets: Race and the Erotics of Cuban Nationalism*. Charlottesville: University Press of Virginia, 1993.

Lange, Matthew, James Mahoney, and Matthias vom Hau. "Colonialism and Development: A Comparative Analysis of Spanish and British Colonies." *American Journal of Sociology* 111, no. 5 (March 2006).

Laskey, Mike Jordan. "Life & Justice Lecture Presenter Charles Camosy." *Catholic Star Herald* April 30, 2015. Accessed June 24, 2015.

http://catholicstarherald.org/life-justice-lecture-presenter-charles-camosy/.

Lee, Jennifer, and Frank D. Bean. *The Diversity Paradox: Immigration and the Color Line in Twenty-First Century America.* New York: Russell Sage Foundation, 2010.

Lees, Martha A. "Preserving Property Values-Preserving Proper Homes-Preserving Privilege: The Pre-Euclid Debate over Zoning for Exclusively Private Residential Areas, 1916-1926." *University of Pittsburgh Law Review* 56 (1994): 367.

Leonard, William C. "A parish for the black Catholics of Boston." *The Catholic Historical Review* 83, no. 1 (1997): 44–68.

Leong, Nancy. "The Misuse of Asian Americans in the Affirmative Action Debate." *UCLA Law Review* Disc. 90 (2016).

Levad, Amy. *Redeeming a Prison Society: A Liturgical and Sacramental Response to Mass Incarceration.* Minneapolis: Fortress Press, 2014.

Lewis, Oscar. "The culture of poverty." *Society* 35, no. 2 (1998): 7–9.

Lewis, Ronald L. *Black Coal Miners in America: Race, Class, and Community Conflict, 1780-1980.* Lexington: University Press of Kentucky, 1987.

Light, Jennifer S. "Nationality and Neighborhood Risk at the Origins of FHA Underwriting." *Journal of Urban History* 36, no. 5 (September 1, 2010).

Lincoln, C. Eric, and Lawrence H. Mamiya. *The Black Church in the African American Experience.* Durham, NC: Duke University Press, 1990.

Lipsitz, George. *How Racism Takes Place*. Philadelphia: Temple University Press, 2011.

———. *The Possessive Investment in Whiteness: How White People Profit from Identity Politics*, rev. and exp. ed. Philadelphia: Temple University Press, 2006.

Lipski, John M. "Afro-Paraguayan Spanish: The Negation of Non-Existence." *Journal of Pan African Studies (Online)* 2, no. 7 (December 1, 2008): 1–37.

Logan, John R., Wenquan Zhang, and Richard D. Alba. "Immigrant Enclaves and Ethnic Communities in New York and Los Angeles." *American Sociological Review* 67, no. 2 (2002).

Lonergan, Bernard J. F. *Collected Works of Bernard Lonergan.* Toronto: University of Toronto Press, 2000.

Lott, Eric. *Love and Theft: Blackface Minstrelsy and the American Working Class:*

Blackface Minstrelsy and the American Working Class. New York: Oxford University Press, 1993.

Love, Edgar F. "Legal Restrictions on Afro-Indian Relations in Colonial Mexico." *Journal of Negro History* 55, no. 2 (April 1970): 131–39.

Lowery, Wesley. "Six Months after Shooting, Tamir Rice's Family Has Him Cremated." *The Washington Post*, May 13, 2015. http://www.washingtonpost.com/news/post-nation/wp/2015/05/13/six-months-after-shooting-tamir-rices-family-has-him-cremated.

Luongo, Michael T. "Argentina Rediscovers Its African Roots." *New York Times*, September 12, 2014. http://www.nytimes.com/2014/09/14/travel/argentina-rediscovers-its-african-roots.html.

Mac Donald, Heather. "On Child Poverty, MSM Ignores the Basic Truth." *National Review*, September 11, 2011. http://www.nationalreview.com/corner/277977/child-poverty-msm-ignores-basic-truth-heather-mac-donald.

Madden, Janice Fanning, and Matthew Ruther. "Has the NFL's Rooney Rule Efforts 'Leveled the Field' for African American Head Coach Candidates?" *Journal of Sports Economics* 12, no. 2 (2010).

Madhani, Aamer, and Rudolph Bush. "Catholics Launch Donation Boycott: Archdiocese Urged To Adopt Reforms." *Chicago Tribune*, April 30, 2002.

Marcelin, Louis Herns. "Identity, Power, and Socioracial Hierarchies Among Haitian Immigrants in Florida." In Anani Dzidzienyo and Suzanne Oboler, eds., *Neither Enemies nor Friends*. New York: Palgrave Macmillan, 2005.

Marrow, Helen B. "New Immigrant Destinations and the American Colour Line." *Ethnic and Racial Studies* 32, no. 6 (July 1, 2009): 1037–57.

Martin, Charles H. *Benching Jim Crow: The Rise and Fall of the Color Line in Southern College Sports, 1890-1980*. Champaign: University of Illinois Press, 2010.

Martin, Dale. *The Corinthian Body*. New Haven: Yale University Press, 1995.

———. *Sex and the Single Savior: Gender and Sexuality in Biblical Interpretation*. Louisville: Westminster John Knox, 2006.

Martinez, Demetria. "The Future Is Mestizo, the Future Is Now." *National Catholic Reporter*, March 6, 2009. Accessed January 12, 2017. https://www.ncronline.org/news/people/future-mestizo-future-now.

Martinot, Steve, and Jared Sexton. "The Avant-Garde of White Supremacy." *Social Identities* 9, no. 2 (June 1, 2003): 169–81.

Massaro, Thomas. *Living Justice: Catholic Social Teaching in Action.* Lanham, MD: Rowman & Littlefield, 2011.

Massey, Douglas. "The Legacy of the 1968 Fair Housing Act." *Sociological Forum* 30, no. S1 (June 2015).

Massey, Douglas, and Nancy Denton. *American Apartheid: Segregation and the Making of the Underclass*. Cambridge, MA: Harvard University Press, 1993.

———. "Hyper-segregation in U.S. Metropolitan Areas: Black and Hispanic Segregation along Five Dimensions." *Demography* 26, no. 3 (August 1, 1989): 373–91.

———. "Residential Segregation of Blacks, Hispanics, and Asians by Socioeconomic Status and Generation." *Social Science Quarterly* 69, no. 4 (January 1988): 797.

Massingale, Bryan N. *Racial Justice and the Catholic Church.* Maryknoll, NY: Orbis, 2014.

———. "Response: The Challenge of Idolatry and Ecclesial Identity." In Dennis M. Doyle, Timothy J. Furry, and Pascal D. Bazzell, eds., *Ecclesiology and Exclusion: Boundaries of Being and Belonging in Postmodern Times.* Maryknoll, NY: Orbis, 2012.

———. "Vox Victimarum Vox Dei: Malcolm X as Neglected 'Classic' for Catholic Theological Reflection." *Proceedings of the Catholic Theological Society of America* (2010).

Matthews, T. J., and M. F. MacDorman. *Infant Mortality Statistics from the 2004 Period Linked Birth, Infant Death Data Set.* US Department of Health & Human Services, Centers for Disease Control and Prevention, National Center for Health Statistics, 2007.

McCabe, Herbert. *The Good Life: Ethics and the Pursuit of Happiness.* London: Continuum, 2005.

McDonald, Dale. "United States Catholic Elementary and Secondary Schools, 2000-2001: The Annual Statistical Report on Schools, Enrollment and Staffing." http://www.eric.ed.gov/ERICWebPortal/contentdelivery/servlet/ERICServlet?accno=ED454614.

McFarland, Pancho. "Chicano Rap Roots: Black-Brown Cultural Exchange and the Making of a Genre." *Callaloo* 29, no. 3 (2006): 939–55.

McGreal, Chris. "Blame Poverty, Not Race, Say Ferguson's White Minority." *The Guardian*, August 23, 2014, sec. US news. http://www.theguardian.com/world/2014/aug/23/ferguson-michael-brown-blame-poverty-not-race.

McGreevy, John T. *Parish Boundaries: The Catholic Encounter with Race in the Twentieth-Century Urban North*. Chicago: University of Chicago Press, 1998.

———. "Racial Justice and the People of God: The Second Vatican Council, the Civil Rights Movement, and American Catholics." *Religion and American Culture: A Journal of Interpretation* 2, no. 4 (Summer 1994)

McGuckin, N. A., and N. Srinivasan. "Journey to Work in the United States and Its Major Metropolitan Areas—1960–2000." Washington, DC, Federal Highway Administration. June 30, 2003.

McMahon, Eileen M. *What Parish Are You From?: A Chicago Irish Community and Race Relations*. Lexington: University Press of Kentucky, 1996.

McWhirter, Cameron. *Red Summer: The Summer of 1919 and the Awakening of Black America*. New York: Henry Holt, 2011.

Medina, Nestor. *Mestizaje: Remapping Race, Culture, and Faith in Latina/o Catholicism*. Maryknoll, NY: Orbis, 2009.

Menchaca, Martha. *Recovering History, Constructing Race: The Indian, Black, and White Roots of Mexican Americans*. Austin: University of Texas Press, 2010.

Metcalf, George R. *From Little Rock to Boston: The History of School Desegregation*. Westport, CT: Greenwood, 1983.

Mikulich, Alexander, Laurie Cassidy, and Margaret Pfeil. *The Scandal of White Complicity in US Hyper-Incarceration: A Nonviolent Spirituality of White Resistance*. New York: Palgrave Macmillan, 2013.

Mitchell, Nathan. *Eucharist as a Sacrament of Initiation*. Chicago: Liturgy Training Publications, 1994.

———. *Real Presence: The Work of Eucharist*. Chicago: Liturgy Training Publications, 2007.

Mock, Brentin. "Latino Gang Members in Southern California are Terrorizing and Killing Blacks," *Southern Poverty Law Center Intelligence Report* January 16, 2007. Accessed June 21, 2017. https://www.splcenter.org/fighting-hate/intelligence-report/2007/latino-gang-members-southern-california-are-terrorizing-and-killing-blacks.

Mohl, Raymond A. "Stop the Road: Freeway Revolts in American Cities." *Journal of Urban History* 30, no. 5 (July 1, 2004): 674–706.

Morgan, Edmund S. *American Slavery, American Freedom*. New York: W. W. Norton, 2003.

Morgan, Kenneth. *Slavery and the British Empire: From Africa to America*. New York: Oxford University Press, 2008.

Morgan-Trostle, Juliana, and Kexin Zheng. "The State of Black Immigrants: Part I: A Statistical Portrait of Black Immigrants in the United States." *New York University Law School Immigrants' Rights Clinic.*

———. "The State of Black Immigrants: Part II: Black Immigrants in the Mass Criminalization System." *New York University Law School Immigrant Rights Clinic*, 19. Accessed January 3, 2017. http://www.stateofblackimmigrants.com/assets/sobi-deportation-sept27.pdf.

Morrill, Bruce T., Susan Rodgers, and Joanna E. Ziegler, eds. *Practicing Catholic: Ritual, Body, and Contestation in Catholic Faith*. New York: Palgrave Macmillan, 2006.

Morrow, Diane Batts. *Persons of Color and Religious at the Same Time: The Oblate Sisters of Providence, 1828-1860*. Chapel Hill: University of North Carolina Press, 2002.

Moore, Cecilia A. "Dealing with Desegregation: Black and White Responses to the Desegregation of Raleigh, North Carolina, 1953." In M. Shawn Copeland, LaReine-Marie Mosely, and Albert J. Raboteau, eds., *Uncommon Faithfulness: The Black Catholic Experience*. Maryknoll, NY: Orbis, 2009.

Moss, Candida. "The Man with the Flow of Power: Porous Bodies in Mark 5:25-34." *Journal of Biblical Literature* 129, no. 3 (September 1, 2010): 507–19.

Moten, Fred. "Blackness and Nothingness (Mysticism in the Flesh)." *South Atlantic Quarterly* 112, no. 4 (September 21, 2013): 737–80.

———. "The Case of Blackness." *Criticism* 50, no. 2 (2008): 177–218.

Myers, Kristen A. *Racetalk: Racism Hiding in Plain Sight*. Lanham, MD: Rowman & Littlefield, 2005.

Nash, Nathaniel C. "Montevideo Journal; Uruguay Is on Notice: Blacks Want Recognition." *New York Times*, May 7, 1993. http://www.nytimes.com/1993/05/07/world/montevideo-journal-uruguay-is-on-notice-blacks-want-recognition.html.

Neary, Timothy B. "Black-Belt Catholic Space: African-American Parishes in Interwar Chicago." *US Catholic Historian* 18, no. 4 (2000): 76–91.

Newman, Mark. "The Catholic Church in Arkansas and Desegregation, 1946-1988." *The Arkansas Historical Quarterly* 66, no. 3 (2007): 293–319.

The New Oxford Annotated Bible: New Revised Standard Version with the Apocrypha. Fully Revised Fourth Edition.

Nightingale, Carl H. *Segregation: A Global History of Divided Cities*. Chicago: University of Chicago Press, 2012.

Nirenberg, David. "Enmity and Assimilation: Jews, Christians, and Converts in Medieval Spain." *Common Knowledge* 9, no. 1 (January 1, 2003): 138–46.

Nopper, Tamara K. *Beyond the Bootstrap: How Korean Banks and U.S. Government Institutions Contribute to Korean Immigrant Entrepreneurship in the United States*. ProQuest, 2008.

———. "Minority, Black and Non-Black People of Color: 'New' Color-Blind Racism and the US Small Business Administration's Approach to Minority Business Lending in the Post-Civil Rights Era." *Critical Sociology* 37, no. 5 (September 1, 2011).

———. "Where to Look: A Response to Min and Park Regarding Korean Immigrant Entrepreneurship, the Disadvantage Thesis, and Colorblind Racism." *Critical Sociology* (2010).

Nopper, Tamara K., and Mariame Kaba. "Itemizing Atrocity." *Jacobin*. Accessed May 20, 2016. https://www.jacobinmag.com/2014/08/itemizing-atrocity/.

Nordheimer, Jon. "Riots Discomfit the Cubans of Miami." *New York Times*, November 26, 1987.

Nothwehr, Dawn. *That They May Be One: Catholic Social Teaching on Racism, Tribalism, and Xenophobia*. Maryknoll, NY: Orbis, 2008.

Nowatzki, Robert. "Paddy Jumps Jim Crow: Irish-Americans and Blackface Minstrelsy." *Éire-Ireland* 41, no. 3 (2006): 162–84.

Nussbaum, Martha C. *Upheavals of Thought: The Intelligence of Emotions*. Cambridge: Cambridge University Press, 2003.

Oates, Mary J. *The Catholic Philanthropic Tradition in America*. Bloomington: Indiana University Press, 1995.

Ochs, Stephen J. *A Black Patriot and a White Priest: Andre Cailloux and Claude Paschal Maistre in Civil War New Orleans*. Baton Rouge: Louisiana State University Press, 2006.

———. *Desegregating the Altar: The Josephites and the Struggle for Black Priests, 1871-1960*. Baton Rouge: Louisiana State University Press, 1993.

O'Connell, Maureen. *Compassion: Loving Our Neighbor in an Age of Globalization*. Maryknoll, NY: Orbis, 2009.

O'Donnell, John Hugh. *The Catholic Hierarchy of the United States, 1790-1922*. Washington, DC: Catholic University of America Press, 1922.

Omi, Michael. "Rethinking the Language of Race and Racism." *Asian Law Journal* 8 (2001).

O'Toole, James M. *Passing for White: Race, Religion, and the Healy Family, 1820-1920*. Amherst: University of Massachusetts Press, 2003.

Older, Daniel José. "Why U.S. Latinos Need to Get Loud About the Dominican Republic." *BuzzFeed*. Accessed June 19, 2015. http://www.buzzfeed.com/danieljoseolder/us-latinos-need-to-get-loud-about-the-dominican-republic.

Olusoga, David, and Casper W. Erichsen. *The Kaiser's Holocaust: Germany's Forgotten Genocide and the Colonial Roots of Nazism*. London: Faber & Faber, 2011.

Øverland, Orm. "Becoming White in 1881: An Immigrant Acquires an American Identity." *Journal of American Ethnic History* 23, no. 4 (2004): 132–41.

Painter, Nell Irvin. *The History of White People*, reprint. New York: W. W. Norton, 2011.

Pasnau, Robert. *Thomas Aquinas on Human Nature: A Philosophical Study of Summa Theologiae* Ia 75–89. Cambridge: Cambridge University Press, 2002.

Pasquier, Michael. "Catholic Southerners, Catholic Soldiers: White Creoles, the Civil War, and the Lost Cause in New Orleans." PhD diss., Florida State University, 2003.

———. *Fathers on the Frontier: French Missionaries and the Roman Catholic Priesthood in the United States, 1789-1870*. New York: Oxford University Press, 2010.

———. "'Though Their Skin Remains Brown, I Hope Their Souls Will Soon Be White': Slavery, French Missionaries, and the Roman Catholic Priesthood in the American South, 1789–1865." *Church History* 77, no. 2 (2008): 337–70.

Paton, Alan. *The Negro in America Today: A Firsthand Report*. National Association for the Advancement of Colored People, 1954.

Patterson, Orlando. "Race by the Numbers." *New York Times*, May 8, 2001.

———. *Slavery and Social Death: A Comparative Study*, 1st ed. Cambridge, MA: Harvard University Press, 1985.

Pattillo-McCoy, Mary. *Black Picket Fences: Privilege and Peril Among the Black Middle Class*, 1st ed. Chicago: University of Chicago Press, 2000.

Paul VI, Pope. *Lumen Gentium: Dogmatic Constitution on the Church.*

Peabody, Sue. "'A Dangerous Zeal': Catholic Missions to Slaves in the French Antilles, 1635-1800." *French Historical Studies* 25, no. 1 (2002): 53–90.

Peach, Ceri. "The Ghetto and the Ethnic Enclave." In David P. Varady, ed., *Desegregating the City: Ghettos, Enclaves, and Inequality*. Albany: State University of New York Press, 2005.

———. "Urbanization: Ethnic and Religious Segregation." In *The Encyclopedia of Global Human Migration*. Oxford: Blackwell, 2013.

Penyak, Lee Michael. "Criminal Sexuality in Central Mexico, 1750-1850." PhD diss., University of Connecticut, 1993.

Perkinson, James W. *White Theology: Outing Supremacy in Modernity*. New York: Palgrave Macmillan, 2004.

Phelps, Jamie Therese. *Black and Catholic: The Challenge and Gift of Black Folk: Contributions of African American Experience and Thought to Catholic Theology*. Milwaukee: Marquette University Press, 1997.

———. "Communion Ecclesiology and Black Liberation Theology." *Theological Studies* 61, no. 4 (2000): 672–99.

———. "Joy Came in the Morning: Risking Death for Resurrection." In Emilie Townes, ed., *A Troubling in My Soul: Womanist Perspectives on Suffering and Evil.* Maryknoll, NY: Orbis, 1993.

———. "Moral Development in an African-American Catholic Context." *U.S. Catholic Historian* 7, no. 2/3 (1988).

Pinckaers, Servais. *The Pinckaers Reader: Renewing Thomistic Moral Theology*. Washington, DC: Catholic University of America Press, 2005.

Pinn, Anthony B., and Benjamin Valentin, eds. *The Ties That Bind: African American and American/Latino/a Theologies in Dialogue.* London and New York: Bloomsbury Academic, 2001.

Poché, Justin D. "The Catholic Citizens' Council: Religion and White Resistance in Post-War Louisiana." *US Catholic Historian* 24, no. 4 (2006): 47–68.

Polednak, Anthony P. "Trends in US Urban Black Infant Mortality, by Degree of Residential Segregation." *American Journal of Public Health* 86, no. 5 (1996): 723–26.

Porter, Jean. *Natural and Divine Law: Reclaiming the Tradition for Christian Ethics.* Grand Rapids, MI: Eerdmans, 1999.

Pramuk, Christopher. *Hope Sings, So Beautiful: Graced Encounters Across the Color Line.* Collegeville, MN: Liturgical, 2013.

Prevot, Andrew. "Beyond White Privilege: Toward an Uncensored, Subaltern, and Aporetic Theological Response to the Crises of Race and Racism." Catholic Theological Society of America, June 2014 Conference.

Prevot, Andrew, and Vincent Lloyd. *Antiblackness and Christian Ethics*. Maryknoll, NY: Orbis, 2017.

Proctor, Frank T. *Damned Notions of Liberty: Slavery, Culture, and Power in Colonial Mexico, 1640-1769*. Albuquerque: University of New Mexico Press, 2010.

Quijano, Aníbal. "Coloniality of Power and Eurocentrism in Latin America." *International Sociology* 15, no. 2 (June 1, 2000): 215–32.

Quillian, Lincoln. "The Decline of Male Employment in Low-Income Black Neighborhoods, 1950-1990." *Social Science Research* 32, no. 2 (2003): 230–34.

———. "Why Is Black-White Residential Segregation So Persistent?: Evidence on Three Theories from Migration Data." *Social Science Research* 31, no. 2 (June 2002):

Quinn, John F. "'Three Cheers for the Abolitionist Pope!': American Reaction to Gregory XVI's Condemnation of the Slave Trade, 1840-1860." *The Catholic Historical Review* 90, no. 1 (2004): 67–93.

Quinones, Sam. "Attack on Family in Compton Latest Incident in Wave of Anti-Black Violence." *Los Angeles Times*, January 25, 2013. http://articles.latimes.com/2013/jan/25/local/la-me-0126-compton-20130126.

Raboteau, Albert J. *A Fire in the Bones*. Boston: Beacon, 1996.

Rasmussen, Brander. *The Making and Unmaking of Whiteness*. Durham, NC: Duke University Press, 2001.

Rector, Robert. "The Poverty Solution: Marriage or Bust." *National Review*, September 20, 2010. http://www.nationalreview.com/corner/247138/poverty-solution-marriage-or-bust-robert-rector.

Reséndez, Andrés. *The Other Slavery: The Uncovered Story of Indian Enslavement in America*. New York: Houghton Mifflin Harcourt, 2016.

Rice, Lincoln. *Healing the Racial Divide: A Catholic Racial Justice Framework Inspired by Dr. Arthur Falls*. Eugene, OR: Wipf & Stock, 2014.

Rodriguez, Cindy Y. "Mexican-American Boy's National Anthem Sparks Racist Comments—CNN.com." CNN, September 16, 2013. Accessed June 8, 2015. http://www.cnn.com/2013/06/12/us/mexican-american-boy-sings-anthem/index.html.

Rodríguez, Ruben Rosario. *Racism and God-talk: A Latino/a Perspective*. New York: New York University Press, 2011.

Rodríguez-Silva, Ileana M. *Silencing Race: Disentangling Blackness, Colonialism, and National Identities in Puerto Rico*. New York: Palgrave Macmillan, 2012.

Roediger, David. *The Wages of Whiteness: Race and the Making of the American Working Class*. London: Verso, 1991.

Román, Miriam Jiménez, and Juan Flores, eds. *The Afro-Latin@ Reader: History and Culture in the United States*. Durham, NC: Duke University Press, 2010.

Ross, Brian. "Trump's Toxicity & the Death Throes of White Power." *Huffington Post*, August 4, 2016. Accessed January 12, 2017. http://www.theatlantic.com/magazine/archive/2009/01/the-end-of-white-america/307208/.

Rothenberg, Paula S. *Race, Class, and Gender in the United States: An Integrated Study*, 9th ed. New York: Worth, 2013.

Rothstein, Richard. *The Color of Law: A Forgotten History of How Our Government Segregated America* (New York: W.W. Norton & Co., 2017).

Rubio, Philip F. *There's Always Work at the Post Office: African American Postal Workers and the Fight for Jobs, Justice, and Equality*. Chapel Hill: University of North Carolina Press, 2010.

Ruether, Rosemary Radford. "Mariology as Symbolic Ecclesiology: Repression or Liberation?" In *Sexism and God-Talk: Toward a Feminist Theology: With a New Introduction*. Boston: Beacon, 1993.

Rumbaut, Rubén. "Debunking the Myth of Immigrant Criminality: Imprisonment among First-and Second-Generation Young Men." *Migration Information Source*, 2006. http://www.fosterglobal.com/policy_papers/DebunkingTheMythOfImmigrantCriminality.pdf.

Russell, John. "Race and Reflexivity: The Black Other in Contemporary Japanese Mass Culture." *Cultural Anthropology* 6, no. 1 (March 18, 2013): 3–25.

Russell-Wood, A. J. R. "Iberian Expansion and the Issue of Black Slavery: Changing Portuguese Attitudes, 1440-1770." *The American Historical Review* 83, no. 1 (1978): 35.

Rzeznik, T. "The Church in the Changing City: Parochial Restructuring in the Archdiocese of Philadelphia in Historical Perspective." *US Catholic Historian* 27, no. 4 (2009): 73–90.

Saad, Lydia. "Americans Misjudge U.S. Abortion Views: Perception that pro-choice position dominates contrasts with even split in actual views." *Gallup Politics*, May 5, 2013. http://www.gallup.com/poll/162548/americans-misjudge-abortion-views.aspx.

Sallas, August. "Where's Ricardo? Housing Matters, Public Housing Project in Little Village, Little Village Community Meeting, Vote 2014 TV

Show, Endorsed Cook County Democrats, Job Fair, Movie Review." *The Hispanic Times.* Accessed June 22, 2015. http://www.thehispanic-times.com/2014/01/wheres-ricardo-housing-matters-public.html.

Sallaz, Jeffrey J. "Talking Race, Marketing Culture: The Racial Habitus in and out of Apartheid." *Social Problems* 57, no. 2 (2010): 294–314.

Sanburn, Josh. "U.S. Steps Closer to a Future Where Minorities Are the Majority." *Time Magazine,* June 25, 2015.

Sanders, Katrina M. "Black Catholic Clergy and the Struggle for Civil Rights." In M. Shawn Copeland, LaReine-Marie Mosely, and Albert J. Raboteau, eds., *Uncommon Faithfulness: The Black Catholic Experience.* Maryknoll, NY: Orbis, 2009.

Satter, Beryl. *Family Properties: How the Struggle over Race and Real Estate Transformed Chicago and Urban America,* 1st ed. New York: Picador, 2010.

Saunders, A. *A Social History of Black Slaves and Freedmen in Portugal, 1441-1555.* New York: Cambridge University Press, 1982.

Saunders, R. Frank Jr., and George A. Rogers. "Bishop John England of Charleston: Catholic Spokesman and Southern Intellectual, 1820-1842." *Journal of the Early Republic* 13, no. 3 (October 1, 1993).

Sautman, Barry. "Anti-Black Racism in Post-Mao China." *The China Quarterly,* no. 138 (June 1, 1994): 413–37.

Schillebeeckx, Edward. *The Eucharist.* London: Sheed & Ward, 1968.

Schmidt-Nowara, Christopher. *Slavery, Freedom, and Abolition in Latin America and the Atlantic World.* Albuquerque: University of New Mexico Press, 2011.

Schorr, Daniel. "A New, 'Post-Racial' Political Era in America." NPR.org. Accessed January 18, 2016. http://www.npr.org/templates/story/story.php?storyId=18489466.

Schorsch, Jonathan. *Jews and Blacks in the Early Modern World.* Cambridge: Cambridge University Press, 2004.

Schüssler Fiorenza, Elisabeth, and David Tracy. *Concilium 175: The Holocaust as Interruption.* New York: T&T Clark, 1984.

Schwalm, Leslie A. *Emancipation's Diaspora: Race and Reconstruction in the Upper Midwest.* Chapel Hill: University of North Carolina Press, 2009.

Scott, Rebecca J. *Degrees of Freedom: Louisiana and Cuba after Slavery.* Cambridge, MA: Belknap, 2008.

Shaw, Jenny. *Everyday Life in the Early English Caribbean: Irish, Africans, and the Construction of Difference.* Athens: University of Georgia Press, 2013.

Shaw, Stephen Joseph. *The Catholic Parish as a Way-Station of Ethnicity and Americanization: Chicago's Germans and Italians, 1903-1939*. Brooklyn, NY: Carlson, 1991.

Seager, James Schofield. "Survival and Abolition: The Eighteenth Century Paraguayan Encomienda." *The Americas* 38, no. 1 (July 1, 1981).

Sears, David O., and Harris M. "The Trajectory of Local Desegregation Controversies and Whites' Opposition to Busing." *Groups in Contact: The Psychology of Desegregation* (1984).

Serrato, Jackie. "Little Village Leaders Differ on Vision for 26th and Kostner." *The Gate Newspaper*, February 5, 2014. Accessed June 22, 2015. http://www.chicagonow.com/el-arco-press/2014/03/little-village-leaders-differ-on-vision-for-26th-and-kostner/.

Sexton, Jared. *Amalgamation Schemes: Antiblackness and the Critique of Multiracialism*. Minneapolis: University of Minnesota Press, 2008.

———. "People-of-Color-Blindness Notes on the Afterlife of Slavery." *Social Text* 28, no. 2 103 (June 20, 2010): 31–56.

———. "Proprieties of Coalition: Blacks, Asians, and the Politics of Policing." *Critical Sociology* 36, no. 1 (2010): 887–908.

———. "The Social Life of Social Death: On Afro-Pessimism and Black Optimism." *InTensions* 5 (2011).

Slabodsky, Santiago. *Decolonial Judaism: Triumphal Failures of Barbaric Thinking*. New York: Springer, 2014.

Sparrow, Tom, and Adam Hutchinson. *A History of Habit: From Aristotle to Bourdieu*. Lanham, MD: Lexington, 2015.

Splendiani, Anna María, and Tulio Aristizabál. *Proceso de beatificación y canonización de San Pedro Claver*. Bogotá: Pontificia Universidad Javeriana, 2002.

Southern, David W. *John Lafarge and the Limits of Catholic Interracialism, 1911–1963*. Baton Rouge: Louisiana State University Press, 1996.

Starobin, Robert S. "Privileged Bondsmen and the Process of Accommodation: The Role of Houseservants and Drivers as Seen in Their Own Letters." *Journal of Social History* 5, no. 1 (1971): 46–70.

Stout, Jeffrey. *Democracy and Tradition*. Princeton: Princeton University Press, 2004.

Sullivan, Shannon. *Revealing Whiteness: The Unconscious Habits of Racial Privilege*. Bloomington: Indiana University Press, 2006.

Susteren, Greta van. "Is George Zimmerman White or Hispanic? He checked off Hispanic on his voter registration." Gretawire, July 15, 2013. Comments.

Taylor, Alan. *The Internal Enemy: Slavery and War in Virginia, 1772–1832.* New York: W. W. Norton, 2013.

Teel, Karen. *Racism and the Image of God.* New York: Palgrave Macmillan, 2010.

Tessman, Lisa. *Burdened Virtues: Virtue Ethics for Liberatory Struggles.* New York: Oxford University Press, 2005.

Titus, Craig Steven. *Resilience and the Virtue of Fortitude: Aquinas in Dialogue with the Psychosocial Sciences.* Washington, DC: Catholic University of America Press, 2006.

Tombs, David. "Crucifixion, State Terror, and Sexual Abuse." *Union Seminary Quarterly Review* 53 (Autumn 1999): 89–109.

———. "Prisoner Abuse: From Abu Ghraib to *The Passion of the Christ.*" In Linda Hogan and Dylan Lee Lehrke, eds., *Religion and the Politics of Peace and Conflict.* Eugene, OR: Wipf & Stock, 2009.

Traxler, Sister Margaret Ellen. "American Catholics and Negroes." *Phylon (1960–)* 30, no. 4 (1969): 355–66.

Trouillot, Michel-Rolph. *Silencing the Past: Power and the Production of History.* Boston: Beacon, 1997.

United States Department of Justice, "Sexual Victimization in Prisons and Jails Reported by Inmates, 2011-12." http://www.bjs.gov/content/pub/pdf/svpjri1112.pdf.

Unnever, James D., and Francis T. Cullen. "The Racial Divide in Support for the Death Penalty: Does White Racism Matter?" *Social Forces* 85, no. 3 (March 1, 2007): 1281–1301.

Vallejo, Jody Agius. *Barrios to Burbs: The Making of the Mexican American Middle Class.* Stanford, CA: Stanford University Press, 2012.

Valtierra, Angel. *Peter Claver: Saint of the Slaves.* Westminster, MD: Newman, 1960.

Vasko, Elisabeth T. *Beyond Apathy: A Theology for Bystanders.* Minneapolis: Fortress Press, 2015.

Vasquez, Irene A. "The Longue Durée of Africans in Mexico: The Historiography of Racialization, Acculturation, and Afro-Mexican Subjectivity." *Journal of African American History* 95, no. 2 (April 1, 2010): 183–201.

Vaughn, Bobby. "Blacks, Indígenas, and Politics." In Anani Dzidzienyo and

Suzanne Oboler, eds., *Neither Enemies nor Friends: Latinos, Blacks, Afro-Latinos.* New York: Palgrave Macmillan, 2005.

Vaughn, Bobby, and Ben Vinson III. "Unfinished Migrations: From the Mexican South to the American South—Impressions on Afro-Mexican Migration to North Carolina." In Darién J. Davis, ed., *Beyond Slavery: The Multilayered Legacy of Africans in Latin America and the Caribbean.* Lanham, MD: Rowman & Littlefield, 2005.

Vellon, Peter G. *A Great Conspiracy against Our Race: Italian Immigrant Newspapers and the Construction of Whiteness in the Early 20th Century*. New York: New York University Press, 2014.

Wacquant, Loïc J. D. "A Janus-Faced Institution of Ethnoracial Closure: A Sociological Specification of the Ghetto." *The Ghetto: Contemporary Global Issues and Controversies* (2011).

———. *Deadly Symbiosis: Race and the Rise of the Penal State*. Cambridge: Polity, 2009.

———. "From Slavery to Mass Incarceration." *New Left Review* 13 (2002): 42–60.

———. *Punishing the Poor: The Neoliberal Government of Social Insecurity*. Durham, NC: Duke University Press, 2009.

———. "Race as Civic Felony." *International Social Science Journal* 57, no. 183 (2005): 127–42.

———. "Three Pernicious Premises in the Study of the American Ghetto." *International Journal of Urban and Regional Research* 21, no. 2 (December 16, 2002): 341.

Walker, Alan W., and Julian Parkhill. "Fighting Obesity with Bacteria." *Science* 341, no. 6150 (September 6, 2013): 1069–70.

Waller, Gary. *The Virgin Mary in Late Medieval and Early Modern English Literature and Popular Culture.* Cambridge: Cambridge University Press, 2011.

Wacquant, L. "A Janus-Faced Institution of Ethnoracial Closure: A Sociological Specification of the Ghetto." In Ray Hutchison and Bruce D. Haynes, eds., *The Ghetto: Contemporary Global Issues and Controversies.* New York: Avon, 2012.

Water, David. "Jubilant Occasion: First Students of Reopened Inner-City Catholic Schools Graduating, Heading to College." *Memphis Commercial Appeal*, May 19, 2012. Accessed June 21, 2017. https://www.highbeam.com/doc/1P2-31402351.html.

Watras, Joseph. *Politics, Race, and Schools: Racial Integration, 1954–1994.* New York: Routledge, 1997.

———. "The Racial Desegregation of Dayton, Ohio, Public Schools, 1966–2008." *Ohio History* 117, no. 1 (2010): 93–107.

Waugh, Scott L., and Peter Diehl. *Christendom and Its Discontents: Exclusion, Persecution, and Rebellion, 1000-1500.* New York: Cambridge University Press, 2002.

Wawrykow, Joseph Peter. *The Westminster Handbook to Thomas Aquinas.* Louisville: Westminster John Knox, 2005.

We Charge Genocide. "UN Shadow Report." Accessed June 23, 2015. report.wechargegenocide.org/index.html.

Welsh, Thomas G. *Closing Chapters: Urban Change, Religious Reform, and the Decline of Youngstown's Catholic Elementary Schools, 1960-2006.* Lanham, MD: Lexington, 2011.

Wemple, Erik. "Why Did New York Times Call George Zimmerman 'white Hispanic'?" *The Washington Post*, March 28, 2012.

West, Cornel. *Prophesy Deliverance! An Afro-American Revolutionary Christianity.* Philadelphia: Westminster, 1982.

West, Traci C. *Disruptive Christian Ethics: When Racism and Women's Lives Matter.* Louisville: Westminster John Knox, 2006.

White, Kevin. "The Passions of the Soul." In Stephen Pope, ed., *The Ethics of Aquinas.* Washington, DC: Georgetown University Press, 2002.

White, C. Vanessa. "Keeping Current: Somebody's Calling: The Liturgy, Discernment, and Christian Discipleship." *New Theology Review* 20, no. 1 (2013).

Wilderson III, Frank B. *Red, White & Black: Cinema and the Structure of US Antagonisms.* Durham, NC: Duke University Press, 2010.

Wilkerson, Isabel. *The Warmth of Other Suns: The Epic Story of America's Great Migration.* New York: Vintage, 2011.

Williams, Eric Eustace. *Capitalism & Slavery.* Chapel Hill: University of North Carolina Press, 1944.

Wilson, William Julius. *When Work Disappears: The World of the New Urban Poor*, 1st ed. New York: Vintage, 1997.

Wilstein, Matt. "'Brutally Honest' Or 'Brutally Ignorant'? Fox Guests Take On Rachel Jeantel's Zimmerman Trial Testimony." *Mediate*, June 27, 2013. Accessed June 8, 2015. http://www.mediaite.com/tv/brutally-honest-or-brutally-ignorant-fox-guests-take-on-rachel-jeantels-zimmerman-trial-testimony/.

Winant, Howard. *The World Is a Ghetto: Race and Democracy Since World War II*. New York: Basic Books, 2002.

Winder, R. L. "Conscripting the Breast: Lactation, Slavery and Salvation in the Realms of Aragon and Kingdom of Majorca, c. 1250–1300." *Journal of Medieval History* 34, no. 2 (2008): 164–84.

Wolf, Kenneth. "The 'Moors' of West Africa and the Beginnings of the Portuguese Slave Trade." *Pomona Faculty Publications and Research* (January 1, 1994).

Wofle-Simon, Felisa, et al. "A Bacterium That Can Grow by Using Arsenic Instead of Phosphorus." *Science* 332, no. 6034 (June 3, 2011): 1163–66.

Wolfinger, James. *Philadelphia Divided: Race and Politics in the City of Brotherly Love*. Chapel Hill: University of North Carolina Press, 2011.

Wolterstorff, Nicholas. *Justice: Rights and Wrongs*. Princeton: Princeton University Press, 2010.

Woods, Tryon. "The Fact of Anti-Blackness: Decolonization in Chiapas and the Niger River Delta." *Human Architecture: Journal of the Sociology of Self-Knowledge* 5, no. 3 (June 21, 2007).

Yancy, George A. *Black Bodies, White Gazes: The Continuing Significance of Race*. Lanham, MD: Rowman & Littlefield, 2008.

———. "Introduction: Framing the Problem." In *Christology and Whiteness: What Would Jesus Do?* New York: Routledge, 2012.

———, ed. *White Self-Criticality beyond Anti-racism: How Does It Feel to Be a White Problem?* Lanham, MD: Lexington, 2014.

Yancey, George. *Who Is White?: Latinos, Asians, and the New Black/Nonblack Divide*. Boulder, CO: Lynne Rienner, 2003.

Yeager, Timothy J. "Encomienda or Slavery? The Spanish Crown's Choice of Labor Organization in Sixteenth-Century Spanish America." *Journal of Economic History* 55, no. 4 (December 1, 1995): 842–59.

Yun, Lisa. *The Coolie Speaks: Chinese Indentured Laborers and African Slaves in Cuba*. Philadelphia: Temple University Press, 2009.

Zanca, Kenneth J. *American Catholics and Slavery, 1789-1866: An Anthology of Primary Documents*. Lanham, MD: University Press of America, 1994.

Ziedenberg, Jason, and Vincent Schiraldi. "Race and Imprisonment in Texas: The Disparate Incarceration of Latinos and African Americans in the Lone Star State." Justice Policy Institute http://www.justicepolicy.org/images/upload/05-02_rep_txraceimprisonment_ac-rd.pdf.

Zugibe, Frederick T. *The Crucifixion of Jesus: A Forensic Inquiry*. Lanham, MD: Rowman & Littlefield, 2005.

Index